In Memoriam

Kenneth Burke

1897-1993

Landmark Essays

Landmark Essays

on
Kenneth Burke

Edited by Barry Brummett

Hermagoras Press
1993

Landmark Essays Volume Two

Published 1993 by Hermagoras Press,
P.O. Box 1555, Davis, CA 95617

Cover design by Kathi Zamminer

Typesetting and Camera-ready Production
by Graphic Gold, Davis, California
Manufactured in the United States of America
by KNI Inc., Anaheim, California

ISBN 1-880393-05-0

2 3 4 5 6 7 8 9 0

Acknowledgements

First, of course, I gratefully acknowledge the life and work of Kenneth Burke. Sometimes inspiring, sometimes exasperating, always provocative, Burke is an influence on the work of every scholar of language, whether we know it or not.

Professor James J. Murphy's leadership of Hermagoras Press is truly a labor of love: the love of learning. The Landmark Essays series of books will become an invaluable reference for learners in many fields, and for that we should all gratefully thank him. Thanks also to the members of the Kenneth Burke Society, many of whom suggested essays that I would not have thought of, or confirmed the choice of essays that I had thought of. Anybody interested in studying Burke should seriously consider joining this vital association.

Thanks to Professors Margaret Carlisle Duncan and Kathryn Olson for their valuable reading of an early draft of the introduction, and for their collegiality in general. And thanks to Professor Robert L. Scott, who first taught me, and many others, about Kenneth Burke.

-Barry Brummett

About the Editor

Barry Brummett is Professor of Communication at the University of Wisconsin-Milwaukee. He received his B.A. from Macalester College and his M.A. and Ph.D. from the University of Minnesota. His teaching and research interests include rhetorical theory and criticism, popular culture, and of course, Kenneth Burke. Brummett has published several essays of critical analyses using Burkean methodology in journals such as *Quarterly Journal of Speech, Journal of Communication,* and *Critical Studies in Mass Communication.* He is the author of *Rhetorical Dimensions of Popular Culture* (Alabama), *Contemporary Apocalyptic Rhetoric* (Praeger), and *Rhetoric in Popular Culture* (St. Martin's).

Table of Contents

Introduction

Landmark Essays on Kenneth Burke

by Barry Brummett

In the inaugural series of "Landmark Essay" books, this is the only volume focused on the work of one scholar. Kenneth Burke is the major figure in American humanities in the twentieth century. Poet, scholar, critic, iconoclast, eccentric, and Yankee crank, he fits tidily into no philosophical school, nor is he reducible to any simple set of principles and ideas. Scholars from many fields, Communication, English, History, Sociology, and more, have studied Burke's theories and critical methods. Burke's provocative work has spawned reams of commentary, extension, debate, and application from those scholars. Kenneth Burke is more than a single intellectual worker; he is the ore for a scholarly industry. This book contains a few outstanding examples of the products of that industry. You will find here models of what it means to be Burkean, to study Burke, and to use Burke in developing our understanding of the human condition.

Burke proposes grand theories and principles for understanding symbol systems, principally language. He shows how being human is inseparable from using symbols. He applies those same principles in criticism, to explain and analyze discourse.

Burke is fundamentally, as he has characterized himself, a "word man," working to understand language and literature.[1] Yet his methods have been used to study texts and discourses that are more than only verbal. His major work was done in the second and third quarters of this century, yet his work anticipates most or all of the critical and scholarly movements that are considered "cutting edge" as we move into the next millennium. As the essays included in this volume show, one can borrow ideas from Burke, or one can become wholly immersed in him. But Burke and his work cannot be reduced to or equated with any other figure, method, or school of thought.

The reader may find striking some similarities among the essays in this book. Written by scholars from several disciplines, they nevertheless address many of the same themes during the course of their exposition. What is also striking, however, is the fact that most of the essays enter that Burkean system of themes from different starting points. By starting with rhetoric, one writer will come around to victimage. Beginning with poetry, another essayist

---

[1] Quoted in Carline Romano, "A Critic Who Has His Critics—Pro and Con," *Philadelphia Inquirer,* 6 March, 1984, 1D.

arrives at dialectic. Thus, they are models of what Burke claims for any critical vocabulary, including his own: that they are cycles of terms, any one of which leads into another. However, some generalizations can be made about the terms at the heart of Burke's vocabulary. If one enters Burke's system, which ideas will one repeatedly circle around?

Words and Kenneth Burke

Some systems of thought are grounded in materialism, some in idealism, some in pragmatism, and so forth. The grounding of each school is an article of faith, or a fundamental presupposition, about the most basic reality for humans. In other words, each system of thought has an ontology. Burke's thinking defies easy reduction to a single ontology, as reflected in his description of humans as animals that use symbols,[2] an aphorism that teeters between the realizations that some of what we do is motivated by animality and some of it by symbolicity. That ambivalence can be found running throughout Burke's writings. So the best one can do, in searching for the heart of Burke's thought, is to find a partial ontology, a grounding-for-the-most-part. For Burke, people *mainly* do what they do, and the world is *largely* the way it is, because of the nature of *symbol systems themselves*.

Burke's symbolic ontology is keyed to the idea that human thought, perception, and especially motivation follow the dances, maneuvers, and tendencies of the symbol systems that humans use. Language is the most important of those symbol systems and is of course the kind of *symbolicity* with which Burke is most concerned. Language, as social creation and a cultural possession; it works in different ways for different communities of speakers. People use and shape their language intentionally. But on the other hand, speakers are used and shaped by the languages that they speak. It might be most accurate to say that, for Burke, language takes on a life of its own, and pulls human motivation in its train. Most Americans summon up negative motivations in response to the term "drug abuse," yet the term popularly covers only illegal drugs such as cocaine and marijuana. Language can be shaped by those who use it; if it could not be, the critic would be out of a job. But critical intervention is rare and difficult. Despite years of educational efforts, public health officials have yet to persuade most of the public to include under the term "drug abuse" the misuse of legal substances such as alcohol or tranquilizers. For the most part, the possibilities and the constraints upon what we think and do *follow* the possibilities and the constraints given to us by our languages.

Burke's largely linguistic ontology can be difficult to grasp because for many students, it seems counter-intuitive. It often takes students several readings of his dictum, "motives are shorthand terms for situations," to get it

---

[2] Kenneth Burke, *Language as Symbolic Action* (Berkeley: University of California Press, 1966) 3.

right.[3] We want to read it as, "motives are *named by* (or reflected by, or summed up by) shorthand terms for situations." But Burke really means to say that the shorthand terms come first, and *then* we get the motives. The motives really *are* the terms themselves. When confronted by situations that demand choice, we form the motives that guide those choices *as* we form ways to say what the situations are to begin with. Once in place, if a language system cannot "say" a motive easily, then we are unlikely to have that motive.[4] If the expression of two or more motives are, aurally or visually, puns for one another, then the motives themselves will be puns for, or linked with, one another.[5] The essays reprinted here will all, in one way or another, develop the idea of the primacy of symbol systems for motivation, perception, and thought.

Words and Dramatism

Burke's system of thought is often called *dramatism*, although he did not use that term from the very start, nor is it clear that all of his concepts can be summed up under that or any other single word. For our purposes, though, it will be useful to take dramatism as a summarizing term for Burke's thought. We should think about what is implied by dramatism and by its root term, drama. Drama is a good metaphor for what Burke wants to say about language, for three reasons.

First, dramatism signals an intention to engage in broadly-based, wide-ranging theorization. Burke makes few timid or limited claims; he means to tell us about the whole range of human experience. Drama is a good metaphor to express that range. The way in which drama confounds reality and representation has, of course, become a commonplace metaphor. The metaphor is especially useful in describing human relations, because it depends upon the portrayal of interaction. It is both about relationships and it models relationships. Burke is far from the first to observe that "all the world's a stage," nor to turn that metaphor into systematic thought.

The drama is peculiar in its ability to span both reality and representation. Drama is symbolic in that it represents something that might well be happening in "real life": *Hamlet* seems to be about something that might have gone on in reality. On the other hand, drama is its own reality, enacted on stage. *Hamlet* and his cohorts need never have existed for a play about him to do its work with an audience, motivating them and shaping their attitudes. Drama bridges reality and representation of reality, and in fact confounds that distinction. Burke makes that claim for what language does in general.

---

[3] Kenneth Burke, *Permanence and Change,* 2nd rev. ed. (Indianapolis: Bobbs-Merrill Company, Inc., 1954; originally published 1935) 29.

[4] As explained through the concept of "terministic screens," in Burke, *Language as Symbolic Action,* 44-62.

[5] Kenneth Burke, *The Philosophy of Literary Form,* 3rd ed. (Berkeley: University of California Press, 1973; originally published 1941) 57.

Second, drama as a central metaphor for Burke is important because it is highly formal or patterned. Drama tends to be generic, that is, each dramatic production is usually of a recognizable type: a comedy, a drama, a musical, and so forth. Even departures from standard patterns are understood in terms of how they vary from those norms. Also, the sheer logistics of drama are highly patterned. The production of any one play involves a run of shows, each following the same general form with a few differences from show to show depending upon mood and circumstance. These characteristics of drama are useful in helping Burke make claims about how language works. Throughout his writings, he is concerned with form and pattern in discourse.

Burke analyzes form at the microscopic level. Every trope or figure of speech is a pattern waiting to be infused with content. Burke would study the words and sentences of a text so as to identify patterns of repetition, progression, rhetorical device, and so forth.[6] Every utterance that attributes motives may be understood as expressing an orientation to one or more terms of his pentad: act, agent, scene, agency, or purpose. (Burke added "attitude" to this list some decades later to make a *hexad*, but most scholarship has used the original *pentad*.) The pentadic terms are formal, too, expressing types of motivational attributions.[7]

Words string out into patterned discourses at the macroscopic level of whole texts or discourses. Burke argues that recurring patterns underlying texts partially account for how those texts move us. Although Burke focuses on forms of standard literary genres such as the epic, tragedy, comedy, and so forth,[8] the basic principle is that few or no discourses exist *sui generis*. The way that texts manifest established and culturally held patterns accounts for their appeal, indeed, for their comprehensibility.

Third, drama is always addressed to an audience; the thought of a fully prepared play being performed only in secret is absurd. Drama is therefore *rhetorical*, and its use as a metaphor signals Burke's concern for that key concept in Western thought. Even when he does not use the term, Burke studies what literature is *doing* for both writer and reader, for speaker and listener. He views "literature as equipment for living," while not denying that it may also be experienced for pleasure or for its own sake.[9] Texts are always also speaking to the real-life problems that people experience, helping them to craft responses to those problems through language. Good drama does this for its audience, and therefore dramatism will study the ways in which all language speaks to audiences.

Burke analyzes how words are used, yet he does not spare his own use of words from scrutiny. This self-consciousness, this reflexivity, runs through-

---

[6] Kenneth Burke, *Counter-Statement,* 2nd ed. (Berkeley: University of California Press, 1968; originally published 1931) 123-183.
[7] Kenneth Burke, *A Grammar of Motives* (Berkeley: University of California Press, 1969; originally published 1945).
[8] Kenneth Burke, *Attitudes Toward History* (NY: The New Republic, 1937) Vol. I.
[9] Kenneth Burke, *Philosophy of Literary Form,* 293-304.

out his work. In studying how language works to motivate people, Burke understands that he also is using language to intervene in that process and therefore to motivate his audiences, his students. For Burke, being a theorist and being a critic is thus inseparable from being a rhetorician. He is an activist of language, and his works show an activism toward the issues of his day. Because he understands that there is never any possibility of asking questions outside the domain of language, Burke anticipates by several decades those critical theorists who are currently at work showing the circularity or undecidability of meaning.[10] There is simply no strain of recent critical or cultural studies that cannot find an ancestral vocabulary in Burke.

Words About Kenneth Burke

Despite a grounding (partially, maybe) in an ontology of symbolicity, Burke's work is probably not totally systematizable. It was published over a span of several decades. We would wonder if a mind of this caliber and originality did *not* change, develop, even contradict itself over that period of time. As a critic and rhetorician, Burke writes to the problems of his time rather than in an aesthetic vacuum. The world changed over and over during Burke's life, and so did his thoughts and writings in response to change.

Perhaps the most important reason why Burke cannot be completely systematized is that systematization is most compatible with a few relatively simple and incontrovertible principles. But ordinary language does not work like that; as Burke pointed out decades before today's critical theorists, meanings are always shifting, terms always spread out into other terms. Burke avoids the irony of writing a static vocabulary about the fluidity of words and their meanings. Because Burke's critical terms rarely mean *just this* or *only that,* it is not only difficult but also contradictory to try to coordinate most of his terms and concepts in a tidy scheme. Even his symbolic ontology constantly "leaks," admitting the influence of the physical, the animal, and the biological upon human experience.

Many different academic disciplines have spun off planets from Burke's unstable constellation of themes and have planted intellectual colonies on them. The term *interdisciplinary,* so often misused, seems to have been invented for Burke especially. His own work incorporates the writing and thinking of an eclectic mix of philosophers, scientists, critics, divines, and business tycoons from every perspective. He has no earned college degree in any field, yet scholars from many fields use his ideas. The appropriation of Burke is facilitated by his grounding in symbolicity, a concept that is perhaps the major currency of intellectual exchange within the humanities today. The ease and frequency with which diverse scholars incorporate Burke is another indication of the extent to which Burke cannot be systematized tidily.

---

[10]As in Jacques Derrida, *Writing and Difference* (A. Bass, Trans.) (Chicago: University of Chicago Press, 1978).

Not every scholar who works with Burke agrees with him entirely, as can be seen in the essays in this volume. While his influence is such that his work is sometimes taken as a sacred text, that is not true of the selections reprinted here. The authors respect Burke enough to spar, play, and dance with him; they agree and disagree with his work, and they find ways to extend it further.

How were these essays chosen, and by which criteria? In keeping with the title of the series from Hermagoras Press, the essays must have landmark status. A landmark, of course, is a prominent feature of the landscape that a traveller makes note of so as not to get lost when going into a wilderness. One never identifies landmarks while going down a highway or clearly marked path; there is little point in it, since the road itself shows you where to go. Landmarks are for the intrepid explorer who *makes* the path. If we want to understand where we are and how we are moving, we must keep checking over our shoulders to compare where we are with where the landmark is.

A landmark is most often useful when it is *not* where one is at present, when it is where one *was*. In that sense, some of the landmark essays in this volume, such as Nichols's and Hyman's, do not reflect the cutting edge of Burkean scholarship *now*. They are summarizing essays, written at a time when scholars in a given discipline needed to be introduced to Burke's work. These older essays typically survey an extremely broad range of Burke's ideas. They are nevertheless useful as a general map and an introduction to the new student of Burke who is just heading off into the wilds of Burkean studies. And they are useful reminders to those who have progressed beyond them, each one a brief refresher course in basic principles and concepts.

On the other hand, every landmark was once new. The traveller determines that *this* tree will be a landmark for the future, something to look back upon later. Not any tree or rock formation will serve that purpose, however. It must be recognized at the time to be extraordinary and noteworthy. Some of the essays in this volume are "new landmarks" in that sense. Chapters such as Condit's and Lentricchia's are on the cutting edge of Burkean scholarship. Because they suggest extensions of, or even departures from, the current understanding of Burke, they may well be landmarks for Burkean scholarship in the next century.

The essays in this volume also share another characteristic which was necessary so as to create a manageable pool of works to consider for inclusion. They are all exclusively theoretical. There are a number of excellent critical, analytical essays that use Burkean concepts to understand texts. Many of those papers are theoretical as well, in that they advance and improve our understanding of theory as they model its application in criticism. But there are so many essays of that sort that they constitute a pool of works for a potential volume of their own. For reasons of focus, only landmark essays that are strictly theoretical were included in this volume.

The present essays were also chosen to represent a wide range of academic disciplines that are now involved in Burkean studies. Scholars from

Communication, English, Sociology, and the eclectic mix of Critical Studies have contributed chapters to this book. Finally, these are essays about, not by, Burke. Readers of this book may come to it after reading Burke himself, or they may use it to prepare for Burke, but it should not be read by itself, without experiencing the original source.

The essays in this book are grouped in three units. First, there is a collection of introductions to, and surveys of, Burke's work. These are the most general and for the most part the earliest, of the essays collected here. Marie Hochmuth Nichols reviews Burke's work up through *A Rhetoric of Motives*. Her essay provided an early introduction of Burke to scholars in Communication. It is therefore a systematic review of Burke's basic theoretical principles, and follows Burke's own terms and phrases as much as possible. Nichols's essay presents Burke as a rhetorician, in keeping with her own training and with the interests of her discipline.

Stanley Edgar Hyman's chapter is a similar review of Burke that was written somewhat earlier than was Nichols's, as it takes the reader only up through *A Grammar of Motives*. Addressing an audience primarily of English Literature scholars, Hyman focuses on Burke's role as a critic and as a methodologist of criticism. Like Nichols, Hyman attempts to systematize Burke as much as possible, but from the perspective of a critic of literature. Hyman shows us that Burke sees human action as inextricable from the ways that people use symbols in discourse.

Another scholar in English, the poet and critic Howard Nemerov, presents Burke to his readers as a creator of vocabularies and terminologies. In this essay, we are asked to consider vocabularies as interrelated systems in which one term leads circularly to another. Nemerov takes the reader closer to Burke's concern specifically with language than do the first two essayists.

Communication scholars Jane Blankenship, Edward Murphy, and Marie Rosenwasser extend the theme of Nemerov's essay with a more focused discussion of the key terms in Burke's own critical vocabulary. They concentrate on Burke's early works, and isolate four key terms with related clusters of terms and concepts subsumed under each. Moving through Burke's early works, they show how similar ideas are expressed in different ways through succeeding systems of terms. Their essay is thus a Burkean approach to Burke that uses the spirit of his own critical system to examine his vocabularies.

The final introductory, survey essay is Michael Overington's argument for why Burke should have a larger presence in the literature of Sociology. Overington presents Burke as a methodologist of criticism, specifically recommending dramatism as method for sociologists. Overington explores Burke's linguistic ontology, explaining the symbolic basis of actions and motives. In this essay we see heavy use of the term "dialectic" as a description of how language works.

The second major section of this book is also the shortest. It presents two essays that are what Burke would call "representative anecdotes" of what may in fact be the most common kind of Burkean essay. Most of what Burkean scholars do is to explore the implications of particular issues, terms, or concepts in his writing. Their work is published in essays that are more focused than are the broad introductions found in part one. Here, we find two premier examples of such studies, by two Communication scholars, Richard B. Gregg and James W. Chesebro.

Gregg focuses on Burke's idea of form, pulling together theoretical work from several books. Form is described here as a natural human capacity. Discourse appeals to audiences by exercising that capacity. Gregg discusses the links among form, knowing, and rhetoric in Burke and explains how Burke's critical methods can be used to understand form in discourse.

Chesebro argues that many scholars of Burke's work unnecessarily limit their understanding of his thought by seeing it as only epistemological or only ontological. Chesebro contends that epistemology and ontology are dialectically related themes in Burke. He urges a balanced consideration of those two philosophical concepts so as to avoid a reductionist treatment of Burke.

Part three of this book is the longest, containing six essays. In this section, Burke's conception of the critic as an activist intervening in politics comes to the foreground. Burke's own work sometimes seems mired in the literary and the aesthetic, but that perception will be understood to be false when compared with the arguments of these essays.

William H. Rueckert develops Burke's idea that a "better life" may be obtained through attention to discourse. He locates Burke as primarily motivated by the Great Depression and by the need to understand the economic and political motivations that led to that social disaster. We see here how Burke analyzes capitalism, mechanism, scientism, and other ideological props of a failed economic order. Rueckert emphasizes Burke's concern for the self and how it is constructed in discourse, which of course anticipates more recent postmodern theories, such as those concerned with subject positions.[11]

The sociologist Hugh Dalziel Duncan makes heavy use of Burke in his own work. Here, he explicitly discusses how Burke's ideas can be used by academic activists to create a more just social order. This article features Burke's use of religious metaphors in his theories.

Leland Griffin studies the communication that constitutes social and political movements. In this essay, he adapts Burke's ideas to develop a theory of the rhetoric of movements. Griffin exploits Burke's concepts of order and the denial of order, especially through discourse. Like Duncan, he points to Burke's use of religious metaphors. Burke's ideas of hierarchy are especially well developed in this essay.

A prominent postmodern scholar, Frank Lentricchia, has written an essay titled with a pun. On the one hand, he discusses Burke's views of history, reading history *along* with Burke. Lentricchia notes, much as did Rueckert,

---

[11]Such as Louis Althusser, *Lenin and Philosophies and Other Essays* (B. Brewster, Trans.) (New York: Monthly Review Press, 1971).

that Burke is a person of the 1930's. Burke's *Attitudes Toward History* is presented as a crucial work for historical thinking. But Lentricchia also uses Burke as an instrument for historical thinking, hence the pun: he reads history *with* (using) Burke's critical method. Lentricchia shows how Burke's theory of comedy anticipated much postmodern critical theory as an instrument for understanding how discourse works in late capitalist societies.

Burke's focus on comedy is then further discussed by Wayne C. Booth's essay. Booth argues that Burke's theory of comedy is useful for managing the conflict, fragmentation, and pluralism that are increasingly characteristic of the postmodern condition. Burke's refusal to settle on any one terminology (except for his own unsettled one) is presented by Booth as comedic and as wholesomely pluralistic.

Finally, Celeste Condit points the way for future studies of Burke. She takes *substance* as a key term in Burke and focuses on gender, culture, and class as the most important aspects of human substance in our time. Burke, she argues, did not adequately theorize those dimensions of human experience. Condit suggests ways to extend Burke so as to account for these issues that are of vital concern to contemporary critics.

Landmarks are only useful if one travels. These essays are meant to be read by students, professors, the general public—by anyone who is one the move intellectually. The thoughts and arguments presented here are not meant to provide a shade within which to recline. They are reference points from which to do some thinking!

Part One:
Overviews and Surveys

Kenneth Burke and the "New Rhetoric"

by Marie Hochmuth Nichols

"We do not flatter ourselves that any one book can contribute much to counteract the torrents of ill will into which so many of our contemporaries have so avidly and sanctimoniously plunged," observes Kenneth Burke in introducing his latest book, *A Rhetoric of Motives,* but "the more strident our journalists, politicians, and alas! even many of our churchmen become, the more convinced we are that books should be written for tolerance and contemplation."[1] Burke has offered all his writings to these ends.

Burke's first work, *Counter-Statement,* published in 1931, was hailed as a work of "revolutionary importance," presenting "in essence, a new view of rhetoric."[2] Since that time, he has written a succession of books either centrally or peripherally concerned with rhetoric: *Permanence and Change,* 1935; *Attitudes toward History,* 1937; *The Philosophy of Literary Form,* 1941; *A Grammar of Motives,* 1945; and his latest, *A Rhetoric of Motives,* 1950. An unfinished work entitled *A Symbolic of Motives* further indicates his concern with the problem of language.

Sometimes thought to be "one of the few truly speculative thinkers of our time,"[3] and "unquestionably the most brilliant and suggestive critic now writing in America,"[4] Burke deserves to be related to the great tradition of rhetoric.

Although we propose to examine particularly *A Rhetoric of Motives* we shall range freely over all his works in order to discover his principles. We propose to find first the point of departure and orientation from which he approaches rhetoric; next to examine his general concept of rhetoric; then to seek his method for the analysis of motivation; and finally, to discover his application of principles to specific literary works.

In 1931, in *Counter-Statement,* Burke noted, "The reader of modern prose is ever on guard against 'rhetoric,' yet the word, by lexicographer's definition, refers but to 'the use of language in such a way as to produce a

Reprinted from *The Quarterly Journal of Speech,* 38 (1952), with permission of the Speech Communication Association.

[1] Kenneth Burke, *A Rhetoric of Motives* (New York: Prentice-Hall, Inc., 1950), p. xv.
[2] Isidor Schneider, "A New View of Rhetoric," *New York Herald Tribune Books,* VIII (December 13, 1931), 4.
[3] Malcolm Cowley, "Prolegomena to Kenneth Burke," *The New Republic,* CXXII (June 5, 1950), 18, 19.
[4] W. H. Auden, "A Grammar of Assent," *The New Republic,* CV (July 14, 1941), 59.

desired impression upon the reader or hearer.'"[5] Hence, accepting the lexicographer's definition, he concluded that "effective literature could be nothing else but rhetoric."[6] In truth, "Eloquence is simply the end of art, and is thus its essence."[7]

As a literary critic, representing a minority view, Burke has persisted in his concern with rhetoric, believing that "rhetorical analysis throws light on literary texts and human relations generally."[8] Although Burke is primarily concerned with literature "as art,"[9] he gives no narrow interpretation to the conception of literature. He means simply works "designed for the express purpose of arousing emotions,"[10] going so far as to say, "But sometimes literature so designed fails to arouse emotions—and words said purely by way of explanation may have an unintended emotional effect of considerable magnitude."[11] Thus a discussion of "effectiveness" in literature "should be able to include unintended effects as well as intended ones."[12] "By literature we mean written or spoken words."[13]

As has been observed, the breadth of Burke's concepts results "in a similar embracing of trash of every description. . . . For purposes of analysis or illustration Burke draws as readily on a popular movie, a radio quiz program, a *Herald Tribune* news item about the National Association of Manufacturers, or a Carter Glass speech on gold as on Sophocles or Shakespeare. Those things are a kind of poetry too, full of symbolic and rhetorical ingredients, and if they are bad poetry, it is a bad poetry of vital significance in our lives."[14]

Sometimes calling himself a pragmatist, sometimes a sociological critic, Burke believes that literature is designed to "do something"[15] for the writer and the reader or hearer. "Art is a means of communication. As such it is certainly designed to elicit a 'response' of some sort."[16] The most relevant observations are to be made about literature when it is considered as the embodiment of an "act,"[17] or as "symbolic action."[18] Words must be thought of as "acts upon a scene,"[19] and a "symbolic act" is the *dancing of an attitude*,"[20] or incipient action. Critical and imaginative works are "answers to

[5] *Counter Statement* (New York, 1931), p. 265.
[6] *Ibid.*, p. 265.
[7] *Ibid.*, p. 53.
[8] *A Rhetoric of Motives*, pp. xiv, xv.
[9] *Counter-Statement*, p. 156.
[10] *Ibid.*
[11] *Ibid.*
[12] *Ibid.*
[13] *Ibid.*
[14] Stanley Edgar Hyman, *The Armed Vision* (New York, 1948), pp. 386, 387.
[15] *The Philosophy of Literary Form* (Louisiana, 1941), p. 89.
[16] *Ibid.*, pp. 235, 236.
[17] *Ibid.*, p. 89.
[18] *Ibid.*, p. 8.
[19] *Ibid.*, p. vii.
[20] *Ibid.*, p.9.

questions posed by the situation in which they arose." Not merely "answers,"
they are "*strategic* answers," or "*stylized* answers."²¹ Hence, a literary work
is essentially a '*strategy for encompassing a situation.*"²² And, as Burke
observes, another name for strategies might be "*attitudes.*"²³ The United
States Constitution, e.g., must be thought of as the "*answer*" or "*rejoinder*"
to "assertions current in the situation in which it arose."²⁴

Although Burke distinguishes between literature "for the express purpose
of arousing emotions" and "literature for use," the distinction is flexible
enough to permit him to see even in such a poem as Milton's *Samson
Agonistes,* "moralistic prophecy" and thus to class it as "also a kind of
'literature for use,' use at one remove. . . ."²⁵

In further support of his comprehensive notion of art is his conception
that since "pure art makes for acceptance," it tends to "become a social
menace in so far as it assists us in tolerating the intolerable."²⁶ Therefore,
"under conditions of competitive capitalism there must necessarily be a large
corrective or *propaganda* element in art."²⁷ Art must have a "hortatory
function, an element of suasion or inducement of the educational variety; it
must be partially *forensic.*"²⁸

Burke thus approaches the subject of rhetoric through a comprehensive
view of art in general. And it is this indirect approach that enables him to
present what he believes to be a "New Rhetoric."²⁹ In part, he has as his
object only to "rediscover rhetorical elements that had become obscured when
rhetoric as a term fell into disuse, and other specialized disciplines such as
esthetics, anthropology, psychoanalysis, and sociology came to the fore (so
that esthetics sought to outlaw rhetoric, while the other sciences . . . took
over, each in its own terms, the rich rhetorical elements that esthetics would
ban)."³⁰

II

Sometimes thought to be "intuitive" and "idiosyncratic"³¹ in his general
theories, Burke might be expected to be so in his theory of rhetoric.
"Strongly influenced by anthropological inquiries,"³² and finding Freud

---

²¹*Ibid.*, p. 1.
²²*Ibid.*, p. 109.
²³*Ibid.*, p. 297.
²⁴*Ibid.*, p. 109.
²⁵*A Rhetoric of Motives*, p. 5.
²⁶*The Philosophy of Literary Form*, p. 321.
²⁷*Ibid.*
²⁸*Ibid.*
²⁹*A Rhetoric of Motives*, p. 40.
³⁰*Ibid.*, pp. xiii, 40.
³¹*The Philosophy of Literary Form*, p. 68.
³²*A Rhetoric of Motives*, p. 40.

"suggestive almost to the point of bewilderment,"[33] Burke, essentially a classicist in his theory of rhetoric, has given the subject its most searching analysis in modern times.

According to Burke, "Rhetoric [comprises] both the *use* of persuasive resources (*rhetorica utens,* as with the philippics of Demosthenes) and the *study* of them *(rhetorica docens,* as with Aristotle's treatise on the 'art' of Rhetoric)."[34] The "basic function of rhetoric" is the "use of words by human agents to form attitudes or to induce actions in other human agents. . . ."[35] It is *"rooted in an essential function of language itself, a function that is wholly realistic, and is continually born anew; the use of language as a symbolic means of inducing cooperation in beings that by nature respond to symbols."*[36] The basis of rhetoric lies in "generic divisiveness which, being common to all men, is a universal fact about them, prior to any divisiveness caused by social classes." "Out of this emerge the motives for linguistic persuasion. Then, *secondarily,* we get the motives peculiar to particular economic situations. In parturition begins the centrality of the nervous system. The different nervous systems, through language and the ways of production, erect various communities of interests and insights, social communities varying in nature and scope. And out of the division and the community arises the 'universal' rhetorical situation."[37]

Burke devotes 131 pages to a discussion of traditional principles of rhetoric, reviewing Aristotle, Cicero, Quintilian, St. Augustine, the Mediaevalists, and such more recent writers as De Quincey, De Gourmont, Bentham, Marx, Veblen, Freud, Mannheim, Mead, Richards, and others,[38] noting the "wide range of meanings already associated with rhetoric, in ancient texts. . . ."[39] Thus he comes upon the concept of rhetoric as "persuasion"; the nature of rhetoric as "addressed" to an audience for a particular purpose; rhetoric as the art of "proving opposites"; rhetoric as an "appeal to emotions and prejudices"; rhetoric as "agonistic"; rhetoric as an art of gaining "advantage"; rhetoric as "demonstration"; rhetoric as the verbal "counterpart" of dialectic; rhetoric, in the Stoic usage, as opposed to dialectic; rhetoric in the Marxist sense of persuasion "grounded in dialectic." Whereas he finds that these meanings are "often not consistent with one another, or even flatly at odds,"[40] he believes that they can all be derived from "persuasion" as the "Edenic" term, from which they have all "Babylonically" split, while persuasion, in turn, "involves communication by the signs of consubstantiality, the appeal of

---

[33] *The Philosophy of Literary Form,* p. 258.
[34] *A Rhetoric of Motives,* p. 36.
[35] *Ibid .,* p. 41.
[36] *Ibid.,* p. 43.
[37] *Ibid.,* p. 146.
[38] *Ibid.,* pp. 49-180.
[39] *Ibid.,* p. 61.
[40] *Ibid.,* pp. 61, 62.

identification."[41] As the "simplest case of persuasion," he notes that "You persuade a man only insofar as you can talk his language by speech, gesture, tonality, order, image, attitude, idea, *identifying* your ways with his."[42]

In using *identification* as his key term, Burke notes, "Traditionally, the key term for rhetoric is not 'identification,' but 'persuasion.' . . . Our treatment, in terms of identification, is decidedly not meant as a substitute for the sound traditional approach. Rather, . . . it is but an accessory to the standard lore."[43] He had noted that "when we come upon such aspects of persuasion as are found in 'mystification,' courtship, and the 'magic' of class relationships, the reader will see why the classical notion of clear persuasive intent is not an accurate fit, for describing the ways in which the members of a group promote social cohesion by acting rhetorically upon themselves and one another."[44] Burke is completely aware that he is not introducing a totally new concept, observing that Aristotle had long ago commented, "It is not hard . . . to praise Athenians among Athenians,"[45] and that one persuades by "identifying" one's ways with those of his audience.[46] In an observation of W. C. Blum, Burke found additional support for his emphasis on *identification* as a key concept. "In identification lies the source of dedications and enslavements, in fact of cooperation."[47] As for the precise relationship between identification and persuasion as ends of rhetoric, Burke concludes, "we might well keep it in mind that a speaker persuades an audience by the use of stylistic identifications; his act of persuasion may be for the purpose of causing the audience to identify itself with the speaker's interests; and the speaker draws on identification of interests to establish rapport between himself and his audience. So, there is no chance of our keeping apart the meanings of persuasion, identification ('consubstantiality') and communication (the nature of rhetoric as 'addressed'). But, in given instances, one or another of these elements may serve best for extending a line of analysis in some particular direction."[48] "All told, persuasion ranges from the bluntest quest of advantage, as in sales promotion or propaganda, through courtship, social etiquette, education, and the sermon, to a 'pure' form that delights in the process of appeal for itself alone, without ulterior purpose. And identification ranges from the politician who, addressing an audience of farmers, says, 'I was a farm boy myself,' through the mysteries of social status, to the mystic's devout identification with the source of all being."[49] The difference

---

[41] *Ibid.*, p. 62.
[42] *Ibid.*, p. 55.
[43] *Ibid.*, p. xiv.
[44] *Ibid.*
[45] *Ibid.*, p. 55.
[46] *Ibid.*
[47] *Ibid.*, p. xiv.
[48] *Ibid.*, p. 46.
[49] *Ibid.*, p. xiv.

between the "old" rhetoric and the "new" rhetoric may be summed up in this manner: whereas the key term for the "old" rhetoric was *persuasion* and its stress was upon deliberate design, the key term for the "new" rhetoric is *identification* and this may include partially "unconscious" factors in its appeal. Identification, at its simplest level, may be a deliberate device, or a means, as when a speaker identifies his interests with those of his audience. But *identification* can also be an "end," as "when people earnestly yearn to identify themselves with some group or other." They are thus not necessarily acted upon by a conscious external agent, but may act upon themselves to this end. Identification "includes the realm of transcendence."[50]

Burke affirms the significance of *identification* as a key concept because men are at odds with one another, or because there is "division." "Identification is compensatory to division. If men were not apart from one another, there would be no need for the rhetorician to proclaim their unity. If men were wholly and truly of one substance, absolute communication would be of man's very essence."[51] "In pure identification there would be no strife. Likewise, there would be no strife in absolute separateness, since opponents can join battle only through a mediatory ground that makes their communication possible, thus providing the first condition necessary for their interchange of blows. But put identification and division ambiguously together . . . and you have the characteristic invitation to rhetoric. Here is a major reason why rhetoric, according to Aristotle, 'proves opposites.' "[52]

As a philosopher and metaphysician Burke is impelled to give a philosophic treatment to the concept of unity or identity by an analysis of the nature of *substance* in general. In this respect he makes his most basic contribution to a philosophy of rhetoric. "Metaphysically, a thing is identified by its *properties*,"[53] he observes. "To call a man a friend or brother is to proclaim him consubstantial with oneself, one's values or purposes. To call a man a bastard is to attack him by attacking his whole line, his 'authorship,' his 'principle' or 'motive' (as expressed in terms of the familial). An epithet assigns substance doubly, for in stating the character of the object it . . . contains an implicit program of action with regard to the object, thus serving as motive."[54]

[50]Kenneth Burke, "Rhetoric—Old and New," *The Journal of General Education,* V (April 1951), 203.
[51]*A Rhetoric of Motives,* p. 22.
[52]*Ibid.,* p. 25.
[53]*Ibid.,* p. 23.
[54]*A Grammar of Motives* New York, 1945), p. 57. For discussion of *substance* as a concept, see, *ibid.,* pp. 21-58; Aristotle, *Categoriae,* tr. by E. M. Edghill, *The Works of Aristotle,* ed. by W. D. Ross, I, Ch. 5; Aristotle, *Metaphysics,* tr. by W. D. Ross, Book Δ, 8, 1017b, 10; Spinoza, *The Ethics,* in *The Chief Works of Benedict De Spinoza,* tr. by R. H. M. Elwes (London, 1901), Rev. ed., II, 45ff; John Locke, *An Essay Concerning Human Understanding* (London, 1760), 15th ed., I, Bk. II, Chs. XXIII, XXIV.

According to Burke, language of all things "is most public, most collective, in its substance."[55] Aware that modern thinkers have been skeptical about the utility of a doctrine of substance,[56] he nevertheless recalls that "substance, in the old philosophies, was an *act;* and a way of life is an *acting-together;* and in acting together, men have common sensations, concepts, images, ideas, attitudes that make them *consubstantial.*"[57] "A doctrine of *consubstantiality* . . . may be necessary to any way of life."[58] Like Kant, Burke regards substance as a "necessary form of the mind." Instead of trying to exclude a doctrine of substance, he restores it to a central position and throws critical light upon it.

In so far as rhetoric is concerned, the "ambiguity of substance" affords a major resource. "What handier linguistic resource could a rhetorician want than an ambiguity whereby he can say 'The state of affairs is substantially such-and-such,' instead of having to say 'The state of affairs *is* and/or *is not* such-and-such'"?[59]

The "commonplaces" or "topics" of Aristotle's *Rhetoric* are a "quick survey of opinion" of "things that people generally consider persuasive." As such, they are means of proclaiming *substantial* unity with an audience and are clearly instances of identification.[60] In truth, *identification* is "hardly other than a name for the function of sociality."[61] Likewise, the many tropes and figures, and rhetorical form in the large as treated by the ancients are to be considered as modes of identification.[62] They are the "signs" by which the speaker identifies himself with the reader or hearer. "In its simplest manifestation, style is ingratiation."[63] It is an attempt to "gain favor by the hypnotic or suggestive process of 'saying the right thing.'"[64] Burke discusses form in general as "the psychology of the *audience,*"[65] the "arousing and fulfillment of desires."[65] The exordium of a Greek oration is an instance of "conventional"[67] form, a form which is expected by the audience and therefore satisfies it. Other recognizable types of form are "syllogistic progression," "repetitive" form, and "minor or incidental" forms which include such devices as the metaphor, apostrophe, series, reversal, etc.[68] The

---

[55] *The Philosophy of Literary Form*, p. 44.
[56] *A Rhetoric of Motives*, p. 21.
[57] *Ibid.*
[58] *Ibid.*
[59] *A Grammar of Motives*, pp. 51, 52.
[60] *A Rhetoric of Motives*, pp. 56, 57.
[61] *Attitudes toward History* (New York, 1937), II, 144.
[62] *A Rhetoric of Motives*, p. 59.
[63] *Permanence and Change* (New York, 1935), p. 71.
[64] *Ibid.*
[65] *Counter-Statement*, pp. 38-57.
[66] *Ibid.*, p. 157.
[67] *Ibid.*, p. 159.
[68] *Ibid.*, pp. 157-161.

proliferation and the variety of formal devices make a work eloquent.[69]

Reviewing *A Rhetoric of Motives,* Thomas W. Copeland observed, "It gradually appears that there is no form of action of men upon each other (or of individuals on themselves) which is really outside of rhetoric. But if so, we should certainly ask whether rhetoric *as a term* has any defining value."[70] The observation is probably not fair, for Burke does give rhetoric a defining value in terms of persuasion, identification, and address or communication to an audience of some sort, despite his observation, "Wherever there is persuasion, there is rhetoric. And wherever there is 'meaning' there is 'persuasion.' "[71]

It is true that in his effort to show "how a rhetorical motive is often present where it is not usually recognized, or thought to belong,"[72] Burke either points out linkages which have not been commonly stressed, or widens the scope of rhetoric. A twentieth-century orientation in social-psychological theory thus enables him to note that we may with "more accuracy speak of persuasion 'to attitude,' rather than persuasion to out-and-out action." For persuasion "involves choice, will; it is directed to a man only insofar as he is _free_." In so far as men "*must* do something, rhetoric is unnecessary, its work being done by the nature of things, though often these necessities are not of natural origin, but come from necessities imposed by man-made conditions,"[73] such as dictatorships or near-dictatorships. His notion of persuasion to "attitude" does not alter his generally classical view of rhetoric, for as he points out, in "Cicero and Augustine there is a shift between the words 'move' *(movere)* and 'bend' *(flectere)* to name the ultimate function of rhetoric." And he merely finds that this shift "corresponds to a distinction between act and attitude (attitude being an incipient act, a leaning or in-clination)."[74] His notion of persuasion to "attitude" enables him to point out a linkage with poetry: "Thus the notion of persuasion to *attitude* would permit the application of rhetorical terms to purely *poetic* structures; the study of lyrical devices might be classed under the head of rhetoric, when these devices are considered for their power to induce or communicate states of mind to readers, even though the kinds of assent evoked have no overt, practical outcome."[75]

In his reading of classical texts, he had noted a stress "upon *teaching* as an 'office' of rhetoric." Such an observation enables him to link the fields of rhetoric and semantics. He concludes that "once you treat instruction as an aim of rhetoric you introduce a principle that can widen the scope of rhetoric beyond persuasion. It is on the way to include also works on the theory and

---

[69]*Ibid.,* pp. 209-211.
[70]Thomas W. Copeland, "Critics at Work," *The Yale Review,* XL (Autumn 1950), 167-169.
[71]*A Rhetoric of Motives,* p. 172.
[72]*Ibid.,* p. xiii.
[73]*Ibid.,* p. 50.
[74]*Ibid.*
[75]*Ibid.*

practice of exposition, description, *communication* in general. Thus, finally, out of this principle, you can derive contemporary 'semantics' as an aspect of rhetoric."[76]

As he persists in "tracking down" the function of the term *rhetoric,* Burke notes an ingredient of rhetoric "lurking in such anthropologist's terms as 'magic' and 'witchcraft,' "[77] and concludes that one "comes closer to the true state of affairs if one treats the socializing aspects of magic as a 'primitive rhetoric' than if one sees modern rhetoric simply as a 'survival of primitive magic.' "[78] Whereas he does not believe that the term *rhetoric* is a "substitute" for such terms as *magic, witchcraft, socialization,* or *communication,* the term *rhetoric* "designates a *function* . . . present in the areas variously covered by those other terms."[79] Thus, one can place within the scope of rhetoric "all those statements by anthropologists, ethnologists, individual and social psychologists, and the like, that bear upon the *persuasive* aspects of language, the function of language as *addressed,* as direct or roundabout appeal to real or ideal audiences, without or within."[80] All these disciplines have made "good contributions to the New Rhetoric."[81]

In "individual psychology," particularly the Freudian concern with the neuroses of individual patients, "there is a strongly rhetorical ingredient."[82] Burke asks the question, "Indeed, what could be more profoundly rhetorical than Freud's notion of a dream that attains expression by stylistic subterfuges designed to evade the inhibitions of a moralistic censor? What is this but the exact analogue of the rhetorical devices of literature under political or theocratic censorship? The *ego* with its *id* confronts the *super-ego* much as an orator would confront a somewhat alien audience, whose susceptibilities he must flatter as a necessary step towards persuasion. The Freudian psyche is quite a parliament, with conflicting interests expressed in ways variously designed to take the claims of rival factions into account."[83]

By considering the individual self as "audience" Burke brings morals and ethics into the realm of rhetoric. He notes that "a modern 'post-Christian' rhetoric must also concern itself with the thought that, under the heading of appeal to audiences, would also be included any ideas or images privately addressed to the individual self for moralistic or incantatory purposes. For you become your own audience, in some respects a very lax one, in some respects very exacting, when you become involved in psychologically stylistic subterfuges for presenting your own case to yourself in sympathetic terms

---

[76]*Ibid.,* p. 77.
[77]*Ibid.,* p. 44.
[78]*Ibid.,* p. 43.
[79]*Ibid.,* p. 44.
[80]*Ibid.,* pp. 43-44.
[81]*Ibid.,* p. 40.
[82]*Ibid.,* p. 37.
[83]*Ibid.,* pp. 37, 38.

(and even terms that seem harsh can often be found on closer scrutiny to be flattering, as with neurotics who visit sufferings upon themselves in the name of very high-powered motives which, whatever their discomfiture, feed pride." Therefore, the "individual person, striving to form himself in accordance with the communicative norms that match the cooperative ways of his society, is by the same token concerned with the rhetoric of identification."[84]

By considering style as essentially a mode of "ingratiation" or as a technique by which one gives the signs of identification and consubstantiality, Burke finds a rhetorical motive in clothes, pastoral, courtship, and the like.[85]

Burke links dialectics with rhetoric through a definition of dialectics in "its most general sense" as "linguistic transformation"[86] and through an analysis of three different levels of language, or linguistic terminology.[87] Grammatically, he discusses the subject from the point of view of linguistic merger and division, polarity, and transcendence, being aware that there are "other definitions of dialectics":[88] "reasoning from opinion"; "the discovery of truth by the give and take of converse and redefinition"; "the art of disputation"; "the processes of 'interaction' between the verbal and the non-verbal"; "the competition of coöperation or the coöperation of competition"; "the spinning of terms out of terms"; "the internal dialogue of thought"; "any development . . . got by the interplay of various factors that mutually modify one another, and may be thought of as voices in a dialogue or roles in a play, with each voice or role in its partiality contributing to the development of the whole"; "the placement of one thought or thing in terms of its opposite"; "the progressive or successive development and reconciliation of opposites"; and "so putting questions to nature that nature can give unequivocal answer."[89] He considers all of these definitions as "variants or special applications of the functions"[90] of linguistic transformation conceived in terms of "Merger and division," "The three Major Pairs: action-passion, mind-body, being-nothing," and "Transcendence."[91]

Burke devotes 150 pages to the treatment of the dialectics of persuasion in the *Rhetoric*,[92] in addition to extensive treatment of it on the grammatical level.[93] Linguistic terminology is considered variously persuasive in its Positive, Dialectical, and Ultimate levels or orders.[94] "A positive term is most

---

[84] *Ibid.*, pp. 38, 39.
[85] *Ibid.*, pp. 115-127; see, also, p. xiv.
[86] *A Grammar of Motives*, p. 402.
[87] *A Rhetoric of Motives*, p. 183.
[88] *A Grammar of Motives*, pp. 402, 403.
[89] *Ibid.*, p. 403.
[90] *Ibid.*
[91] *Ibid.*, p. 402.
[92] *A Rhetoric of Motives*, pp. 183-333.
[93] *A Grammar of Motives*, pp. 323-443.
[94] *A Rhetoric of Motives*, p. 183.

unambiguously itself when it names a visible and tangible thing which can be located in time and place."[95] Dialectical terms "have no such strict location."[96] Thus terms like "Elizabethanism" or "capitalism" having no positive referent may be called "dialectical."[97] Often called "polar" terms,[98] they require an "opposite"[99] to define them and are on the level of "action," "principles," "ideas."[100] In an "ultimate order" of terminology, there is a "guiding idea" or "unitary principle."[101]

From the point of view of rhetoric, Burke believes that the "difference between a merely 'dialectical' confronting of parliamentary conflict and an 'ultimate' treatment of it would reside in this: The 'dialectical' order would leave the competing voices in a jangling relation with one another (a conflict solved *faute de mieux* by 'horse-trading'); but the 'ultimate' order would place these competing voices themselves in a *hierarchy,* or *sequence,* or *evaluative series,* so that, in some way, we went by a fixed and reasoned progression from one of these to another, the members of the entire group being arranged *developmentally* with relation to one another."[102] To Burke "much of the *rhetorical* strength in the Marxist dialectic comes from the fact that it is 'ultimate' in its order,"[103] for a "spokesman for the proletariat can think of himself as representing not only the interests of that class alone, but the grand design of the entire historical sequence. . . ."[104]

In his concept of a "pure persuasion," Burke seems to be extending the area of rhetoric beyond its usual scope. As a metaphysician he attempts to carry the process of rhetorical appeal to its ultimate limits. He admits that what he means by "pure persuasion" in the "absolute sense" exists nowhere, but believes that it can be present as a motivational ingredient in any rhetoric, no matter how "advantage-seeking such a rhetoric may be."[105] "Pure persuasion involves the saying of something, not for an extraverbal advantage to be got by the saying, but because of a satisfaction intrinsic to the saying. It summons because it likes the feel of a summons. It would be nonplused if the summons were answered. It attacks because it revels in the sheer syllables of vituperation. It would be horrified if, each time it finds a way of saying, 'Be damned,' it really did send a soul to rot in hell. It intuitively says, 'This is so,' purely and simply because this is so."[106] With such a concept Burke

---

[95] *Ibid.*
[96] *Ibid.,* p. 184.
[97] *Ibid.*
[98] *Ibid.*
[99] *The Philosophy of Literary Form,* n. 26, p. 109.
[100] *A Rhetoric of Motives,* p. 184.
[101] *Ibid.,* p. 187.
[102] *Ibid.*
[103] *Ibid.,* p. 190.
[104] *Ibid.,* pp. 190, 191.
[105] *Ibid.,* p. 269.
[106] *Ibid.*

finds himself at the "borders of metaphysics, or perhaps better 'meta-rhetoric.' . . ."[107]

III

Of great significance to the rhetorician is Burke's consideration of the general problem of motivation. Concerned with the problem of motivation in literary strategy,[108] he nevertheless intends that his observations be considered pertinent to the social sphere in general.[109] He had observed that people's conduct has been explained by an "endless variety of theories: ethnological, geographical, sociological, physiological, historical, endocrinological, economic, anatomical, mystical, pathological, and so on."[110] The assigning of motives, he concludes, is a "matter of *appeal*,"[111] and this depends upon one's general orientation. "A motive is not some fixed thing, like a table, which one can go to and look at. It is a term of interpretation, and being such it will naturally take its place within the framework of our *Weltanschauung* as a whole."[112] "To explain one's conduct by the vocabulary of motives current among one's group is about as self-deceptive as giving the area of a field in the accepted terms of measurement. One is simply interpreting with the only vocabulary he knows. One is stating his orientation, which involves a vocabulary of ought and ought-not, with attendant vocabulary of praiseworthy and blameworthy."[113] "We discern situational patterns by means of the particular vocabulary of the cultural group into which we are born."[114] Motives are "distinctly linguistic products."[115]

To Burke, the subject of motivation is a "philosophic one, not ultimately to be solved in terms of empirical science."[116] A motive is a "shorthand" term for "situation."[117] One may discuss motives on three levels, rhetorical, symbolic, and grammatical.[118] One is on the "grammatical" level when he concerns himself with the problem of the "intrinsic," or the problem of "substance."[119] "Men's conception of motive . . . is integrally related to their conception of substance. Hence, to deal with problems of motive is to deal with problems of substance."[120]

---

[107] *Ibid.*, p. 267.
[108] *The Philosophy of Literary Form*, p. 78.
[109] *Ibid.*, p. 105.
[110] *Permanence and Change*, p. 47.
[111] *Ibid.*, p. 38.
[112] *Ibid.*
[113] *Ibid.*, p. 33.
[114] *Ibid.*, p. 52.
[115] *Ibid.*
[116] *A Grammar of Motives*, p. xxiii.
[117] *Permanence and Change*, p. 44.
[118] *A Grammar of Motives*, p. 465.
[119] *Ibid.*
[120] *Ibid.*, p. 337.

On the "grammatical" level Burke gives his most profound treatment of the problem of motivation. Strongly allied with the classicists throughout all his works in both his ideas and his methodology, Burke shows indebtedness to Aristotle for his treatment of motivation. Taking a clue from Aristotle's consideration of the "circumstances" of an action,[121] Burke concludes that "In a rounded statement about motives, you must have some word that names the *act* (names what took place, in thought or deed), and another that names the *scene* (the background of the act, the situation in which it occurred); also, you must indicate what person or kind of person *(agent)* performed the act, what means or instruments he used *(agency)*, and the *purpose*."[122] Act, Scene, Agent, Agency, Purpose become the "pentad" for pondering the problem of human motivation.[123] Among these various terms grammatical "ratios" prevail which have rhetorical implications. One might illustrate by saying that, for instance, between *scene* and *act* a logic prevails which indicates that a certain quality of scene calls for an analogous quality of act. Hence, if a situation is said to be of a certain nature, a corresponding attitude toward it is implied. Burke explains by pointing to such an instance as that employed by a speaker who, in discussing Roosevelt's war-time power exhorted that Roosevelt should be granted "unusual powers" because the country was in an "unusual international situation." The scene-act "ratio" may be applied in two ways. "It can be applied deterministically in statements that a certain policy *had* to be adopted in a certain situation, or it may be applied in hortatory statements to the effect that a certain policy *should be* adopted in conformity with the situation."[124] These ratios are "principles of determination."[125] The pentad would allow for ten such ratios: scene-act, scene-agent, scene-agency, scene-purpose, act-purpose, act-agent, act-agency, agent-purpose, agent-agency, and agency-purpose.[126] Political commentators now generally use *situation* as their synonym for *scene,* "though often without any clear concept of its function as a statement about motives."[127]

Burke draws his key terms for the study of motivation from the analysis of drama. Being developed from the analysis of drama, his pentad "treats language and thought primarily as modes of action."[128] His method for handling motivation is designed to contrast with the methodology of the physical sciences which considers the subject of motivation in mechanistic terms of "flat cause-and-effect or stimulus-and-response."[129] Physicalist terminologies are proper to non-verbalizing entities, but man as a species should

---

[121] *Ethica Nicomachea,* tr. by W. D. Ross, III, i, 16.
[122] *A Grammar of Motives,* p. xv.
[123] *Ibid.*
[124] *Ibid.,* p. 13.
[125] *Ibid.,* p. 15.
[126] *Ibid.*
[127] *Ibid.,* p. 13.
[128] *Ibid.,* p. xxii.
[129] *The Philosophy of Literary Form,* pp. 103, 106.

be approached through his specific trait, his use of symbols. Burke opposes
the reduction of the human realm to terms that lack sufficient "coordinates";
he does not, however, question the fitness of physicalist terminologies for
treating the physical realm. According to Burke, "Philosophy, like common
sense, must think of human motivation dramatistically, in terms of action and
its ends."[130] "Language being essentially human, we should view human
relations in terms of the linguistic instrument."[131] His "vocabulary" or "set of
coordinates" serves "for the integration of all phenomena studied by the
social sciences."[132] It also serves as a "perspective for the analysis of history
which is a 'dramatic' process. . . ."[133]

One may wonder with Charles Morris whether "an analysis of man
through his language provides us with a full account of human motives."[134]
One strongly feels the absence of insights into motivation deriving from the
psychologists and scientists.

IV

Burke is not only philosopher and theorist; he has applied his critical
principles practically to a great number of literary works. Of these, three are
of particular interest to the rhetorician. In two instances, Burke attempts to
explain the communicative relationship between the writer and his audience.
Taking the speech of Antony from Shakespeare's *Julius Caesar*,[135] Burke
examines the speech from "the standpoint of the rhetorician, who is
concerned with a work's processes of appeal."[136] A similar operation is
performed on a scene from *Twelfth Night*.[137]

Undoubtedly one of his most straightforward attempts at analysis of a
work of "literature for use," occurs in an essay on "The Rhetoric of Hitler's
'Battle.'"[138] "The main ideal of criticism, as I conceive it," Burke has
observed, "is to use all that there is to use."[139] "If there is any slogan that
should reign among critical precepts, it is that 'circumstances alter
occasions.'"[140] Considering *Mein Kampf* as "the well of Nazi magic,"[141] Burke
brings his knowledge of sociology and anthropology to bear in order to
"discover what kind of 'medicine' this medicine-man has concocted, that we

---

[130] *A Grammar of Motives*, pp. 55, 56.
[131] *Ibid.*, p. 317.
[132] *The Philosophy of Literary Form*, p. 105.
[133] *Ibid.* p. 317.
[134] Charles Morris, "The Strategy of Kenneth Burke," *The Nation*, CLXIII (July 27, 1946), 106.
[135] "Antony in Behalf of the Play," *Philosophy of Literary Form*, pp. 329-343.
[136] *Ibid.*, p. 330.
[137] "Trial Translation (from *Twelfth Night), ibid.*, pp. 344-349.
[138] *Ibid.*, pp. 191-220.
[139] *Ibid.*, p. 23.
[140] *Ibid.*
[141] *Ibid.*, p. 192.

may know, with greater accuracy, exactly what to guard against, if we are to forestall the concocting of similar medicine in America."[142] He considers Hitler's "centralizing hub of *ideas*"[143] and his selection of Munich as a "mecca geographically located"[144] as methods of recruiting followers "from among many discordant and divergent bands. . . ."[145] He examines the symbol of the "international Jew"[146] as that "of a *common enemy*,"[147] the " 'medicinal' appeal of the Jew as scapegoat. . . ."[148]

His knowledge of psychoanalysis is useful in the analysis of the "sexual symbolism" that runs through the book: "Germany in dispersion is the 'dehorned Siegfried.' The masses are 'feminine.' As such, they desire to be led by a dominating male. This male, as orator, woos them—and, when he has won them, he commands them. The rival male, the villainous Jew, would on the contrary 'seduce' them. If he succeeds, he poisons their blood by intermingling with them. Whereupon, by purely associative connections of ideas, we are moved into attacks upon syphilis, prostitution, incest, and other similar misfortunes, which are introduced as a kind of 'musical' argument when he is on the subject of 'blood poisoning' by intermarriage or, in its 'spiritual' equivalent, by the infection of 'Jewish' ideas. . . ."[149]

His knowledge of history and religion is employed to show that the *"materialization"* of a religious pattern is "one terrifically effective weapon . . . in a period where religion has been progressively weakened by many centuries of capitalist materialism."[150]

Conventional rhetorical knowledge leads him to call attention to the "power of endless repetition";[151] the appeal of a sense of "community";[152] the appeal of security resulting from "a world view" for a people who had previously seen the world only "piecemeal";[153] and the appeal of Hitler's "inner voice"[154] which served as a technique of leader-people "identification."[155]

Burke's analysis is comprehensive and penetrating. It stands as a superb example of the fruitfulness of a method of comprehensive rhetorical analysis which goes far beyond conventional patterns.

---

[142] *Ibid.*, p. 191.
[143] *Ibid.*, p. 192.
[144] *Ibid.*
[145] *Ibid.*
[146] *Ibid.*, p. 194.
[147] *Ibid.*, p. 193.
[148] *Ibid.*, p. 195.
[149] *Ibid.*
[150] *Ibid.*, p. 194.
[151] *Ibid.*, p. 217.
[152] *Ibid.*
[153] *Ibid.*, p. 218.
[154] *Ibid.*, p. 207.
[155] *Ibid.*

Conclusion

Burke is difficult and often confusing. He cannot be understood by casual reading of his various volumes. In part the difficulty arises from the numerous vocabularies he employs. His words in isolation are usually simple enough, but he often uses them in new contexts. To read one of his volumes independently, without regard to the chronology of publication, makes the problem of comprehension even more difficult because of the specialized meanings attaching to various words and phrases.

Burke is often criticized for "obscurity" in his writings. The charge may be justified. However, some of the difficulty of comprehension arises from the compactness of his writing, the uniqueness of his organizational patterns, the penetration of his thought, and the breadth of his endeavor. "In books like the *Grammar* and the *Rhetoric*," observed Malcolm Cowley, "we begin to see the outlines of a philosophical system on the grand scale. . . . Already it has its own methodology (called 'dramatism'), its own esthetics (based on the principle that works of art are symbolic actions), its logic and dialectics, its ethics (or picture of the good life) and even its metaphysics, which Burke prefers to describe as a meta-rhetoric."[156]

One cannot possibly compress the whole of Burke's thought into an article. The most that one can achieve is to signify his importance as a theorist and critic and to suggest the broad outlines of his work. Years of study and contemplation of the general idea of effectiveness in language have equipped him to deal competently with the subject of rhetoric from its beginning as a specialized discipline to the present time. To his thorough knowledge of classical tradition he has added rich insights gained from serious study of anthropology, sociology, history, psychology, philosophy, and the whole body of humane letters. With such equipment, he has become the most profound student of rhetoric now writing in America.

---

[156]Malcolm Cowley, "Prolegomena to Kenneth Burke," *The New Republic*, CXXII (June 5, 1950), 18, 19.

Kenneth Burke
and the Criticism of Symbolic Action

by Stanley Edgar Hyman

If, as Kenneth Burke has sometimes insisted, a book is the indefinite expansion of one sentence, then a critical method is only the securing of material to document that sentence. Actually, Burke has a number of sentences—that is, a number of methods—in each of his books, but if he had to stand or fall by one sentence it would probably be: Literature is symbolic action. To use his own stress-shifting technique, his earlier work emphasized it as *symbolic* action, his later work as symbolic *action*. With a kind of limitless fertility Burke has done everything in criticism's bag of tricks, including several things he put there, but the choice is either to let him represent every aspect of modern criticism, in which case he has written your book for you, or else to restrict him arbitrarily to that critical area, symbolic expression, in which he has particularly specialized, with the additional factor that it is something no one else covers adequately. In his essay "The Problem of the Intrinsic," reprinted as an appendix to *A Grammar of Motives,* Burke is incautious enough to write: "I began by speaking of the three fields: Grammar, Rhetoric, and Symbolic. It is perhaps only in the third of these categories that modern criticism has something vitally new to offer the student of literature." This is not true (even hedged by the word "vitally"), as his own work demonstrates, but it does point at the tremendous shock of novelty in Burke's studies of symbolic action, so that anyone reading him for the first time has the sudden sense of a newly discovered country in his own backyard.

Burke's first book of criticism, *Counter-Statement,* published in 1931, set up most of the principles and procedures he later developed, termed "counter" because they were then (as always) a minority view. The book is a collection of essays, some of them revised periodical pieces, dealing with general literary problems, including the political program implicit in his aesthetic, and with specific writers: Flaubert, Pater, de Gourmont, Mann, and Gide. The concept of symbolic action is as yet undeveloped, but Burke makes constant glancing suggestions of it: Gide's concern with homosexuality made him a

Reprinted from *The Armed Vision* (New York: Alfred A. Knopf, 1948). Used by permission of Phoebe Pettingell Hyman.

political liberal by training "his sense of divergence," Gourmont's "paper" transgressions resulted from his leprosy and seclusion, the biographer "symbolizes" his own problems in choosing to write of Napoleon, and so on. Some of the techniques later developed for studying symbolic action are also suggested, particularly the contextual associations of imagery, as when he notes the malevolent contexts of the word "future" in Shakespeare, in contrast to its confident use in Browning, and the power of "demon" in Keats, opposed to its innocuousness in Tennyson.

The book's chief concern, however, is with rhetoric, and its dichotomous terms are concerned with demarcating rhetoric from grammar: "pamphleteering" versus "inquiry," "declamatory" versus "realistic," "the psychology of form" versus "the psychology of information," with no third term for "symbolic." In fact, Burke's insistence in the book that art is not experience, but *something added* to experience, puts the emphasis in opposition to the concept of symbolic action, but then in a modification, attacking the concept of vulgar economic causation, he presents the germ of the later view. He writes:

> In one sense, art or ideas do "reflect" a situation, since they are a way of dealing with a situation. When a man solves a problem, however, we should hardly say that his solution is "caused" by the problem to be solved. The problem may limit somewhat the *nature* of his solution, but the problem can remain unsolved forever unless he *adds* the solution. Similarly, the particular ways of feeling and seeing which the thinker or the artist develops to cope with a situation, the vocabulary they bring into prominence, the special kinds of intellectual and emotional adjustment which their works make possible by the discovery of appropriate symbols for encompassing the situation, the kinds of action they stimulate by their attitudes towards the situation, are not "caused" by the situation which they are designed to handle.

Here, minus the military metaphor, is the whole concept of works of art as "strategies" for encompassing situations; that is, symbolic action. Besides its great importance for developing the concept of rhetoric in art and its hints of the later symbolic, *Counter-Statement* is chiefly interesting for the passion of its concern with art. "The Status of Art" is an elaborate *Apologie for Poetrie* against subtler detractors than Sidney or Shelley had to cope with; "Thomas Mann and André Gide" is an exercise in scrupulosity that spends ten pages erecting an ethical distinction between them and then demolishes it as oversimple; "Program," "Lexicon Rhetoricae," and "Applications of the Terminology" are an ironic triptych the parts of which, respectively, set the aims of the good life as Burke sees them, define the concepts that underlie the program, and apply them to problems of art.

Burke's next critical book, *Permanence and Change,* subtitled *An Anatomy of Purpose,* appeared in 1935. It is the least "literary" of his books, although precisely how it would classify is hard to say: as social psychology, social history, philosophy, moral possibility, "secular conversion," or what. Its central concern is, as with Burke's latest book, "purpose" (that is, "motives," the situations underlying "attitudes" and "strategies"). The book's three sections are: "On Interpretation," a survey of "criticism" in areas of life rather than art; "Perspective by Incongruity," an exploration of the metaphoric nature of strategies and systems of meaning; and "The Basis of Simplification," Burke's own sketch for a critical frame that would clarify and resolve the confusions he has discussed earlier. Thus, it is a book about society and social communication, but its key metaphor (what Burke would later call its "representative anecdote") is Man as Artist, and it treats social problems in terms of poetic and critical techniques (characteristically, its topic sentence is "All living things are critics"—a greater democratization of criticism than Burke's namesake Edmund ever planned—and its last section states: "all men are poets"). Fittingly, most of what Burke has to say about symbolic action in the book comes in the "Perspective by Incongruity" section. He notes that felling a noble tree (a theme that has always particularly interested him) may be a symbolic parricide; that Darwin's intense attacks of vertigo, like Joyce's blindness, would seem to be the symbolic self-punishment for the "impiety" of his work; that acts from mountain-climbing and bull-fighting to empire-building contain substantial symbolic ingredients; that McDougall's integration-dissociation psychology, analogically related to the structure of the British Empire, is actually a projection of it, and would be particularly curative for British patients. Despite these frequent symbolic readings, the concept of works of art as strategies has not yet coalesced, and the book tends to use the term "strategy" simply to mean a trick, so that rationalizing one's motives as diplomatically as possible is "strategic."

The central concept of *Permanence and Change* is the concept of perspective by incongruity, or metaphor, the seeing of one thing in terms of something that, to a greater or lesser extent, it is not. Burke writes:

> Indeed, as the documents of science pile up, are we not coming to see that whole works of scientific research, even entire schools, are hardly more than the patient repetition, in all its ramifications, of a fertile metaphor? Thus we have, at different eras in history, considered man as the son of God, as an animal, as a political and economic brick, as a machine, each such metaphor, and a hundred others, serving as the cue for an unending line of data and generalizations.

"Perspective by incongruity," as Burke defines it, is a method he first noted in Nietzsche and his pupil Spengler, the switching of a term from its natural context to another where it is revealing although impious, like speaking of Arabian Puritanism, or Eliot's phrase "decadent athleticism," or Veblen's term "trained incapacity." As Burke extends its application in the book, it eventually comes to include even concepts like "rebirth," the principal symbolic action in his later work:

Once a set of new meanings is firmly established, we can often note in art another kind of regression: the artist is suddenly prompted to review the memories of his youth because they combine at once the qualities of strangeness and intimacy. Probably every man has these periods of rebirth, a new angle of vision whereby so much that he had forgot suddenly becomes useful or relevant, hence grows vivid again in his memory. Rebirth and perspective by incongruity are thus seen to be synonymous, a process of conversion, though such words as conversion and rebirth are usually reserved for only the most spectacular of such reorientations, the religious.

One of Burke's own characteristic perspectives by incongruity in the book, later developed into a major source of insight or irony, is etymology, going back to the root meanings of words for a fresh or "reborn" slant, as where he notes that "theory" means "vision of God," that "caricature" comes from a root meaning to "overload," that "property" and "propriety" "are not etymologically so close by mere accident."

Permanence and Change contains a good deal of general literary discussion, but its specific literary references tend to be incidental, used as examples or analogies, and not discussed in any detail. Burke refers glancingly to the Nietzschean symbol of the mountain in *The Magic Mountain;* some of Shakespeare's techniques of stylistic ingratiation; the planned incongruity of Hemingway's descriptions of violence in terms of Jane Austen delicacies; the inadequate exorcism of their private monsters in the work of Nietzsche and Swift; the "abyss-motif" in Eliot, Milton, and Hart Crane: Lawrence's "ethical universe-building." The only work of imaginative literature quoted from in the book and discussed at any length, curiously enough, is Edwin Seaver's sociological novel *The Company,* and no line of poetry is anywhere quoted.

Burke's next book, *Attitudes toward History* in 1937, is his most significant work in terms of symbolic action and will be discussed below at some length. *The Philosophy of Literary Form,* subtitled *Studies in Symbolic Action,* appeared in 1941 and might be considered almost a supplement of practical applications of the concepts in *Attitudes.* Except for the long title essay, the book is a collection of articles and reviews done in the preceding decade. The essays are united by their common concern with "speculation on the nature of linguistic, or symbolic, or literary action—and in a search for more precise ways of locating or defining such action," or, more generally, Burke's purpose is "to identify the substance of a particular literary act by a theory of literary action in general." In the course of this, Burke is centrally occupied with what he calls "strategies," related to the "attitudes" of his previous book (note the progress of his key metaphor from Man as Declaimer in *Counter-Statement,* to Man as Artist in *Permanence and Change,* Man as Gesturer in *Attitudes toward History,* and Man as Warrior in *The Philosophy of Literary Form*). The first page of the book begins by distinguishing between "strategies" and "situations":

So I should propose an initial working distinction between "strategies" and "situations," whereby we think of poetry (I here use the term to include any work of critical or imaginative cast) as the adopting of various strategies for the encompassing of situations. These strategies size up the situations, name their structure and outstanding ingredients, and name them in a way that contains an attitude towards them.

This point of view does not, by any means, vow us to personal or historical subjectivism. The situations are real; the strategies for handling them have public content; and in so far as situations overlap from individual to individual, or from one historical period to another, the strategies possess universal relevance.

In "Literature as Equipment for Living," an essay attempting to define a sociological criticism, Burke proposes the classification of sophisticated works of art in terms of the basic strategies he finds in proverbs: "strategies for selecting enemies and allies, for socializing losses, for warding off evil eye, for purification, propitiation, and desanctification, consolation and vengeance, admonition and exhortation, implicit commands or instructions of one sort or another."

These and other strategies are the basic symbolic actions of art. Burke defines the symbolic act as "the dancing of an attitude" and carefully distinguishes it from what we think of as the "real" act:[1]

Still, there is a difference, and a radical difference, between building a house and writing a poem about building a house—and a poem about having children by marriage is not the same thing as having children by marriage. There are practical acts, and there are symbolic acts (nor is the distinction, clear enough in its extremes, to be dropped simply because there is a borderline area wherein many practical acts take on a symbolic ingredient, as one may buy a certain commodity not merely to use it, but also because its possession testifies to his enrollment in a certain stratum of society).

Burke classifies symbolic action on three levels: the bodily or biological, from insomnia to the over-all sensory experience of a poem (like the sense of drought in reading "The Ancient Mariner"); the personal or familistic, chiefly relations to parents and other "familiar" persons; and the abstract, as in symbolic enrollment or re-enrollment built around rebirth. As a way of getting around resistance to a term as dubious as "symbolic" (and, more seriously, of advancing toward a useful methodological criterion), Burke proposes the substitution of the ultra-respectable word "statistical," in the sense that the "statistical" inspection of a body of images or a body of works

---

[1] Allen Tate has a wonderful reference in *Reactionary Essays* to a man who discovers oil under his land and, instead of digging, writes a poem saying: "O Oil, make me thy conduit!"

will reveal a trend of symbolic significance, whereas any isolated image or work might seem purely "practical." Thus a statistical study of associations and clusters will show the structure of motivation operating. Later in the same essay Burke lists a number of his "rules of thumb," techniques for studying poetic strategies that he uses throughout the book. They include isolating the basic "dramatic alignment" and obtaining its supplementary "equations" inductively from the work; charting associative clusters and structural relations; noting "critical points" or "watershed moments," especially beginnings, endings, peripeties, discontinuities, weaknesses of motivation, and particular strengths of dramatic organization; noting the imagery of "agon" or rebirth; and then, in all these classifications, introducing the "differentia" that gives each symbolic act in literature its unique character.

The chief new terms Burke produces in *The Philosophy of Literary Form* are the concepts of the "Power family" (used throughout, but only so named in the book's Introduction), whereby powers in all areas are related so that any one can do symbolic service for any other; and the naming of the three ingredients in art as: "dream," the symbolic factors; "prayer," the rhetorical factors; and "chart," the factors of realistic sizing up (which would probably coincide with "grammatical"). In terms of the "Power family," Burke is able to translate rapidly and efficiently from literary to non-literary areas and back again in terms of symbolic action, so that, as he says, "one may marry or rape by politics, wage war in argument, be mentally superior by the insignia of social privilege, bind or loose by knowledge, show one's muscle or enhance one's stature by financial income, etc." In terms of the dream-prayer-chart division, Burke is able to achieve a balance of symbolic, rhetorical, and grammatical emphasis in treating any given work (whereas before, in *Counter-Statement* and *Permanence and Change,* he had leaned particularly toward the rhetorical, and in *Attitudes* toward the symbolic).

At the same time Burke develops purely grammatical techniques of analysis (that is, not concerned particularly with either how the device affects the reader or how it expresses the poet, but simply with what it is and how it operates), as in his study "On Musicality in Verse," which explores subtle, almost unnoticeable phonetic effects in poetry, involving such things as cognate variation, augmentation, diminution, and chiasmus. The piece that Burke considers the "most complete" example of analysis focused on a single work in the book, "The Rhetoric of Hitler's *Battle,*" is a balanced chart-dream-prayer analysis of *Mein Kampf:* showing in purely grammatical terms to what extent it reflected realities in Germany and the world situation, in symbolic terms to what extent it was Hitler's great evil poem, and in rhetorical terms to what extent and through what devices it captured the German people, thus ironically converting Hitler's already completed symbolic act of world domination into something that just missed being the real thing. Burke explores the relationship between these emphases, showing the way, for example, that a symbolic factor in Hitler, like the Jew as scapegoat, enters the work as a formal structure, produces a comparable symbolic action in the reader, and thus operates rhetorically to "convert." In thus emphasizing an understanding of the precise nature of Hitler's "snake-oil," valuable pragmatically in coping with it and native variants, Burke ends with the problem returned constructively from the symbolic to the real world.

Most of his studies, however, deal with a "purer" literature. In this book the literary discussion is central rather than peripheral as in *Permanence and Change*. He analyzes Coleridge, particularly "The Ancient Mariner," at great length, as dramatic ritual of major importance; discusses the *Eumenides* of Æschylus in detail to illustrate the sort of full poetic meaning he would oppose to "semantic" meaning; studies Iago's rhetoric as a caricature of the dramatist's art, and Antony's rhetoric as a triumph of it; explores two contemporary novels, Robert Penn Warren's *Night Rider* and John Steinbeck's *The Grapes of Wrath*, to demonstrate the analytic techniques he has listed as "rules of thumb"; and analyzes authors from Homer and Lucretius to Flaubert and Lewis Carroll in the course of exploring other critical problems. In the book's Appendix he includes reviews that demonstrate his critical practice on contemporary fiction, poetry, drama, and even paintings.

Burke's latest book, *A Grammar of Motives,* published in 1945, is the first volume of a gigantic trilogy, planned to include *A Rhetoric of Motives* and *A Symbolic of Motives,* which will be called something like *On Human Relations*. The aim of the whole series is no less than the comprehensive exploration of human motives and the forms of thought and expression built around them, and its ultimate object, expressed in the epigraph: *"Ad bellum purificandum,"* is to eliminate the whole world of conflict that can be eliminated through understanding. The method or key metaphor for the study is "drama" or "dramatism," and the basic terms of analysis are the dramatistic pentad: Act, Scene, Agent, Agency, and Purpose. The *Grammar,* which Burke confesses in the Introduction grew from a prolegomena of a few hundred words to nearly 200,000, is a consideration of the purely internal relationship of these five terms, "their possibilities of transformation, their range of permutations and combinations," as reflected in statements about human motives, chiefly as expressed in "theological, metaphysical and juridical doctrines." The *Rhetoric* is to deal with the audience-effect aspect of utterances, drawing its material chiefly from "parliamentary and diplomatic devices, editorial bias, sales methods and incidents of social sparring"; and the *Symbolic* with the psychological-expression aspects, drawing its material principally from "the forms and methods of art."

It is not relevant to our topic here, nor within my competence, to discuss Burke's treatment of all the major philosophic views man has evolved, except to note that his aim is not to debunk or defend them, but to characterize or "place" them, to show which key terms they feature while slighting the others. "It is not my purpose at this late date merely to summarize and report on past philosophies," he writes. "Rather, I am trying to show how certain key terms might be used to 'call the plays' in any and all philosophies." This "placing" requires what Burke calls a "representative anecdote," a key metaphor, and he opens the book with the representative anecdote of the Creation (that is, God as Creator) and concludes it with political Constitutions (that is, Man as

Constitutor), while the entire book is framed around Drama as the representative anecdote (Man as Acter or Actor—a great improvement at least in generality over such earlier metaphors as Man as Warrior). He notes that "modern war" would make an unwieldy anecdote, "since it is more of a *confusion* than a *form*," and that the characteristic scientific terminology that uses Man as Laboratory Animal as its representative anecdote is inevitably "reductive." In selecting Drama as his representative anecdote, Burke acquires a terminology and framework with which he can discuss anything from the closet drama of a man tying his shoelace to the big-spectacle drama of Genesis.

Undismayed by the whole corpus of organized philosophic thought, Burke draws his analytic material from his usual widespread and informal sources, including the familiar introspective memories of his own behavior (he remembers first reading Santayana and dreaming "of a tourist life in white flannels along the Mediterranean"), and conjectures about his unconscious processes (in looking for "terms" that "grandly converge," he notes that he may have been inspired by thinking of "terminals" and "Grand Central"). He quotes, as usual, the revealing remarks, questions, even dreams, of his children, to illuminate the philosophers' problems; and leans heavily on his old etymological trick of casting light on a term by going back to its root meaning; noting, for example, that "investing" means that "one *clothes oneself* in the severe promises of future yield, *donning* the idealizations of what one would like to be, *dressing up* in the symbols of lien and bond."

For a book devoted to "placing" philosophies, the *Grammar* manages to spend a surprising amount of space on literature. It begins and ends on Ibsen (Burke has noted that beginnings and endings are particularly significant), illustrating the scene-act ratio in the opening pages with Ibsen's *An Enemy of the People* and concluding with an analysis of *Peer Gynt* to illustrate "essence." In the course of the book he draws on examples from Pope and Wordsworth to Caldwell, Hemingway, and Richard Wright, and studies the *Phaedrus* at length to demonstrate dialectic transcendence.

After the publication of *The Philosophy of Literary Form* Ransom had suggested his doubts that the dramatistic method could handle lyric poetry. Picking up the challenge, Burke analyzes Shelley's "Ode to the West Wind" and Wordsworth's "Composed upon Westminster Bridge" as examples of incipient or arrested "action" in the text of the book, and includes three appendices illustrating the method in practice on various lyric forms: "The Problem of the Intrinsic," a general discussion of the dramatistic method in analyzing lyrics, in contrast to the disguised and unformulated dramatism of the neo-Aristotelian school; "Motives and Motifs in the Poetry of Marianne Moore," the method applied to a body of lyric poetry; and "Symbolic Action in a Poem by Keats," a remarkable tour de force following the development of the action in the "Ode on a Grecian Urn," which, like the essay on *Mein Kampf* in the previous book, is probably the best illustration of the detailed application of Burke's method in its totality.

A Grammar of Motives makes occasional rhetorical and symbolic readings, which Burke was apparently unable to resist, giving a substantial foretaste of what the *Rhetoric* and *Symbolic* will be like. By way of rhetorical meanings Burke notes that there are constant rhetorical motives behind the manipulations of the grammar (as where one deflects attention from an evil in society, the scene-act "ratio" or principle of determination, by situating it as a factor in people, the act-agent ratio); that "whatever speculation and investigation may precede Marxist assertions, there is the pressure to make them serviceable as a Rhetorical inducement to action on the part of people who have slight interest in speculation and investigation *per se*"; that legislatures adopt the "Hamletic" strategy of endless investigations to avoid embarrassing decisions; that "political platforms are best analyzed on the rhetorical level, as they are quite careless grammatically." By way of hints of the *Symbolic*, Burke notes: that "purely philosophic theories of power" may be inspired "by personal problems of potency"; that Henry Adams's *Education* is a rebirth ritual, and *Murder in the Cathedral* a purification ritual; that Arnold's "Sohrab and Rustum" (for obvious reasons in the son of Thomas Arnold) reverses the Jack the Giant Killer pattern of fantasy and has the son slain in combat by the father; that Hume's questioning of "ancestry" in attacking causality and Bentham's "neutral" or "sterilized" vocabulary are significantly "bachelors'" theories; that pragmatism, instrumentalism, operationalism, and similar philosophies featuring "agency" all point at a fixation on the mother, whereas "purpose" philosophies point at the erotic woman of maturity; that the turn from verse to prose in a writer's work may be a similar development from the "maternal" or "familial" to the "erotic" or adult. One brief section of the book, the last part of the chapter on "Scene," consists of "a few observations" on rhetorical and symbolic meanings in regard to Stoic and Epicurean philosophies, inserted "to illustrate how the other levels impinge upon the Grammatical," and suggesting for the later books a bewildering and wonderful array of possibilities in similar analysis.

Burke's uncollected periodical and symposium pieces have more or less followed the development of his books. The articles prior to 1941 not collected in *The Philosophy of Literary Form,* with the exception of the essay on "Surrealism" in *New Directions 1940,* tend to repeat other work, and the "Surrealism" essay seems largely a foretaste of "placing" material that will probably be handled in the *Symbolic.* The reviews not collected tend to be on other critics, from Tate and Ransom to Mary Colum, and only two of them are still significant: one the review of Spender's *Forward from Liberalism* in the *New Republic,* 1937, because on the basis of Spender's "non-collective" Communism Burke predicted his later disillusionment; and the other the review of two studies of Coleridge, in the *New Republic,* 1939, because it is one of the rare examples of Burke's use of his symbolic-action readings for "debunking," when he disparages the Kafka and Kierkegaard fads because they represent "the stage of masturbatory adolescence" and "quarrels with the father," which is "trivial" compared to the complexity of Coleridge's symbolic action.

Burke's pieces written since the *Philosophy* include three articles that did not find a place in the *Grammar:* "The Character of our Culture" in the *Southern Review,* Spring 1941, a comment on a symposium held by the American Philosophical Society (Blackmur commented in the same issue), with Burke chiefly interested in showing the symposium's avoidance of the "monetary"; "On Motivation in Yeats," in the *Southern Review,* Winter 1942, a preliminary exercise in the dramatistic analysis of lyric poetry; and "The Tactics of Motivation," in *Chimera,* Spring and Summer 1943, a work-out of the whole pentad in commenting on the manifesto for naturalism of the Failure of Nerve series in *Partisan Review.* His recent reviews have dealt briefly with contemporary criticism in reviews of books by Alfred Kazin and Eric Bentley, as well as Ransom, Tate, Warren, and others, and with a number of historical, linguistic, and philosophic works where he has been content to add levels of meaning to the book (finding more symbolic interpretations for Marguerite Young's *Angel in the Forest,* adding a rhetorical level to Cassirer's magical and semantic levels in *The Myth of the State*). One of Burke's briefer reviews, in the *New Republic* in 1943, of Downes's and Siegmeister's *Treasury of American Song,* reveals an unbecoming ignorance of the material (Burke's only display of that occupational disease of reviewers, so far as I know). In addition, in "Kinds of Criticism" in *Poetry,* August 1946, and "Ideology and Myth" in *Accent,* Summer 1947, Burke has published what seem to be fragments of the *Rhetoric.*

2

In *Attitudes toward History,* 1937, despite the title, literature is central, (whereas in *Permanence and Change* it is peripheral and illustrative). The book is a study of literary attitudes as symbolic action or ritual, and the "history" of the title only points up the concern with grounding literature in society and showing the interrelationships of its attitudes to "the curve of history," politics, and economics. The book's basic division of attitudes is into those of "acceptance" and "rejection" (Schopenhauer's *Bejahung und Verneinung*), and—growing out of them, combining the best features of both—acceptance-rejection, which Burke calls "the comic." "Frames of Acceptance" are orthodoxies and include philosophies like those of William James, Whitman, and Emerson; literary forms like epic, tragedy, comedy, and lyric; and ritual structures in general centering in incest-awe and symbolic castration. "Frames of Rejection" are heresies, the emphasis shifting against the symbols of authority, and include philosophies from Machiavelli to Marx and Nietzsche; literary forms like the elegy, satire, burlesque and the grotesque; and ritual structures in general centering on symbolic parricide. The comic frame is an attitude of ambivalence "neither wholly euphemistic nor wholly debunking." Burke writes:

> A comic frame of motives avoids these difficulties, showing us how an act can "dialectically" contain both transcendental and material ingredients, both imagination and bureaucratic embodiments, both "service" and "spoils." But it also makes us sensitive to the

point at which one of these ingredients becomes hypertrophied, with the corresponding atrophy of the other. A well-balanced ecology requires the symbiosis of the two.

The name "comic" has confused many readers, principally through confusion with "comedy." As a matter of fact, the name was probably chosen as Burke's ironic observation that being an accepter-rejecter in a world of ravening accepters and ravening rejecters is a pretty funny thing to be. He admits in the book to choosing "comic" when he might just as well have chosen "humanistic" because it "sounds better" to him (exploring his subconscious to find that it is principally a way of saying his own name, Kenneth, and a preoccupation with death by choking or gagging). Whatever the source of the term, the attitude it represents is basic to Burke's values, and the book concludes with a plea for the framing of comic vocabularies. It seems to connote not only "ironic," "humanistic," and "sceptical," but all the implications of truth emergent out of an *agon* in "dialectic" and "dramatistic."

The basic concept of the book, underlying all three frames or attitudes, is the concept of "symbolic action," that act "which a man does because he is interested in doing it exactly as he does do it." These symbolic acts, as Burke sees them, center in initiation, change of identity, rebirth, purification, and other related magical ceremonies. He writes:

> Our basic principle is our contention that all symbolism can be treated as the ritualistic naming and changing of identity (whereby a man fits himself for a role in accordance with established coordinates or for a change of role in accordance with new coordinates which necessity has forced upon him). The nearest to a schematic statement that we might come is this:
>
> In general, these rituals of change or "purification" center about three kinds of imagery: purification by ice, by fire, or by decay. "Ice" tends to emphasize castration and frigidity. . . . Purification by fire, "trial by fire," probably suggests "incest-awe." . . . Redemption by decay is symbolized in all variants of the sprouting seed, which arises in green newness out of filth and rot. . . . We may also note the two symbols of perspective, the mountain and the pit (sometimes merged in symbols of bridges, crossing, travel, flying). The mountain contains incestuous ingredients (the mountain as the mother, with frigidity as symbolic punishment for the offense). So also does the pit (ambivalence of womb and "cloaque," the latter aspect tending to draw in also ingredients of "purification by decay").

Thus each work of art tends to be a ritual of death and rebirth with identity changed, organized in relation to accepting or rejecting a key symbol of authority. In terms of these rituals Burke analyzes innumerable works of literature, of which his scattered interpretations of Thomas Mann's symbolic actions (which have interested him greatly in all his writings) probably add up to the clearest picture. Burke reads *The Magic Mountain* as a rebirth ritual

in which Hans Castorp is prepared for "resocializing" in the war at the end
by his seven years on the maternal mountain, for which he is punished by
symbolic castration, death, and rebirth in a new existence in the snow
scene—the whole a ritual in which Mann himself is reborn from pacifist
liberal to supporter of the German cause in the first World War. *Death in
Venice* and *Mario and the Magician* are scapegoat rituals for Mann as artist,
in the first of which the erotic criminality of the artist, represented by
Aschenbach, is punished by death; in the second of which Mann dissociates
the artist into two: the bad artist, Cippola, erotic and criminal (as well as
Fascist symbol) is punished by death; and the good artist, the narrator, freed
of criminality by Cippola's expiatory death, goes off "liberated." The *Joseph*
books are rebirth in the pit, as *The Magic Mountain* was rebirth on the
mountain. In them Joseph, an endlessly recurring identity, carries Mann to a
broader collectivity than the earlier German nationalism, as, purged of the
criminality of the artist, he takes on a larger criminality, the bisexuality of the
prophetic "nourisher," of which he is finally in turn purged.

Burke sums up the nature of literary ritual for the writer in general:

> The change of identity (whereby he is at once the same man and
> a new man) gives him a greater complexity of coordinates. He "sees
> around the corner." He is "prophetic," endowed with "perspective."
> We need not here concern ourselves with the accuracy of his
> perspective; we need only note its existence. It makes him either
> "wiser" or "more foolish" than he was—in any case, it forms the
> basis upon which the ramifications of his work are based. Thus, in
> Mann's novels, Joseph is not equipped to be a "prophet" until he has
> been reborn in the pit.
>
> Rebirth is a process of socialization, since it is a ritual whereby
> the poet fits himself to accept necessities suggested to him by the
> problems of the forensic. It will also, as regression, involve concern
> with the "womb-heaven" of the embryo, and with the "first
> revolution" that took place when the embryo developed to the point
> where its "shelter" became "confinement." Hence, when you examine
> this ritual, you find such symbols as the "pit" a symbolic return-to,
> and return-from, the womb.
>
> This involves "incest-awe," since the adult can return to the
> mother not as a sexually inexperienced infant, but as a lover. It
> involves homosexuality (actual or symbolic) since it involves an
> affront to the bipolar relationships of mother and father, and since a
> shift in allegiance to the symbols of authority equals the symbolic
> slaying of a parent. It involves castration symbolism, connotations of
> the "neuter," by way of punishment for the symbolic offense. The
> "neuter" may also take on connotations of the "androgynous,"
> because of the change in identity effected by the ritual.

Just as the individual rituals of specific works are symbolic actions, so are the
poetic forms themselves: thus tragedy is a formalized ritual of expiation,

humor is a ritual for reducing the burden of the situation, satire a ritual for "projecting" one's vice onto a scapegoat and killing it off. The writer also expresses himself symbolically in the choice of subject (as *Counter-Statement* noted about the biographer of Napoleon writing of his own Napoleonism): he expresses his "deep-lying sympathy" in the passages he quotes from other writers, even when attacking them; he writes "what is necessary to sustain him." The most rational-seeming activities have symbolic ingredients, as Burke notes in regard to the "bachelor" philosophies of Hume and Bentham, or the elements of ritual purification and castration in Pasteur's campaign for medical sterilization. Even the most corrupt or evasive hack production contains these same symbolic ingredients, which tell the truth despite its author. Burke writes, in a variant of Blake's criterion for asserting that Milton was "of the Devil's party":

> A writer may *profess* allegiance to a certain cause, for instance, but you find on going over his work that the *enemies* of this cause are portrayed with greater vividness than its advocates. Here is his "truth" about his professions of belief.

And in another place:

> By charting clusters, we get our clues as to the important ingredients subsumed in "symbolic mergers." We reveal, beneath an author's "official front," the level at which a lie is impossible. If a man's virtuous characters are dull, and his wicked characters are done vigorously, his *art* has voted for the wicked ones, regardless of his "official front." If a man talks of *glory* but employs the imagery of *desolation,* his *true subject* is desolation.

The mention of "cues" and "clusters" brings up the question of Burke's techniques for discovering and exploring symbolic action in a writer's work. He summarizes:

> We get cues as to his "non-realistic" or "symbolic" meaning in two ways. By examining the internal organization, noting what follows what, we disclose the content of a symbol in disclosing its *function....* We can check such disclosures by "metaphorical analysis," as we note the tenor of the imagery which the author employs.... And we can interpret the symbolic content of one book by comparing it with kindred symbols in other books.

The most obvious cue or clue is imagery or symbols, particularly in associated "clusters" of images, of which the mention of any one tends inevitably to call up others (the sort of thing Caroline Spurgeon found in Shakespeare and around which Armstrong later built his method), or in a developmental "curve." There are many other points of particular significance. One is the title of the work (Burke has noted, for example, that in Huysmans's transition from naturalism to Catholicism, all the titles of his naturalistic work are nouns, all the titles of his Catholic work are nouns, and

all the titles of his transitional work are prepositions or prepositional).
Beginning and endings are particularly strategic, "the first setting the tone for
the reception of one's message, the second clinching the thesis for a final
parting" (and we might note that Burke's own beginnings and endings,
perhaps more consciously than most, are not only "strategic" but always
particularly eloquent). Breaks in continuity in a writer's work are always
significant: either formal breaks, as when *Murder in the Cathedral* shifts from
verse to prose; or logical breaks, as when a Wyndham Lewis metaphor is
insistently inadequate; or discontinuities in subject-matter. Even puns and
sound-relationships are of symbolic significance, so that the name
"Desdemona," sounding like "death" and "moan," foretells her fate. In the
section on "Cues" in the book Burke has a long discussion of the symbolic
mimesis of sounds, based on Sir Richard Paget's work in *Human Speech* and
admittedly tentative, in which he suggests symbolic possibilities of "dancing"
acceptance in the repetition of the "m" sound and its cognates, rejection in
the "p" sound and its cognates, choking from the "k" sound, etc. Finally,
history itself is an important clue to symbolic meaning, as Burke demonstrates by tracing the historical transformations of the symbolic action in his
poetic forms, and the historical "curve" behind Shakespeare's shifts in
imagery.

The core of the book is the last third, the "Dictionary of Pivotal Terms."
Burke explains why he has put it at the end of the book rather than at the
beginning, remarking that the alphabetical convention of a dictionary is
specious, since the definition of the words in "a" requires a prior knowledge
of all the words to "z," and consequently he is defining his terms only after
they have been displayed in action. He writes:

> In our own case, we have found it advisable to pursue a catch-as-catch-
> can policy, introducing our terms where there is an opportunity to disclose at
> the same time something of their function. We hope to make apparent first
> their general slant or drift, and to sharpen their explicitness as we proceed
> (showing their function by introducing them into various contexts). Formal
> definitions should thus be relegated to a final summary, where each term can
> draw upon the reader's knowledge of *all* the terms.

Burke has frequently used a dictionary of terms to sum up what each of his
books has to say, since he believes that his views *are* the terms, and this
Dictionary continues the tradition of the Lexicon Rhetoricae in *Counter-
Statement* and the list of concepts on page 337 of *Permanence and Change*.
In this case the Dictionary is a formalized alphabetical listing of the thirty-
three key concepts of the book and Burke's work up to 1937. Some of them
are principally the basic devices of symbolic action, like Alienation, Bridging
Device, Casuistic Stretching, Communion, Identity, Rituals of Rebirth,
Secular Prayer, Transcendence; some of them are principally the basic
techniques of his criticism, like Clusters, Cues, Discounting, Essence,
Imagery, Lexicological; some are principally social phenomena, like Good
Life, which expresses his social program, and Problem of Evil; some, like

Perspective by Incongruity, are at a high enough level of generality to cover all three categories, being at once symbolic actions in the work, devices for criticizing the work, and social phenomena. There is no way to summarize or paraphrase these pivotal terms in less space than they take up, and the only way to get a sense of their tremendous value and fruitfulness is to read them in the context of the book. It may be possible, however, to show how interrelated they are in operation by quoting a conveniently short one, on "Sect":

> Those who, faced with the danger of being "driven into a corner," counter by forming a new collectivity. Their cooperation gives them a new positive campaign base, from which they may sally forth to steal the recognized symbols of authority from their opponents. A sect is always threatened with defensive, negativistic, "splintering" tendencies so long as the ingredient of rejection is uppermost.
>
> Troeltsch has pointed out the part that the spread of literacy has played in sectarianism. Sectarianism is "colony thinking." It attains full expression when the group of like-minded forms some material cooperative enterprise that gives the bureaucratic equivalents of its Utopia. The spread of literacy, however, led to a subtler kind of colony, usually lacking material body: the "colonies of the mind." By his preferences in reading, one "recruits his band," and they may be scattered across all the earth and through all periods of history.
>
> The nineteenth century was particularly prolific in sectarian colonies, of both the material and spiritual sorts. There were the colonies of special scientific disciplines. And here and there a lonely man, off by himself, shaped his identity by membership in one or another of such vaguely corporate units.

Although the richest of these terms are abstract enough to include collective social as well as individual literary behavior, the examples are consistently literary. Managing to include both the classic and the contemporary (sometimes, the sublime and the ridiculous), Burke illustrates Alienation with examples from Shakespeare and an Albert Bein play, Cues with Shakespeare and Cummings, Identity with Shakespeare and Mann's *Joseph* novels, Imagery with Shakespeare and Aragon's *Bells of Basle,* etc.

The central concern of *Attitudes toward History* is with charting attitudes and framing "a comic vocabulary of motives"—that is, with public materials, literary or forensic—and characteristically its chief theoretical reliance is on such authorities on the forensic as Bentham, Marx, Peirce, Veblen, and Malinowski. At the same time, as Burke has made clear "no statement about motives can ever be anything other than symbolic action" itself, and he has sketched out in the book the ways his system and terminology express himself. In addition to tracing "comic" as a way of saying, among other things, "Kenneth," he finds that one of his other principal terms, "bureaucratization," is a way of saying "Burke" or "burking" the issue, and he suggests that his preference for "p" terms, "poetry," "piety," "petition," "propriety," "possession," "prayer," and "perspective," is a survival of his earlier period "as an aesthete, to whom poetry was synonymous with rejection." Under "Cues" in the book, Burke devotes ten pages to an elaborate introspection into some of the underlying motives revealed in his own work. He pursues his "apparently neutral" title for one section, "The Curve of History," through an early story, "The Book of Yul" in *The White Oxen,* and other writings, finding that the word "curve" has extremely complex associations for him, so that his title is actually "The Mountain-Woman-Church of History," with features of guilt, death, and eroticism smuggled in.

Burke finds that "bureaucratization of the imaginative" is a way of saying that things "die" and are "reborn"; that "perspective by incongruity," in its concern with "neutralization," involves symbolic castration and is consequently a fitting rebirth transition between the first section of *Permanence and Change,* its keynote "the fish, under water," and the third section, a heaven of the secularization of religious terms. He then investigates the "arbitrary" names he gave characters in the stories in *The White Oxen* and finds that they have a "tonal logic"; that his character named Treep, whose role was to cut down a tree, was precisely named "tree-rejection," and when, become gigantic, he is renamed Arjk, the name still fits. Burke explains:

> Looking at these syllables, we speculated: the "r" is the growl of his pugnacity. The "j" is his new *genius* as *gigantic,* as is the "ah" of "a," in contrast with the "ee" of his name before "rebirth." And the "k" is the initial of our given name. Thus, "a-r-j-k" means: "Kenneth, formerly a little man, made big and pugnacious."

He then finds that the same principles are involved in the nicknames he has given his children (so that his third daughter, nicknamed "Jake," has all of "Arjk" but the growl), in his poems, and in the key terms of his conceptual vocabulary. He concludes with the reservation that the same symbolic expressions could be found in other fashions:

> Of course such matters "radiate" in many directions. We could have begun with Treep's felling of the tree, for instance, and developed a line of thought from this ritualistic murder, relating it to subsequent symbolizations of rape and redemption in the same story....
>
> We could, in other words, have considered critical concepts as symbols, looking for the ways in which the later pattern of ideas parallels the pattern of plot in these early fantasies. Hence, we should regret it if the reader carried away the impression that the organization of character by the fitting together of verbalizations involves "tonal puns" alone.

Burke has used introspection into his own motivations and past experience in all his books since *Counter-Statement:* in *Permanence and Change,* noting his "great resentment as a child upon learning that lions were cats, whereas to me they were purely and simply the biggest dogs"; in *The*

Philosophy of Literary Form, recalling that the name of a character in an early story he wrote underlies an arbitrary obscene word he made up for a hypothetical illustration; in *A Grammar of Motives,* exploring the adolescent images a reading of Santayana called up and the probable line of association behind his term "grandly converge." To a certain extent this is a critical trick, even a cheat, since by admitting the most tenuous meanings, sometimes of an extremely unattractive nature, about his own writing, Burke can then go on to find similar things in the work of other writers with the technique to some extent justified. Actually, of course, nothing is proved (which Burke would be the first to admit, since he is trying to "suggest" meanings, not "prove" them), and in the long run these introspective revelations will probably turn out to be the more valuable as insights into the mind and working methods of an utterly scrupulous and supersubtle artist and critic than they will be as grounds for methodological generalization. In the discussion of his own underlying motivations Burke writes:

> Perhaps we are here making "admissions" that we should make men hire expensive detectives to find out. Our only way of defense is to say *"tu quoque."* We hold that, insofar as any man's writings contain sincerity of organization, being something more than mere disjunct psittacism, we can disclose analogous processes at work. We'll even accept an offer to disclose them, if any one cares to come forward with the proud claim that his work is psittacism pure and unadulterated. A man can, on the surface, maintain any insincerity he prefers. But in the depths of his imagery, he cannot lie. When being sufficiently *engrossed* in a subject to give it organized expression, the poet or philosopher must embody his variants of such basic psychological processes. He could not do otherwise unless he had a *different kind of body* from other men. So, if any enlightened philosopher or critic cares to challenge us, contending that his own work is free of puns, we are willing, for a consideration, to go on a search for "cues."

So far as I know, no one has ever taken him up on this offer. In thus losing the positive proof of demonstration on a skeptic, we probably get the equally impressive negative proof of the unanswerable conviction the book carries; that many have scoffed, but none remained to pay.

3

Despite the novelty and shock-value of Burke's methods, the study of literature as symbolic action has quite a respectable ancestry. Plato's concern with the ill effects of poetry in *The Republic* is in large part a concern with symbolic action in the audience. Socrates says (Jowett translation): "If you consider, I said, that when in misfortune we feel a natural hunger and desire to relieve our sorrow by weeping and lamentation, and that this feeling which is kept under control in our own calamities is satisfied and delighted by the

poets . . ." Aristotle, however, is the true father of symbolic action, as of so
many things. In his emphasis on *action,* his insistence in *The Poetics* (Lane
Cooper translation) that "happiness and misery are not states of being, but
forms of activity," that being good is *acting* good, he laid the groundwork for
our reading "pity" and "terror" not as audience states but as audience
symbolic actions, responding to the symbolic action in tragedy. Coleridge,
whose own poems, particularly "The Ancient Mariner" and "Kubla Khan,"
are so complete a text of symbolic action, halted on the verge of the concept,
perhaps from a kind of "resistance," although he had independently
discovered its principal theoretical basis, the concept of nonconscious mental
areas. In his *Lectures on Shakespeare* he notes that Shakespeare's titles and
opening scenes are particularly significant, as Burke would, but decides that
they are significant in terms of conscious artistry. Ruskin continued the
tradition with a very Burkian analysis of the symbolic action implicit in the
etymological meanings (some of them perhaps dubious) of the names of
Shakespeare's characters (I have taken the liberty of printing the Greek
transliterated):

> Of Shakespeare's names I will afterwards speak at more length;
> they are curiously—often barbarously—mixed out of various
> traditions and languages. Three of the clearest in meaning have been
> already noticed. Desdemona—*"dusdaimonia,"* *miserable fortune*—is
> also plain enough. Othello is, I believe, "the careful"; all the calamity
> of the tragedy arising from the single flaw and error in his
> magnificently collected strength. Ophelia, "serviceableness," the true,
> lost wife of Hamlet, is marked as having a Greek name by that of her
> brother, Laertes; and its signification is once exquisitely alluded to in
> that brother's last word of her, where her gentle preciousness is
> opposed to the uselessness of the churlish clergy:—"A *ministering*
> angel shall my sister be, when thou liest howling." Hamlet is, I
> believe, connected in some way with "homely," the entire event of
> the tragedy turning on betrayal of home duty. Hermione *(herma),*
> "pillar-like" ... ; Titania *(titēnē),* "the queen"; Benedick and Beatrice,
> "blessed and blessing"; Valentine and Proteus "enduring or strong"
> *(valens),* and "changeful." Iago and Iachimo have evidently the same
> root—probably the Spanish Iago, Jacob, "the supplanter."

In so far as the general assumptions behind the analysis of symbolic
action in art are basic psychological generalities, many of them have been
anticipated by shrewd students of human nature in the past. To mention a few
at random, Goethe noted, according to Eckermann, that the talents of women
seem to cease with marriage and children, raising the possibility that their
works of art are some form of what we would now call "sublimated" (or
symbolic) sexuality or maternal impulse. Around the turn of the century
Ferdinand Brunetière insisted in his essay on "The Philosophy of Molière"
that Tartuffe "is an act as much as a work: a work of combat, as we would

now say, and an act of declared hostility"; and Bernard Shaw noted in *The Quintessence of Ibsenism* that a writer's use of scriptural quotation tends to signalize bad conscience at those reinforced points (and is thus symbolic denial through overassertion). Since Freud, of course, these conceptions have become psychoanalytic commonplaces, and analysts deal constantly with problems of symbolic action. Erich Fromm, for example, has developed a concept of religious or political doctrines as symbolic expressions of the character structure and personality traits of their creators, and as satisfying similar psychic needs in the character structure of those won over to them.

In a similar fashion a number of Burke's key concepts have been anticipated by other writers. Tolstoy, for example, in *What Is Art?* clearly anticipates the condition of psychological dispossession Burke describes under "alienation": "In regard to religion the upper circles of the Middle Ages found themselves in the position educated Romans were in before Christianity arose, that is, they no longer believed in the religion of the masses but had no beliefs to put in place of the worn-out Church doctrine, which for them had lost its meaning"; and also the Burkian concept of "being driven into a corner": "The Church doctrine is so coherent a system that it cannot be altered or corrected without destroying it altogether." Irving Babbitt, in *Rousseau and Romanticism,* precedes Burke in noting how psychic alienation results in movements of negativism, Satanism, Byronism; and in the same book also approximates the Burkian special sense of "communion." Even I. A. Richards, whose interests are so completely turned on the communicative function of language and so little on the expressive, at least once pushed his own concept of the actions implicit in attitudes to its logical conclusion in symbolic action. In *Coleridge on Imagination* (under a Burkian aegis, that is) he writes:

> The saner and greater mythologies are not fancies; they are the utterance of the whole soul of man and, as such, inexhaustible to meditation. They are no amusement or diversion to be sought as a relaxation and an escape from the hard realities of life. They are these hard realities in projection, their symbolic recognition, coordination and acceptance. Through such mythologies our will is collected, our powers unified, our growth controlled. Through them the infinitely divergent strayings of our being are brought into "balance or reconciliation." The "opposite and discordant qualities" of things in them acquire a form; and such integrity as we possess as "civilized" men is our inheritance through them.

Finally, D. H. Lawrence's famous remark: "One sheds one's sicknesses in books," only expresses what many artists throughout history have recognized as the symbolic action in their own work.

The men Burke is most indebted to, however, are not the forerunners of symbolic action, with the exception of Coleridge, but a group of relatively eccentric philosophers and philosophic writers (very similar to Richards's

group) who tend to resemble him in a curious fashion. One of them is Jeremy
Bentham. It is hard to read Hazlitt's account of Bentham in *The Spirit of the
Age* without thinking of Burke seen from an antagonistic point of view, even
to the "barbarous philosophical jargon" that "is not mere verbiage, but has a
great deal of acuteness and meaning in it, which you would be glad to pick
out if you could." Like Richards, Burke sees Bentham as the founder of the
serious study of language, and in *Permanence and Change* he classes him
with Darwin in having become "thousands of selves." He has little faith in
Bentham's project for a "neutral" speech and metaphor that would eliminate
"poetry" and "rhetoric" (or in the doctrines that have succeeded it in
semantics), seeing the project as essentially a vast castration-symbolism; as
he sees Bentham's antireligious utilitarianism as essentially a secularized
religious pattern, a variant of the Golden Rule. At the same time he finds
Bentham's analysis of speech and classification of its types in *Table of the
Springs of Action* an invaluable exploration of these matters, eminently usable
once its bias in favor of "neutrality" is discarded; while in Bentham's
utilitarian analysis of "interests" and "motives" constituting the "springs" of
human action lie the roots of Burke's lifelong attempt to "place" motives,
again with the invidious connotations eliminated. In *Attitudes,* announcing:
"The best of Bentham, Marx and Veblen is high comedy," he credits Bentham
with having developed "debunking" to the point where "epigons" have had to
do nothing but cash in on his genius for a century, and in *The Philosophy of
Literary Form* he makes it clear that the "epigons" he is talking about are
men like Thurman Arnold and Stuart Chase. In *A Grammar of Motives,* while
using Bentham a number of times, he adds to his debunking of Bentham's
debunking (that it is a "bachelor's" castration symbol) a new symbolic
explanation gleefully picked up from Bentham himself (that it is rooted in his
childhood, in an abnormally intense fear of ghosts, which became the
"fictions" in language that he feared as an adult).

Coleridge is perhaps the man of all the group whom Burke most
resembles, and one cannot read Coleridge's writings, particularly the
Biographia, without being struck by the resemblances: in ideas, methods,
even eccentricities. As a study in symbolic action, Coleridge and his work
have fascinated Burke, and the core of the long title essay of *The Philosophy
of Literary Form* is the analysis of "The Ancient Mariner," just as Coleridge's
high degree of consciousness in the subtleties of sound makes him the logical
choice for a text on delicate musicality in verse, and his extreme linguistic
preoccupation generally makes him perhaps the most frequently quoted writer
in Burke's books. Burke has classed Coleridge among the greatest critics of
world literature," and he regards his emphasis as directly opposed to
Bentham's debunking, in that it is tragic" or "dignifying," treating material
interests as a limited aspect of "higher" interests. In "The Philosophy of
Literary Form" Burke mentions being at work on a monograph entitled "The
Particular Strategy of Samuel Taylor Coleridge," which has never appeared (it
may have turned into his course on Coleridge during the 1938 summer
session at the University of Chicago). He notes the problems and rewards

involved:

> At present I am attempting such a "symbolic" analysis of Coleridge's writings. His highly complex mind makes the job of charting difficult. . . .
> However, there are two advantages about the case of Coleridge that make the job worth trying. In the first place, there is the fact that he left so full a record, and that he employed the same imagery in his poems, literary criticism, political and religious tracts, letters, lectures, and introspective jottings. Thus we have objective bridges for getting from one area to another; these images "pontificate" among his various interests, and so provide us with a maximum opportunity to work out a psychology by objective citation, by "scissor work.". . .
> The second advantage in the case of Coleridge is that, along with his highly complex mind (perhaps one of the most complex that has left us a full record) you have an easily observable *simplification.* I refer to the burden of his drug addiction. . . .

Coleridge is not only Burke's favorite subject; he is a kind of banner for him. Thus in his essay on "Surrealism" he puts Coleridge forward as the father of surrealism and the writer of "the great Surrealist masterpiece" ("Kubla Khan"), and then proposes Coleridge's distinction between "imagination" and "fancy" as basic to an analysis of the movement. In the *New Republic* review mentioned above he insists that the current Kierkegaard-Kafka fad should properly be a Coleridge fad. In "The Problem of the Intrinsic" he takes up the charge made by the neo-Aristotelian critics that their opponents are too "Coleridgean," Platonic, or deductive about poetry, converts it into a banner, and shows that precisely at the point where the neo-Aristotelians are making the most critical sense and producing the most valuable readings, they are being most "Coleridgean."

A third thinker on whom Burke has based a good deal of his work is Thorstein Veblen, the only American of the three, and consequently the only one he does not share as a source with Richards. The Veblen influence, however, seems to be more or less wearing off. In *Permanence and Change* Burke relies heavily on Veblen's concept of "trained incapacity," taking it as a basic "perspective by incongruity" or metaphor, and extending its reference until it becomes a major social, psychological and literary phenomenon somewhat similar to what the gestaltists speak of as a "bad *Gestalt.*" Unlike almost everyone else but the economists, Burke does not find *The Theory of the Leisure Class* Veblen's "greatest contribution to our thinking," but *The Theory of Business Enterprise,* seeing it as our finest analysis of the "metaphysics" of capitalism. *Permanence and Change* also makes a good deal of some of Veblen's other ideas, particularly his device for avoiding the Manichean dualism implicit in his view of institutions, by postulating opposed "instincts," predatory and altruistic. In *Attitudes toward History* Burke does little with Veblen, except to note that at his best, like Bentham and Marx, he is "high comedy;" and to develop Veblen's "planned incapacity" into his own

term "planned incongruity." In *The Philosophy of Literary Form,* although
Veblen is quoted frequently, it is almost always as a social thinker; not, as he
was originally for Burke, a metaphoric critic of our whole culture. In *A
Grammar of Motives* he is not referred to at all (although it can be presumed
that both later volumes will have places for him).

Less heavily Burke has drawn on a number of other philosophers and
philosophic thinkers, among them two—John Stuart Mill and Charles S.
Peirce—who also resemble him somewhat (Blackmur has pointed out the
latter resemblance, meaning for "the buoyancy and sheer remarkableness of
his speculations," not, one hopes, for his terminology). Burke is one of the
few contemporary critics who have made use of A. O. Lovejoy's *Great Chain
of Being;* and among more traditional philosophers, he has regularly utilized
James, Dewey, Bergson, and a number of other moderns (before the
Grammar, in which, of course, he surveyed the bulk of philosophy). The
general pattern of Burke's philosophic indebtedness, however, is rarely more
than the adoption of a basic concept or two, combined with widespread
"discounting" or outright attack, and until the emergence of Aristotle as his
major influence in the latest book, no philosopher was ever recognizably his
master.

Burke's effect on contemporary criticism is, at least in America, fully as
pervasive as that of Richards. In addition to R. P. Blackmur (whose
relationship to him has been noted above) the men whose work is most
closely related to his in this country are Malcolm Cowley, Francis Fergusson,
and Harry Slochower. Cowley has not so far published a volume of criticism,
but his forthcoming book on American literature, from fragments that have
appeared in periodicals, seems to be a major piece of work. In magazine
pieces over the past two decades he has utilized many of Burke's concepts,
terms, and insights, turning them to his own uses, popularizing them
somewhat, and applying them to writers untapped by Burke. His introductory
studies of Hemingway and Faulkner for the Viking Portable Library, in
particular, are first-rate studies in symbolic action, and almost the first serious
examination either writer has received.

Like Cowley, Francis Fergusson is now engaged in writing his first book
of criticism after many years of periodical writing. Unlike Cowley, he has
been affected by Burke only recently, and then more or less on his own
terms. The title "drama critic" has been badly debased until it now means a
semi-literate reviewer of plays for a newspaper, but for two decades
Fergusson has been a drama critic in the proper sense, a critic of both
dramatic literature and performance, and probably the best in America. His
criticism has three principal strands. The first is a sharp aesthetic morality, a
concept of art as disinterested, digested, measured, disciplined, and final,
derived in part from the modern classicist, neo-humanist, and traditionalist
critics Maritain, Benda, Fernandez, Babbitt, Eliot—and in part from the
classics and writers like Dante, with which concept he has relentlessly
punctured the windy and immature, from Eugene O'Neill to Selden Rodman.

(This has not kept him, incidentally, although he is generally scornful of the moderns as "spirit-maiming" or "demoralizing," from valuing highly some very unclassical writers like D. H. Lawrence.) At the same time he has applied the comparative technical standard of the rounded and complete Greek ritual drama, as interpreted by Aristotle and best exemplified by Sophocles' *Œdipus the King,* to the study of the serious modern drama, from Ibsen and Chekhov to Lorca and Cocteau.

The third strand is his use of dramatism and the pattern of the Sophoclean ritual drama as a way of reading non-dramatic literature; which he stated in *Hound & Horn,* as early as July-September 1933, in a review of Boleslavsky's *Acting: the First Six Lessons,* when he proposed the method as a way of reading lyric poetry; and illustrated in the *Hound & Horn* James number the next year with a reading of "The Drama in *The Golden Bowl.*" It is this third strand which has principally served to unite Fergusson and Burke, and as Burke's method developed into "dramatism" and the "pentad," Fergusson took advantage of many of its conceptual formulations, particularly its *"poiema-pathema-mathema"* formulation, which he converted into "purpose-passion-perception," the three essential stages of the ritual drama, and made the cornerstone of his own work. Fergusson's review of Burke's *Grammar,* the ablest one to appear, announced in terms of high praise their wide area of agreement as well as their limited areas of disagreement (chiefly his objection to Burke's "rationalistic" slighting of medieval realism and "abstractionist" retreat from the earlier concrete "ritual drama as hub"). Fergusson's forthcoming book (some of which I have had the opportunity of reading in manuscript, and one chapter of which has so far appeared in the *Kenyon Review,* Spring 1947), a study of post-Shakespearian drama as partial developments of "purpose," "passion," or "perception" rather than the Sophoclean ritual whole, gives evidence of being an important literary event.

The man whose books make the most explicit use of Burke is Harry Slochower. Slochower's combination of Marx, Freud, and Gestalt is similar to Burke's socio-psychological integration, although Slochower draws much more heavily on Marxism and on a German philosophic tradition. Some time before the publication of his first book in English, *Three Ways of Modern Man* in 1937 (I have not read his first book, *Richard Dehmel,* written in German), Slochower discovered Burke's terminology, and found it, as did Cowley, Fergusson, and others, an efficient and consistent critical frame for expressing his own ideas. The book appeared with an appreciative Foreword by Burke, and displays a number of Burkian terms, concepts, insights, direct quotes, and even Burke's characteristic quotation marks. At the same time its central emphasis, on novels as expressing formal philosophic "ideologies" (Slochower's three bins are Feudal Socialism, Bourgeois Liberalism, and Socialist Humanism, but in the course of the work they get phrased as Monist, Dualist, Dialectic, even Father, Son, Holy Ghost), is very unlike Burke's personalist "symbolic action" emphasis. Slochower's second book, *Thomas Mann's Joseph Story* (1938) is more like Burke's own work, the lengthy analysis of a single complex work of art in a number of levels, translated into a number of vocabularies, but again with Slochower's distinctive collective-ideology emphasis. His third and most ambitious book, *No Voice is Wholly Lost* ... (1945) is an attempt to survey almost the whole mass of contemporary literature instead of exploring a few texts in detail. The book is full of brilliant insights, but Slochower has too much ground to cover to be able to integrate them, the treatment of contemporary Americans is frequently weak (hacks like Steinbeck are classed with Malraux and Mann, windy bores like Wolfe are treated as comparable to Kafka and Rilke, and major writers like Hemingway and Faulkner tend to be slighted), and the book as a whole is disappointing. Its extension and application of Burke's terms in what by now has become a very different perspective is an excellent job, however, and in general Slochower is informed, perceptive, and methodologically equipped enough to make his importance certain any time he chooses to desert the survey-course type of book and settle down to do what he has shown he can do best, dig into a major book at length.

One of the oddest and most amusing applications Burke has had was by Yvor Winters, surely the last convert anyone would have predicted. Winters's first book, *Primitivism and Decadence,* appeared in 1937 with the introductory Note, in his characteristic churlish tone:

> I have wherever possible employed the terminology of Kenneth Burke, and have acknowledged it, in order to avoid the unnecessary multiplication of terms; my own analysis of rhetorical devices began, however, about as early as his own, and was dropped for a time while his continued, because it did not seem especially fruitful. My own analysis was resumed when I discovered the key to the ethical significance of rhetoric and the possibility of creating an aesthetic on such an analysis; my quarrel with Mr. Burke, which will appear fully in this volume, is precisely that he has failed to do this.

Winters went on in the book to make desultory use of a number of Burke's terms from *Counter-Statement,* particularly one that seems to have charmed him: "qualitative progression," for a type of poetic structure; but the attempt to use a set of terms while quarreling violently with the ideas for which they are shorthand formulas was obviously foredoomed, and after the first book Winters gave it up and created an ethically weighted vocabulary of his own.

In crediting Burke while quarreling with him, Winters was being more generous than a number of other critics, Edmund Wilson and Philip Rahv among them, who have repeatedly drawn on Burke's concepts and insights without credit. (One of the Rahv cases is particularly amusing, in that it appeared in a review in the December 1937 issue of *Partisan Review*, on the page following the only formal notice the magazine has ever taken of Burke's work, Sidney Hook's venomous attack.) Several young poets and critics in England, among them Francis Scarfe and Christopher Hill, are either familiar with Burke's work or have independently worked out many of his symbolic-action concepts. In America almost every critic has been influenced by him.

Ransom, Tate, Brooks, and Warren have all drawn on Burke somewhat and praised him highly, while generally disagreeing with him; and Burke has in turn drawn on their insights, praised them, and, in the case of Ransom in particular, engaged in elaborate and endless literary polemic with him. Warren's study of "The Ancient Mariner" uses a good deal of Burke's work on the poem as well as the general structure of his method, while quarreling strongly with his "personal" emphasis on Coleridge's drug-addiction and marital troubles. (Burke's review of the book, in *Poetry,* April 1947, replies in kind, praising Warren's reading as having "exceptional merit" and then going on to oppose its central contention with Burke's own detailed reading, even more explicitly "personal" than before in its emphasis, and sweeping over the whole body of Coleridge's other writings for correlations.)

Randall Jarrell has written at least one first-rate Burkian analysis, "Changes of Attitude and Rhetoric in Auden's Poetry," in the *Southern Review,* Autumn 1941, announcing in the opening paragraph: "I have borrowed several terms from an extremely good book—Kenneth Burke's *Attitudes toward History*—and I should like to make acknowledgements for them," and then going on to apply the terms brilliantly in exploring Auden's symbolic and rhetorical action. Delmore Schwartz and a number of other young poets have utilized Burke in their criticism, and Muriel Rukeyser has used his concepts in her poetry, acknowledging material from *Attitudes* in *A Turning Wind.* Herbert Muller relies even more heavily on Burke's concepts and insights in his *Modern Fiction* and *Science and Criticism* than he does on those of Richards, and identifies Burke as "perhaps the most acute critic in America today." Some idea of the spread of Burke's influence in America can be had from noting the wide variety of critics who have at one time or another acknowledged some degree of indebtedness to him. In addition to the ones discussed above, the list would include: Philip Wheelwright, Newton Arvin, Arthur Mizener, Lionel Trilling, David Daiches, John L. Sweeney, Joseph Warren Beach, Ralph Ellison, Morton Dauwen Zabel, and innumerable others.

The criticism Burke's work has received makes almost as melancholy a record as that of Richards's, and like Richards he has been most enthusiastically attacked by some of the men he has influenced most profoundly. At the low end of the scale, of course, he has received the honor reserved for only the best contemporary critics, attack by Henri Peyre, Alfred Kazin, J. Donald Adams, and company. The bitterest of all these was the above-mentioned review by Sidney Hook in *Partisan Review*, which dismissed him as an apologist for Stalin and a "weak man of minor talent." (Burke's reply, in the January 1938 issue, confined itself chiefly to quoting the section of his book Hook had distorted, and Hook's counter-reply in the same issue, which continued to misconstrue Burke's term "bureaucratization" as pejorative, made it clear that the distortion was fundamental.) At the other end of the scale Burke has received a number of sympathetic studies: by Gorham B. Munson in *Destinations,* a series of studies of prominent writers of the twenties (1928); by Austin Warren in the *Sewanee Review* (Spring and

Summer 1933); by Henry Bamford Parkes in *The Pragmatic Test,* which treats him as a major modern thinker along with men like James, Dewey, Nietzsche, Bergson, and Eliot; and by Howard Nemerov in "The Agon of Will as Idea: a note on the terms of Kenneth Burke," in *Furioso* (Spring 1947), which, recognizing "the impertinence of trying to compass into this brief note the vast complexities and ironies of Burke's writing," instead ingeniously added some of Nemerov's own to them. Somewhere between these two extremes no reviewer has ever quite succeeded in coping with more than one aspect of a Burke book, depending on whether the reviewer (according to the whims of editors) was a semanticist or a linguist, a social psychologist, a philosopher, a critic, a sociologist, or a plain bewildered reviewer.

4

The reason reviewers and editors have had such trouble fastening on Burke's field is that he has no field, unless it be Burkology. In recent years it has become fashionable to say that he is not actually a literary critic, but a semanticist, social psychologist, or philosopher. A much more accurate statement would be that he is not *only* a literary critic, but a literary critic *plus* those things and others. In his article "The Tactics of Motivation" Burke suggests the general problem of synthesis on a higher level than any single field could handle. He writes:

> But if one offered a synthesis of the fields covered by the various disciplines, which of the disciplines could possibly be competent to evaluate it? Where each specialty gets its worth precisely by moving towards diversity, how could any specialty possibly deal with a project that offered a *unification* among the diversities? Or, otherwise put: if one were to write on the *interrelatedness* among ten specialties, one would be discussing something that lay outside the jurisdiction of them all.

The lifelong aim of Burke's criticism has been precisely this synthesis, the unification of every discipline and body of knowledge that could throw light on literature into one consistent critical frame. Opposing every pious or conventional view that would exclude one critical tool or another as "improper," Burke has insisted: "The main ideal of criticism, as I conceive it, is to use all that is there to use." In another place, defending the use of biographical information on a poet, he writes: "we should use whatever knowledge is available," and explains:

> I grant that such speculations interfere with the symmetry of criticism as a game. (Criticism as a game is best to watch, I guess, when one confines himself to the single unit, and reports on its movements like a radio commentator broadcasting the blow-by-blow description of a prizefight.) But linguistic analysis has opened up new possibilities in the correlating of producer and product—and these concerns have such important bearing upon matters of culture and

conduct in general that no sheer conventions or ideals of criticism should be allowed to interfere with their development.

What modern criticism seems to resemble most is pre-Baconian science, as described by Taine in his *History of English Literature:*

> So long as it [science] limited its effort to the satisfying of an idle curiosity, opening out speculative vistas, establishing a sort of opera in speculative minds, it could launch out any moment into metaphysical abstractions and distinctions: it was enough for it to skim over experience; it soon quitted it, and came all at once upon great words, quiddities, the principle of individuation, final causes. Half proofs sufficed science; at bottom it did not care to establish a truth, but to get an opinion. . . .

Like Bacon, Burke has set out to do no less than to integrate all man's knowledge into one workable critical frame. In the course of that, he has set out to turn psychology on literature, has discovered that he would first have to synthesize one consistent psychology from the warring schools, has done it; then discovered the same need to integrate sociologies; then work both together as a social psychology; then add linguistics and semantics to the formula; still later add philosophies and theologies; finally, to turn the whole tremendous mass on a poem. His aim, as stated in the conclusion to *Permanence and Change,* has been "to show an integral relationship existing among a great variety of cultural manifestations which are often considered in isolation." The showiest part of Burke's work has been in the vitally necessary task of integrating Marx and Freud, or what he calls "economics" (I would prefer "sociology") and psychology. Thus he offers "a theory of the psychological processes that go with the economic ones," or proposes to unite Marx and Freud on the basic concept of "the symbols of authority," or treats Machiavelli, Hobbes, Voltaire, Bentham, Marx, and Veblen as "great formulators of economic psychoanalysis."

Burke has drawn heavily on Marxism in all his books while at the same time criticizing its mechanical simplifications in *Counter-Statement,* noting its covert "god-function" in *Attitudes,* and so forth; and all his analyses tend to have a sociological dimension, although they are rarely only that (one or two of the shorter articles in *The Philosophy of Literary Form* are exceptions). At the same time Marx himself is one of Burke's heroes, a great "dramatist" or "impresario" in "Twelve Propositions"; the great poet and rhetorician who made *The Communist Manifesto* "a masterpiece" in *A Grammar of Motives.* Burke has also drawn enthusiastically on a wide variety of other social views, from the historical tragic opera of Spengler to the philosophic social psychology of George Herbert Mead.

Similarly, his psychology is integrative and mediative, what Richards would call "centrist" and which Burke has distinguished as "a *phenomenological* science of psychology, rather than the tenuousness of the purely introspective or the impoverishment of the purely behavioristic." Its chief source is psychoanalysis, although a psychoanalysis socialized somewhat along the lines of the revisionist Freudians, since "the coordinates of individual psychology invariably place a wrong emphasis upon symbolic acts." Burke has used a tremendous amount of Freudian theory and terminology in his work since *Counter-Statement,* which canonized as permanent parts of a critical vocabulary concepts like "compensation," "transference," and "adjustment." He has written two lengthy evaluations of psychoanalysis, one in *Permanence and Change* under "Secular Conversions," and one, "Freud—and the Analysis of Poetry," in *The Philosophy of Literary Form,* reprinted from the *American Journal of Sociology.* The first attempts to "place" psychoanalytic therapy as a type of "conversion downward by misnomer," the second is a specifically literary application, attempting to suggest "how far the literary critic should go along with Freud and what extra-Freudian material he would have to add." Burke concludes that dream mechanisms like "condensation" and "displacement" are the basic mechanisms of poetry, key terms in poetic analysis, and that psychoanalysis is an approach of great value and subtlety to "poem as dream." Beyond that,

> I should say that, for the explicit purposes of literary criticism, we should require more emphasis than the Freudian structure gives (1) to the proportional strategy as against the essentializing one, (2) to matriarchal symbolizations as against the Freudian patriarchal bias, (3) to poem as prayer and chart, as against simply the poem as dream.

Burke's discussions of psychoanalysis deal not only with the theories of Freud, but also with those of the chief dissenters: Jung, Adler, McDougall, Rivers, Stekel, and Rank (he quarrels particularly with the last two, preferring Freud's free-association dream readings before Stekel's arbitrary "dream book" symbology was imposed on it, and rejecting Rank's oversimple application of the concept of the "death wish" to art in favor of a fuller "death-and-rebirth" concept). At the same time he sees Freud as he sees Marx, a titanic figure, a great tragic poet who "deserves the eternal respect of mankind because of the profound imaginativeness and methodical skill" by which he brought us face to face with the chthonic and the "cloacal" underlying apparently transcendent concerns.

Next to psychoanalysis Burke's greatest psychological indebtedness has been to the gestaltists, although he tends to see their work as a more usable extension of the experimentation of behaviorists like Watson and Pavlov rather than as a sharp break with the behavioral tradition; and it is in keeping with this that he seems to be more familiar with the laboratory work of men like Köhler and Koffka than with the theoretical work of Wertheimer. Some of Burke's most effective exercises in psychological integration have been translating back and forth among behavioral, Gestalt, and Freudian vocabularies to establish their essential agreement at key points. As much as it can be identified, Burke's own psychology seems to be a Gestalt framework with extensive Freudian additions. At the same time he has drawn on almost every other psychology, and has made particular use of Jaensch's *Eidetic Imagery,* Kretschmer's *Physique and Character,* and the laboratory work of Sherrington with animals and Piaget with children. From the frequency with which he has quoted it, Piaget's study *Language and Thought of the Child* seems to be particularly important to him (this conjecture is borne out in his review in the *New Republic* of Mrs. Colum's *From These Roots,* where he reproaches her specifically with ignoring Gestalt, Bentham and his successors, Piaget, and critics like Richards and Empson—a distinguished assortment.)

Burke has been much more critical of the theoreticians of language, although here too he has found it possible to integrate a number of disparate schools. The theory he has accepted most uncritically is the gesture-origin theory of speech of Sir Richard Paget, which he transforms into a gesture-essence theory.[2] Burke first used it in *Attitudes toward History,* exploring some significant consonant-sounds in writings, including his own, with the reservation that "most of our vocabulary has come from the accretions of *social* layers that carry us far from biological mimetics." Under attack by Margaret Schlauch and other philologists for holding a theory that is essentially that of the Platonic archetypes and in any case doesn't seem to fit the evidence, Burke defended Paget's theory in "The Philosophy of Literary Form" as not philology but "poetics," philology being the field studying *"the ways in which, if Paget's theory were 100 per cent correct, such linguistic mimesis as he is discussing would become obscured by historical accretions."* This is ingenious, and it may very well be true, but unfortunately Burke has himself discredited precisely this sort of escape-clause argument in *Counter-Statement:*

> Let us further note the "heads I win, tails you lose" mechanism which the psychoanalysts have at their disposal. Having defined the nature of a man's psychosis, they can fit any act into the scheme. For if the act follows the same pattern as the psychosis, they can explain it as consistent—but if it does not follow this pattern, they can account for it as "sublimated" or "compensatory." With such *vaticinium post eventum* (such explanation by epicycles) at their command, there is no reason why they should ever be at a loss for explanations in keeping with their tenets.

---

[2] This translation of theories about "origin" into theories about "essence" has become one of the major tactics in Burke's recent work. In "Ideology and Myth" in *Accent,* Summer 1947, he points out that the savage, having no way to express concepts of "substance," "essence," or logical priority in general, expresses them in terms of temporal priority, as myths of "origin." For a number of years, apparently, Burke has been treating aspects of nineteenth-century evolutionary thinking like Paget's theory of the origins of speech in gesture, Freud's theory of the origin of the Œdipus complex in the slaying of the primal father, the Cambridge theory of the ritual origin of drama, as higher types of this savage myth-making, and translating them back into statements about the gesture-*nature* of speech, the ritual-*nature* of drama, etc. The process is discussed at some length under "The Temporizing of Essence" in the *Grammar,* pp. 330-40.

Modern semantics has had short shrift from Burke. His long essay "Semantic and Poetic Meaning" in *The Philosophy of Literary Form* is an eloquent exploration of the barrenness of the semantic ideal of a "neutral" vocabulary. His own ideal, like theirs, is the "purification of war," but he would achieve it, not through a wild-goose chase after "terms that avoid ambiguity," but by seeking "terms that clearly reveal the strategic spots at which ambiguities necessarily arise." Where the semantic ideal would "eliminate," Burke would "rechannelize," and the most eloquent sentence in *A Grammar of Motives* (which was written all through the war years) is the statement:

> And so human thought may be directed towards "the purification of war," not perhaps in the hope that war can be eliminated from any organism that, like man, has the motives of combat in his very essence, but in the sense that war can be refined to the point where it would be much more peaceful than the conditions we would now call peace.

Nevertheless, while quarreling somewhat with Korzybski and his followers (for nominalism, a "reductive" frame, falling into their own "two-valued orientation" pit, and so on) and Carnap and Morris (for their barren positivist ideal), Burke manages to use a number of concepts and insights from both semantic schools; as distinguished from Ogden and Richards, whom he uses pretty much without attack, and such popularizers as Thurman Arnold and Stuart Chase, whom he attacks without using (although he has credited Arnold with one "serviceable" insight, the distinction between "political government" and "business government").

Into his integration of sociologies, psychologies, linguistics, semantics, and some physical and biological science, Burke has recently added philosophies and theologies. Characteristically, his imagery in *A Grammar of Motives* is of "bargaining with" the philosophers, as where he writes: "It is an important spot to haggle over, however, if you are going to haggle at all. For once you let this point go by unquestioned, you give Kant some important advantages." Burke must have lost his shirt in the deal, because his integrative frame now draws heavily on Aquinas, Augustine, and great numbers of the saints; philosophers from Plato and Aristotle to Nietzsche, Bergson, and Santayana; and he himself has a philosophy or metaphysic, of "substance," which is chiefly defined in terms of the positivism it opposes. Burke even has a curious kind of theology, not of "gods" but of "god-terms," since "gods" are only "names for motives or combinations of motives" common to a group, and every man has the right to worship God "in his own metaphor." Burke's gods are metaphors, terms, or even words (it is amusing and typical that his reference to "the good book" should be to the dictionary). In "The Tactics of Motivation," he speaks of animals transcending the animal dimension at times "just as complex dialectical operations, developing imagery to conceive beyond imagery, may enable men slightly to transcend the human dimension." In an older theology this would have been to the third realm, the angelic or the divine; it is characteristic of Burke to make it to the "dialectic" or "poetic." (For the record, it might be noted that Burke's angels, in an early story in *The White Oxen,* spend their time in heaven singing their own compositions.)

The most complete integration of all these strains Burke has so far achieved is his concept of "dramatism." In a sense, it follows from all his previous work and all the previous methods he has absorbed. In "The Five Master Terms" in *View,* Series III, No. 2, he writes: "'Dramatism' is certainly no invention of ours. We lay claim only to have looked at the matter a bit more quizzically than usual, until the meditation yielded some results. Instead of saying, 'Life is a drama and the world is its theatre,' then hurrying on, we tried to ponder this metaphor long and hard." It has developed out of his constant antinomian dichotomies in *Counter-Statement,* out of the concept of attitudes as incipient "actions" in *Permanence and Change,* most particularly out of the dialectic that runs through all of Burke's work from the first as a basic principle. Burke sometimes equates all of these ("that 'attitudinal action' which we have called the dramatistic, but which might also be called the dialectical"), but actually they are a deepening and a progression, from dichotomy to attitudinal-action to dialectic to dramatism. To some extent it is the idealist dialectic of Coleridge and Hegel; to a much greater extent it is Marx's historical materialist dialectic; it is even the rationalist dialectic of "that great modern dialectician, Sigmund Freud" (although Burke has elsewhere protested that Freud "is not dialectical enough"). With Marx and Freud, Burke gets beyond dialectic into dramatism, noting that "for all the talk of 'mechanism' in the Freudian psychology, we may see its underlying dramatistic nature," and proposing a union of Marx and Freud in terms of "an over-all theory of drama," since "Freud gives us the material of the closet drama, and Marx the material of the problem play, the one worked out in terms of personal conflicts, the other in terms of public conflicts." More than any of these, of course, it is the dialectic of Plato's Socrates, "*the act of definition* in his conversation," as inherited by Aristotle.

Philosophically Burke's "dramatism" is derived most completely from Aristotle, and the Aristotelian realism of scholastic thinkers like Aquinas, in their philosophy of "action."[3] In literary terms he seems to have been chiefly influenced by Henry James's Prefaces. As early as his Yeats article in the *Southern Review,* Winter 1942, Burke wrote: "It is a dramatist's concept, the sort of concern we read much of in Henry James's prefaces, where he is offering us an analysis of the novelist's motives in terms of the dramatist's

---

[3] It may be relevant here to mention a remarkable and characteristically scholastic book, Scott Buchanan's *Poetry and Mathematics* (1929), which may have influenced Burke toward dramatism, and certainly, if he read it, suggested his listing of such "reductive" metaphors for man as "Man is a machine," "Man is an animal," etc. Buchanan's book is a treatment of imaginative literature in terms of the metaphors of mathematics, and eventually a treatment of mathematics and science themselves as contemporary expressions of the pattern of Greek tragic drama.

exigencies." In "Motives and Motifs in the Poetry of Marianne Moore," in *Accent,* Spring 1942, one of his earliest uses of the terms "act," "scene," and "agent," he explains them as "the three terms central to the philosophy of drama embodied in Henry James's prefaces." In "The Tactics of Motivation," *Chimera,* Summer 1943, he amplifies these references:

> Henry James's prefaces as a whole, however, exemplify a much wider use of "dramatistic" co-ordinates than this. Many of his notes deal with the relation between agent and scene (in the sense of the relation between a given work and the situation under which he wrote it). Many others deal with the author's mind as the source of the work, relations between agent and act. And many deal with the purely internal relationships prevailing among act, scene, and agent in a given novel. But throughout the prefaces, he consciously and systematically considers the novel in dramatistic terms.

As a full dramatistic perspective this is an insistence on "*ritual drama* as the Ur-form, the hub," and all of Burke's earlier frameworks fit into it (even Paget, whose "theory of 'gesture speech' obviously makes a perfect fit with this perspective"). "Human affairs being dramatic, the discussion of human affairs becomes dramatic criticism." This ritual drama is the *agon,* with competing protagonist and antagonist, and it must be complete, "take us into-and-out-of," not incomplete, taking us into and seeking "to leave us there" (what Francis Fergusson has called, describing Wagner, "the luxury of running down a steep place into the sea"). It must be the full rhythm of "purpose to passion to perception," or "poiema, pathema, mathema," which Burke describes in "The Tactics of Motivation": "Out of the agent's action there grows a corresponding passion, and from the sufferance of this passion there arises a knowledge of his act, a knowledge that also to a degree transcends his act."

The individual ritual of "symbolic action" is thus clearly based on the pattern of ancient collective ritual, is in fact modern society's substitute for it (so that, for example, hypersexuality would be a private "erotic dance" to replace the lost tribal erotic dance). Consequently a good deal of Burke's dramatism relies on anthropology and ethnology. "He begins by considering the poet as a medicine man, and the poem as the medicine," Ransom has written, adding that he is "wonderfully keen at sniffing out ritualistic vestiges—taboo, fetish, name-calling, and so on." Burke has made a great deal of the pattern of the sacrificial king, from concluding *The Philosophy of Literary Form* with a long burlesque treating the democratic President as sacrificial king to proposing it as a ritual pattern that would have added another dimension to Bentley's study of figures like Nietzsche and D. H. Lawrence in *A Century of Hero Worship.* Burke has been greatly concerned in general with the behavior of primitive groups, drawing equally on the sweeping formulations of theorists like Frazer and the concrete and scientific reporting of modern field workers like Malinowski. He has called *The Golden Bough* "comic," his highest term of praise, since, "by showing us the rites of magical purification in primitive peoples," it "gives us the necessary cues for the detection of similar processes in even the most practical and non-priestly of contemporary acts." To my knowledge, Burke has never directly referred to the Cambridge school of classical scholars who have applied Frazer to the detection of the patterns of ancient dramatic ritual underlying Greek art and thought (Gilbert Murray, Jane Harrison, F. M. Cornford, A. B. Cook, etc.), and he seems never to have read them. Nevertheless, particularly in the *Grammar,* in his perception of "tribal patterns" behind philosophic notions, the *"agon"* behind the "dialectic," the property concepts behind the Greek *"Moira,"* the "Dionysian dramas that underlay the patterns of Greek thought," he is clearly following in their line; and his appreciative review of Lord Raglan's *The Hero* (a somewhat diluted but more ambitious assertion of the same theory) and his willingness to call his work "folk criticism" suggest either some acquaintance with their work or a striking pattern of identical thinking.

The matter of Burke's terminology in general requires some consideration. In his proliferation of terms Burke is in the tradition of Bentham, Peirce, and Veblen, and their credo was stated ironically by Peirce in a letter to William James (and quoted by Burke, who calls it "these uncomfortable rigors"):

> It is an indispensable requisite of science that it should have a recognized technical vocabulary, composed of words so unattractive that loose thinkers are not tempted to use them; and a recognized and legitimate way of making up new words freely when a new conception is introduced; and that it is vital for science that he who introduces a new conception should be held to have a *duty* imposed upon him to invent a sufficiently disagreeable series of words to express it. I wish you to reflect seriously upon the moral aspect of terminology.

Burke has not, however, like Peirce, made up new words as a matter of principle, but rather, like Veblen, restored and redefined old ones wherever possible. (Chinese lawmakers, Richards informs us, recommend "that those who introduce new terms or make unauthorized distinctions should be put to death.") In this use of old words in a new precise sense, there is a loss as well as a gain. Joubert, who insisted on the employment of the common words of everyday speech even for such subjects as metaphysics, noted the gain: people are shown "what they do really think" in their own terms, the writer gives a greater impression of having assimilated "life and its concerns." Coleridge, who made up a great many words, like "intensify," which have since become current, noted the loss:

> In such [scientific] discourse the instructor has no other alternative than either to use old words with new meanings (the plan adopted by Darwin in his Zoönomia;) or to introduce new terms, after the example of Linnaeus, and the framers of the present chemical nomenclature. The latter mode is evidently preferable, were it only

that the former demands a twofold exertion of thought in one and the same act. For the reader, or hearer, is required not only to learn and bear in mind the new definition; but to unlearn, and keep out of his view, the old and habitual meaning; a far more difficult and perplexing task, and for which the mere semblance of eschewing pedantry seems to me an inadequate compensation.

He conceded, however, that where "it is in our power to recall an unappropriate term that had without sufficient reason become obsolete, it is doubtless a less evil to restore than to coin anew." Burke thus gains a number of real values from his use of common terms in a transformed, unfamiliar, or obsolete sense; but the fact that his "comic" does not mean what people think of as comic, and his "prayer" does not mean what people think of as prayer, is undoubtedly responsible for some confusion in his readers, and probably contributes to the numerical limitation of his audience.

On the other hand, Burke's terms have been moving toward greater and greater clarity, each developing out of the set before, and the current dramatistic pentad—act, scene, agent, agency, purpose—would probably come closest to satisfying Joubert as being the language of common speech. Burke writes:

> It must be our purpose ever to perfect our terminology—for in an adequate terminology there are adequate exhortations and admonitions. And basic to the structure of a terminology is the need for an essential complexity or pliancy—not merely complexity got by the accumulation of terms, but complexity *at the start.* . . .

A curious device of this development in Burke's work is the nursing along, in each book, of the metaphor that eventually burgeoned as "dramatism." Thus *Counter-Statement* defines form as "the psychology of the audience," and concludes on the development of dramatic form as "representative anecdote." *Permanence and Change,* in its conclusion, suggests that the "ultimate metaphor" for discussing the universe and man's relations to it would be "poetic or dramatic man." *Attitudes toward History* speaks of the inventor's "drama," Burke's own historical "drama," and argues in a footnote:

> In brief, we contend that "perspective by incongruity" makes for a *dramatic* vocabulary, with weighting counter-weighting, in contrast with the liberal ideal of a *neutral* naming in the characterization of processes. . . .
>
> The neutral ideal prompts one to forget that terms are *characters,* that an essay is an *attenuated play.* . . .
>
> The element of dramatic *personality* in essayistic *ideas* cannot be intelligently discerned until we recognize that names (for either dramatic characters or essayistic concepts) are shorthand designations for certain fields and methods of action.

By 1941, when *The Philosophy of Literary Form* was published, Burke's dramatist metaphor had developed the two basic terms of the pentad, and he trots out the act-scene terminology on the first page of the Foreword and continues it through the title essay, discussing symbolic action in terms of "agons" and, in a footnote, explaining all five terms of the pentad and what his next work will do with them. At the same time the essay "Semantic and Poetic Meaning" distinguishes the poetic ideal as going "through" drama rather than around it, and the eleventh proposition of Burke's "Twelve Propositions on the Relation between Economics and Psychology" is flatly: "Human relations should be analyzed with respect to the leads discovered by a study of drama," while the development of this proposition announces Freud and Marx as "impresarios."

The only other terminological metaphor that Burke has carried through from his earliest books is the ironic use of the terminology of business and finance for markedly non-financial matters, a device he shares with Thoreau. He speaks of "investment," "socialization of losses," "cashing in on," "discounting," "mergers," as though matters of art and ideas were important enough to get on ledgers. "Once the comic proviso is added," he notes, "the whole terminology of capitalism is found remarkable for its clear simplification of social processes." In "Character of Our Culture" in the *Southern Review,* Spring 1941, Burke calls his attitude "speculative," with the melancholy note:

> I use the word "speculative" with full awareness of its monetary pun, for in calling myself here a "speculator" I fully believe that I am exemplifying a social value that has been affected by the monetary motivation—though I must speak, alas! as one who has not had the advantage of much original field work in this subject, one whose knowledge of it is at best second-hand, indeed, one who has money much more on his mind than in his purse.

Burke's dramatist pentad is an attempt to find a set of terms so basic and so all-embracing that they can handle any area of discourse. As such, it is the successor of a long line of triads, tetrads, pentads, etc. The most obvious relationship, to which Burke himself calls attention in the book, is to Aristotle's Four Causes—formal, material, efficient, and final—which Burke equates respectively with act, scene, agent, and purpose, with agency also included under "final." Burke also equates his pentad with Aristotle's six elements of tragedy, plot as act, character as agent, thought as purpose, melody and diction as agency, and spectacle as scene. After Aristotle, Ben Jonson had a more or less Aristotelian triad in *Discoveries*—poem, poesy, poet—which would probably correspond to Burke's agency, act, and agent. Lessing's bodies-actions dichotomy in the *Laocoön* is a very close approximation of scene-act, and Lessing later fills out the other terms. Emerson's triad of cause-operation-effect in "The Poet," which he translates poetically as Jove-Pluto-Neptune, Father-Spirit-Son, and Knower-Doer-Sayer, would probably be the equivalents of purpose, act, and either scene or agent. Santayana, in *Interpretations of Poetry and Religion,* in describing the way in which nature, an "engine" under paganism, becomes "a temporary stage, built for the exigencies of a human drama" under Christianity, clearly has a dramatist set of terms that includes at least act and scene. Finally, Ernest Fenollosa, in his essay on "The Chinese Written Character as a Medium for Poetry," has an agent-act-object triad very close to Burke's pentad.

One major aspect of Burke's work has been somewhat slighted in the discussion above: his treatment of "rhetoric," the poem-audience relationship, which has been arbitrarily assigned as Richards's territory. Actually Burke has been concerned with rhetorical action almost as much as with symbolic action in his work, and in *Counter-Statement* and *Permanence and Change* much more. In "The Philosophy of Literary Form," he proposes a relationship between the poet-poem and the poem-audience ratios that involves rhetoric with a kind of symbolic action in the audience. He writes:

> Many of the things that a poet's work does for *him* are not things that the same work does for *us* (i.e., there is a difference in act between the poem as being-written and the poem as being-read). Some of them are, some of them are not. . . .
>
> But my position is this: That if we try to discover what the poem is doing for the poet, we may discover a set of generalizations as to what poems do for everybody. With these in mind, we have cues for analyzing the sort of *eventfulness* that the poem contains. And in analyzing this eventfulness, we shall make basic discoveries about the *structure* of the work itself. . . .
>
> And I contend that the kind of observation about structure is more relevant when you approach the work as the *functioning* of a structure. . . . And I contend that some such description of the "symbolic act" as I am here proposing is best adapted for the disclosure of a poem's function.

A poem is thus designed to "do something" for the poet and his readers, and the poet's manipulation of this symbolic action in the reader is rhetoric, or what is more generally called "communication" as distinguished from "expression." Burke also identifies it with "prayer" in his dream-prayer-chart triad, or "the choice of gesture" to embody the poet's attitude "for the inducement of corresponding attitudes." The poem is thus a symbolic act of the poet, but "surviving as a structure or object, it enables us as readers to re-enact it," so that reading too is the enactment of symbolic "rites."

Burke has two elaborate studies of rhetoric in *The Philosophy of Literary Form*, "Antony in Behalf of the Play," a long monologue by Antony to the audience explaining Shakespeare's mechanisms as they focus in his oration over Caesar's body, and "Trial Translation (from Twelfth Night)," a less ambitious but similar explanation by the Duke. Burke has called these studies of the "reader-writer relationship," but more properly they are studies of the reader-poem relationship, since they work from the text rather than from Shakespeare. His fuller study, "The Rhetoric of Hitler's 'Battle,'" is more accurately a study of the reader-writer relationship, since it covers Hitler's symbolic expression in the book, the audience's symbolic action in reading it, and the rhetorical relation between the two. It unites the private and public, the introspective (conjectural in this case) psychology best designed for getting at the author's symbolic expression, and the behavioral psychology best designed for getting at what is rhetorically communicated.

Counter-Statement attempts to develop the concept of rhetoric, first through a distinction between "clinical" and "songful" handling, then between "realistic" and "declamatory," "observation" and "ritual," "information" and "ceremony"; finally fixing on the distinction (later "chart" versus "prayer") between "the psychology of information" and "the psychology of form." "Form," which *Counter-Statement* defines as "the psychology of the audience" and "the creation of an appetite in the mind of the auditor, and the adequate satisfying of that appetite," or "the arousing and fulfillment of desires," is thus equivalent to "rhetoric," which is no more than "effective literature." By his next book, *Permanence and Change,* Burke was calling this phenomenon "stylistic ingratiation," to leave room in the term "form" for structure symbolically as well as rhetorically determined.

Edmund Wilson quotes H. L. Mencken as saying that he even enjoys the prospectuses put out by bond houses, because everything written is an attempt to express the aspirations of some human being. Burke's concepts of "symbolic action" and "rhetoric" result in a similar embracing of trash of every description (although we can doubt that he "enjoys" it as Mencken does), which frequently illustrates the mechanisms of more significant works in a fashion easier to follow. For purposes of analysis or illustration Burke draws as readily on a popular movie, a radio quiz program, a *Herald Tribune* news item about the National Association of Manufacturers, or a Carter Glass speech on gold as on Sophocles or Shakespeare. Those things are a kind of poetry too, full of symbolic and rhetorical ingredients, and if they are bad poetry, it is a bad poetry of vital significance in our lives. In immersing himself in this cheap "forensic" material as much as he does (we can presume that *A Rhetoric of Motives* will consist largely of it), Burke is himself a kind of sacrificial king, bored to death that the tribe's crops may grow.

5

Finally, a brief look at Burke's own situation, strategies, attitudes, motives, symbolic actions, purposes, is in order. One factor of great importance is his non-critical writing, of which he has been moderately prolific. He has published two works of fiction, *The White Oxen,* a collection of short stories, in 1924, and *Towards a Better Life,* a novel written as "a Series of Epistles, or Declamations," in 1932. Both works are subtle, ambiguous, fairly obscure, stylized, and highly eloquent: the former progressing from fairly realistic stories to stories bewilderingly symbolic and rhetorical, as a kind of "counter-statement" at a time "when rhetoric is so universally despised"; the latter a gesture of return "to more formalized modes of writing," "from the impromptu to the studied," its concern with plot "peripheral," its central concern with what Burke calls the Six Pivotals: "lamentation, rejoicing, beseechment, admonition, sayings, invective." Both books have been little read or recognized, although they have clearly influenced such writers as Robert M. Coates and Nathanael West, have been praised by William Carlos Williams and attacked as "duller than Thackeray" by Yvor Winters, and *Towards a Better Life* at least seems to me one of the important works of fiction in our time. In relation to his criticism, the only ground for discussing them here, they echo many of the ideas, demonstrate many of the theories in practice, function as the same imaginative "placing" of human motives from a different angle; and while they were written chiefly as rhetorical action, they have given his later criticism endless material for identifying symbolic action.

Wilde, I believe, somewhere remarks that he got his education in public, as a reviewer, and Burke has used his reviewing in a similar fashion. As a comparison of the articles in *The Philosophy of Literary Form* with the reviews printed as an Appendix reveals, the subject of this year's review becomes the subject of next year's references, and by going far afield from imaginative literature in his reviews, he has consistently broadened the horizons of his work. At the same time Burke gets critical ideas directly from problems that arise out of his reviewing ("It was in the attempt to review two books of this sort that we first found ourselves confronting what we consider the typical properties of constitutions"); and in some cases he even writes his reviews in whole or part into his later text. Burke has also written music criticism, including a stint as music critic for the *Nation,* and occasional art criticism, so that his work, particularly *Counter-Statement,* is larded with authoritative musical and plastic references and analogies (although it must be admitted that his art references, unlike his music references, tend to be to rather literary, rarely abstract or modern, works). Burke has also done a great deal of translating from the German, including some of Mann's short stories, and works by Spengler, Schnitzler, von Hoffmannsthal, Emil Ludwig, and others, which then too became grist for his critical mill. Finally, he has published a number of poems, most of them free in form, rhetorical, and emphasizing irony and social protest, which have never been collected in book form.

Burke's social ideas, as expressed most directly in his poetry and in a more complex fashion in his criticism, form a complicated and ambiguous pattern. The chief element is an outspoken dislike for technology and our machine civilization, with its cults of "efficiency," "the higher standard of living," and so on; with a remarkable consistency all of his works from the earliest to the latest have constituted a "counter-statement" to the technological ideal, opposing it with "negativism," "opposition," "interference"; in short: "the aesthetic would seek to discourage the most stimulating values of the practical, would seek—by wit, by fancy, by anathema, by versatility—to throw into confusion the code which underlies commercial enterprise, industrial competition, the 'heroism' of economic warfare; would seek to endanger the basic props of industry." This is from the "Program" in *Counter-Statement,* Burke's early manifesto for aestheticism, but the same themes continue in the Conclusion to *Permanence and Change,* formalized as a poetic communism; and in the section on "Good Life" in *Attitudes toward History,* stated more positively in terms of ideals of active participation and ecological balance. In *The Philosophy of Literary Form* they become more bitter, with references to "our despicable economic structure" making us do "despicable things"; and more pessimistic, with Burke seeing "a dismal political season" in store for us, the only hope temporarily "a campaign base for personal integrity, a kind of beneath-which-not," which is actually Eliot's last-ditch ideal, to "keep something alive." By *A Grammar of Motives,* the social view becomes at once less bitter and less pessimistic. Burke is still antagonistic to our cult of the "gadget," "the higher standard of living,"[4] the "fantastic hardships" that men undergo to have technological "conveniences," but the industrial system and the money motive are now "poignant" rather than "despicable," and he finds an ironic hope:

> At a time when the liars, the stupid, and the greedy seem too greatly in control of a society's policies, philosophies of materialistic reduction may bring us much solace in reminding us that *the very nature of the materials* out of which a civilization is constructed, or in which it is grounded, will not permit such *perfection* of lies, stupidity, and greed to prevail as some men might cause to prevail if they could have their way.

His conclusion is the proposal of "a kind of 'Neo-Stoic resignation,'" since "For better or worse, men are set to complete the development of technology."

There are two strains in this attitude, which after a time separated. One is an objection to machinery, technology, industrialization per se, in any society, with Burke opposing to them a "maximum of physicality," less button-pressing, less mobility and more action, biological adaptation and "metabiology," and a larger ecological efficiency opposed to the limited "efficiency" of technology. This is the most "reactionary" (in the pure sense of the word) strain in Burke, an agrarian, backward-looking ideal that he shares with Thoreau, the Jeffersonians and Populists, and less savory groups, and which has led Henry Bamford Parkes to write, with a certain accuracy: "he would like to have lived in Confucian China." At its most extreme this is even a dislike of science itself, and there is some truth in a reviewer's charge that Burke, like the old ladies of the anti-vivisection societies, tends to see laboratory scientists as "sadistic rat-torturers." At the other extreme he is

---

[4] By 1947, in an article on "The American Way" in the December *Touchstone,* Burke was describing the whole of American culture as derived from the generalizing principle of "the higher standard of living," used in a non-pejorative sense, with American philosophic and aesthetic concepts either expressions of it or reactions to it.

prepared to find some good in technology, even defending it against an archaeologist named Kidder in his article "Character of Our Culture," finding such real, if negative values as its lessening the ravages of crop failure, pestilence, and other natural disasters. Somewhere in the middle he himself lives ("His life itself is a design," William Carlos Williams wrote in the *Dial*), combining the simple, immobile, and agrarian life with the technology necessary to get him, by car, train, and subway, to the New York Public Library.

The other strain in Burke's social attitude is his objection, not to industrialization per se, but to the specific features of the capitalistic system. In *Permanence and Change* he embraces Communism (largely of an out-of-the-world variety), proposing a dialectical materialism altered into a "dialectical biologism," and a "poetic" and "stylistic" life achieved through and beyond the Communist society. He argues that Communism is "the only coherent and organized movement making for the subjection of the technological genius to human ends," and that it polarizes such valuable c-words (or "Kenneth-words") as co-operation, communication, communion, collectivism, and communicant. In *Attitudes toward History* he finds collectivism inevitable as the next stage in his curve of history, but presents his collectivist communism with "comic correctives," and the section on the "Good Life" made it clear that his social ideal is actually much more Confucian (if not more confused). Although he still refers approvingly to such orthodox Communist equipment as "dialectical materialism," his later works have veered away from calling his agrarian and decentralized Jeffersonian social ideal "Communism." Fordism is apparently to his mind still Fordism, whether of the American or the Soviet variety.

Burke's ideas on poetry and criticism are inextricably tied up with his ideas on life (he defines art, for example, as "biological adaptation," thus the "good life") and are frequently on a high enough level of abstraction to be both at once. On criticism his keynote is the topic sentence of *Permanence and Change:* "All living things are critics," with the example of the trout, becoming a critic after his jaw is ripped, learning "a nicer discrimination between food and bait." His critic, like Matthew Arnold's, is, in the last analysis, a critic of life; and his job: "to present as many counter-influences as possible," "to integrate technical criticism with social criticism," "to look a gift horse in the mouth." Where the "poet" hypnotizes, it is "the function of criticism to supply the sharp sound that awakens us"; and "whatever poetry may be, criticism had best be comic."

This view is not, however, contemptuous of poetry. The theme that "poetry" (whether as a written lyric, a world-view, or a way of life) is very close to the central value of our existence runs through all of Burke's writing; it is "equipment for living," it "comforts," "protects," and "arms" us. At the same time he insists on the importance of the poetic sensibility, what Blackmur calls "the symbolic imagination," as the ultimate feature of criticism, writing:

The objection arises when philosophers of science are loath to grant that this very capacity of science demands a compensatory counterpart, variously named "intuition," "imagination," "vision," "revelation," etc. For though one could scientifically break a work of art into many ingredients, and by test arrive at some extremely subtle and perfectly just discriminations about these ingredients, it is when confronting the *synthesis* of the ingredients that the scientific method becomes inadequate.

The other essential ingredient in Burke's scheme is the element in irony, humor, "the comic." He defines humor as the "humanization" that "enables us to accept our dilemmas"; irony as the "humility" that comes from "a sense of fundamental kinship with the enemy"; the comic as a "charitable" attitude containing the paradox of acceptance-rejection, give and take. Essentially all these are aspects of the same thing: an attitude of scrupulosity, reservation, "getting off before the end of the line," counterstating, corrective discounting, "rolling with the punch." Burke's good life would not only be good; it would be comic, ironic, perhaps even funny. In any case it would certainly be undignified. Burke writes in an early essay:

Dignity? Yes, there seems to be a thirst for personal dignity. There is a trace of the hysterical, the devious, in this need of dignity. Dignity belongs to the conquered; one leaves the room with dignity when he has been routed; the victor can romp. Dignity is a subjective adjustment. It is objectively unpliant; it is unbiological, a dignified man could not run from a lion. One meets facts objectively without dignity. One sacrifices his authority, first asking what mean task the outside thing demands of him. Dignity is Ptolemaic, indignity is Copernican. The development of man in Europe, some one has said, has been a loss of personal dignity in proportion to his mastery of nature.

Finally, there is the matter of Burke's critical writing itself. He has always had a relatively small audience, although it has been a regularly increasing one, and the sale of *A Grammar of Motives* was substantial enough to constitute, finally, a kind of public recognition and success, the sort that artists of unyielding integrity (Martha Graham comes to mind as another example) tend to achieve late in life, after a generation of popular "sell-outs" have had their brief fames and blown away. The chief reason, in my experience, given for resistance or inability to read him is the charge of "obscurity" or "jargon." Not referring to himself, Burke answered the "obscurity" charge in *Counter-Statement,* writing: "There are some forms of excellence (such as complexity, subtlety, remote inquiry, stylistic rigor) which may limit a book's public as surely as though it were a work on higher mathematics." Actually Burke's writing itself is very clear and very straightforward, the obscurity being entirely a matter of the concepts and terms. Even John Crowe Ransom, who has sometimes been his severest critic, has granted him a prose of "literary distinction." The charge of "jargon" is somewhat more accurate. Although Burke has frequently kidded the German philosophic style (he notes that Kant, Fichte, Schelling, and Hegel "write like the shifting of cars in a freight yard"), he is at the same time somewhat drawn to it, defends its "cumbersome nomenclature" as "a form of poetry," and in such terms as "Neo-Malthusian Principle," "Bureaucratization of the Imaginative," and "Perspective by Incongruity" comes very close to its characteristic jargon.

A number of his stylistic habits and devices have been known to irritate readers. The trick of stress-shifting, the distinction between "knowledge of the *Good*" and "*knowledge* of the Good," although a meaningful and effective dialectic device, tends to be used enough in the late work to be irritating. The distinction between "what are years?" and "what all are years?" is a barbarism, pure and simple. Less justifiable reader annoyance is sometimes felt at two of his most characteristic and most brilliantly effective devices: his use of words in a special sense by putting them in quotation marks, and his footnotes. The quotation marks ("And the childless priest could be named a 'father' because he had 'spiritual' progeny, the 'children' of the church") are a way of emphasizing, pointing up double meanings, marking off a special sense. The footnotes rise in an arc from a few in *Counter-Statement,* more in *Permanence and Change,* and most in *Attitudes toward History;* and then fall off, with fewer in *The Philosophy of Literary Form* and almost none in *A Grammar of Motives*. At their height, in *Attitudes,* where the footnotes bulk almost as large as the text, they serve as a wonderful counterpoint melody: the specific against the general, the peripheral against the central, the random against the planned, the suggestive against the explored (Burke has thrown off in footnotes enough suggestions regarding things he has never had a chance to investigate to keep a flotilla of critics busy for a lifetime). Nevertheless, the constant footnotes carrying along another story occasionally get the reader feeling a little schizoid, and there is no doubt that at their apogee they represented some similar unreconciled dissociation in Burke, which he seems to have reconciled since. Finally Burke's style sometimes tends to be unnecessarily repetitious, as when he restates a thing three times, using a slightly different figure each time, rather than stating it fully once and for all; he splits infinitives without qualm; and he mixes metaphors wickedly (Margaret Schlauch, who pointed some out in a review, noted that the issue is not a grammarian's purism, but that Burke tends to blunt the usefulness of his metaphors by mixing them, as in his "frames" that "melt," "struggle," and "contend").

On the other hand, one of the most ingratiating features of Burke's style is his constant reliance on the joke and the pun, even the elaborate burlesque, to make serious points. His jokes, when they are successful, are wonderful, a wry and ironic humor that always bites; but the pun has an even more important and serious function in his work. Like the ancient Egyptians, who used to fill their sacred rituals with puns to increase their magic effectiveness, Burke puts into his puns the heart of what he has to say. Like Shakespeare's,

Burke's puns are lightning metaphors, Empsonian ambiguities, perspectives by incongruity, reinforced by his passionate interest in etymology and awareness of linguistic significance on a great number of levels, including the psychoanalytic.

Another feature of Burke's writing, which has markedly increased in the recent books, is a concern with the scatological. Burke is insistent on the need for "making peace with," alternately, "the soil" and "the faeces." He has identified Freud's work as "an interpretative sculpting of excrement"; Stoicism as "the transcendence of offal"; Eliot's *"Merdes" in the Cathedral,* an "ecclesia super cloacam." One section of *A Grammar of Motives* explains his concept of the "Demonic Trinity," the interrelationship of the erotic, urinary, and excremental, and he has increasingly tended to translate back and forth among all three and related motifs like the mystical vision and the monetary. Burke's scatalogical concern unquestionably represents a serious and profound attempt, like Freud's, to confront the "cloacal" underlying our "transcendent" activities, but at times the flippancy of his presentation makes it seem merely another "counter" or antinomian expression; to try a Burkian pun (encouraged by his "latent patent, covert overt"), we might say that he has received so little of the world's "increment" that he has been forced to devote himself to its "excrement."[5]

The final question about Burke's work is what it all adds up to. If it has seemingly had a lack of focus, gone after a bewildering number of quarries in no apparent sequence, it has had the compensatory virtue of endless fertility, suggestiveness, an inexhaustible throwing off of sparks. This view would seem to be borne out by the readiness with which Burke seems reducible to aphorisms: the "Flowerishes" printed in the *Rocky Mountain Review,* Winter 1943; the facility with which brief excerpts from the *Grammar* stood alone in a publisher's brochure called "The Burke Sampler" and *Accent,* Autumn 1945; the "memorability" of isolated lines from his work: America as a country in which death "is in exceptionally bad repute," "Thou shalt not commit adulteration," the right of each man "to worship God in his own metaphor," "Die as a mangled wasp dies," "The man did good for the oppressed? Then he made them oppressors," and so on.

And yet, valuable as this quality is, it is more likely that Burke's work is intensely organized and that with the conclusion of his current trilogy a total pattern will emerge to embrace all his previous work. It will be probably the most all-embracing critical system ever built up for turning on a single poem, and we can expect a period of unequaled critical fruitfulness as Burke and his followers turn it on poem after poem in succession. What would not one give, for example, for a full-length study by Burke of such a work of endless fertility as *Moby Dick,* never satisfactorily explored? (He has, incidentally, in

---

[5] It has been suggested to me that Burke's critical preoccupation with the cheap forensic material of the movies, the radio, and the newspapers may not represent the sacrificial boredom to which I attribute it so much as another aspect of this fascinated scatological concern.

several places mentioned making notes on it.) To raise the obvious objection immediately, suppose the poem or work collapses flat under the tremendous weight of the critical system? Our faith here must lie in Burke's genuine humility, the ironic humor that keeps him always backing away from his own machinery. in *Towards a Better Life* his hero aphorizes: "Watch the mind as you would eye a mean dog";[6] and in the sobering conclusion of *Permanence and Change* Burke reminds us "that men build their cultures by huddling together, nervously loquacious, at the edge of an abyss."

In "A Critic's Job of Work" R. P. Blackmur charges that Burke's method "could be applied with equal fruitfulness to Shakespeare, Dashiell Hammett, or Marie Corelli." In *The Philosophy of Literary Form* Burke admits the charge (after he "got through wincing"), adding: "You can't properly put Marie Corelli and Shakespeare apart until you have first put them together. First genus, then differentia. The strategy in common is the genus. The *range* or *scale* or *spectrum* of particularizations is the differentia." What we can expect with the completion of Burke's system is the detailed studies of "differentiae," what Burke elsewhere calls "the miracle of evaluation," built on the present somewhat indiscriminate lumping by genus. From the brief samples of it Burke occasionally vouchsafes us, we can be sure that it will be literary criticism almost unequaled for power, lucidity, depth, and brilliance of perception. In the ultimately unclassifiable man who once had a protagonist remark: "One is not quite at rest when he has accounted for so much nobility by trivial mechanisms," all we can be sure of beyond that is that it will be a literary criticism constituting a passionate avowal of the ultimate and transcendent importance of the creative act.

---

[6] As Burke would be the first to point out, this terrifying relationship of "mind" to "*mean* dog" was probably inspired by a tonal pun.

Everything, Preferably All At Once:
Coming to Terms with Kenneth Burke

by Howard Nemerov

In one perhaps accidental symbolic act, Burke expressed his essence: he had some of his early books reissued by *Hermes* Publications. Hermes, originally a boundary stone, presently grew a face and a beard and went on to become the Roman god of boundaries, Terminus. Rising still further, he became Hermes Trismegistus, "the fabled author of a large number of works (called Hermetic books) most of which embody Neo-Platonic, Judaic, and Cabalistic ideas, as well as magical, astrological and alchemical doctrines". In other words, everything, and preferably all at once.

The dictionary from which I drew this description of Burke in his aspect as Hermes identifies him with the Egyptian scribe Thoth, who above all "created by means of words", and "appears sometimes . . . as exercising this function on his own initiative, at other times as acting as the instrument of his creator". That is a doubt one may properly have about any scribe whose *oeuvre* is imposing enough to make one wonder whether he is representing the world or proposing to replace it; Milton, for instance, invoking his heavenly muse, claims to merit the instruction by reason of his "upright heart and pure"; and yet through the intended humility I have always heard a certain obstinacy in "upright", and thought of it as comparable with another Miltonic epithet, "erected". But the doubt may be peculiarly appropriate to Burke, who "above all creates by means of words" in the special sense that he creates words, terms, terminologies—the business of Hermes. And when you ask whether he does this on his own initiative or as the instrument of his creator, you get the somewhat cryptic though certainly comprehensive reply from his address to the Logos:

> For us
> Thy name a Great Synecdoche,
> Thy works a Grand Tautology.

Schopenhauer once called the world a vast dream dreamed by a single being, but in such a way that all the people in the dream are dreaming too. A lovely figure, and in its logological translation it might do for Burke's world as well: a vast dream dreamed by a single Word, but in such a way that all the words in the dream are dreaming too.

Reprinted from *The Sewanee Review* 79 (1971). Used by permission.

But I have just remembered that part of my title, "preferably all at once", is about Burke intensively: it comes from him. (Somewhat as when you make what seems a good pun you can never be certain it isn't waiting for you in *Finnegans Wake*.) There is a passage late in *A Rhetoric of Motives* that I had been meaning to cite somehow, as an instance of Burke's excessiveness about terms and of one's appreciation of his rightness if one would only think about it (as I. A. Richards said, a book is a machine for thinking with).

The passage is called "Rhetorical Names for God", and after some introductory talk a page-and-a-bit goes to a listing of terms you might use when appealing to the Deity. The range is indeed extensive, as is proper to the All in All, going from "ground of all possibility" around to "nothing" and taking in *en route* such things as real estate, money, sleep, excrement, and death. But now I especially note: "Center, circumference, apex, base (preferably all at once)."

By this example I mean only that when you speak of the writers you care most for, you not only speak about them—you also speak them.

Here is a sort of monkish metaphor for what Burke does: he illuminates texts. In its application to criticism the figure tell us one of the things we most expect from critics, that they should offer us particular enlightenment about particular works, showing us things we had not seen and that, once seen, compel us to acknowledge their truth and significance. In its more medieval aspect the figure suggests an independent activity integral to the other and, in Burke's criticism, identical with it: as in the illuminations of the *Book of Kells*, Burke is using the text while weaving up his own designs.

Most simply put, he can get more thoughts out of a book than anyone else can, evoking in his reader time after time a mixed attitude of surprise, gratitude, and chagrin—"yes, of course, why couldn't I have seen it for myself?"—while at the same time, in the same gestures, often in the very same sentences, he is developing a method and a terminology which the reader, if he will, can master for application elsewhere.

For this reason, there is very little in Burke's writing of what Whitehead stigmatized as "inert knowledge". Everything is in movement, in development; everything is always being used for all it's worth, and sometimes maybe more.

There is an enthusiasm in all this that sometimes comes near enough to madness: criticism as rhapsody, or *furor poeticus*. Nor do I mean that in disparagement, though aware that some writers would; for among the most appealing things about Burke, to my mind, is the sense he has, the sense I get from reading him, that thought, if it is to matter at all, must be both obsessive and obsessively thorough, that thinking, if it is to salvage anything worth having from chaos, must adventure into the midst of madness and build its city there. Also that this action never really ends until the thinker does; everything is always to be done again. Also this: that system begins in inspiration, order in improvisation, method in heuristic. Here is one of Burke's own and somewhat breathless descriptions:

So we must keep trying anything and everything, improvising, borrowing from others, developing from others, dialectically using one text to comment upon another, schematizing; using the incentive to new wanderings, returning from these excursions to schematize again, being oversubtle where the straining seems to promise some further glimpse, and making amends by reduction to very simple anecdotes.

That seems characteristic, even to "we must"—for Burke makes many and difficult demands upon his readers—and even to "make amends"—for he is as magnanimous as he is demanding.

Back in days when such things mattered more to the literary community at large than perhaps they do just now, there was much debate upon a question, raised I believe by T. S. Eliot, as to whether criticism could be, or should be, "autotelic". Much debate, but relatively little illumination, probably because that forbidding word "autotelic" implied the expected answer, that criticism had better humbly confine itself to the ancillary task of digging nuggets of wisdom, or pure form, or whatever, out of the superior materials provided by the poets and novelists, and not set up in business on its own. And indeed there was much local and practical justification for the expected answer, inasmuch as when criticism did its thing, usually under the formidable name of aesthetics, the results were often of a dullness far beyond the call of duty.

But all the same, the very fact that the question was raised indicated some anxiety about the expected answer; and the massive development of criticism as both an art and an industry around that time suggested the perhaps horrifying thought that if the critics went on as they were going there was some remote chance that some one among them might one day actually learn something about literature *in principle,* and not only about this work and that work in snips and snaps and *aperçus.*

Well, in Burke and some others (among whom I should name especially I. A. Richards and William Empson), I conceive that there began to appear ways in which criticism could be "autotelic" in such a style as not in the least to prevent its traditionally imputed function of praising and damning and qualifying the work of "creative" writers; and it appeared indeed that by its new independence criticism was able to perform its traditional function not merely better than before, producing "insights" at such a rate as for a few years almost made people believe in progress once again, but also at depths and over ranges not previously suspected to exist. Having begun with the usual critical attempt to winkle "meanings" out of literary works, Burke and the others (and a good few more than I have mentioned) were led on into quite new questions—at least for the tradition of criticism in English, and in modern times—about meaning in general, what it is and how it arises and in what ways it relates to language. In fact, the same question that had been asked about criticism now appeared about language: was it ancillary to meaning, instrumental to thoughts that somehow had an independent existence? Or was it autotelic, and capable of generating worlds, or the world, primarily by reason of its own internal arrangements, as the language of mathematics, or, more darkly, of music, seemed to suggest?

Kenneth Burke's researches in this area seem to me venturesome, enchanting, and productive. And I have sometimes thought of them as contributing to the development of a new species of epic poetry, a poetry containing its own criticism much as a dream sometimes contains its own interpretation more or less explicitly; this poetry might be that intellectual comedy which Valéry, himself an anticipator of it, said he would value more highly than either the divine or the human. (The question whether such a poetry would have to come in verse seems entirely secondary; from the "creative" side one might cite *The Magic Mountain, Finnegans Wake,* and *Remembrance of Things Past* as works containing their own critique.) In what follows, rather than trying to describe Burke's "system" or "doctrine", which anyhow is always evolving out of and dissolving into method, I shall try a species of rhapsodic impressionism and imitation.

Putting first things first, in accordance with Burke's principle of "the temporizing of essence", the mind's first move upon the world is to assert something, to be active. The assertion will probably be suggested by the world, yet it will also have in it something both arbitrary and peremptory, and at least prospectively insane. This is what writers commonly call "having an idea", a phrase usually treated as ultimate and unquestionable, but which with Burke's help we may see a bit further into.

The essence of "having an idea" is "giving a name". Its effect is always to say to the phenomenon, "Be other than thou art." It is both prayerful and commanding, it both asks and asserts. It challenges, and upon the challenge it moves into a combat with "the world" which at its best it both wins and loses. Wins, in that a more or less large range of particular appearances is brought into patterned clarity, simultaneously articulated and integrated, by coming under the sway of the idea. Loses, in that the victory is only for a time, and more especially in that the idea of its own nature overextends itself and like a tragic hero perishes in its pride, in its triumph, in the *hubris* brought on by success. This happens from two considerations in particular: every One, in becoming many, attempts to become All and falls abroad into chaos, nothingness, the abyss. Or else: every idea, at the end of the line, loses all content and meaning other than itself; it reaches redundancy, tautology, pleonasm, and at last says, uninformatively enough: I am that I am. These two ways of losing may be regarded as the damned and redeemed forms of one single but unsayable thing.

These two ways, moreover, have to do with simple figurations that may stand for the base of all thought: the line and the circle. Nor is it accidental, I think, that line and circle, and the spiral compounded of their motion, make up our ways of thinking about time—bringing us again to the "temporizing of essence".

We do not ordinarily believe we make progress by going 'round in circles; and yet in a round world we may have no other course. Consider how it is precisely, though mysteriously, the circling of the heavens that creates time, whose even progress along a straight line is among the blandest of our metaphysical assumptions, though possibly surpassed in this respect by the one that claims we don't have metaphysics any more. Or a homelier example: almost any literary critic will affirm, if only as costing him nothing, the assertion that "Finally, what the poem means is what the poem says," a pure yet somehow heartening tautology in that he will as readily affirm from experience that our circular course from what the poem says at first to what it says at last, or as near last as we ever get, improves our knowledge in reckonable ways.

Perhaps both line and circle have damned and redeemed forms, or ways of being thought about. The circle, from antiquity a "perfect" and sacred figure, is complete, hence eternal, simple, and rounding upon itself: the mind of God, in a phrase I've heard attributed to half a dozen writers from Bonaventura to Pascal, is a circle whose center is everywhere and whose circumference is nowhere. Alternatively, the circle may stand for futility and unending repetition and the boredom of a bad eternity. In the same way, the line in its optimistic leaping forth suggests progress; but as the progress is from an unknown (or non-existent) past to an unknown (or nonexistent or endless) future, it may likewise engender feelings of hopelessness.

Otherwise put: If a storyteller says to us, in effect, "This happened, and then that happened, and then something else happened . . . " we are bored; no matter how many things happen, we "keep waiting for something to happen". Whereas if a story were limited to the recital of its *idea*, there could be no story; for stories have to be one thing after another. So that a story *is* the compound of line and circle, as Burke indicates in a simple figure:

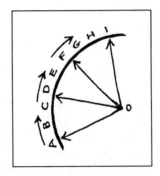

upon which he comments:

> Any narrative form . . . in its necessary progression from one episode to the next is like the stages from A to I along the arc. But as regards the principle of internal consistency, *any* point along the arc is as though generated from center O. And the various steps from A to I can be considered as *radiating* from generative principle O, regardless of their *particular* position along the arc of the narrative sequence.*

What is said of stories holds also for philosophies, which arose out of stories and which retain, using terms for persons, the "dramatistic" cooperations and conflicts, mergers and divisions, of stories. It may hold true in a peculiarly poignant way of Burke's philosophy, a corpus of mythology relating how certain heroes or demigods, called by the family name of *terms*, incarnated themselves in the world of action where they overcame the old dragon of chaos, established order, gave laws, and so on, until at last defeated by the dragon's mother, once named by Burke as "material recalcitrance". But, happily, new generations of terms arose . . . and the story is always beginning just as it is always ending.

Burke's mind must be a fascinating but terrifying place to live in. So it would seem, anyhow, from the homeopathic experience of it in small doses that one gets from his books. Despite the order imposed by narrative, despite a grand friendliness of manner and a most beguiling disposition to admit mistakes, to begin again, to reveal not only the result of thought but much of its process as well, the chief thing I note about his mind is that it cannot stop exploding. In the early books the footnotes, like large dogs leashed to dwarfish masters, often marched along for pages under a few homeless-looking lines of text; in the later books this habit has been overcome by the expedient of relegating the footnotes into appendices (the dogs get bigger, but are kept in their own kennels); while after *A Grammar of Motives* and *A Rhetoric of Motives* (1945 and 1950 respectively) the completion of the proposed grand design has been deferred by a huge volume called *Language as Symbolic Action,* a smaller though still substantial one called *The Rhetoric of Religion,* and an unpublished though mimeographed *Poetics* of three hundred pages, not to mention numerous uncollected articles, unpublished notes, etc. (the dogs are beginning to wag their kennels?).

Once, when asked to make suggestions about a Burke essay in manuscript, I indicated a few places where it might be cut. Some weeks later a letter announced earnestly that after thoroughly considering my remarks he had rewritten the whole thing and cut it from sixty-five pages to seventy-six. And during the question period after a recent lecture in which he had been talking about the cycle of terms and the generative power of any dialectical term to spawn a terminology, I heard Burke tell the class: "Any term will lead you to the others. There's no place to start." Ah, I thought, that means there's no place to stop, either. And I wondered: which half of Burke's mind will win? The linear, progressive, orderly half that proposes to itself systematic philosophy and sequential argument from beginning to end? or the radical, explosive half, the lyric and rhapsodic philosopher whose entire effort is to make every poor part contain the glorious, impossible whole, as in the Ptolemaic cosmology the Primum Mobile goes racing 'round at enormous speeds only in order that every place may catch up with every place and be at rest in the peace of the Empyrean? For, certainly and a little remarkably, I still have scarcely any idea of what the proposed third canticle, *A Symbolic of Motives,* may contain, no matter what anticipations of it must inevitably

---

*Kenneth Burke, "Dramatic Form—And: Tracking Down Implications", *Tulane Drama Review* (T 32), Vol. 10, No. 4 (Summer 1966), pages 59-60.

have come up in the story so far. Surely a place where any writer might beseech Apollo for both peaks of Parnassus, where either one had served before.

I mention this because it belongs to the figures of line and circle which I seem to have got stuck with, and because it is at the heart of that cooperative conflict between narrative and essence, image and concept, myth and philosophy, that Burke calls "the temporizing of essence".

Language, for Burke, not merely mirrors the world it seems to see, but also generates it. This is the sticking point at which over and over he divides from all philosophies proposing to base on scientific models; and not only divides from, but undercuts and gets beyond, seeing the human hope precisely in the rich polyvalence of terms, the Shakespearean equivocations, which those philosophies propose to exclude.

That language in any sense makes the world is a thought intolerable to those who view the world, implicitly or otherwise, as a solid existent (like Descartes's *res extensa*) which the mind passively records as a camera does in univocal concepts which it may then manipulate as a computer does.

For Burke, language is literally making, constitutive, or *poetic* of "reality". To the extent that its terms are not only positive ones, such as "house", but dialectic ones, such as "good" or "high" or "sinful", capable of division into and merger with other terms, it is language itself that makes the symbolic world. This is the distinctively human world in which we struggle along on the guidance of phantasy, the world of human action as over against the world of sheerly physical motion described by physics according to models that positivist philosophers constantly claim to emulate by various "reductionist" schemes according to which human motives are viewed as mechanisms, and according to which "God", "soul", and "spirit" are progressively read out of the act until at last, by a miracle comparable with the stomach's digesting itself and emitting a satisfied belch, "mind" too is read out of the act by the very mind that claims to be doing the reading.

Yet there is an important way in which Burke, while at odds with "scientistic" philosophers if not with science itself, is adventured on somewhat the same quest as that of physics: he would bring the world of human action, as it would the world of physical motion, under the dominion of few, simple, and elegant laws. It is tempting to wonder what would happen if his discoveries in this line educed the kind of cooperation among the learned that routinely goes on in physics; but they do not. And besides, this kind of thought may be peculiarly related to its thinker; as I have heard it observed of another original and self-made philosopher, Rudolf Steiner, that he was everywhere and his disciples nowhere.

The sense in which the internal resources of language themselves generate views of the world formed the subject of *A Grammar of Motives;* whereas *A Rhetoric of Motives* studied the ways in which these same resources might be wilfully manipulated for conflicting purposes. Between the two there was already noticeable a considerable area of overlap, which will perhaps extend also to *A Symbolic of Motives* in its presumable "transcendence" of the area of competitive identifications—the marketplace, the human barnyard, as Burke says—by considering the forms and methods of literature as "timeless" patterns.

So we have a triad, and the progression through it, something like Inferno-Pugatorio-Paradiso, and something like the equally celebrated id-ego-superego. Something like, at least, in the important respect that the outer terms are represented as eternal fixities while the middle one is the scene of conflict, development, and playing-out in time and history of the patterns beneath and above. As if, to adapt one of Burke's analogies, the grammar is a chord which the rhetoric breaks into linear form as an arpeggio, while the symbolic, the chord again and newly understood in relation to its constituent notes, will be but a moment in time, the ear of corn reaped in silence before the initiates at Eleusis, whose trials had brought them to that wordless understanding upon which even Plato and Aristotle agree.

That seems a good place to stop, a high note to sustain so that we know this particular aria is over. Of the much more that might be said, I will bring us down to the ground by only one further reflection.

It was during the normal confusions of sophomore year that a friend gave me a copy of *Attitudes toward History*—"two mouse-grey volumes," he said, "containing all knowledge." And I could see what he meant. The two things in especial that Burke said to a young man of eighteen were "Everything is interesting" and "Everything is a language." The sense in which those two things are one might well take thirty years or more to put together, but I'll try to put my results into a small anecdote and an emblem.

Most of one's education in those days was not only liberal education but self-education, and permissive extremely. The Great Books were the ones we thought our teachers had never read; at least, they were never mentioned in lectures. Still, I once confided in an admired professor that I'd been reading Kenneth Burke. "Ah," he said, and there came upon his face an expression of solemnity which ever since I've identified with Harvard Square—when you meet it elsewhere it's derivative—as he said: "Brilliant; brilliant, yes. But hardly solid."

I have sometimes unworthily thought—for that professor was admirable at teaching—that some people found solidity so universal a value they even wanted it between the ears. But thirty years later I found my emblem in an invention that was new when the world—the symbolic real one, of course—was new:

> Rounding upon itself, it became a perfect sphere when closed. It was made mostly of nothing, its critics pointed out that it was full of holes; besides, they said, it obviously leaks. Philosophers added that it was vain to suppose you could encompass the Void with bits of string, and as a final blow they said it was a tautology.

All the same, it caught fish.

Pivotal Terms in the Early Works of Kenneth Burke

by Jane Blankenship, Edward Murphy, and Marie Rosenwasser

Twenty years ago Kenneth Burke was termed "the most profound student of rhetoric now writing in America."[1] After the intervening years of "new rhetoric(s)" and considerable agreement that they have produced nothing like a comprehensive theory of rhetoric, this assessment of Burke still rings true.

In addition to his major contributions to rhetorical theory, Burke has also left his mark in such disciplines as philosophy, psychology, political science, sociology and literary criticism.[2] Much of this pervasive influence has been due to *A Grammar of Motives* and *A Rhetoric of Motives* and by such later works as *Language as Symbolic Action* and *The Rhetoric of Religion*.[3]

Most readers of Burke would agree that he is difficult to understand. As Nichols has observed: "In part the difficulty [in comprehending Burke] arises from the numerous vocabularies he employs. His words in isolation are usually simple enough, but he often uses them in new contexts. To read one of his volumes independently, without regard to the chronology of publication, makes the problem of comprehension even more difficult because of the specialized meanings attaching to various words and phrases."[4] We believe it is important to reexamine Burke's early works where his terminological development can be traced. By early works we refer to *Counter-Statement*

Reprinted from *Philosophy and Rhetoric,* 7 (1974), 1-24. Copyright 1974 by The Pennsylvania State University. Reproduced by permission of The Pennsylvania State University Press.

[1] Marie Hochmuth Nichols, "Kenneth Burke and the 'New Rhetoric,'" *Quarterly Journal of Speech* (April, 1952), p. 144.

[2] Reference to Burke's writings has proliferated in recent years in journals such as *The Quarterly Journal of Speech;* e.g., four of the essayists in the February, 1973, issue refer specifically to certain Burkean assumptions. See Robert E. Sanders, "The Question of A Paradigm for the Study of Speech-Using Behavior," p. 8, n. 15; Stanley Deetz, "Words without Things: Toward a Social Phenomenology of Language," p. 51, n. 28; Parke G. Burgess, "Crisis Rhetoric: Coercion vs. Force," p. 62, n. 1; and Karlyn Kohrs Campbell, "The Rhetoric of Women's Liberation: An Oxymoron," p. 78, n. 21.

The influence in both rhetorical theory and other disciplines is illustrated by the variety of contributors in William Rueckert, ed., *Critical Responses to Kenneth Burke: 1924-1966* (Minneapolis: University of Minnesota Press, 1969). See also Hugh Duncan, *Symbols in Society* (New York: Oxford University Press, 1968), and Murray Edelman, *The Symbolic Uses of Politics* (Urbana: University of Illinois Press, 1964).

[3] *A Grammar of Motives* (New York: Prentice-Hall, Inc., 1945); *A Rhetoric of Motives* (New York: Prentice-Hall, Inc., 1950); *The Rhetoric of Religion: Studies in Logology* (Boston: Beacon Press, 1961); and *Language as Symbolic Action: Essays in Life, Literature, and Method* (Berkeley: University of California Press, 1966).

[4] Nichols, "Kenneth Burke and the 'New Rhetoric,'" p. 144.

(1931), *Permanence and Change* (1935), *Attitudes Toward History* (1937), and *Philosophy of Literary Form* (1941).[5] Not only is such a reexamination important to provide additional insights into Burke's later work, it is also useful because the key terms grappled with by Burke remain essential terms in any attempt at formulating a comprehensive theory of rhetoric.

In this paper we will examine the four early works in order to provide a lexicon of key terms and sketch the relationships that these terms have with each other. First, we will focus on four pivotal terms: Orientation, Motive, Symbolic Action, and Form. In discussing these key terms we will introduce other terms which are associated with them. We will call these associations "clusters." This is not to suggest that these associations are neatly drawn by Burke or by these authors; for example, "strategy" is associated with Motive, where it receives the fuller treatment, but also with Form. After dealing with these associational clusters, we will touch briefly on two other essential terms introduced but not as fully developed—Identification and Transcendence.

Some preliminary observations ought to be made about this approach to Burke. While we do not wish to press the view of Burke as a *systematic* thinker, we do suggest that he writes from an emerging perspective. As he observed: "If one builds a vocabulary at random, it lacks the value of a perspective, or rationale, being merely eclectic."[6] Eclecticity in Burke ought not to be mistaken for randomness nor to mean that he works without central vision. Burke may well have provided a useful visual image to use when approaching his work this way:

> Imagine a circle—outside of it, imagine a series of dots—and outside these dots, imagine another circle. The inner circle represents an established structure of meanings, the familiar meanings with which one has grown up. They are 'intimate.' They name the important factors and relationships of one's experience, and they shape attitudes toward these factors. But in time, outside this circle of meanings, new material accumulates. This new material is not adequately handled by the smaller circle of meanings. . . . People then must strive to draw a wider circle that will encompass this new matter, left inadequately charted or located by the smaller circle.[7]

---

[5] Editions of the four books used in this paper are as follows: *Counter-Statement* (Berkeley: University of California Press, 1968) copyright 1931; *Permanence and Change: An Anatomy of Purpose* (Indianapolis: The Bobbs-Merrill Co., Inc., 1965), copyright 1935, copyright second revised edition 1954; *Attitudes Toward History* (Boston: Beacon Press, 1961), copyright 1937, copyright revised second edition 1959; *The Philosophy of Literary Form,* revised edition abridged by the author (New York: Vintage Books, 1957), copyright 1941. We have used these editions primarily because they are the ones most readily accessible to readers of Burke.

[6] Kenneth Burke, "The Tactics of Motivation," *Chimera,* I (Spring, 1943), p. 28.

[7] Kenneth Burke, "The Relation between Literature and Science," in Henry Hart, ed., *The Writer in A Changing World* (New York: Equinox Cooperative Press, 1936), p. 165. The tactic of clustering is, thus, one Burke suggests himself.

Or, as Burke sums it up in *Permanence and Change:* "To think through a matter is to trace an ever-widening circle of interrelationships."[8]

Further, Burke's early works cannot be understood without some reference to the methodology that informs them. In "perspective by incongruity" Burke has a method that extends "the use of a term by taking it from the context in which it [is] habitually used and applying it to another."[9] Such planned incongruity provides "a method for gauging situations by verbal 'atom cracking.'"[10] In it one deliberately wrenches loose a word belonging customarily to a certain category and applies it to a different category. Thus, we come to form new classifications and realignments.[11] We can "characterize events from a myriad shifting points of view...."[12] We can see more possibilities, see new relationships, crack old myths, decrease rigidity and increase fluidity.[13] Via this process of conversion and rebirth, of "cutting across the bias," we come to have "a new angle of vision."[14]

Perspective by incongruity is so essential to Burke's method that he recommends:

> ... planned incongruity should be deliberately cultivated for the purpose of experimentally wrenching apart all those molecular combinations of adjective and noun, substantive and verb, which still remain with us. It should subject language to the same 'cracking' process that chemists now use in their refining of oil.[15]

Metaphor is essential for the functioning of a Perspective by Incongruity because:

> ... the metaphor always has about it precisely this revealing of hitherto unsuspected connectives which we may note in the progressions of a dream. It appeals by exemplifying relationships between objects which our customary vocabulary has ignored.[16]

---

[8] *Permanence and Change*, p 230. Hereafter *PC*.

[9] *Ibid.*, p 89.

[10] *Attitudes Toward History*, p 308. Hereafter *ATH*.

[11] *PC*, p. 113. See same source (pp. 90-93) for a discussion of Nietzsche's and Bergson's methods of incongruity.

[12] *PC*, p. 102.

[13] A related term to Perspective by Incongruity is Bureaucratization of the Imaginative. See *ATH*, pp. 225-269.

[14] *PC*, p. 154 n.

[15] *PC*, p. 93. Perspective by Incongruity is Burke's recommended method for "doing everything from metaphysics to poetry to criticism." He urges his readers to realize that: the great syntheses of the metaphysicians have been schemes for cosmically joining logical or conceptual distinctions which were not justified by the nature of the universe at all, but were merely verbal distinctions applied by us for our practical dealings with reality. Metaphysics in this sense ... is the mere solving of pseudo-problems, as the metaphysician works out an elaborate system for reconciling differences which never existed in the first place, but were invented for purposes of convenience. (*Ibid.*, p. 93)

[16] *Ibid.*, p. 90. "Causistic stretching" is another term for "metaphorical expansion" (*ATH*, p. 230) and is done by "transcendence" (*ATH*, p. 309). See *Philosophy of Literary Form* (hereafter *PLF*), pp. 327-28 for a discussion of dialectic and metaphor.

Philosophers are urged to seek out the "master metaphors" they are employing as the cue to organizing their work and to say why they chose the metaphors they did choose.[17] Of his own work he observes:

> We choose the 'man as communicant' metaphor, for instance, because we feel that it brings out the emphases needed for handling present necessities. We modify it with the dead, mixed metaphor 'bureaucratization of the imaginative' because we think that people thereby are kept from being too sensitively exposed to disillusionment as they are affronted by the 'let down' that necessarily occurs when a tender imaginative-Utopian possibility is implemented by being given its practical embodiment in 'this imperfect world.'[18]

Every perspective, Burke argues, requires a metaphor, explicit or implicit, for its organizational base.[19]

Perspective by Incongruity is the method of his early work. It is the process by which he invents the dramatistic metaphor that is fully developed in his later works. The term itself disappears in Burke's later work—in large measure precisely because it has birthed the metaphor around which Burke centers his work.

Against the background of this methodological term, we will now examine four pivotal substantive terms. The structure of this section of the paper might best be illustrated as follows:

Major Term	Minor Terms in the Cluster
Orientation	Trained incapacity, piety, frames of acceptance, symbolic synthesis.
Motive	Situation, strategy, attitude.
Symbolic Action	Symbol, synecdoche, naming, meaning, act.
Form	Psychology of form, psychology of information, style, manner, strategy.

We do not maintain that there is only one way to order the major terms. As Burke, himself, has observed: "When working with a set of terms that mutually or circularly imply one another, we must necessarily pick one of them to begin with, though we might as well have begun with any of the others."[20] Moreover, we do not maintain that the relationship among these terms is the same within each cluster, for Burke is not always clear about whether relationship is hierarchical or coordinate. What we do maintain is that they *are* related in associational clusters.

---

[17] *ATH,* p. 262.
[18] *Ibid.,* pp. 262-263.
[19] *Ibid.,* p. 262.
[20] *Language as Symbolic Action* (Berkeley: University of California Press, 1966), p. 365.

Orientation

An individual's Orientation is his way of looking at the world, and is defined as "a bundle of judgments as to how things were, how they are, and how they must be," "a sense of relationships, developed by the contingencies of experience," "a schema of serviceability," a system of "new meanings," and an "*interpretative attitude.*"[21] Further, within all Orientation is the process of linkage.[22]

Orientation functions in a variety of ways. It "involves matters of expectancy, and affects our choice of means with reference to the future," is concerned with judgment of what is proper which is bound up with motives, and influences one's judgment of "*likeness.*"[23] An Orientation either trains or incapacitates us. It helps us interpret our interpretations, permits us to test experiences by serving as a criterion of service and disservice, allows us to verbalize our oughts and ought-nots, to praise and blame, and lets us get at our motives, for a motive "is a term of interpretation."[24] An Orientation, Burke reminds us, is "a self perpetuating structure, creating the measures by which it shall be measured."[25] Each part "tends to corroborate the other parts."[26]

Orientation is affected by our "trained incapacity" which affects the means we select to achieve our ends. According to Burke's interpretation of Veblen, "trained incapacity" is "that state of affairs whereby one's very abilities can function as blindnesses."[27] The poet, for example, will look at the ocean and see its anger, the chemist will see its iodine. Means-selecting and trained incapacity are so important that Burke concludes, "Faulty means-selecting, on the basis of an inadequate orientation, would seem enough to account for everything."[28]

Intimately related to Orientation is "piety" which operates as a guide for establishing our system of Orientation and is described as: "a system-builder, a desire to round things out, to fit experiences together into a unified whole . . . *a sense of what properly goes with what,*" a "schema of orientation, since it involves the putting together of experiences," "*the yearning to conform with the 'sources of one's being'. . . .*"[29] Piety forms those "linkages" of experiences which bring "all the significant details of the day into co-ordination,

---

[21]*PC,* pp. 14, 18, 21, 80-81, 118. Burke also refers to Orientation as a "general view of reality" and as an "accumulation and inter-working of characters" (p. 4). It is also discussed as "a view of how the world is put together" (p. 81).

[22]*Ibid.,* p. 10.

[23]*Ibid.,* pp. 18, 23.

[24]*Ibid.,* pp. 6, 22, 21, 25.

[25]*Ibid.,* p. 262.

[26]*Ibid.,* p 169.

[27]*PC,* p. 7. See p. 10 for a discussion of "trained incapacity" and "means selecting."

[28]*Ibid.,* p. 17.

[29]*Ibid.,* pp. 74, 76, 69. See also p. 83 for a summary of style and piety. Burke further states that "The Orientation may be right or wrong; it can guide or misguide" (p. 76).

relating them integrally with one another."[30] These pious linkages operate as complex "interpretative" networks.[31]

Intense conflicts may arise, Burke observes, when the "rational order of symbols [establishes] a congruity wholly alien to the emotional order of symbols."[32] Burke points to Darwin as "the supreme instance of the tendency to construct rational categories which are at variance with the categories of linkage formed in emotional experience" and refers to Darwin's attacks of vertigo as evidence of such a conflict.[33]

If "piety" is conforming, it follows that "impiety" is the reorganizing of "one's orientations from the past" or any attempt to attack "the kinds of linkage already established."[34] New Orientations are obtained impiously because Orientation involves expectancy as does "piety."

In *Attitudes Toward History* Burke introduces the phrase "frames of acceptance" which turns out to be a synonym for Orientation. "Frame of acceptance" is defined as "the more or less organized system of meanings by which a thinking man gauges the historical situation and adopts a role with relation to it."[35]

There are, according to Burke, two *essential* frames: acceptance and rejection.[36] Rejection is judged to be "less well rounded" and "less complete" than acceptance.[37] Rejection frames "make for fanaticism, the singling-out of one factor above others in the charting of human relationships."[38] There may be, however, treachery lurking in certain acceptance frames; for example, Burke cautions against acceptance frames that are "chemically pure," for they too may be "incomplete" or partial.[39]

A term that is associated with "frames of acceptance" and appears in *Attitudes Toward History* but not in *Permanence and Change* is "symbolic synthesis." "One must," Burke urges, "erect a vast symbolic synthesis, a rationale of imaginative and conceptual imagery that 'locates' the various aspects of experience."[40] A symbolic synthesis guides social purpose, provides cues as to what we should get and how we should try to get it and how to resign ourselves to renouncing things we can't get. Symbolic syntheses are "designed to produce . . . 'acceptance' in one form or another."[41]

---

[30] *Ibid.*, p. 75.

[31] *Ibid.*

[32] *Ibid.*, p. 73.

[33] *Ibid.*

[34] *PC*, pp. 80, 87.

[35] *ATH*, p. 5. The "comic frame" is recommended as the most "serviceable" (pp. 106, 143, 170-171). It is the most serviceable because it enables people "to be observers of themselves while acting" (p. 106).

[36] *Ibid.*, pp. 19-24.

[37] *Ibid.*, p. 28.

[38] *Ibid.*, pp. 28-29.

[39] *Ibid.*, p. 33.

[40] *Ibid.*, p. 179.

[41] *ATH*, pp. 19-20. See p. 184 for a discussion of "symbolic superstructure," p. 194 for "natural tendency toward integration," p. 20 for "frames functioning actively not passively," p. 20 for close relation between acceptance and rejection, p. 58 for an explanation of why epic, tragedy, and comedy are art forms of acceptance and the elegy, satire, and burlesque are art forms that stress the negative.

To summarize, an Orientation is developed by a sense of "piety" and the "symbolic synthesis" we create within our "frames of acceptance." Our Orientation helps us "locate" a situation, adopt a role with relation to it, "gauge" our activities, derive a vocabulary of motives and thus implicit programs of action and attitudes.[42]

Motive

It is not until the later works that Burke fully develops Motive in relationship to hierarchy. Still, Burke's observation that Motive "is not some fixed thing, like a table, which one can go and look at . . ." is an indication of the difficulty implicit in the term.[43] And, even though we have to wait until the later works for a full account of Motive, Burke does lay considerable groundwork in the works we are considering.

At the outset of *Permanence and Change* Burke makes it clear that *"motives are subdivisions in a larger frame of meanings"*; this larger frame of meaning is what we have previously identified as an Orientation.[44] This motivational machinery is used to comprehend, describe, and define the circumstances and events in which human beings find themselves because Motive is "a term of interpretation."[45]

Our "words for motives are in reality words for situation" and our "introspective words for motives are rough, shorthand descriptions for certain typical patterns of discrepant and conflicting stimuli."[46] For example:

> If we say we perform an act under the motivation of duty, for instance, we generally use the term to indicate a complex stimulus-situation wherein certain stimuli calling for one kind of response are linked with certain stimuli calling for another kind of response. We act out of duty as against love. . . .[47]

There is, then, a serviceability about an account of motives because it permits us to predict certain responses rather than others, once we have identified the stimulus-situation.[48] The *names* we give to motives "shape our relations with our fellows."[49] Since they provide interpretations, they "prepare us *for* some functions and *against* others, *for* or *against* the persons representing these functions."[50] Moreover, they suggest *how* we shall be for or against. For example: "Call a man a villain, and you have the choice of either attacking

---

[42]*Ibid.*, pp. 20, 92.
[43]*PC*, p. 25.
[44]*Ibid.*, p. 19.
[45]*Ibid.*, p. 25.
[46]*Ibid.*, pp. 30-31. See also *PLF:* ". . . *situation* is but another word for motives" (p. 18).
[47]*Ibid.*
[48]*Ibid.*
[49]*ATH*, p. 4.
[50]*Ibid.*

or cringing. Call him mistaken and you invite yourself to attempt setting him right."[51] This leads Burke to suggest that motives are, in this sense, "distinctively linguistic products."[52]

Since individuals have their own Orientations, Motives are subjective things. The Motive which we assign to any given situation derives its character from the entire framework of interpretation (Orientation) by which we judge it.[53] So, in a sense, a Motive is a response to a situation; but Burke is quick to point out that it is more than that:

> One tends to think of a duality here, to assume some kind of breach between a situation and a response. Yet the two are identical. When we wish to influence a man's response, for instance, we emphasize factors which he had understressed or neglected, and minimize factors which he had laid great weight upon. This amounts to nothing other than an attempt to redefine the situation itself. In this respect our whole vocabulary of motivation is tautological.[54]

While a motivational schema may be peculiar to an individual or group of individuals, it is not to be considered evasive or self-deceptive. On the contrary, our motivational schema is shaped to fit our general orientation as to purposes, instrumentalities, the "good life."[55] Indeed,

> In such vicissitudinous times as ours . . . with the advances of technology straining against the political, social, economic, aesthetic, moral orientations established at a period when the needs of society were radically different, is it not to be expected that the entire matter of motivation would again become liquid?[56]

Burke has now established the general outlines of his theory of motivation, and he has made clear that motives, or interpretations of a situation, may vary with an individual's own orientation. But, he reasons,

> if there is *one underlying motive or set of motives that activates all men* there must be *one underlying situation common to all men.* It seems obvious that before we could establish the existence of a common situation or motive for all men, we should have *to define the cosmic situation and man's place in it.*[57]

---

[51]*Ibid.*
[52]*PC,* p. 35. Burke argues this point thus: our interpretation of reality involves a vocabulary of "ought" and "ought not" terms. These names in turn shape the relationships on which our interpretations are based. He says: "Our minds, as linguistic products, are composed of concepts (verbally molded) which select certain relationships as meaningful" (*ibid.*).
[53]*PC,* p. 25.
[54]*Ibid.,* p 220.
[55]*Ibid.,* p. 29.
[56]*Ibid.,* p. 33.
[57]*Ibid.,* p. 221.

"Situations," Burke tells us, "do overlap, if only because men now have the same neural and muscular structure as men who have left their records from past ages" for we and they "are in much the same biological situation."[58] Insofar as situations *do* overlap from individual to individual, or from one historical period to another, strategies used to encompass them possess "universal relevance."[59]

There are within the early works some abortive attempts to provide us with a terminology of motives. For example, at one point in *Attitudes Toward History*, if we take Burke literally, his "Seven Offices" (Govern, Serve, Defend, Teach, Entertain, Cure, Pontificate) are precisely that—"one more terminology of motives."[60] But it is not until later that his schema of universal motives (Guilt, Redemption, Hierarchy, and Victimage) fully emerges.[61] And, although he hints at the centrality of the entelechical motive, that too fully emerges at a later stage in Burke's development.[62]

Burke *is*, however, explicit and consistent about the relationship between situation and strategy; for example, he says: ". . . strategies size up the situations, name their structure and outstanding ingredients, and name them in a way that contains an attitude toward them."[63] He illustrates this point by saying that when a person enrolls in a cause, he sizes up the situation and decides on a strategy of action to encompass it. Situation and strategy are interwoven in these early works as are the later scene and act of Burke's pentad.[64]

Another name for strategies might be "attitudes."[65] The most basic of attitudes are "Yes, No, and the intermediate realm of Maybe."[66]

The attitude much discussed by Burke is the *"attitude towards* life" which he terms the *"integrative* attitude" or the strategy of containment.[67] He refers us, for example, to Thomas Mann's "assertion that one must 'contain his enemies.' "[68] The strategy of containment seems to be the strategy most admired by Burke himself and best illustrated by his work. In this case as in many other instances, the influences of Coleridge would appear strong: ". . . in the universe of thought . . . no blind alleys exist; this village road

---

[58]*PLF*, p. 3.
[59]*Ibid.*
[60]*ATH*, p. 353.
[61]*Rhetoric of Motives*, pp. 260-294; *Rhetoric of Religion*, pp. 4-5. See also "On Human Behavior Considered 'Dramatistically' " *PC*, pp. 274-294. We have not considered this section of *PC* in our paper because it was based on a paper not given until 1951.
[62]See Burke's discussion of entelechy in *RM*, pp. 13-15; *GM*, pp. 260-262; *RR*, pp. 246, 300.
[63]*PLF*, p 3.
[64]*Ibid.*, pp. 93, 111, 54.
[65]*Ibid.*, p. 54.
[66]*ATH*, Intro., np.; *PLF*, p. 84n. Many of the major terms in Burke's first four books appear to be "strategies." In *ATH*, for example, he labels as strategies: Identification, Acceptance and Rejection, Rituals of Purification and Rebirth, Transcending Upward or Downward, and Bureaucratization of the Imaginative (pp. 225-338).
[67]*ATH*, p. 47n.
[68]*Ibid.*

enters one upon a system of highways which encircle the world."[69]

Throughout Burke's discussion of Motive (and the associated terms "situation," "strategy," "attitude") there are statements that are clearly essential to his later works and which do not substantially change in his maturing years. For example, in *Attitudes Toward History* he reminds us that "implicit in a theory of motives is a program of action."[70] For Burke, to name (and hence to describe) a motive is to describe briefly and subjectively a stimulus situation. That description itself suggests, implicitly at least, a response to the situation. "Attitudes," or strategies, "size up" these situations and in so doing, help us decide on a way to encompass them.

Symbolic Action

Concomitant with Burke's early interest in the relationship between motive and action was his interest in language as symbolic action. In *Counter-Statement* "symbol" is called "the verbal parallel to a pattern of experience."[71] It can be a "formula," and it is a "generating principle which entails a selection of different subtilizations and ramifications."[72] Symbols function in at least six ways: (1) as the "interpretation of a situation"; (2) by "favoring the acceptance of a situation"; (3) as the "corrective of a situation"; (4) as the "exercise of 'submerged experience'"; (5) as an "emancipator"; and (6) as a "vehicle for 'artistic' effects."[73] First, a symbol provides us with "a terminology of thoughts, actions, emotions, attitudes, for codifying a pattern of experience."[74] Second, a symbol may "enable us to admit, for instance, the existence of a certain danger which we had emotionally denied."[75] For example, a humorous symbol "enables us to admit [a] situation by belittling it. . . ."[76] Third, situations may be "corrected" by symbols. "Life in the city arouses a compensatory interest in life on a farm, with the result that symbols of farm life become appealing. . . ."[77] Fourth, symbols may touch on "submerged patterns" in the receiver and "may 'stir remote depths.'"[78] Thus, "symbols of cruelty, horror, and incest may often owe their appeal to such causes."[79] Fifth, symbols, when they are "effective," may manipulate the "values in our codes" and thereby shift terms in such a way as to replace indolence with leisure, foolhardiness with bravery, miserliness with thrift, and

---

[69]Samuel Taylor Coleridge, *Aids to Reflection,* as cited in Rueckert, *Critical Responses to Kenneth Burke, op. cit.,* pp. 56-57.
[70]*ATH,* p. 92.
[71]*Counter-Statement,* p 152. Hereafter CS.
[72]*Ibid.,* p 157.
[73]*Ibid.,* pp. 153-156.
[74]*Ibid.,* p 154.
[75]*Ibid.*
[76]*Ibid.*
[77]*CS,* p. 155.
[78]*Ibid.*
[79]*Ibid.*

the like, thus "emancipating" us from rigid stereotyping of conduct.[80] And sixth, insofar as "everybody yearns to say one brilliant thing," the symbol may appeal as a vehicle for " 'artistic' effects."[81] Burke labels this the "most poignant" of the ways in which a symbol appeals.

The relationship between symbols and "situations" is thus clear; the symbol provides either an orientation to a situation, or an adjustment to it, or both.[82] Burke illustrates the powerful implications of such orienting adjustments: ". . . once a man has integrated his whole life about his business (interweaving it with a full texture of social relationships and personal transcendences) you will be far from knowing what is going on if you try to analyze his motives as merely the 'desire for monetary profit.' His business has become a 'vessel,' it is 'charismatic.' "[83]

Symbols also function as vessels, and this metaphorical expression may be one of Burke's most complete ways of discussing the function of symbols. In *Attitudes Toward History* he says symbols are "mergers" and "vessels."[84] "[T]hey are acts of synthesis, capable of infinite analysis."[85] The symbol as vessel unites opposites.[86] The symbol as "vessel" may not be complete until it performs "this merger of opposites by 'transcendence' " because "a symbol is a vessel of much more content than is disclosed by its 'face value' as a label."[87] Thus symbols are both labels and vessels but as vessels they carry "unchartable emotional implications."[88] For example, a symbol "may transcendentally fuse an author's attitude towards his parents, his friends, his State, his political party, his métier, his memories of childhood, his hopes for the future, etc. If you try to consider these various components analytically, there is no 'logical order' by which to progress. *You should talk about them all at once.*"[89]

In "its essence" language is not neutral; it is "loaded with judgments."[90] It is "intensely moral—its names for objects contain the emotional overtones which give us the cues as to how we should act toward these objects."[91] Language "takes its shape from the fact that it is used by people acting together. It is an adjunct of action—and thus naturally contains the elements of exhortation and threat which guide and stimulate action."[92] Nouns, Burke

---

[80]*Ibid.*, p. 156.
[81]*Ibid.*
[82]*Ibid.*
[83]*ATH*, p. 329.
[84]Ibid., p. 106.
[85]*Ibid.*
[86]*Ibid.*, pp. 233-234.
[87]*Ibid.*, pp. 234, 329.
[88]*Ibid.*, p. 343. While symbols act as merging devices they are also culturally and time bound; see *CS*, pp. 85, 83-84.
[89]*ATH*, p. 198.
[90]*PC*, p. 177. See also, language as public, *PLF*, p. 38; language and shaping of it by group, *CS*, p. 173; language as an implement to action, *PC*, p. 173; as containing a "magical decree," *PLF*, pp. 5-7; as related to act, *ATH*, p. 339; as a way of sizing up reality, *PLF*, p. 5.
[91]*PC*, p. 177.
[92]*Ibid.*, pp. 191-192.

suggests, carry with them "invisible" adjectives and verbs, "invisible" adverbs because "the names for things and operations smuggle in connotations of *good and bad....*"[93] Thus, they tend "naturally toward the use of implicit moral weightings...."[94] It is from *group* relationships that the "weighting of words arises."[95] Language "of all things, is most public, most collective, in its substance."[96] In "its origins" it "takes its shape by the co-operative patterns of the group that uses it."[97] Even when the individual tries to "transform language for his special purposes" he must remember that the "resources with which he begins are 'traditional,' that is: *social.* And such sociality of meaning is grounded in a sociality of material conduct, or co-operation."[98]

He admonishes us not to be content with simple "dictionaries," for words "may contain attitudes much more complex and subtle than could possibly be indicated in the efficient simplifications of a 'practical' dictionary."[99] The tendency of scientists and technologists to construct such dictionaries causes Burke to distrust "scientific language," for it is "devoid of the tonalities, the mimetic reenforcements, the vaguely remembered human situations, which go to make up the full, complex appeal of the poetic medium."[100] Those who espouse "a purely 'neutral' vocabulary" attempt "to make a totality out of a fragment...."[101] Such attempts at neutralizing language envision "a vocabulary that *avoids* drama."[102]

Burke would have us remember the synecdochic nature of words, for words tend to deal imperfectly with continuous reality and are only acts upon a scene.[103] Of this partial nature of words, Burke says:

> We find our way through this everchanging universe by certain blunt schemes of generalization, conceptualization, or verbalization—but words have limited validity. Their very purpose being to effect practical simplifications of reality, we should consider them inadequate for description of reality as it actually is.[104]

While cautioning us that words are but "aspects of a much wider communicative context, most of which is not verbal at all," he reminds us that "words also have a nature peculiarly their own."[105] Thus, "when dis-

---

[93] *Ibid.*, p. 192.
[94] *Ibid.*
[95] *Ibid.*, p. liii.
[96] *PLF*, p. 38.
[97] *PC*, p. 173.
[98] *Ibid.*, p. liii.
[99] *ATH*, p. 329.
[100] *PC*, p. 58.
[101] *PLF*, p. 121.
[102] *Ibid.*, p. 129. Burke would have us remember the synecdochic nature of words since words deal imperfectly with reality (*ibid.*, p. 24) and must be considered in relation to their nonverbal scene (*ibid.*, p. vii). See *ATH* for discussion of the Negative as a useful linguistic product, p. 374.
[103] *PLF*, pp. vii-ix.
[104] *PC*, p. 92.
[105] *PLF*, p. vii.

cussing them as modes of action, we must consider *both* this nature as words in themselves *and* the nature they get from the nonverbal scenes that support their acts."[106]

In *Permanence and Change,* Burke tells us that there are two main functions in the "communicativeness" of language: *communion* and *action.*[107] "Speech is communicative in the sense that it provides a common basis of feeling—or it is communicative in the sense that it serves as the common implement to action."[108]

There is a "magical decree" which is "implicit in all language. . . ."[109] Burke explains: ". . . the mere act of naming an object or situation decrees that it is to be singled out as such-and-such rather than something-other."[110] And, ". . . if you size up a situation in the name of regimentation you *decree* it an essence other than if you sized it up in the name of planned economy."[111] The "command" that one acts one way rather than another is "*implicit* in the name."[112]

Naming and interpreting are linguistic acts, but what is an Act? A developed answer is not given in these four books, but we do learn several things about the nature of Act. An Act has two features, "co-operative" or "competitive," and one or the other must be selected as the "essence" of the given act.[113] Further, act involves both meaning and doing, for as Burke says, "the subject demands a predicate as resolutely as the antecedent of a musical phrase in Mozart calls for its consequent."[114] Just as naming calls for an act, there is a capacity within us that calls for the naming. When we use symbols, we are using all of ourselves—both our capacity or potential to act and our ability to perform or execute an act; for as Burke says, "a capacity is not something which lies dormant until used—a capacity is a command to act in a certain way."[115] The following passage summarizes this relationship:

> We have the original emotion, which is channelized into a symbol. This symbol becomes a generative force. . . . The originating emotion makes for *emotional* consistency within the parts; the symbol

---

[106] *Ibid.*

[107] *PC,* p. 176.

[108] *Ibid.,* pp. 175-176.

[109] *PLF,* p. 5.

[110] *Ibid.*

[111] *PLF,* p. 7.

[112] *ATH,* p. 339.

[113] *Ibid.,* pp. 252-253. Because naming implies doing and "names embody attitudes" and "cues of behavior" which are "implicit in the attitude," Burke says that we may "act" in the names and attitudes we give to our children *(ATH,* p. 4). Hence it is an act to change your own or others' attitudes *(ibid.).* Acts have their counterparts in attitudes *(ATH,* p. 340) and are physical (e.g., the act of walking) as well at attitudinal *(PC,* p. 105). In *PLF,* p. 144, Burke says "The ideal word is in itself an act. . . ." See *ATH,* p. 5 for "faith" and "rationality" in relation to "power of action" and method for act.

[114] *CS,* p. 140.

[115] *Ibid.,* p. 142.

demands a *logical* consistency within this emotional consistency.[116]

Symbols, then, are verbal parallels to patterns of experience and, as such, are synecdochic in nature. Even so, symbols are vessels loaded with logical and emotional implications. Thus, when we give a thing a name (attach a symbol to it) we are committing an act of considerable complexity and consequence. That symbol will henceforth determine our attitude toward the thing. To "name" is therefore to call to action.

Form

Form is a way of uniting motive and symbol, situation and act. It is a term that lets us begin, branch out, and then return to the term from which we started at the beginning of the paper, Orientation. In *Counter-Statement*, Burke defines Form as a "creation of an appetite in the mind of the auditor, and the adequate satisfying of that appetite. . . ."[117] It is "an arousing and fulfillment of desires."[118] Thus, a "work has form insofar as one part of it leads a reader to anticipate another part. . . ."[119] Burke continually stresses the receiver-oriented aspect of Form and he goes so far as to say that "form would be the psychology of the *audience*."[120] For example, he writes:

> . . . in the case of Antony's speech, the value lies in the fact that his words are shaping the future of the audience's desires, not the desires of the Roman populace, but the desires of the pit. This is the psychology of form as distinguished from the psychology of information.[121]

A work that has form is clearly preferable to a work that has information and Burke warns the artist to be careful lest "form" be overwhelmed by "information." "The hypertrophy of the psychology of information is accompanied by the corresponding atrophy of the psychology of form."[122] The arousal and satisfaction of an appetite is, according to Burke, a "natural" process which is continually pleasurable. We do not find such pleasure in a continuous stream of new information.

It is interesting to note that "natural" is a word which appears frequently in Burke's discussion of Form. Although psychologists and philosophers may argue over whether forms are "innate or resultant," Burke declares that all is settled so far as a work of art is concerned.[123] They (forms) "simply *are*."[124]

---

[116] *Ibid.*, p. 61. See *PLF*, pp. 8-11 for a discussion of poetry as symbolic action and brief treatment of "enactment."
[117] *CS*, p. 31.
[118] *Ibid.*, p. 124.
[119] *Ibid.*
[120] *Ibid.*, p. 31.
[121] *Ibid.*, p. 33.
[122] *Ibid.*
[123] *CS*, p. 141. Burke's underlining.
[124] *Ibid.*

He says:

"... when one turns to the production or enjoyment of a work of art, a formal equipment is already present. . . ."[125] These "innate forms" are the "'potentiality for being interested by certain processes or arrangements'" or the "'feeling for such arrangements of subject-matter as produce crescendo, contrast, comparison, balance, repetition, disclosure, reversal, contraction, expansion, magnification, series, and so on.'"[126] He concludes: "So the formal aspects of art appeal in that they exercise formal potentialities of the reader."[127] In this use of the term Burke implies that Form is both stimulus and response, both a conscious and unconscious process; it is "inherent in the very germ-plasm of man."[128]

In his "Lexicon Rhetoricae" he discusses five aspects of Form: syllogistic progression, qualitative progression, repetitive form, conventional form, and minor or incidental form.[129] He illustrates:

> ... the lines in *Othello* beginning, 'Soft you, a word or two before you go,' and ending 'Seized by the throat the uncircumcized dog and smote him thus *(stabs himself)*' well exemplify the vigorous presence of all five aspects of form, as this suicide is the logical outcome of his predicament (syllogistic progression); it fits the general mood of gloomy forebodings which has fallen upon us (qualitative progression); the speech has about it that impetuosity and picturesqueness we have learned to associate with Othello (repetitive form), it is very decidedly a conclusion (conventional form), and in its development it is a tiny plot in itself (minor form).[130]

The main function of Form is to allow us to gratify appetites. What are the *conditions* of form as appeal? Apparently the reindividuating of the psychological universals. Psychological universals would appear not just as balance, contrast, and the like, but also as universal situations, fundamental attitudes, typical actions, patterns of experience, and the like. For as Burke comments "any particular cluster of conditions will involve the recurrent emotions . . . and fundamental attitudes. . . ."[131] Since the artist's symbols and the experiences they represent are not precisely the same as those of the audiences, the reader reinterprets and personalizes the symbol. However, the kind of individuation on which Burke dwells refers to the artist's particularization of the crescendo in any of the myriad aspects possible to human experience, localizing or channeling it according to chance details of his own life and vision. Individuation and reindividuation are possible because of

---

[125] *Ibid.*
[126] *Ibid.*, p. 46.
[127] *Ibid.*, p. 142.
[128] *Ibid.*, p. 46.
[129] *CS*, pp. 124-128.
[130] *Ibid.*, p. 128.
[131] *Ibid.*, p. 107.

innate formal potentialities.

In *Counter-Statement,* Burke maintains that style is a constituent of Form: ". . . those elements of surprise and suspense are subtilized, carried down into writing of a line or a sentence, until in all its smallest details the work bristles with disclosures, contrasts, restatements . . . , in short all that complex wealth of minutiae which in their line-for-line aspect we call style and in their broader outlines we call form."[132]

He explicitly relates style, "ingratiation" and "inducement" to "identification." As "ingratiation," style is "an attempt to gain favor by hypnotic or suggestive process of 'saying the right thing' "[133] and an "elaborate set of prescriptions and proscriptions for 'doing the right thing'. . . ."[134] We see the relationship between identification and style when Burke says that one "hypnotizes" a man by "ringing the bells of his response."[135]

Further, style is the "ritualistic projection or completion of manners. . . ."[136] It has to do with "custom"; with the "meeting of obligations," with "what goes with what."[137] Burke explains in some detail that when a person cannot "justify" himself by spontaneously using such "congregational" responses as ingratiation and inducement, he will likely be driven to justify himself through "segregational" attitudes and acts. The "loss of style" results not only in "segregational" acts and attitudes but it reinforces completion and violence and fosters superiority rather than solidarity.[138] Burke further explains that style can have its own kind of "deterioration." He observes:

> . . . in societies greatly marked by class prerogatives, style itself tends to become a competitive implement, as a privileged group may cultivate style to advertise its privileges and perpetuate them. Style then ceases to be propitiatory. It becomes boastful. It is no longer a mode of ingratiation, but a device for instilling fear, like the emperor's insignia. (Such fear is generally called respect.) As style assumes this invidious function, there is a corresponding social movement from inducement toward dominance.[139]

Another aspect of style appears to be "manner" which in *Counter-Statement* is defined as "power without monotony" and is described as a "restriction of the means by which formal and Symbolic saliency is obtained."[140] It diffuses rather than restricts the means by which the "bells of response" are rung. The notion of manner as restrictive is developed in

---

[132] *Ibid.,* pp. 37-38.
[133] *PC,* p. 50. See also *PLF,* p. 266.
[134] *PC,* 268.
[135] *Ibid.,* p. 52.
[136] *ATH,* p. 201.
[137] *Ibid.*
[138] *PC,* p. 268.
[139] *Ibid.,* p. 270n.
[140] *CS,* p. 181.

Attitudes Toward History: "Style is the ritualistic projection or completion of manners (as when the need of 'push' and 'drive' in selling attains its stylistic counterpart in the breezy hero)."[141]

By 1941 in *The Philosophy of Literary Form,* Burke associated stylization with strategy. For example, he identifies sentimentalization, brutalization, neutral description, and ennoblement[142] as kinds of stylization and explains the relationship between it and strategy in this example:

> Suppose that some disaster has taken place, and that I am to break the information to a man who will suffer from the knowledge of it. The disaster is a *fact,* and I am going to *communicate this fact.* Must I not still make a choice of *stylization* in the communication of this fact? I may communicate it 'gently' or 'harshly,' ... I may try to 'protect' the man somewhat from the suddenness of the blow; or I may so 'strategize' my information that I reinforce the blow.[143]

He further relates style to strategy when he suggests that all critical and imaginative works are answers to situational questions and that the answers are "strategic" or "stylized" because in all work naming is done strategically or stylistically in modes that embody attitudes.[144] Thus, style, as strategy, is a way of *encompassing* a situation.[145]

Style, then, is a ritualistic strategy for obtaining ingratiation or identification. Style is a constituent of form but it is also related to piety in that it is dominated by a sense of what goes with what in a given situation.

Pivotal Terms Introduced But Not Developed

Other pivotal terms introduced in these early works are Identification and Transcendence. These are treated less exhaustively by Burke in the early works, but are pervasive enough to examine briefly.

"Identification" is "one's way of seeing one's reflection in the social mirror."[146] It is "hardly other than a name for the *function of sociality.*"[147] One identifies himself with others "by establishing relationships to groups."[148] It is absolutely essential for human beings to relate to one another; indeed, the man with faulty identifications "is better off than a man who can identify himself with no corporate trend at all."[149]

The breadth (or "resonance" as Burke would say) of the term "identification" is clearly spelled out in *The Philosophy of Literary Form:*

---

[141] *ATH,* p. 201.
[142] *PLF,* pp. 110-111.
[143] *Ibid.,* p. 109.
[144] *Ibid.,* pp. 109-110.
[145] See, for example, *PLF,* pp. 109-111.
[146] *Ibid.,* p. 195.
[147] *ATH,* pp. 266-267.
[148] *PLF,* p. 195.
[149] *ATH,* p. 263.

> By 'identification' I have in mind this sort of thing: one's material
> and mental ways of placing oneself as a person in groups and
> movements; one's ways of sharing vicariously in the role of leader or
> spokesman; formation and change of allegiance; the rituals of suicide,
> parricide, and prolicide; the vesting and divesting of insignia, the
> modes of initiation and purification that are involved in the response
> to allegiance and change of allegiance; . . . clothes, uniforms and their
> psychological equivalents. . . .[150]

Scattered throughout the early works are many examples of the various forms
identification may take; e.g., it may be a way of bragging—for when praising
some corporate unit like church, college, nation—to which one belongs or
with which one is identified—one praises himself and is boasting vicariously.[151]

In epics, "magnification" lends "dignity to the necessities of existence,
'advertising' courage and individual sacrifice for group advantage—and it
enables the humble man to share the worth of the hero by the process of
'identification.' The hero, real or legendary, thus risks himself and dies that
others may be *vicariously* heroic. . . ."[152] Burke argues that there is considerable "social value" in such a pattern; the value "resides in its ability to make
humility and self-glorification *work together*. . . ."[153] Every man, Burke
argues, is represented in "universal tragedy" by "the stylistically dignified
scapegoat."[154] This is true because

> In his offense, he [the scapegoat] takes upon himself the guilt of all—
> and *his* punishment is *mankind's* chastening. We identify ourselves
> with his weakness (we feel 'pity'), but we dissociate ourselves from
> his punishment (we feel 'terror'). The *dis*sociation, however, coexists
> with the *as*sociation. We are not onlookers, but participants.[155]

The fact of "participation" is stressed; e.g., Burke, in discussing *Death in
Venice* suggests that "both author and reader are asked to 'identify'
themselves with Aschenbach in his erotic criminality, which is punished by
death."[156] Thus, there is "no 'spectator' here; there are only 'participants.' "[157]

The sense of a structure's *reasonableness* plays a part in "giving people a
sense of ownership" because "they can *identify themselves* with the insignia
in which that reasonableness is vested."[158] In these instances, implicity at
least, identification is both means and end.

The second term introduced in the early works is "Transcendence." Even

---

[150] *PLF*, p. 195.
[151] *ATH*, pp. 144-145.
[152] *Ibid.*, pp. 35-36.
[153] *Ibid.*, p. 36.
[154] *Ibid.*, p. 188n.
[155] *Ibid.*
[156] *Ibid.*, p. 189n.
[157] *Ibid.*
[158] *ATH*, p. 220n. Parenthesis in text.

in its underdeveloped state, the pervasiveness of the term is clear. It is a symbolic merging and bridging that allows people to transcend their inherent separateness.[159] To transcend is to reconcile opposites by a "higher synthesis," after which one is endowed with a new identity.[160] "[A]bandonment of an old self" is imperative in acts of Transcendence, for "re-creation" is the essence of transcendent acts.[161] Transcendent acts are acts of "transformation."[162] They are "incorporations" and hence are inclusionary rather than exclusionary in nature.[163]

"The stimulus towards transcendence, or symbolic bridging and merging," Burke reminds us, "arises from the many kinds of conflict among values implicit in a going social concern."[164] It is midway "between an old weighting and a new weighting" that we stand in "the realm . . . called 'perspective by incongruity' (a term that designates one way of transcending a given order of weightedness).[165] Transcendence is an act of resolution—a resolution of "contradictions," "opposites"; it involves "transubstantiation."[166] Such resolution or conversions "are generally managed by the search for a 'graded series' whereby we move step by step from some kind of event, in which the presence of a certain factor is sanctioned in the language of common sense, to other events in which this factor had not previously been noted."[167] Burke turns to music as he often does to illustrate this process:

> . . . if one introduces into a chord a note alien to the perfect harmony, the result is a discord. But if you stretch out this same chord into an arpeggio having the same components, the discordant ingredient you have introduced may become but a 'passing note.' 'Transcendence' is the solving of a logical problem by stretching it out into a narrative arpeggio, whereby a conflicting element can be introduced as a 'passing note,' hence not felt as 'discord.'[168]

If dialectical synthesis appears impossible at one level, then we symbolically erect "a 'higher synthesis,' in poetic and conceptual imagery" that helps us "accept" the contraries with which we are confronted.[169] Only those who search for "bridging devices" or "symbolic structure whereby one 'transcends' a conflict in one way or another" *can* yield to new motivations and hence undergo the process of rebirth.[170]

Throughout, Burke implies that language is both the ultimate bridging

---

[159] *Ibid.*, pp. 224, 106.
[160] *Ibid.*, p. 92.
[161] *PLF*, p. 33; *PLF*, p. 53.
[162] *Ibid.*, p. 44.
[163] *Ibid.*
[164] *ATH*, p. 179.
[165] *PC*, p. liv.
[166] *ATH*, pp. 92, 336; *PLF*, pp. 21, 44.
[167] *PC*, p. 142.
[168] *PLF*, p. 84.
[169] *ATH*, p. 92.
[170] *Ibid.*, p. 224.

device and the major obstacle to Transcendence. Yet throughout his work there is a sustaining faith that we may yet transcend temporary divisiveness and together, with him, seek the "good life."[171] For it was in such a "fatal moment of recreation" that Coleridge's "loathsome water snakes" were "proclaimed blessed and beautiful."[172]

Conclusion

Thus, we have come something of a full circle from the first major term considered in this paper, the methodological term, Perspective by Incongruity—a process by which new birth and Transcendence are possible. That there is much overlapping between and among the pivotal terms Orientation, Motive, Symbolic Action, Form, Identification, and Transcendence, is clear. In Burke's work that is to be expected for as he says:

". . . insofar as the terms mutually imply one another, the whole family circle is already contained in one of them. . . ."[173]

Throughout our discussion of the four early works of Kenneth Burke we have included passages and interpretation from all of the works in which the key terms occur. Such an approach rests on the assumption that the question: "What are the pivotal terms in the rhetorical theory of Kenneth Burke?" may help us to answer the larger and more persistent question: "What are the key terms in a comprehensive theory of rhetoric?" Whether such a theory may rest only or even substantially on the work of Kenneth Burke remains to be seen. It is clear, however, that if we are to write anything like a comprehensive theory of rhetoric we will have to deal with terms such as Transcendence, Identification, Form, Symbolic Action, Motive, Orientation, and Perspective by Incongruity: Perspective by Incongruity, because it *does* provide us with new angles of vision; Orientation, because we *do* attempt to make sense out of the disorder into which we are born; Motive, because we *do* need ways of interpreting situations, because in the motives we assign to actions, there *is* at least an implicit "program of socialization";[174] Symbolic Action and Form because we are symbol-using beings and one of the essential ways we act *is* linguistically; Identification and Transcendence because we *do* seek to overcome our generic divisiveness and function socially.

---

[171] *PC,* p. 29.
[172] *PLF,* p. 53.
[173] *LSA,* p. 365.
[174] *ATH,* p. 170.

Kenneth Burke and
the Method of Dramatism

by Michael A. Overington

It is possible that sociologists have read the work of Kenneth Burke and found it neither important nor interesting.[1] One searches in vain for any expository treatment of his work in those journals read by sociologists, or indeed, for any expository treatment of the sociological importance of Burke in other journals. Yet Burke has been lurking in sociologists' footnotes since the 1930s, and recently his system, "Dramatism," has been promoted to equal rank with "Symbolic Interaction" and "Social Exchange" in the coverage given to these aspects of "Interaction" in *the International Encyclopedia of the Social Sciences*.[2] What are we to make of this?

Certainly Kenneth Burke has never regarded himself as a sociologist. Moreover, his wanderings through academia have usually put him in contact with critics, rhetoricians, and philosophers, rather than sociologists. Burke has never been able, therefore, to develop a group of students through his teaching and research supervision who would be able and willing to present the position of their *maître* before a broader sociological audience. Yet, the fact that Burke himself is the author of the *IESS* article on "Dramatism" does give some pause. Was there no other person capable of presenting this systematic position? After some forty years, is dramatism so intimately tied up with Burke as to make it *his* system? Is it, then, merely a brilliantly inventive set of insights held in systemic place by the idiosyncracies of Burke's own mind?

Clearly, Louis Wirth did not think so in 1938 when he said of Burke's *Permanence and Change* (1935) that "It contains more sound substance than any text on social psychology with which the reviewer is familiar." But in his caution that "There is much in this treatise that will appear unsystematic and

Reprinted from *Theory and Society* 4 (1977). Reproduced by permission of Elsevier Science Publishers B.V.

[1] This work incorporates portions of a chapter of a dissertation submitted to the Department of Sociology at the University of Wisconsin, Madison. Joe Elder, Lloyd Bitzer, and Warren Hagstrom met together with Kent Geiger and Nick Danigelis in 1974 to sign away their blame for that project. Failing to persuade George Zollschan that he should take some share of the culpability, the writer is left to acknowledge full responsibility for whatever sins of commission and omission that this latest revision includes.

[2] Kenneth Burke, "Dramatism," in *International Encyclopedia of the Social Sciences* (New York, 1968), pp. 445-452.

irrelevant to those accustomed to a less personal and poetic mode of discourse,"[3] one may find a plausible answer. The full corpus of Burke's work is broader than the social psychological thrust of this volume, but an idiosyncratic style does characterize all his work and has surely proven to be a major stumbling block for sociologically trained readers. Although Wayne Booth is a little strong when he says, "Among anthropologists, sociologists, psychologists, and rhetoricians his 'dramatism' is increasingly recognized as something that must at least appear in one's index, whether one has troubled to understand him or not,"[4] it is long since time for a sociologically interested exposition of Burke's work to be presented to a broad sociological audience, so as to hasten an *informed recognition*. The challenge here is to respect Burke's stylistic *métier,* which is an integral part of his work, while offering a translation of his systematic writings that makes sense to sociologists.

Carving a clear presentation of dramatism from Burke's immense *oeuvre* is made easier by his practice of using major volumes to collect, summarize, and organize his more fragmentary material, which runs to some seventeen pages in the most complete checklist of his writings.[5] Yet even when reduced to his eight major volumes (1957; 1959; 1965; 1966; 1968a; 1969a; 1969b; 1970), the task might still prove unmanageable unless some clear distinction were to be drawn between dramatism as a *method* for analyzing human relationships (which is the way Burke elected to present his system in *IESS*), and the substantive contributions that Burke has made to a sociological understanding of human relationships by applying this "method." In principle, dramatism is a method that is applicable by anyone trained in its usage, and it should be allowed to stand or fall as an analytic methodology quite independent of the substantive conclusions about human conduct that Burke draws from his own usage of the method. For the sake of clarity, therefore, this present essay will restrict itself to an exposition of the problematic and logic of inquiry of dramatism as a method. A companion piece provides a reconstruction of Burke's substantive position.[6]

In the *IESS* article, the most sociologically pertinent summary of dramatism as a method, Burke defines the system as follows:

> a method of analysis and a corresponding critique of terminology designed to show that the most direct route to the study of human relations and human motives is via a methodical inquiry into cycles or clusters of terms and their functions.[7]

---

[3] Louis Wirth, "Review of *Permanence and Change,*" *American Journal of Sociology* 43 (1938), pp. 483-486.
[4] Wayne Booth, "Kenneth Burke's Way of Knowing," *Critical Inquiry* 1 (September 1974), p. 2.
[5] See Armin Paul Frank and Mechthild Frank, "The Writings of Kenneth Burke," in William Rueckert, ed., *Critical Responses to Kenneth Burke: 1924-1926* (Minneapolis, 1969), pp.495-512.
[6] See Michael A. Overington, "Kenneth Burke as Social Theorist: He's Got Some Explaining to Do," St. Mary's University, Halifax, Canada (1975).
[7] Kenneth Burke, "Dramatism," *op. cit.,* p. 445.

Yet in contrast to this definition of his enterprise as an analysis of the *terms* implicated in the analysis of action, he offers another stipulation of dramatism "in a wider sense [as] any study of human relations in terms of 'action.'...."[8] Although in this wider sense, Burke certainly includes the early work of Parsons, and perhaps the writings of Weber, Simmel, Schutz, Mead and other theorists of social *action,* Abraham Kaplan has clarified the ambiguity in these two definitions:

> Burke explicitly declares his concern to be with the analysis of language, not 'reality'. But it remains doubtful whether he has in fact clearly distinguished the two and successfully limited himself to the linguistic level.[9]

Much of Burke's work shuttles between these two positions, and the reader is not always clear whether a given analysis is addressed to *terms* about action or to *action itself.* In practice, this unclarity beclouds the use of dramatism as a *meta-method* for talking about the explanatory (in his language, *motivational)* terms of theories of social *action,* with its employment as a *method* (with its own terms) for *explaining* social action. As a method, dramatism addresses the empirical questions of how persons explain their actions to themselves and others, what the cultural and social structural influences on these explanations might be, and what effect connotational links among the explanatory (motivational) terms might have on these explanations, and hence, on action itself. As a meta-method, dramatism turns from common sense explanatory discourse to that of the social scientist, in an effort to analyze and criticize the effect of a "connotational logic" on social scientific explanations of action. Thus, dramatism attempts to account for the motivational (explanatory) vocabulary of ordinary discourse and its influence on human action *and* for particular sociological vocabularies when they are used to explain human action. In the first case, Burke is addressing the influence of explanatory language on *human action;* in the second, he is dealing with the influence of explanatory language (its connotational logic) on the *social scientific explanation* of human action.

But whether as meta-method or method, dramatism aims to be a logic of inquiry, an instrumental logic which may be used to investigate hypotheses about particular problems. Therefore, sociological examination of Burke's dramatistic "method" will require both a brief specification of Burke's problematic, and a rather more extensive treatment of his logic of inquiry both in terms of its development and the intersubjectivity of dramatistic practice.

---

[8] *Ibid.,* p. 448.
[9] Abraham Kaplan, "A Review of *A Grammar of Motives,*" in William Rueckert, ed., *op. cit.,* p. 170.

In the most fundamental sense Burke's object of inquiry is *motive:* the language *of* motives, motives *in* language, language *as* motive. Yet motive is a concept which has several usages in the social sciences. The formulation of the concept as a cause, or as some drive state of the individual, is the most familiar in sociological discourse. Burke's conception of motive is like neither of these, and it has provided the basis for the symbolic interactionist understanding of motives as the accounts people give for their action: "rationalizations," if you will, as motives.[10] Nonetheless, his view of motives is not simply that of the individual's verbal justification or explanation of his own or another's action. Certainly, this formulation of motive would cover "language *of* motives" and "motives *in* language." It handles Burke's emphasis on the cultural and structural bases for particular vocabularies of motive and the process by which some verbal explanation becomes the sufficient justification for the individual's own action or for the persuasion of others to act. What is omitted from this approach (which might be thought of as the study of vocabularies of motive) is the emphasis Burke places on the motivational influence of sheer terms. Words *qua* words, he suggests, because of the connotations which hold clusters of terms together, can become justifications for action.

Whether or not there is a relation between things, Burke argues that if there is a connotational relation between the terms which symbolize these things, then the embedment of such a connotational relation in the linguistic structures of human mental processes is sufficient to influence people to translate this symbolic relation into action (by providing a sufficient justification, by making sense for them of the projected action). For example, to call some occurrence of a death "murder" is to justify (explain, motivate) the search for an individual who intended to kill; to call some property loss "theft" is to sanction a police dragnet for a thief. Murder and theft are criminal acts because of the statutory decision of some political body; they are not *inherently* criminal. No matter what took place at the scene of the crime, calling the situation "murder" or "theft" brings into play the terminological relations which inhere in the meaning of these words. Thus, if there was a "murder," then there was a "murderer"—a person who, having constructed the "intention," put it into action by killing an individual. Whatever took place to bring about this death, the attachment of meaning to

---

[10]The classic essay here is C. Wright Mills, "Situated Actions and Vocabularies of Motive," in Irving Louis Horowitz, ed., *Power, Politics and People* (New York, 1963), pp. 439-452. Here Mills acknowledges his debt to Burke's *Permanence and Change,* first published in 1935. This paper by Mills in 1940 was the debut of Burke's ideas in sociology. The most recent analytic attention to the issue of motives from a similar position may be found in George K. Zollschan and Michael A. Overington, "Reasons for Conduct and the Conduct of Reason," in George K. Zollschan and Walter Hirsch, eds., *Social Change: Conjectures, Explanations and Diagnoses* (Boston, 1975).

it as a "murder" requires, because of the connotational relations which inhere in this term, that we look for an individual who planned and executed the act, whether or not such an individual exists. It is not the fact of the act as murder, but the fact of *calling* it "murder" which leads to the search for an intentional killer. Language is itself the motive for the search.[11]

This may be a rather startling idea, and it might help to clarify it if we look at some consequences of Burke's view as it could apply to something as familiar as the sociologist's language of explanation. We are fond of talking, for example, about "explained variance," a concept defined in statistical theory as common covariation between variables. While there is no sense of "explanation" or "cause" in the statistical definition, the concept does have those meanings in theoretical discourse (at least, "explained" does). Thus, we find that a statistical measure of explained variance, e.g., R^2, becomes the *explanation* of some relationship, despite that measure's purely statistical nature. Again, "significance tests" refer only to the improbability of some statistical hypothesis; yet, the temptation, a temptation brought on by the other connotations of "significance," to treat statistical significance substantively has lured many a researcher from the paths of technical purity.[12] All of which is to illustrate Burke's view that the implicit coherency which makes terms "stick together" (our sense of what terms go with what) is as important an influence on the explanation we give for social behavior *and* action as are the actual relations which social phenomena bear to each other.[13]

Thus, it is to this tripartite understanding of motives, to the language *of* explanation, explanation *in* language, language *as* explanation, that Burke

---

[11]It is interesting here to compare David Matza's treatment of the "essential thief." Matza points out that the common sense view of the way in which police investigate crimes is hardly in keeping with their practice. They do not tackle such matters with a Holmesian technique, i.e., inductive clue collection leading to a deduction of the identity of the culprit; rather, they have a pre-selected collection of individuals in the community who are, by their reputation, thieves, what Matza calls "essential thieves." The police turn to this group for their suspect. As Burke would expect, an act which is "essentially" that of theft, requires for its motivational complement (its explanation) a person who is "essentially" a thief. A person and his acts become so confounded that the person's identity is seen as nothing more than his actions written large. This identification of a person with his acts is the result, Burke would say, of the power of motivational terms to create a coherent justification which will have consequences for people. The "essential thief" is the necessary dramatistic complement to the act of theft, when the connotative logic implied by the term "theft" is worked out in practice.

The use of deviant acts in this example will surely remind the reader of some of the concerns of "labeling theory" which has commonalities with Burke's position. Nonetheless, his understanding of the motivational force of verbal labels is a good deal broader than the position of the labeling theorists.

[12]See also K. W. Taylor and James Frideres, "Issues versus Controversies: Substantive and Statistical Significance," *American Sociological Review* 37 (August 1972), pp. 464-472.

[13]I agree with Burke that "things" and the symbols for things are not the same; but what one can know about "things" without symbols, apart from their resistance, is quite mysterious. Thus, what the actual relations between phenomena might be is always an hypothesis; the only way to address this is in the selection of a set of terms by means of which to conduct an analysis. If *human* knowledge is acquired through symbols, then the "actual" state of affairs of the world is not open to human knowledge, only that "actuality" which enters in its symbolic "transformation."

turns his attention. His problematic is to describe the fundamental roots of motives in the social world, to explicate the changes in motivational frameworks which can be traced across Western history, to show the importance for all human society of the fact that persons' actions are influenced by words of explanation and justification, and finally, to offset the possible influence of inadequate languages of explanation employed by sociologists. To this problematic, Burke addresses the analytic tool of dramatism.[14]

While motive is the object of dramatistic inquiry, dialectic is the method. But to say that Burke's method is dialectical is, as Louis Schneider has commented,[15] to say nothing very clear; "dialectic" and "dialectical" are ambiguous terms. Among the various meanings that Schneider finds attached to the conception of dialectic in sociology, one has notions like the unanticipated consequences of human action, which is linked to questions of reification and alienation (when persons "find" themselves confronting these unintended creations as something more than human fabrications); goal displacement, the emergence of means as ends; successful societal adaptations as blockages to further change; development through conflict; contradiction, paradox, dilemma; and the dissolution of conflict by a melding of opposites. Yet Burke's notion of dialectic involves but one of these, the concept of contradiction and the ironic presupposition that one approaches a fuller, more true, explanation for social action by taking opposing perspectives on that action.

It is not unreasonable to ask why Burke argues for a dialectical rather than positive method for understanding the social world. I suspect that the answer to that question reveals how similar his basic ontological assumptions about the world are to those of Wilhelm Dilthey, although Burke does not evidence awareness of the likeness. Like Dilthey he assumes that physical and social objects are different kinds of realities. The physical world is whatever it is, independent of human action, thought, belief or values. The social world, however, is an interpreted reality erected through action, belief and thought on the raw physical material. The consequence of this for both Burke and Dilthey is a presupposition that the methodology of the social sciences will be different from that of the physical sciences. For Burke, who takes the social world to be constituted through a dialectical (contradictory) process of interest-oriented action, this means electing a methodology which traces the multiplicity of interests and orientations possible in any situation. A dialectical ontology *requires* a dialectical epistemology. His dialectic thus

---

[14] See further, Overington, "Kenneth Burke as Social Theorist: He's Got Some Explaining to Do," *op. cit.*
[15] Louis Schneider, "Dialectic in Sociology," *American Sociological Review* 36 (August 1971), pp. 667-678.

involves an epistemological perspectivism[16] as the methodology to grasp the "essential" reality of the human world of action. His irony of contradiction, however, does not at all lead him to a "debunking" critique of the social realm. Rather it operates as a protection from the powerful influence of modal vocabularies of motives which have their roots in the property relations of society. If, as Marx says, "The ideas of the ruling class are, in every age, the ruling ideas: i.e. the class which is the dominant *material* force in society is at the same time its dominant *intellectual* force,"[17] then only through a deliberate and seemingly perverse entertainment of contradictory explanations can the social analyst construct an understanding of social relations (or, taking dramatism as meta-method, erect a vocabulary of terms) broader than that legitimated by the ruling class and its intellectual servants. While this latter point may well be a little stronger than Burke's view, it is a consistent conclusion drawn from two Burkean premises. First, vocabularies of motive are rooted in the property structure and the influence of men of property; and second, multiplying such vocabularies will lead, through a dialectic of contradiction, to an "essentially" true explanation.

Perhaps the most *formally* accurate characterization of this dialectic is in terms of its relation to the Platonic dialogue. Charles Morris, for example, described Burke's *A Grammar of Motives* as:

> a dramatic dialectic in which philosophers, political theorists, economists, poets, theologians, and psychologists all have their say, and each mode of saying is shown to need correction by each other mode. The book is experienced as a vast dialogue.[18]

Indeed, Burke's dialectic is a conversation of many voices, each having its place and its perspective, no voice supplanting or replacing another: it is the dialogue as a whole, the voices in harmony and discord, which is the end of the dialectic. There is here no question of a synthesis as the culmination of the dialectic; there is no single authoritative perspective; it is only the multiplicity of elements in the dialectic which offers an accurate account.[19]

---

[16]"Epistemological perspectivism" is a locution chosen to express a philosophical view of knowledge of the social world as fundamentally available only *within* personal, social, and ideological perspectives; to claim that there is no knowledge of social objects, no knowledge of persons, no social *knowledge*, therefore, which is complete, absolute, unconditioned by intellectual frameworks and language. One should not be tempted to see Burke as idiosyncratic in his perspectivism. Others who have advocated similar positions are Karl Mannheim, George Mead, Alfred Schutz, and Maurice Merleau-Ponty, a distinguished collection of people who have had some influence on the development of sociological thinking.

[17]Karl Marx, *Selected Writings in Sociology and Social Philosophy,* T. B. Bottomore and Maximilien Rubel, eds. (New York, 1956), p. 78.

[18]Charles Morris, "The Strategy of Kenneth Burke," in William Rueckert, ed., *op. cit., p.* 164.

[19]Here Burke differs from both Plato and Hegel, for, of any one voice in the dialogue (or dialectic, the terms are equivalent for him), "[It is] necessarily a restricted perspective, since it represents but one voice in the dialogue, and not the perspective-of-perspectives that arises from the cooperative competition of *all* the voices as they modify one another's assertions, so that the whole transcends the partiality of its parts." [Kenneth Burke, *A Grammar of Motives* (Berkeley, California, 1969), p. 89.]

The reader should not yield to the temptation to dismiss lightly Burke's use of this particular method (logic of inquiry); it is not a literary critic's whim but an essential philosophical and political principle which underlies its usage. Burke finds in the institutionalizing of the dialectical process (as he conceived it) the only chance for a society to continue to function in its contacts with the obdurate character of the natural world. The natural world is whatever it is inherently; to define the world incorrectly, to act in the world on a false hypothesis has, as the limit, destructive consequences. A perspectival approach to the world offers, at least for Burke, more probability of an accurate interpretation of, and, thus, adaptive action on the natural and social world. This point is most clearly made where Burke says:

> I take democracy to be a device for institutionalizing the dialectic process by setting up a political structure that gives full opportunity for the use of competition to a cooperative end . . . I should contend that the dialectic process *absolutely must* be unimpeded, if society is to perfect its understanding of reality by the necessary method of give and take.[20]

Now we should turn to an examination of the development of this dialectical logic of inquiry and then to a consideration in more detail of the publicly available rules for using dramatistic procedures.

Clearly, this dialectic did not appear fully developed in his work in the nineteen twenties and thirties. Yet, even in *Counterstatement,* his earliest critical volume, the operation of his logic is clear, and Burke's own comment on the seminal nature of this volume is essentially accurate, both with respect to its system and its method.[21] Indeed, his later work may be seen as a development of the method and substance of this first volume, although it would be misleading to claim that there is anything in this work but the conceptual possibility of the final system.

Counterstatement propounds the view that the creative artist should be an advocate of values antithetical to those advanced by his particular time and society. Every era and culture will be marked by one overwhelming set of values, Burke claims, and this emphasis leads to a lack of attention to other "perennial" aspects of human experience. Given, he suggests, the technological emphasis, the appeal to motives like "money" and "efficiency" which characterize the modal culture of the contemporary Western world, there is a neglect of motives (explanations, justifications) drawn from art, religion, mythology, and a celebration of motives taken from property, war, government, and social organization. In the face of this, it is the artist's task to speak "dialectically," to speak in opposition to this emphasis, in effect to speak for "inefficiency!"

---

[20]Kenneth Burke, *The Philosophy of Literary Form* (New York, 1957), p. 328.
[21]Kenneth Burke, *Counterstatement* (Berkeley, California, 1968), pp. xi, 22.

When one connects this oppositional concept of dialectic with the interest-based theory of ideational association that Burke takes explicitly from De Gourmont, then the adumbration of his method of inquiry stands forth in this first volume. From it, one can conclude that inquiry into human action is to be conducted by examining the interest bases for people's ideas and ideational relations through a deliberate introduction of a contradictory perspective into the interaction of this action. Understanding is to be achieved by ironic illumination. Yet it is not at all clear in this book why it is that a contradictory perspective will lead one to a more accurate view, save that it can bring into analytic focus other aspects of human life which are obscured by the modal motivational framework legitimated by the "industrial" division of property and labor. Nor is it obvious what a contradictory perspective would be, or how one might construct it. However, in his next two volumes *Permanence and Change* (1965) and *Attitudes Toward History* (1959), Burke offers a more helpful account of the process of his dialectic. Indeed, he makes an effective presentation of a particular dialectical technique that he calls "perspective by incongruity." This is a method that operates by bringing together terms and concepts which are normally never found together and which, in their ironic juxtaposition, undermine the "taken for granted" character of the motivational force of the terms in their conventional relations. In his words: "Perspective by incongruity [is] a method for gauging situations by verbal atom cracking. That is, a word belongs by custom to a certain category—and by rational planning you wrench it loose and metaphorically apply it to a different category."[22] Burke notes that this technique is closely connected to De Gourmont's notion of the "dissociation of ideas," which "was concerned with the methodic blasting apart of verbal particles that had been considered inseparable; [whereas on the other hand] 'perspective by incongruity' refers to the methodic merger of particles that had been considered mutually exclusive."[23]

Nonetheless, these two techniques are hardly independent. They are a kind of early version of the "merger and division" technique, a device for exploring connotational transformations which flowers in his later work,[24] and which Burke traces back to the *Phaedrus* and Plato's distinction between the twin processes of the dialectic—organization into unity and division into

---

[22]Kenneth Burke, *Attitudes Toward History* (Boston, Mass., 1959), p. 308.
[23]Kenneth Burke, *Permanence and Change* (Indianapolis, Indiana, 1965), pp. liv-lv. When not applied too narrowly, this conception of "perspective by incongruity" is not strange to sociology. Most familiar to American sociologists, perhaps, will be its application by the *Chicago School*. Although the *University of Chicago Sociological Series,* which is the best collection of the work of the researchers at Chicago, contains around thirty-five volumes, it is the studies of deviance which are best known and are seen as best representative of the *School.* It is in these volumes that irony can be seen in the use of terms like "profession," "career," "morality," etc., to analyze the activity of deviants and criminals. This linking of "respectable" terms with deviant activity quite clearly captures the sense of verbal incongruity to which Burke is referring.
[24]Burke, *A Grammar of Motives, op. cit.,* pp. 402-418.

parts—which work together to produce truthful discourse. But there must surely be many incongruous meldings of terms that one could use. Why one incongruity rather than another? Is Burke arguing for a "verbal cubism," or does the atomic imagery he uses to define this technique expose a desire to be taken scientifically?

The best answer one can extract from this context suggests that "'perspective by incongruity' makes for a *dramatic* vocabulary, with weighting and counter-weighting, in contrast with the liberal ideal of *neutral* naming in the characterization of processes."[25] Yet, we can only guess at the basis for the "weighting." While it is moral and aesthetic, and it seems to be informed by "a Marxism so tolerant, so tentative that he must find it a bit uncomfortable . . . ,"[26] we have no explicit rules for it. However, it would not be inaccurate to read Burke as offering us a three-step guide to motivational analysis. First, identify the modal motivational framework, both its terms and the weighting of these terms on behalf of the ruling elites. Second, construct an ironic motivational terminology weighted in opposition to the interests of property by constructing incongruous motivational phrases from the modal vocabulary of motives and from whatever terms one's own inventive genius will supply. Finally, offer this analysis in public discourse, in order to give a truer explanation for human action *and* to provide people with a liberating alternative justification for their action. This logic of inquiry, therefore, is not simply an instrument for interpreting the social world; it also gives the possibility of *changing* that world!

A penetrating example of this ironic technique is Burke's account of psychoanalysis as a form of "secular conversion" which "effects its cures by providing a new perspective that dissolves the system of pieties lying at the root of the patient's sorrows or bewilderments."[27] If we translate that into a less Burkean vocabulary, then we may take him to be claiming that the therapist uncovers the patient's neurotic tendencies and effects a "cure" by teaching the patient to use a different vocabulary to talk about them. The therapeutic vocabulary of motives is organized about a different "system of pieties," a different moral order, and the analytic language works a cure as patients learn to talk about their problems in a new vocabulary with new moral values. Through this they discover the therapeutic effect of a new set of motives which frees them from the old motivational framework and, thus, from the old neurotic determination.[28]

---

[25] Burke, *Attitudes Toward History, op. cit.,* p. 311.
[26] Crane Brinton, "What is History?," *Saturday Review of Literature* 15 (August, 1937), pp. 3-4, 11.
[27] Burke, *Permanence and Change, op. cit.,* p. 125.
[28] For similar accounts of the procedures of psychoanalysis, *cf.* O. Hobart Mowrer, *The Crisis in Psychiatry and Religion* (Princeton, New Jersey, 1961) and Jerome Frank, *Persuasion and Healing* (New York, 1961). A parallel description of conversion through the provision of new vocabularies of motive is to be found in a study of brainwashing in China by Robert Jay Lifton, *Thought Reform and the Psychology of Totalism* (London, 1961).

However, Burke did not produce this ironic perspectivism *de novo;* indeed, he relates it to the basic orientation of Nietzsche and to the system of Bergson. Burke traces to Nietzsche the sense of perspectives as interpretations from a particular position, which become "true" insofar as they encourage a creative praxis to bring the "mythic" orientation into reality.[29] It is to Bergson, however, that he turns for his justification of "incongruity as a system." For Bergson, the life process is a continuous flow within which we make distinctions by the use of language. The existent world *is* a continuity of unified being; we find our way through it with the abstracting power of words. But these abstract verbal systems are not reality; if we want to get closer to reality, we must find a technique to unify the many different abstractions. Burke summarizes: "As the nearest verbal approach to reality, M. Bergson proposes that we deliberately cultivate the use of contradictory concepts."[30] Here is the fundamental distinction between *things* and *words about* things, and the further emphasis on the priority of things, which Burke insists on through all his work. Despite what he has to say about the necessity of using abstractions and metaphors to describe facts, he does appear to believe that the "isness" of the world exists independently of words about that "isness." Yet what that "isness" might be without language is not very clear. Could it have more than what he calls recalcitrance,[31] the capacity to resist our interpretations? That's hardly sufficient justification for him to give such priority to "things in themselves"; surely the "isness" of things is their least interesting quality to persons. Nonetheless, one cannot grasp Burke's devoted attention to the study of language as it influences human conduct without understanding, at the same time, his fundamental assumption of the ontological priority of the physical, material world.

---

[29]It is not altogether clear that Burke's essentialist and substance-oriented philosophy is a comfortable bedmate with Nietzsche's perspectivist and process vision. Surely Burke is also a perspectivist, but one always feels that he is struggling to an understanding of the essence of persons and their world. On the other hand, Nietzsche's "myths" appear to be instruments through which he seeks to realize his own potential. It may well be that Frederick Copleston's summary of the importance of Nietzsche's work as "a dramatic expression of a lived spiritual crisis" [*A History of Philosophy,* Vol. VII (New York, 1963), p. 199] captures the real common ground between these two men. Burke's works published before the Second World War speak of the effect of the economic depression on the artist's mind (his own): the Depression overturned a whole system of values and motives and threw into chaos the minds which had been socialized to these same values and motives. These volumes further speak of Burke's attempt to use them to put his "world" back together (see particularly, *Permanence and Change, op. cit.,* p. xlvii). It may well be that the common spiritual crisis which he shared with Nietzsche led to his electing a similar perspectivist orientation which would insulate him from the collapse of another absolute system of values and motives. Yet, in *Language as Symbolic Action* (Berkeley, California, 1966), pp. 3-24, one finds Burke endorsing his own perspectival analysis as that best suited to tracking down the *essence* of human conduct. In the culmination of the dramatistic system, therefore, perspectivism is swallowed up in a dialectical method which no longer requires ironic counterpoint.
[30]Burke, *Permanence and Change, op. cit.,* p. 94.
[31]*Ibid.,* pp. 255-261.

This formulation of the "perspective by incongruity" was not the final statement of Burke's dialectic; this is to be found in the "Pentad," a codification of the many possible perspectives into five basic questions that are to be asked when explaining any human action. *A Grammar of Motives* is devoted to these questions. The development to this last stage is best traced by Daniel Fogarty in his effort to place Burke as a rhetorical theorist.[32] The dialectic of verbal incongruities in its initial statement, Fogarty suggests, allowed him to formulate a position. However, Burke quickly realized that such a simple thesis-antithesis-synthesis form neglected the potential of verbal irony, and he began to play with the etymological (connotative) possibilities of terms as a way of increasing the perspectives he could bring to bear, all the time searching for an "essential" definition of his terms.[33] With the many possible "starts" provided by this etymological approach, he was able to move "from the dialectical to the symposium type of inner personal discussion. It is as though Burke were a five or six-man discussion group taking all the speaking parts himself until he has sifted the best resultant formulation of the idea in question... 'Ideally [Burke writes in a letter], all the various voices are partisan rhetoricians whose partial voices 'competitively cooperate' to form the position of the dialogue as a whole...' "[34]

The pentad retains both the "inner symposium" and the etymological approach at the same time as it offers the final reconstruction of the dialectic. However, in this reconstruction, the "tolerant Marxism" of the earlier dialectic is incorporated into a procedure wherein incongruity is almost entirely teased out of motivational frameworks themselves, without explicit attention to their social or cultural roots in property relations. Yet, the pentad does codify the dramatistic logic of inquiry; it does provide rules, albeit of a general kind, for the explanation of human action. As Burke summarizes it:

> In any rounded statement about motives, you must have some word that names the *act* (names what took place, in thought or deed), and another that names the *scene* (the background of the act, the situation in which it occurred); also, you must indicate what person or kind of person *(agent)* performed the act, what means or instruments he used *(agency)*, and the purpose.[35]

---

[32]Daniel Fogarty, *Roots for a New Rhetoric* (New York, 1959). This work gains its authority from Burke's comments on Fogarty's reconstruction of his method, which are included in the volume.

[33]One should note the parallels between Burke and Durkheim, *The Rules of the Sociological Method* (New York, 1938), p. 35, and Aristotle's method of many beginnings and the search for an "essential" definition for the concept under investigation, *cf.* Richard McKeon, "Aristotle's Conception of the Development and the Nature of Scientific Method," *Journal of the History of Ideas* 8 (January, 1947), pp. 4-5.

[34]Daniel Fogarty, "Kenneth Burke's Theory," in William Rueckert, ed., *op. cit.*, p. 326.

[35]Burke, *A Grammar of Motives, op. cit.*, p. xv.

The five terms of the pentad are therefore Act, Scene, Agent, Agency, Purpose, to which he later added Attitude (as incipient act) to make a hexad. He notes that, as terms, they are neither positive nor dialectical, defined neither lexically nor oppositionally; rather they are collapsed questions, e.g., *Act* is equivalent to "What was done?"; *Scene* is the same as "In what sort of a situation was it done?" and so on.[36]

Nor, he comments, is there anything particularly original about the pentad. It is parallel with Aristotle's four causes; we can correlate material cause and *Scene*, efficient cause and *Agent*, formal cause and *Act*, final cause and *Purpose*, and, as a subdivision of final cause, means and *Agency*. The pentad has a similar relation to the "hexameter" of the mediaeval schoolmen, which was used as a mnemonic guide for rhetors when they were discussing an event, i.e., who, what, where, by what means, why, how, when. In the hexameter, "who" correlates with *Agent*, "what" with *Act*, "where" and "when" go with *Scene*, "why" with *Purpose* and "by what means" with *Agency*.[37] Finally, a similar correlation can be found between the pentad and the journalist's catechism: who, what, when, where and how. It is these similarities which give Burke such confidence in the *basic* nature of his terms.[38] Thus, it is the pentad which provides the fundamental dramatistic technique for methodic analyses of human action, or for the meta-methodological critique of the terminology about human action.

In the relationships among these five terms there is a whole series of word pairs, correlations, or "ratios," which may be used to explain action or to explicate explanations of action. The *Scene-Act* ratio, for example, is an assertion that particular acts correlate with particular scenes, and "sensible" explanations will exhibit a consistency between acts and their scenes. Likewise, the *Scene-Agent* ratio explains action as a result of a correlation between agents and scenes: "It is a principle of drama that the nature of acts and agents should be consistent with the nature of the scene."[39] However, the original "consistency" of the ratios has, in the latest formulation, become "correspondence," such that with respect to a *Scene-Act* ratio he is talking about "a proposition such as: Though agent and act are necessarily different in many of their attributes, some notable element of one is implicitly or analogously present in the other."[40]

The context in which we can best make sense of these explanatory correspondences between various terms of the pentad is to be found in Burke's early work, *The Philosophy of Literary Form*. There he notes that dramatism is an heuristic for the analysis of human *action;* it is

---

[36]Kenneth Burke, *The Rhetoric of Religion* (Berkeley, California, 1970), p. 26.
[37]Burke, *A Grammar of Motives, op. cit.,* p. 228.
[38]Fogarty, "Kenneth Burke's Theory," *op. cit.,* p. 327.
[39]Burke, *A Grammar of Motives, op. cit.,* p. 3.
[40]Burke, "Dramatism," *op. cit.,* p. 446.

a *calculus*—a vocabulary, or set of coordinates, that serves best for the integration of all phenomena studied by the social sciences. We propose it as the logical alternative to the treatment of human acts and relations in terms of the mechanistic metaphor (stimulus, response, and the conditioned reflex). And we propose it, along with the contention that mechanistic considerations need not be *excluded* from such a perspective, but take their part in it, as a statement about the predisposing structure of the *ground* or *scene* upon which the drama is enacted.[41]

Burke recognizes that only a mechanistic explanation, perhaps in terms of "equilibria,"[42] will be appropriate for human *aggregates* and their *behavior.* Indeed, "Man's involvement in the natural order makes him in many respects analyzable in terms of sheer motion. . . ."[43] However, the dramatistic analysis of action is intended as a corrective to mechanistic perspectives and aggregate analysis. Through it, Burke hopes to rescue the human person, *as a concept,* from collapse into a conceptual universe suitable only for particles or organisms; and human persons, *as living, acting symbolizing animals,* from the *"temptation* to become sheer automata."[44]

The basic, corrective principles of dramatism and the ratios are taken from drama because human action is "essentially" dramatic, for Burke. The drama presumes human action; the playwright's task is to offer a plausible account of the acts of agents in terms of scenes, purposes, and agencies. As Burke puts it in "Dramatism," "drama is employed, not as a metaphor but as a fixed form that helps us discover what the implications of the terms 'act' and 'person' *really are.*"[45] In other words, the drama is Burke's choice for an analytic model of the social world. What makes drama work is the ability of playwrights to call upon cultural expectations of consistency between scenes and both acts and agents. Burke is saying that drama provides a form for the analysis of human action; drama "works" only when it draws on these cultural expectations so as to build plot and characters around these ratios. Thus, the drama is a major research site to which Burke has turned for his insight into motives. When he understands how a play operates, he knows about the expectations of both audience and playwright with respect to a convincing explanatory framework. It was precisely from his study of the drama that he was able to abstract the terms of the pentad as the major dimensions of the explanation of human action.

The most common ratios used by Burke are Scene-Act and Scene-Agent. When engaged in a dramatistic study, he notes, "the basic unit of action

---

[41]Burke, *The Philosophy of Literary Form, op. cit.,* p. 90.
[42]See Burke, "Dramatism," *op. cit.*
[43]Burke, *Language as Symbolic Action, op. cit.,* p. 60.
[44]*Ibid.,* p. 59.
[45]Burke, "Dramatism," *op. cit.,* p. 448.

would be defined as 'the human body in conscious or purposive motion',"[46] in other words, an *agent acting* in a *situation*. For example, in a mental hospital (scene) one would expect to find insane acts performed by insane agents; and conversely, one would also expect that agents who are insane and so act are properly found in mental hospitals. The correspondence between the pentadic terms is transitive. In this example, we can see that these ratios (linguistically based expectancies) provide guidance for people unsure of how to act in a situation (like a mental hospital), a framework with which to understand and explain the interaction around them, and justification for bringing some consistency into a situation which may lack it. Thus, in addition to their analytic contribution here, dramatistic ratios make explicable placing people into mental hospitals whom we find to be insane. Whether or not such action makes any therapeutic sense, it does bring the situation into line with the cultural expectancies that are encoded in the linguistic structure of mind.

When Burke is analyzing something, he is trying to come to an understanding of its *substance,* its essence, which is equal to the sum of its connotational attributes. Thus, the ratios are used as heuristics to locate the essences of concepts or (methodically) of action. When one views the ratios as tools for uncovering the substance of terms, or the substance of action, i.e., when they are used so as to focus on one of the pentadic terms as it is affected by all the others; when a dialectic of many beginnings, many investigative starts, is used, then it is helpful to follow William Rueckert's lead and take the many ratios as reducible to but four distinct terminological emphases which get at essence, at essential definitions, in different ways.[47]

The first of these four, *contextual definition,* locates the essence of objects (concepts, processes, conduct) in their setting, for example, the use of "organizational climate" as an independent variable. *Genetic definition* locates substance in the origins of things; this can be exemplified in the explanation of a son's occupational status by reference to the father's occupational status. The third of these, *directional (entelechial) definition,* treats essence as a trend or the perfection of a process; this is clearly what Marx is doing when he conceives of the perfecting, the transcending, of the class struggle in the trend toward the revolution and the establishment of a classless society. The last of these four is uniquely Burke's, encompassing the other three, converting contextual, genetic and directional substance into *dialectical essence.* All *terms* locating substance in background, origins, or trends can be shown to form part of a cluster of terms that are related to each other by Burke's use of a dialectic of merger and division, similarity and difference.

---

[46]Burke, *A Grammar of Motives, op. cit.,* p. 74.
[47]William Rueckert, *Kenneth Burke and the Drama of Human Relations* (Minneapolis, 1963), pp. 153-154.

This pursuit of dialectical substance is perhaps the most fundamental operation in Burke's logic of inquiry. With it, he argues, terms of explanation and justification may be shown to cluster together about some master term. For example, in *A Grammar of Motives,* he spends much time arguing that the metaphysical positions of various philosophical schools may be explained as a result of their clustering around a master term (in this case drawn from the pentad); idealism around *Agent,* pragmatism around *Agency,* materialism around *Scene,* and so on.[48] It is here, perhaps, that his logic of inquiry is weakest; there are no explicit rules for accomplishing this analysis of clusters of motivational terms. Yet this particular procedure is central to his work, for he claims that it is the dialectical substance of clusters of any explanatory terms which implies "logically" all the other parts. Thus, an explanation of human action which draws upon one term in any cluster will bring all the other terms to bear upon the explanation through a kind of connotive logic. And further, insofar as the mind is social, is built from, among other things, the motivational commonplaces of a particular social order, then the connotational relations in the cluster become a motivational (explanatory) resource for the individual person. Willy nilly, people are drawn to explain and justify their acts, to urge themselves and others to act, by the internal logic of these dialectical clusters.

Indeed, one of these clusters, "order" (the cluster of terms which are connotatively implicit in this concept), contains, for Burke, the whole drama of human relations—contains, therefore, the essence of the human condition. Through his analysis of the connotations of the term "order," Burke tries to show that the substance of the human social realm is that of an hierarchial order held together by norms, where both hierarchy and norms are rooted in property interests and stabilized by processes of scapegoating through which the reality and morality of the hierarchial order are affirmed.[49] It is the centrality, therefore, of this dialectical procedure which makes Burke's omission of any set of rules for the use of the technique (save the heuristic employment of the pentad) so problematic for his methodic position. However, a careful search of Burke's writings does provide some lead as to the overall critical method he proposes, at least with respect to literature.[50] We must not forget that Burke developed dramatism as a system for the analysis of action (and terms about action) out of a method of literary criticism. His remarks here may be taken, therefore, as a basis for understanding his general method. For Burke, any kind of literary work, any kind of symbolic action, can be analyzed as "dream," "prayer," or "chart," i.e., in terms of its

---

[48]Burke, *A Grammar of Motives, op. cit.,* pp. 127-317.
[49]Kenneth Burke, *A Rhetoric of Motives* (Berkeley, California, 1969), pp. 183-294, and Burke, *The Rhetoric of Religion, op. cit.,* pp. 172-272.
[50]Burke, *The Philosophy of Literary Form, op. cit.,* pp. 56-75, and Kenneth Burke, "Fact, Inference and Proof in the Analysis of Literary Symbolism," in Stanley Hyman, ed., *Terms for Order* (Bloomington, Indiana, 1964), pp. 145-172.

sub-conscious elements, its communicative aspects, or its efforts to give realistic meaning to a personal or social situation.[51] But in any of these cases, the essential facts in a literary work are its *words;* thus, the basic tool for analysis is a selected concordance of terms, a list of words with the frequency and context of their occurrence. From this list, the literary analyst's task is to develop an interpretation of the work's "solution" to some problem in the life of the artist or the society in which he lives.

In constructing an interpretation, Burke acknowledges that the analyst's fundamental assumptions about the social world must play a part. For, he says:

> Facing a myriad possible distinctions, he should focus on those that he considers important for social reasons. Roughly, in the present state of the world we should group these about the 'revolutionary' emphasis involved in the treatment of art with primary reference to symbols of authority, their acceptance and rejection.[52]

Burke also outlines some principles for the selection of words into the "concordance," which are of interest in that they give an idea as to why he focuses on one word rather than another; but they do not help to explicate the relation *between* words, which is crucial to understanding word clusters. Indeed, when he summarizes the essay and its methodological advice, he says to "look for *moments* at which in your opinion, the work comes to *fruition.* Imbue yourself with the terminology of these moments. And spin from them."[53] But it is precisely this "spinning" for which we are trying to discover a logic; it is "spinning" which is his technique for constructing dialectical clusters.

We are not completely without guidance. There is one important clue to the criteria for the relations between words, which may be found in Burke's comment:

> We consider synecdoche to be the basic process of representation, as approached from the standpoint of 'equations' or 'clusters of what goes with what.' To say that one can substitute part for whole, whole for part, container for the thing contained, thing contained for the container, cause for effect, or effect for cause, is simply to say that both members of these pairs belong in the same associational cluster.[54]

"[S]ince substitution is a prime resource available to symbol systems...,"[55] and if the synecdoche is the basis for relations within dialectical clusters, then I would argue that it is to the peculiar logic of the dream, as

---

[51]Burke, *The Philosophy of Literary Form, op. cit.,* pp. 6-7, 241-243.
[52]Burke, *Attitudes Toward History, op. cit.,* p. 200.
[53]Burke, "Fact, Inference and Proof in the Analysis of Literary Symbolism," *op. cit.,* p. 167.
[54]Burke, *The Philosophy of Literary Form, op. cit.,* p. 65.
[55]Burke, "Dramatism," *op. cit.,* p. 450.

understood by Freud,[56] and to the techniques of free association,[57] that we should look to understand the process of dialectical substance. The logical relations in the dream are different from the logic of consciousness. In the dream, logical connections are represented by temporal simultaneity, causal relationships, by the transformation of a causal object into its effect, by the suppression of "either/or," and most importantly, as Freud notes, by the fact that "Dreams feel themselves at liberty... to represent any element by its wishful contrary."[58] The dream is characterized most fundamentally, in fact, by synecdoche and an ironic dialectic of opposites.

Now while, admittedly, Burke's discussion of the logic of the dream, particularly the concepts of "condensation" and "displacement," which he appropriates as "the tendency of one event to become the synecdochic representative of some other event in the same cluster,"[59] takes place in the context of his analysis of his analysis of subconscious elements of poetry (the poem as dream), the synecdoche is the fundamental relational process of his connotational logic, *tout court*. It is the synecdoche together with three other tropes, metonymy, metaphor, and irony, which serve as the *relata* between motivational (explanatory) terms. Thus, in the exploration of the relations within dialectical clusters, terms are shown to be related as parts to wholes, as tangibles for intangibles, by representation, and in paradox and contradiction.[60] Which is to say that, loosely speaking, it is a "figurative" or "metaphorical" logic which underpins the connotational organization of terms in particular dialectical clusters.

Perhaps these comments will become clearer if I provide an example of Burke's own application of a dramatistic procedure to a situation in which his assumptions about the interrelationship of language, mind and action are used to frame the interpretation of a complex social action. Burke claims that, just as language is the unique human capacity, and the mind is formed out of the social process (which is one of communication), so the principles of mental functioning (and the symbolic and social action in which it results) are built on the syntactic and semantic qualities of particular languages.[61] Thus, grammars of motivational terms can also be treated as grammars of human action.

Burke's explanation for the rise of Christian anti-Semitism in Nazi Germany seems a useful example of his method, although no claims are made that this analysis is empirically substantiated. For Burke, as for others like Lipset (1963), anti-Semitism is an example of scapegoating. Burke is here addressing the same problem as social scientists, the correlation between

---

[56] Sigmund Freud, *The Interpretation of Dreams* (New York, 1965).
[57] Burke, *The Philosophy of Literary Form, op. cit.*, p. 229.
[58] Freud, *op. cit.*, p. 353.
[59] Burke, *The Philosophy of Literary Form, op. cit.*, p. 239.
[60] Burke, *A Grammar of Motives, op. cit.*, pp. 503-517.
[61] The parallels here with G. H. Mead, Sapir-Whorf, and the symbolic interactionist tradition, are obvious.

economic depression and anti-Semitism. The problem is familiar to sociologists; it is his analysis which will appear unusual. Let me quote Burke's analysis at some length so that readers may appreciate the flavor of his work and have the text to refer to as I try to provide a fuller explication:

> Economic depression means psychologically a sense of frustration. The sense of frustration means psychologically a sense of persecution. The sense of persecution incites, compensatorily, a sense of personal worth, or goodness, and one feels that this goodness is being misused. One then 'magnifies' this sense of wronged goodness by identification with a hero. And who, with those having received any Christian training in childhood, is the ultimate symbol of persecuted goodness? 'Christ.' And who persecuted Christ? The Jews. Hence, compensatorily admiring oneself as much as possible, in the magnified version of a hero (the hero of one's first and deepest childhood impressions) the native Christian arrives almost 'syllogistically' at anti-Semitism as the 'symbolic solution' of his economically caused frustrations.[62]

Of course, one could see this argument as nothing more than an attempt to fill out the linkages concealed by the "frustration-aggression" hypothesis, and, given Burke's familiarity with Freud, it may well be that this particular explanation of aggressive behavior was a stimulating influence in Burke's development of his own more elaborate theory. Nonetheless, we will not get far in understanding this example of Burke's analytic technique if we treat him as a plagiarizer of Freud. Nor would it greatly assist this illustration of the figurative logic of dramatism if we were to use the merger and division technique, as does Burke himself in a later volume.[63] On the other hand, if we reconstruct this argument and try to amplify the links in the argument by appeal to the pentadic ratios, it may help to bring out the mixture of metaphorical, "logical," *relata* in the theory.

Economic depression leads to psychological frustration. When the *scene* for people is economic depression, then the *acts* of *agents* who take that scene as their frame will exhibit depressive qualities, like frustration, in consistency. Thus is enacted the correspondence of *Scene-Act, Scene-Agent* ratios. When frustration is taken, in its turn, as the scene, the context, for agents acting, it offers only a very limited and constrained frame within which to understand and justify one's ability to act (or rather one's *inability* to act), and this leads to a "Why me?" attitude. The compensatory way in which a sense of persecution can lead to a sense of personal worth and "wronged goodness" appears to be an operation of antithesis: people could equally well be depressed by a sense of persecution. Thus, a feeling of persecution, when it leads to a sense of increased self worth, is achieved

---

[62]Burke, *Attitudes Toward History, op. cit.,* pp. 168-169.
[63]Burke, *A Grammar of Motives, op. cit.,* pp. 406-408.

through the logic of opposites. Compare the ironies of the Sermon on the Mount: the progression to a sense of "wronged goodness" is accomplished through an *Agent-Scene* consistency—good people, good agents, are treated well, operate against a good scene.

From this point, the argument is somewhat more obvious! By identification with the hero-figure, persecuted individuals are able to make their own feelings consequential on a broader scene. They can locate themselves in a cultural rather than personal context: But why Jesus? The subsumption of terms under the connotative influence of a master term is one of the most important elements in motivational grammar. In much the same way that terms "transcend" the things they represent, there is a tendency in grammars of motive to "transcend" motivational (explanatory) terms with one summary, essential, "God term." What more appropriate "God term" for the hero, as a motive, than "Jesus" could we find? The individuals and Christ are now "condensed" for the individuals' motivational understanding of the economic depression. Their sufferings are now synecdochically involved with Christ; they are part of the whole that is Jesus. The rest flows, Burke remarks, "almost 'syllogistically.'" When the individuals *are* Christ, and are identified with him "essentially," then the persecutors, equally "essentially," are the persecutors of Christ: the Jews.

This illustrative reconstruction from Burke's work, selected for its sociological topic, does pose the two questions that remain to be asked about dramatism. First, how are we to separate the methodic use of this system from its employment as a meta-method (as an analytic device for examining explanatory terms)? The illustration, of course, is methodic in character; it implies that this account of anti-Semitism is a description of the process through which individual Germans came to hold their position. Nonetheless, it would take little effort to suggest that, whether or not this description was empirically substantiated, the connotational relations of the terms used by the analyst could produce that same analytic description. Method and meta-method are entwined. Indeed, from another perspective, the distinction between dramatism as a method and as a meta-method could be eliminated, and both modes of analysis could be treated as procedures for interpreting explanations of human action that are different only in terms of the audiences to which these motivational accounts are addressed. Thus, what has been called the *meta-methodic* use of dramatism may be viewed as a sociological procedure for interpreting explanations of action offered to a *sociological audience,* and what has been termed the *methodic* use may be seen as a sociological procedure for interpreting explanations of action (and hence action itself) offered to *any audience other than a sociological one.*[64] In both cases, however, the dramatistic logic of inquiry is directed to the interpretation and analysis of *explanations (motivational accounts),* and the

---

[64]See further, Zollschan and Overington, *op. cit.*

dramatistic procedures of analysis are the same. Thus, in assessing the utility of dramatism, it makes little difference if we draw a distinction between its employment as method or as meta-method.

This moves us to the second, and perhaps more important question, one that relates directly to the sociological efficacy of dramatism. Is there a practical limit, a limit that would make analytic sense, to the kinds of descriptive accounts that could be spun out of the terms of this illustration, or, more generally, *out of any set of analytic terms?* Certainly there is no reason to scorn the pentad as a guiding rule for the critique of analyses of human action. Indeed, Zollschan and Overington (1975) have exhibited the pentad's utility as a rule for assessing the theoretic generality of theories of motivation. Yet, the actual operation of such dramatistic *critiques* of explanations, as well as dramatistic *explanations* themselves through the development of *dialectical clusters of terms,* raises problems.

Clearly, the connotational *relata* of synechdochy, metonymy, metaphor, and irony, which constitute the internal logic of dialectical clusters, precisely because of their figurative (metaphoric) character, make it possible for individuals to present highly personal analyses of explanations for human action. What makes terms *relative* as parts for wholes, as tangibles for intangibles, as representational, and as contradictions is manifestly dependent upon what metaphoric connotations they have for a particular user of the dramatistic critique. Fortunately, we can assume that these figurative *relata* will not be merely idiosyncratic; nonetheless, they will be influenced by the analyst's experience. Yet, surely, this need not condemn the dramatistic logic of inquiry to the realm of the intra-subjective and the merely personal.

Although Burke's discussion of the analysis of literary work, in "Fact, Inference and Proof in the Analysis of Literary Symbolism", may well not be directly applicable here, it does provide a guide to the production of evidence within the dramatistic logic of inquiry. Whatever the nature of a particular dramatistic interpretation, however a person spins the analysis of some explanation of human action (whether that be addressed to a sociological or some other audience), the *text* of the explanation (the motivational account) is always available as a concrete "fact" from which to generate rival interpretations. And here, is the dramatistic analyst worse off than *any* sociologist engaged in the reconstruction, the representation, of another's theory? Are there rules comparable to those applied in the reconstruction of survey, observational, or experimental evidence that one can use in the reconstruction of theories (explanations) of action? Some sociologists have argued that since there are rules for any theorizing *that is addressed to a sociological audience* (usually they mean constructing logically well-formed propositions that are "testable"), one should reconstruct such theorizing according to these same rules. Others have made a practice of reconstructing some aspect of another's explanation so that it will organize a data set with little attention to the relationship that these selected aspects bear to the totality of the other's work. To a degree, therefore, there are rules that some follow in the reconstruction of theories (explanations) that are addressed to sociologists. Nonetheless, the majority of such reconstructions follow neither of the patterns that we have portrayed and rely instead upon the plausibility secured by the interpretation in relation to its audience. Certainly, we know little or nothing about the rules for achieving this plausibility. Our studies of the rhetoric of sociology are barely nascent.

And so to repeat the question: "Is the dramatistic analyst worse off than *any* sociologist engaged in the reconstruction, the representation, of another's theory?" If we restrict the answer to those theories (explanations of action) addressed to a sociological audience, then I believe the answer to be "No." In the first place, we do not know what the rules are for presenting plausible reconstructions (unless stylistic familiarity or sociological fashionability be crucial!); a dramatistic reconstruction has as much *a priori* plausibility as any other interpretation that could be generated with the text. In the second place, to match the claimed reconstructive adequacy of well-formed and testable propositions (either in interrelated nets or wrenched out of any context), the dramatistic logic of inquiry proposes its own criteria. These are twofold. First, identify the key analytic terms in the explanation; and second, explore the connotational links in dialectical clusters formed by these key analytic terms under the pentadic rubric (Remember that "In any rounded statement about motives, you must have some word that names . . . [the act, scene, agent, agency, and purpose]."[65] Performing both of these tasks leads to a rounded dramatistic analysis, and, insofar as the original explanation of action (theory) is inadequately developed with respect to the pentad, makes a dramatistic critique possible.

Thus, to answer our original question as to the possibility of a limit on the dramatistic spinning out of connotational *relata,* it is possible to indicate three limiting factors. First, the text as a "fact" imposes an overall framework within which these dialectical clusters may be explained. Second, the aim of the dramatistic analyst, to spin out the pentadic terms through an exploration of these clusters, directs the analysis. Finally, the audience to whom the dramatistic analysis is directed provides a culture within which some connotations will be more acceptable (perhaps because they are more familiar and fashionable?), and hence the analysis more plausible.

However, although these same three factors provide practical limits in the dramatistic analysis of motivational (explanatory) frameworks that are *not* addressed to sociologists, they do not offer guidance in the sampling of motivational discourse that is to become the "text" for the inquiry. Of course, such a sampling problem does not arise with motivational frameworks (explanations of action) that are offered to a sociological audience. But when it comes to an attempt to analyze the frameworks of motives that members of some group, organization, institution, or even a whole culture[66] employ in

---

[65]Burke, *A Grammar of Motives, op. cit.,* p. xv.
[66]For example, see Burke, *Attitudes Toward History, op. cit.,* pp. 111-165.

explaining their completed or proposed actions, we are very much in need of some rules for sampling. These the dramatistic logic of inquiry fails to offer, and Burke's own practice suggests little more than the rhetorical techniques of example and illustration as procedures for sampling. These are certainly not adequate as systematic rules for selecting items of motivational discourse from socially bounded universes of motivational talk. Yet, surely we have enough theories of sampling in use among sociologists engaged in observational, experimental, and survey research to provide some basis for sampling items of motivational discourse from motivational frameworks. This defect of dramatism is hardly crippling!

We have traced the development of dramatism as a method of inquiry into motivational (explanatory) frameworks of all kinds, from its early formulation as an emancipatory analytic counterpoint against motivational frameworks that serve the interests of property to its last change into an internally self-sufficient procedure for uncovering the connotational influences on explanations of action (particularly, sociological explanatory terminologies). This change (from a "tentative Marxism" to an essential perspectivism) is the last stage in Burke's struggle to formulate a general system for the analysis of motives and language. In this final transformation, he isolates language from its embedment in patterns of interaction in order to treat the "purely" linguistic relationships among words. Of course, such a treatment has to assume the cultural actuality of the metaphorical *relata* through which analysis takes place, much as Lévi-Strauss has to presume the actuality of a binary logic for his analysis of myth.[67] Sociologists concerned to utilize a dramatistic logic of inquiry must decide for themselves whether they will use it to study the purely internal relations of motives and language, or whether they will employ it in an examination of the social and economic roots of motivational discourse. The procedures for analyzing motivational frameworks will be the same in either case.

Clearly, the present brief exposition has not provided an inventory of the techniques to be used in a dramatistic analysis; that was not its purpose. Indeed, from the dearth of sociological commentary on dramatism, it would appear that no sociological audience is yet available for the monographic length that such completeness would entail. Here, rather, we have examined the sociological pertinence of Burke's work through a concentration on the intersubjectivity of his methodology. This intersubjectivity is a necessary condition for the sociological import of dramatism. It is reasonable to conclude from the present reconstruction that dramatism does provide such an intersubjective method for the analysis and critique of explanations of action. Dramatism meets the necessary condition for its sociological importance. Only time will tell if that necessary condition is also "sufficient."

---

[67]See Edmund Leach, *Claude Lévi-Strauss* (New York, 1970).

References

Burke, Kenneth, *The Philosophy of Literary Form*, New York: Vintage, 1957.

Burke, Kenneth, *Attitudes Toward History*, Boston: Beacon Press, 1959.

Burke, Kenneth, "Fact, Inference and Proof in the Analysis of Literary Symbolism," in Stanley Hyman, ed., *Terms for Order*, Bloomington, Indiana: Indiana University Press, 1964, pp. 145-172.

Burke, Kenneth, *Permanence and Change*, Indianapolis, Indiana: Bobbs-Merrill, 1965.

Burke, Kenneth, *Language as Symbolic Action*, Berkeley: University of California Press, 1966.

Burke, Kenneth, *Counterstatement*, Berkeley: University of California Press, 1968a.

Burke, Kenneth, "Dramatism," *International Encyclopedia of the Social Sciences*, New York: Macmillan, 1968b, pp. 445-452.

Burke, Kenneth, *A Grammar of Motives*, Berkeley: University of California Press, 1969a.

Burke, Kenneth, *A Rhetoric of Motives*, Berkeley: University of California Press, 1969b.

Burke, Kenneth, *The Rhetoric of Religion*, Berkeley: University of California Press, 1970.

Lipset, Seymour Martin, "The Sources of the Radical Right," in Daniel Bell, ed., *The Radical Right*, Garden City, New York: Anchor Books, 1963.

Part Two:
A Focus on Critical and
Philosophical Issues

Kenneth Burke's Prolegomena to the Study of the Rhetoric of Form

by Richard B. Gregg

Rhetorical analysts have had difficulty dealing with phenomena of form. Kenneth Burke's ideas regarding the rhetoric of form provide a productive way to begin to conceptualize and analyze the rhetoric of form. Burke traces human forming from the most fundamental level of tacit symbolic "fixing" through more sophisticated kinds of systemic "knowing" to the manipulating of technical forms for the purpose of evoking response. Certain critical operations to account for the rhetoric of form are appropriate in view of Burke's conceptualization.

Questions concerning the nature of form and how to treat it in analysis have long vexed rhetorical critics. In his discussion of criticism, Arnold says, "There are, we must confess, more mysteries than rules about how structures and forms modify explicit contents of discourse."[1] Yet an attempt to shunt aside the mysteries with the observation that the content of a message, what is said, is more important than its form "ignores the fact that we all speak through structures and forms."[2] Arnold suggests that part of the difficulty may be caused by critical perspectives which picture an oversimplified bifurcation of the concepts of "content" and "form." The result is a conceptual misdirection that leads away from an understanding of how structures or forms "mean." In a more positive vein, Arnold describes "form" as emerging shape which transcends pattern, "the outcome of selecting stimuli, noting and perhaps 'editing' their structures, and blending the information with experience to create a more or less holistic perception of 'what it's all about.'"[3]

Years ago John Dewey related forms in art to human perception and experience:

> This is what it is to have form. It marks a way of envisaging, of feeling, and of presenting experienced matter so that it most readily and effectively becomes material for the construction of adequate experience on the part of those less gifted than the original creator.

Reprinted from *Communication Quarterly* 26 (1978), with permission of the Eastern Communication Association.
[1] Carroll C. Arnold, *Criticism of Oral Rhetoric* (Columbus: Charles E. Merrill, 1974), p. 105.
[2] Arnold. p. 103.
[3] Arnold, p. 133.

Hence, there can be no distinction drawn, save in reflection, between form and substance.[4]

There is a noticeable similarity between the perspectives on form offered by Arnold and Dewey; both conceive form to function in ways more significant than the simple "arrangement of materials" view. To think of form as "shape which transcends pattern" or as "a way of envisaging" suggests that we must somehow conceive of form as shaped meaning which may emerge and be perceived in messages by readers or listeners or viewers. To fully understand that forms mean and that all meaning is formed is to bring together what we have heretofore thought of as form and content into a conceptual whole. And such a conceptualization relates form in significant ways to the processes of invention and judgment which are at the heart of the rhetorical act.

Kenneth Burke, in his voluminous writings, has discussed the rhetoric of form in ways compatible with the perspective outlined above. He believes that one of the primary tests of any critical method is its ability to account for form,[5] and there is a sense in which all of Burke's work is devoted to the exploration of symbolic form. Burke's definition of form reveals his rhetorical orientation: "*Form* in literature is an arousing and fulfillment of desires."[6] The appeal of form, says Burke, is correct "in so far as it gratifies the needs which it creates. The appeal of form in this sense is obvious: form *is* the appeal."[7]

Because Burke emphasizes the importance of form, because he never conceptualizes in ways that encourage bifurcation, and because he is interested in the rhetorical function of form, it would seem profitable to examine his ideas regarding form systematically. I propose to undertake such an examination in this paper, with an eye toward understanding what Burke means by "form," what assumptions underlie his position, and what implications for critical method issue therefrom.

Form and Symbolic Behavior

Kenneth Burke's treatment of the rhetoric of form rests upon a basic assumption about the way perception and conceptualization occur. Such concretized and individuated manifestations of form as those experienced in literature or rhetorical discourse partake of the more general, generative, and foundational nature of symbolic form structured by the human mind interacting with its external environment. Several passages from Burke's writings reveal the close association he sees between natural phenomena and symbolic form:

---

[4] John Dewey, *Art As Experience* (New York: G. P. Putnam's Sons, 1958, 3rd impression), p. 109.
[5] Kenneth Burke, *A Rhetoric of Motives* (Cleveland: The World Publishing Co., 1962), p. 686.
[6] *Counterstatement* (Chicago: University of Chicago, 1957, 2nd ed.), p. 124.
[7] *Counterstatement*, p. 138.

> There are formal patterns which distinguish our experience. They apply in art since they apply outside of art. The accelerated motion of a falling body, the cycle of a storm, the gradations of a sunrise, the stages of a cholera epidemic, the ripening of crops—in all such instances we find the material of processional form.[8]

Or again:

> The appeal of form as exemplified in rhythm enjoys a special advantage in that rhythm is more closely allied with 'bodily' processes. Systole and diastole, alternation of the feet in walking, inhalation and exhalation, up and down, in and out, back and forth, such are the types of distinctly motor experiences 'tapped' by rhythm. Rhythm is so natural to the organism that even a succession of uniform beats will be interpreted as a succession of accented and unaccented beats.[9]

We must follow Burke's thinking closely here, for he is not assuming a simple stimulus-response action between man and his environment in which the forms of human cognition grow from sensory awareness. Rather, he assumes man is an active shaper of his knowing. Take, for example, the rather complex notion of crescendo or climax. Burke finds the history of art replete with various arrangements of material embodying the principle of crescendo; that is, they are arrangements distinguished in perception as crescendo. In the natural environment, says Burke, there is no such thing as crescendo, only arrangements susceptible to a perceptual configuration of crescendo or climax. The frequent embodiment of the principle in works of art testifies to the fact that we think in terms of crescendo because such a configuration "parallels certain psychic and physical processes which are at the roots of our experience."[10] Crescendo is but one example of the kind of arrangement or process which is a part of man's perceptual capacity and Burke specifies such others as contrast, comparison, balance, repetition, disclosure, reversal, contraction, expansion, magnification, and series. These are potentialities of appreciation which "would seem to be inherent in the very germ-plasm of man,"[11] and which . . . are not passive, but functionally active phenomena, or commands "to act in a certain way."[12] Thus, when a display of materials is perceived in the configuration of a crescendo, man has performed a mental act upon those materials which forms them in the pattern of crescendo. And by the act of forming, the materials are rendered comprehensible and are comprehended. Burke's perspective on symbolic

---

[8] *Counterstatement,* p. 141.
[9] *Counterstatement,* p. 140.
[10] *Counterstatement,* p. 45.
[11] *Counterstatement,* p. 46.
[12] *Counterstatement,* p. 142.

form: (1) holds that the human "knows" when his perceptual act provides shape to the content of experience and consciousness so that, in a single stroke, what we distinguish as form and content are cast together in complementary, holistic fashion; (2) emphasizes the "action" principle of a perceptual act, thus underscoring the creativity of human forming, the functional aspect of such creativity, and the mediational nature of form. From this perspective form takes on epistemological significance, for we are carried to the level of symbolic activity where fundamental formings, orderings, and integrating processes occur. Here may be found those principles of form that underlie all individuations of forming including the rhetorical function because forming constitutes human actions guided by purposes and characterized by consequent directional stances.[13] As we shall see, Burke distinguishes between the natural symbolic level of fundamental forming and the artistic activity by which materials are manipulated to achieve certain effects of arrangement. But he never forgets that the natural human disposition to form, and the principles underlying that disposition, reach upward and outward to permeate all forms of, and in, discourse, and carry with them the psychological potential for being induced, entertained, and gratified by the manifestations of form.

Form and Language

Burke's discussion of language constantly moves back and forth between the level of fundamental symbolic forming, where principles inherent in man's symbolic nature are constraining, and the level of purposeful manipulation of language forms, where considerable technical and artistic freedom may be exercised. Language is one of man's symbol systems, and therefore necessarily incorporates the essential formative characteristics of symbolism in general. Thus, language is one of man's means of creating fixed contents and patterns of consciousness. It can do more than just represent the contents of experience; it can present experiential contents in the forms of

---

[13]Burke's probe to the symbolic foundation of form in general to illuminate rhetorical form in particular seems justified by Ernst Cassirer's comprehensive theory of symbolic forms. Cassirer undertakes to explore the medium through which all configurations of cultural life pass. In his view, man brings chaos out of the constant flow of impressions around him by acting upon those impressions in an inherently symbolic way. The result of the action is the creation of contents of consciousness which comprise man's reality. "The fluid impression assumes form and duration for us only when we *mould* it by symbolic action in one direction or another. In science and language, in art and myth, this formative process proceeds in different ways and according to different principles, but all these spheres have this in common: that the product of their activity in no way resembles the mere *material* with which they began." Ernst Cassirer, *The Philosophy of Symbolic Forms*, Vol. I (New Haven: Yale University Press, 1955), 107. To appreciate the depth and scope of Cassirer's work, one must read all three volumes under this title. Vol. I, *Language;* Vol. II, *Mythical Thought:* and Vol. III, *The Phenomenology of Knowledge.* Although Cassirer's work supports and enriches the ideas of Burke explicated in this paper, Burke was not directly influenced by Cassirer. He has not read the three volumes, though he did read Cassirer's *Language and Myth* and reviewed *Myth of the State.* Personal correspondence to the author, May 14, 1977.

original shapings. It is, as Burke indicates, considerably more than a sensory significance.

> Symbols are not merely reflections of the things symbolized, or signs for them: they are to a degree a *transcending* of the things symbolized. So, to say that man is a symbol-using animal is by the same token to say that he is a "transcending animal." Thus, there is in language itself a motive force calling man to transcend the "state of nature."[14]

Burke's thinking corresponds with that of Cassirer, who states that the function of language is not to repeat distinctions and definitions but to make them intelligible by formulating them. Such formulations have a bond with the sensory on the one hand, while refining and surpassing it on the other. "Language shows itself to be *at once* a sensuous and an intellectual form of expression."[15]

Burke's treatment of several of the shapings of consciousness encouraged by language reflects his awareness of this duality of language form. He believes, for example, that synecdoche, wherein a part of a meaning context represents the whole, is typical of language meaning because it is one of the basic forms of all symbolic meaning, and he perceives it occurring in many variations other than just the conventional trope. Likewise, the cognitive strategies that search out and create perceptual and conceptual similarities are pervasive symbolic maneuvers, and are manifest on a continuum from simple comparison to subtle metaphor. "A 'metaphor' is a concept, an abstraction— but a specific metaphor, exemplified by specific images, is an 'individuation.' Its appeal as form resides in the fact that its particular subject matter enables the mind to follow a metaphor process."[16] Here, Burke's emphasis is on the metaphoric process as it occurs at the primal symbolic level, though his reference to individuation points us toward the level of artistic manipulation. He emphasizes the manipulative use of the metaphorical principle when he talks of "coaching" the transference of words from one category of associations to another, or the kind of "casuistic stretching which allows us to speak of a 'broadcast network' or the 'head of a corporation.' "[17]

---

[14]Burke, *A Rhetoric of Motives,* p. 716.

[15]Cassirer, Vol. I, p. 319. See also pp. 105-114.

[16]Burke, *Counterstatement,* p. 143. Burke is one among a large number of scholars from various disciplines who believe metaphor to be one of the most fundamental symbolic processes. Gadamer, for example, writes of metaphor in a way very like Burke's metaphorical continua: "Even disregarding all formal similarities that have nothing to do with the generic concept, if a person transfers an expression from one thing to the other, he has in mind something that is common to both of them, but this need not be in any sense generic universality. He is following, rather, this widening experience, which sees similarities, whether of the appearance of an object, or of its significance for us. It is the genius of linguistic consciousness to be able to give expression to the similarities. This is its fundamental metaphorical nature, and it is important to see that it is the prejudice of a theory of logic that is alien to language if the metaphorical use of a word is regarded as not its real sense." Hans Georg Gadamer, *Truth and Method* (New York: The Seabury Press, 1975), pp. 388-389.

[17]Burke, *Attitudes Toward History,* pp. 229-230.

We see in Burke's treatment of the linguistic forms of synecdoche and metaphor assumptions regarding certain principles of symbolic forming that guide his search for form in discourse. There are the creative principles of "thingness" and "attribution" which function symbolically to "fix" shape and image in accordance with certain perceived identifying characteristics. There is the principle of abstraction involved in the formistic removal of the contents of consciousness from the constant flux of sensory stimuli. And these principles, when coupled with the symbolic strategy of perceiving similarity, give man the powers of assimilation and separation, comparison and contrast, analysis and synthesis, which underlie the construction of man's terministic screen. Now we begin to understand the peculiar force of the Burkean pairing of "identification-division" which he believes is central to all of man's symbolic knowing, and particularly his rhetorical activity.

> We have said that man, as a symbol-using animal, experiences a difference between *this* being and *that* being as a difference between *this kind* of being and *that kind* of being. Here is a *purely dialectical* factor at the very center of realism. Here, implicit in our attitudes toward things, is a principle of *classification.* And classification in this linguistic, or formal, sense is all-inclusive, "prior" to classification in the exclusively social sense. The "invidious" aspects of class arise from the nature of man not as a "class animal," but as a "classifying animal."[18]

Burke's reference to attitudes in his discussion of man's capacity for classification brings another of his continua into view, this one having to do with man's critical and evaluative action, which occurs within each phase of his symbolic behavior. At the primal stage, Burke believes that the very act of apprehension is an act of evaluation in which the mind seeks for and creates those perceptually "fixed" forms of consciousness which become the basis for all intellection.[19] There is purpose in the formative symbolic acts of creating distinctive, fixed meanings, prompted by the desire to comprehend. Comprehension contains within it the capacity for further action, for to "know" is to begin to know what to do with or about that which is comprehended. The logic of human symbolic capability leads to the production of language as we know it, and at the linguistic stage, the act of "fixing" terminologically, with its dialectical inclination to identify and divide, constitutes a critical act of a higher intellectual order. According to Burke,

---

[18]Burke, *A Rhetoric of Motives,* pp. 806-807.
[19]Once again, Burke's view corresponds to Cassirer's: "Every *apprehension* of a particular empirical thing or specific empirical occurrence contains within it an act of evaluation. . . . Thus the limits between the objective and the subjective are not rigidly determined from the first but are formed and determined only in the progressive development of experience and its theoretical principles. It is through a constantly renewed intellectual operation that what we call objective reality changes its shape and is re-created in a new form. This operation has essentially a *critical* character." *The Philosophy of Symbolic Forms,* Vol. II, p. 31.

linguistic naming can be thought of as the act of creating "frames of acceptance." "By 'frames of acceptance' we mean the more or less organized system of meaning by which thinking man gauges the historical situation and adopts a role with relation to it." And such behavior is constrained by evaluation and purpose, for names "prepare us *for* some functions and *against* others, *for* or *against* the persons representing those functions. The names go further: they suggest *how* you shall be for or against."[20] As Burke sees it, the critical-evaluative function is an inherent part of man's symbolic forming. It pervades those tacit symbolic strategies which effectuate the structures of man's reality, guides the various stages of language formation and use wherein terministic structures both reflect and shape perception, and reveals itself in the forms employed by the makers of discourse. In short and in sum, "the symbolic act is the *dancing of an attitude*."[21]

The critical action continuum is important to Burke's thinking about language and form. Man's symbolic formings on the primal level are creative and functional acts. These formings so shape the contents of consciousness that ways of knowing include ways of acting toward, operating on, behaving in terms of, in other words, ways of being. Linguistic symbols, following the principles of symbolizing in general, fix and present forms of knowing, being and doing.[22] A terminology is a beseechment to see things in certain ways and at the same time to adopt certain attitudinal and behavioral stances toward what is seen. For Burke, the forms of language are naturally hortatory, are intensely emotional and moral, and may be viewed as actions in and of themselves. Consequently, Burke is led, as a critic, to adopt what he calls a "dramatistic" as opposed to a "scientistic" approach to the study of language. A scientistic approach, explains Burke, puts primary stress upon the propositional form such as "it is" or "it is not." A dramatistic approach on the other hand places primary stress upon the hortatory form such as "thou shalt" or "thou shalt not." The scientistic approach, says Burke, "culminates in the kinds of speculation we associate with symbolic logic, while the dramatistic culminates in the kinds of speculation that find their handiest material in stories, plays, poems, the

---

[20]Burke, *Attitudes Toward History*, pp. 4-5.

[21]*The Philosophy of Literary Form* (Berkeley: University of California Press, 1973), p. 1.

[22]"Speech is communicative in the sense that it provides a common basis of feeling—or it is communicative in the sense that it serves as the common implement of action. In primitive societies these two functions are nearly identical: the emotional overtones of the tribal idiom stimulate the kinds of behavior by which the tribe works and survives. The word for the tribal enemies will contain the overtones of evil that reinforce the organization for combating the enemy. Or the words for the tribal purposes will contain favorable overtones which perpetuate the same purposes. By such an identity between the *communion* and *action* aspects of speech, the vocabulary of doing, thinking, and feeling is made an integer." *Permanence and Change* (New York: Bobbs-Merrill, 1965), pp. 175-176. An excellent critical essay which illustrates the co-active phenomena of knowing, doing, and being in rhetoric is Thomas W. Benson's, "Rhetoric and Autobiography: The Case of Malcolm X," *Quarterly Journal of Speech*, 60 (1974), 1-13.

rhetoric of oratory and advertising, mythologies, theologies, and philosophies after the classic model."[23]

Burke's discussion of "the negative," which he calls a "distinctive linguistic marvel" because it is language which allows man to develop the peculiar possibilities of the negative (the command—"No"; the reality—"Nothing"; the principle—"Negativity"; the attitude—"Negativism"; the doctrine "Nihilism"), emphasizes the actional-hortatory nature of linguistic form, and leads us to those phenomena of form and structure that round out his thinking. The negative, says Burke, is not generated from the impulse to define or inform, but from the urge to command, that is, to say "no."[24] As Burke sees it, the principle of negativity, in its hortatory nature, is implicit in all use of language. To use words properly, we must understand that the word is not what it stands for. There could not be the linguistic form of metaphor to fix the fundamental metaphorical processes of the mind if we did not accept that things are not literally what we say they are. There are whole styles of language usage which rely upon the negativity principle, as with irony, for example, which features the act of linguistic discount. For Burke, the negative lurks about all forms of linguistic meaning, because positive meaning is heightened by the opposing possibility of the negative while the concept of negativity gains potency from its opposition to the positive.[25]

The concept of negativity, whereby an essential aspect of linguistic meaning includes tacit recognition of opposition, diversity, and denial, constitutes a universal principle of dialectic, and has profound implications for the forms of human communication. "Every terminology is dialectical by sheer reason of the fact that it is a terminology."[26] Insofar as terms "name," they become partisan in their shaping of substantive meaning by magnifying some attributes of phenomena at the expense of others. "Even if every

---

[23]Burke, *Language As Symbolic Action*, pp.44-45. I. A. Richards, in his *Principles of Literary Criticism* (New York: Harcourt, Brace and World, 1925) agrees with the essence of Burke's remarks: "Poetry affords the clearest examples of this subordination of reference to attitude. It is the supreme form of *emotive* language. But there can be no doubt that originally all language was emotive; its scientific use is a later development, and most language is still emotive. Yet the late development has come to seem the natural and the normal use, largely because the only people to have reflected upon language were at the moment of reflection using it scientifically" p. 273.

[24]*Language As Symbolic Action*, p. 10.

[25]For Burke's thorough discussion of the importance of the negative, the reader is referred to *Language As Symbolic Action*, pp. 9-15 and in the same work, Chapter 7, "A Dramatistic View of the Origins of Language," pp. 419-479.

[26]*A Grammar of Motives* (New York: The World Publishing Co., 1962), p. 57. Burke's view of the inherently dialectical nature of language is widely shared. "The operation of binary contrast appears to be a linguistic fundamental to which the human mind is uniquely adapted. Binary pairs of adjectives appear in all languages and there are in English as well as related languages formal devices for inventing new adjectival contrasts. When we list the attributes which apply to a given concept, we nearly always imply that these attributes are to be thought of as being contrasted in an opposite state. The notion of opposition is a linguistic fundamental, and despite its dubious logical character, permeates all languages of the world." James Deese, *Psycholinguistics* (Boston: Allyn and Bacon, 1970), p. 103. Cassirer concludes that, "Indeed we find, in language taken as a whole, that every meaning is linked with its opposite, and that only the two together become an adequate expression of reality." *The Philosophy of Symbolic Forms*, Vol. I, p. 120.

terminology is a *reflection* of reality, by its very nature as a terminology it must be a *selection* of reality; and to this extent it must function also as a deflection of reality."[27] The symbolic act of linguistic assertion raises the possibilities of counter assertions, and the carrying out of a physical action implied by the assertion may call forth opposing actions. Thus, the dialectical principle within symbolic formation lies all across the spectrum of symbolic action. It occurs at the foundational level of symbolic action, where the contents of consciousness are shaped according to perceived phenomenal attributes in light of intention, resulting in a modification of the temporal flux. It pervades and constrains language symbols and systems as it heightens distinctions, emphasizes contrasts, and facilitates the expansion of contrasts into oppositions and contradictions. It is an ingredient in the larger systemic cognitions of peoples and cultures, and is discoverable in the forms of acts and artifacts we take to be the manifestations of a culture.[28]

"Perfection" and Hierarchy as Form

When we arrive at Burke's considerations of the forms of system, we discover that he has been tracking a principle of the internal logic of symbolization to its completion. In an early work, Burke discusses the guiding logic of "piety," which he describes as a "system-builder, a desire to round things out, to fit experiences into a unified whole. Piety is *the sense of what properly goes with what*."[29] In one of his essays, where he defines man, he includes the notion that man is "driven by perfection." This is a "formal lure," typified by the urge to round things out, to complete, to reach logical conclusions, to provide closure. "The principle of perfection is essential to the nature of language as motive. The mere desire to name something by its 'proper' name, or to speak a language in its distinctive ways is intrinsically 'perfectionist.'" Again, "A given terminology contains various *implications*, and there is a corresponding 'perfectionist' tendency for men to attempt to carry out those implications."[30]

This motive of piety, of seeking perfection, works its way along through man's formulation of orderings and systems where relationships of equality, subordination, and superordination get symbolically established. The forming principle underlying the orderings is that of "hierarchy" which shares equal status in Burke's perspective with the forms of "identification-division." As principle, hierarchy is ever present. "To say that hierarchy is inevitable is not to say that any particular hierarchy is inevitable: . . . But to say that the

---

[27] Burke, *Language As Symbolic Action*, p. 45.
[28] For example, Burke says, "although we tend to view religions as systems of internally generated doctrines, they are often *polar* terms, being best defined at a given time in history by some other doctrine they are *against*." *Language As Symbolic Action*, p. 397.
[29] *Permanence and Change*, p. 74.
[30] *Language As Symbolic Action*, pp. 16-19. Cassirer also discusses the perfection principle in linguistic systems. See *The Philosophy of Symbolic Forms*, Vol. I, p. 197.

hierarchic principle is indigenous to well-rounded human thinking is to state a very important fact about the rhetorical appeal of dialectical symmetry."[31]

In its most general sense, hierarchy simply refers to "order," a desire to perceive and conceive relationships, connections, parallelisms, cause and effect relationships, and so on. The evaluative and critical function of symbolic forming does not allow orderings to rest in a context of neutrality, however, but infuses the processes of systematizing with valuings. These strategies of hierarchy are the shapers of those contents of consciousness we refer to as "theory," "system," "ideology," "philosophy," and "religion." They lead to holistic forms which give contextual shape to individuated formings. And such shaped content can be dramatically summed up with ultimate terms like "justice," "law," "necessity," and "fate."[32]

Now we are able to sketch an overview of Burke's ideas concerning the nature of form. Man comprehends his environment as he symbolizes about it; that is, he forms images and perceptual patterns and conceptualizations in accordance with the constraints of symbolic capacity. Basic to symbolic capacity are such processes as the fixing of similarities, the shaping of contrasts, the designating of attributes, and the combined analytic-synthesizing movement of the mind which creates "wholeness-partness" understandings. The logic of symbolic strategies of fixing and associating, which incorporates the principle of rounding out, leads to patterns of completion in which the fundamental forms of consciousness are located. Each of these symbolic principles is characterized by great flexibility, and can fix and shape individuations of content in an endless variety of ways.

All of these movements of the mind are acts, characterized by purpose, critical capacity, and psychological consequence. To act is to form and to form is to act; the principles of forming are the principles of action, and they induce and modify future actions as they body forth attitudes and valuings. They may lead to further movements of the mind, or to physical activity, or both. As Burke makes clear, the stress may occur on either term in the phrase, "symbolic act." Activated as they are by intention, and constituting, as they do, actions, they will affect and be affected by such psychological states as fulfillment, gratification, and tension. They will, in fact, arouse and shape such psychological states. In the words of Burke, form will arouse and fulfill expectancies in some fashion; form has rhetorical impact even in its most fundamental dimensions. The Burkean schema provides us with a set of terms which are related by implication, and which we can use when trying to account for form. They are: act, action, intention, inducement, function,

---

[31]*A Rhetoric of Motives,* p. 665. Once again, Cassirer's discussion of the principle of hierarchy provides grounding for Burke's ideas. See his discussion of hierarchy in mythic thought in *The Philosophy of Symbolic Forms,* Vol. 2, p. 73 and pp. 235-261, and Vol. I, p. 118. Throughout Cassirer's discussion, the principle of hierarchy is clearly seen in development that proceeds from the designation of the concrete to the symbolization of the abstract. For example, see Vol. I, p. 190.
[32]*Language As Symbolic Action,* p. 127.

judgment, and fulfillment or gratification. These terms of psychologic not only relate to each other, but also interrelate with another set of terms which refer to the shaping principles of symbolic capacity: identification, division, dialectic, transcendence, order, hierarchy, and completion.

Following his urge for comprehension, man constructs symbols about symbols with each symbol system following the constraints of its own logic. The development of symbol systems provides man with the "tools" which allow him to perform as a technologist or artist as he further constructs his reality by manipulating his fundamental formings. And the rhetorical nature of form becomes more striking when Burke considers the technical and artistic manipulation of forms as they are strategized in discourse.

Symbolic Form and Technical Form

Symbolic form, intention and purpose, and artistry and technique are joined together as the artist (composer of music, maker of fiction, rhetor), works with his materials and tools to shape his product, whatever that might be. The shaping first occurs on the level of imagination and intellection, as the artist symbolizes for himself the moods and claims with which he comprehends situations. Then, he turns to the task of further shaping those private symbols into forms which render them accessible to the thoughts of others.

> If the artist were to externalize his mood of horror by imagining the facts of a murder, he would still have to externalize his sense of crescendo by the arrangement of these facts. In the former case he is individuating an "emotional form," in the latter a "technical form." And if the emotion makes for the consistency of his details, by determining their selection, technique makes for the vigor, or saliency, or power of the artwork by determining its arrangement.[33]

The artist's individual symbolizing provides the emotional and intellectual principles which will logically constrain the technical shaping of a work. In one instance, Burke exemplifies what he means and interrelates the purposes of artist and audience as he discusses the development of the character of Falstaff in Shakespeare's plays. As members of an audience listen to a few of Falstaff's speeches, and watch his characterization develop, they are able to arrive at a perceptual synthesis of Falstaff, to know something about the principles he stands for and his style of coping. Once the perceptual synthesis is formed, the audience knows what to expect of Falstaff each time he puts in an appearance, and enjoys watching ensuing individuated presentations of the Falstaffian synthesis.[34]

---

[33] *Counterstatement*, p. 51.
[34] *Counterstatement*, p. 61.

It will be helpful here to turn the dramatistic perspective on Burke's example, and taking it as a "representative anecdote," pause over it for a moment to understand his vision of form at work. Here we have a playwright, seeking to translate his individual motives, intentions, and claims into forms which will induce public participation. At the level of private rumination, the principles of primal forming discussed earlier are operative. Thus, identifications, divisions, relationships, affirmations, denials, are focused to fix contents of consciousness. These shapings bring certain principles of logical consistency to bear, and entail action constrained by a sense of completion. The playwright goes to work with the technical tools of his trade, language, action, and staging, to structure character, manipulate emotion, and develop and advance the claims we refer to as plot. Burke's example suits our rhetorical perspective very well, for the playwright must keep in mind that he is working on a public presentation and audience considerations must be reflected in his artistry. "In externalizing or impersonalizing his thesis, he seeks to translate it into a system of motivations which will be cogent with his readers, because these motivations belong to the general scientific *Weltanschauung* of his times."[35] If he is successful in his forming of individuated images, then certain ideas or principles are bodied forth in the characters he develops, and may be seized upon, re-translated, and synthesized by members of the audience, who thereafter use the synthesized form to anticipate and gauge the actions of the characters. The playwright creates expectancies with his materials, then fulfills those expectancies as he continues to illustrate character throughout the rest of the play.

We are led by Burke's example to note the several levels of forming involved in the playwright's work. There are the individuated formings of image and act which form larger patterns when perceived in juxtaposition. These large patterns are also forms; they present ideas, and shape and body forth motivational principles. A play is a vehicle of movement over time, as well as action within spatial scene, so that ideas and principles can modify as they develop, form oppositions and contradictions, coalesce to form larger summings-up, undergo reversal (wherein suddenly the imagery of the upward way changes identity to become the imagery of the downward way, or the movement to completion of form suddenly shatters into diversely individuated fragments), and build to an agonistic climax that demands psychological release in denouement. And when the play is over, and all of its actions summed up in retrospect, the actions can be perceived to have formed a holistic tableaux, a patterned phenomenon that can be described without retracing all of the lesser movements of shaping and action.

There is forming at every level of the playwright's work, from the discrete contents of consciousness that can be isolated to the holistic shape

---

[35]*Permanence and Change*, p. 24.

that sums them all up. What is of special interest to the critic of rhetorical discourse is that at each level form involves action, from those fundamental principles of symbolic forming that are covert, primal acts of the mind through the acting of principles and ideas in repetitive, progressive movement, to the summing up act of perceiving the forming structure which encompasses all. At each level, the action includes an inducement to participate; to participate is to act in terms of the building expectancies and to be gratified by the fulfillment provided. The inducement, in this Burkean perspective, is rhetorical; invitation to action involves critical and evaluative faculties at every level and is therefore partisan in stance and tone. The rhetorical outcome will take some manifestation from among the great variety possible on a continuum running from appreciation of a perspective to overt action in behalf of a cause. To accept this perspective is to agree with Burke that form is a "universal locus of appeal," a thoroughly rhetorical phenomenon.[36]

One final note before we move on to outline what all of this means for the rhetorical critic at work. In the Falstaff example, the fulfillment of expectancy is a fairly straight-forward proposition. The audience is led to expect a particular form, and gets it time and again. But the human is a highly complex being, and thus formistic gratification may be experienced in highly complex ways. Burke illustrates this innumerable times in his own critical analyses of various kinds of discourse; one instance will have to make the point for us here. In following the development of *Hamlet*, Burke notes that the appearance of the ghost of Hamlet's father is forecast in Scene 4 of Act I, but the ghost does not actually appear until an unexpected moment. Here is a case, says Burke, when satisfaction follows a temporary set of frustrations, and hence is more complex in form but also more intense where experienced.[37]

The Critique of Form

We indicated earlier that for Burke, the critical focus must be upon form and structure, and as we might surmise, Burke takes what he calls a "pragmatic" approach to critical analysis. It is an approach that assumes that a poem is "designed to 'do something' for the poet and his readers, and that we can make the most relevant observations about its design by considering the poem as the embodiment of this act."[38] From the pragmatic viewpoint, the work is approached "as the *functioning* of a structure (quite as you would make more relevant statements about the distribution of men and postures on a football field if you inspected this distribution from the standpoint of tactics

---

[36]*A Rhetoric of Motives*, p. 583.
[37]*Counterstatement*, pp. 29-30.
[38]*Philosophy of Literary Form*, p. 89.

for the attainment of the game's purposes)."[39]

To advance his critical purpose, Burke proposes what seems a simple formula, but simple only on first glance: the two primary symbols for charting the relationships of form are the "equals sign" and the "arrow." Simply put, "what equals what" would seem to place the critical focus on the identifications and divisions presented in a work, and "from what through what to what" upon the unfolding of such images in a work or a body of works. In the most general sense this is so, but as we watch Burke operate analytically it is obvious that he has his eye more closely attuned to the complex strategies of human forming than a straight-forward statement of his formula reveals. To get at the equations in a work, Burke first undertakes what he calls a "statistical" examination.[40] In other words, he will examine the individuated images that can be found in the work. He notes the way the images begin to gather in clusters, not necessarily in terms of which images occur in close juxtaposition in a work (though this may be important), but in terms of similarities of ideas bodied forth in the combined synecdochic representations of the images. At this level, we begin to see the arguings of form as we find what kind of image goes with what kind of act (style), what kind of act goes with what kind of scene (situation), and with what intention (motive). Now, a kind of hierarchic development may be perceived in a progression moving from individuated images to the level of ideas and on to the level of principle (goal, objective, purpose, value). At this point, Burke cautions the critic to watch for dramatic alignment; the equations must now be described in terms of what opposes what. We can note which images are in opposition, explicitly or implicitly, which acts are in opposition, which ideas are opposed, and which principles clash. Inducements and expectations of form should now be beginning to clarify. Clarification of these rhetorical ingredients of form is furthered as the critical focus couples the equation with the arrow, that is, as the dramatistic movement of "from what—through what—to what" is noted.

In his early book *Counterstatement,* Burke contended that the movements of form could be conceived to occur in terms of three principles; progressive form, repetitive form, and conventional form. He has adhered to this conceptualization in his own criticism since publication of that book. Repetitive form occurs when a principle is consistently maintained in the presentation of various individuated images and ideas. As Burke explains, a series of images may evoke the same mood, or sustain an attitude, or repeat the identity of a character. "By a varying number of details, the reader is led to feel more or less consciously the principle underlying them—he then requires that this principle be observed in the giving of further details."[41]

---

[39]*Philosophy of Literary Form,* p. 74.
[40]See pp. 18-33 for Burke's discussion and illustration of his "statistical" operation.
[41]*Counterstatement,* p. 125.

Progressive form becomes more complicated and follows two patterns, syllogistic progression and qualitative progression. Burke does not equate syllogistic progression with the syllogism of formal logic, though that is one of the forms it may take. Rather, Burke means any form of arguing which advances step by step such that if certain things are accepted certain things must follow, with the keenest manifestations of syllogistic progression being reversal, peripety. "Insofar as the audience, from its acquaintance with the premises, feels the rightness of the conclusion"[42] the syllogistic form is successful. Success is a rhetorical matter. Qualitative progression can become more subtle, warns Burke, for it is not a matter of incident or idea preparing us for another, but a matter of one quality preparing us for another "(the grotesque seriousness of the murder scene preparing us for the grotesque buffoonery of the porter scene)." These progressions lack the sharp anticipatory character of syllogistic progression. "We are prepared less to demand a certain qualitative progression than to recognize its rightness after the event. We are put into a state of mind which another state of mind can appropriately follow."[43]

In progressive form and repetitive form, expectations are created during the interaction of an audience with a work. But the expectancies of conventional form are "categorical" expectancies, and are usually present prior to the interactions of audience and work. For example, well established literary genres impose the demands of conventional form upon authors who would adhere to them, and create categorical expectancies in readers who recognize them. Ceremonial speaking occasions, such as Presidential Inaugural Addresses, create conventional forms and attendant expectancies over time. Perhaps the clearest case of conventional form occurs in ritual, where expectancies, fulfillments, and form join together in a correctness of procedure which promotes the continuance of certain motives and adherence to group norms for behaving and being.[44] As Burke points out, "any form can become conventional and be sought for itself—whether it be as complex as the Greek tragedy or as compact as the sonnet."[45] In any event, the in-ducements of conventional form are just as rhetorical as are progressive and repetitive forms, a fact best recognized, perhaps, when the expectancies of conventional form are not followed completely or correctly in presentation.

These three dynamics of form, the progressive, the repetitive, and the conventional, are not mutually exclusive, but may occur together and within one another. Thus, there can be repetition of progressive forms, progressions

---

[42]*Counterstatement*, p. 125.
[43]*Counterstatement*, p. 125.
[44]The discussion of ritual throughout Burke's work, when synthesized, describes what Burke perceives to be the seven strategies of symbolic fixing which create the conventional forms of myth. They are explicated in Cynthia M. Danel, "The Relationship of Rhetoric and Ritual as Discussed in the Major Works of Kenneth Burke," unpublished M. A. thesis, The Penn State University (May, 1976).
[45]Burke, *Counterstatement*, p. 126.

of conventional forms, repetitions of conventional forms, progressions of repetitive forms, and progressions and repetitions which follow the dictates of convention.

What is most significant here is that the schematics of form outlined by Burke account for two dimensions of dynamics, the technical dynamics of a piece of rhetoric wherein we appreciate the artistry of the rhetor as we note the unfolding of imagery, the building of claims, the placement of concepts, the juxtaposing of styling devices, all of which comprise the structure of the discourse; and the intellectual and motivational dynamics wherein we ascertain the potential development of thought and feeling on the part of auditor or reader in response to the invitations of structure as we note the identifications evoked by concretized patterns of imagery, the more abstract ideas which the image patterns "add up" or "boil down" to, the value laden principles which may be summed up out of the ideas, and the ultimate concept which constrains the whole, the form of forms. It is in this second dynamic that we see the emerging of rhetorical forms within the structure of discourse, culminating in the conceptual shaping of meaning we refer to as a way of knowing, of comprehending. That it is a *way* of knowing indicates that the conceptual shaping is directional; it values, attitudinalizes, motivates action toward or away from phenomena within the shaping. And since symbolic knowing as Burke conceives it is characteristically human knowing, a description of the contents of knowing involves the pentadic ratios Burke develops in his *A Grammar of Motives:* agent, act, agency, scene, and purpose. The pentadic terms refer to the categories of human consciousness which encompass concretized and individuated knowings.

With the addition of this final set of terms, we see that what Kenneth Burke offers us is a calculus for charting the rhetoric of form. The contents of consciousness are embodied in perceptions of actors, acting with purpose, using various means to achieve ends, within contextual scenes (since within the Burkean perspective, one set of terms always implies an opposite set, we may also conceive of the motion of impersonal forces, operations which occur randomly, without apparent cause, and toward no clearly perceived end, which vitiate the bounds of any clearly defined scene). These contents of consciousness are shaped according to volitional constraints and such primal principles of forming as identification-division, hierarchy and piety, into patterns of meaning which are imbued with action directives in relation to perceived contexts. Because volition and action undergird consciousness, symbolic form functions within a grid of such motivational states as intention, judgment, appeal, expectancy, and gratification. The interaction of motive and act, the principles of forming, and the pentadic categories of perception add up to a presentation of consciousness which finds what we have called content and form joined in a meaningful way of knowing. And because these interacting phenomena participate in the fundamental modes of symbolic forming they constitute invitations to know for all who interact with them. By tracking the valences among these interacting elements, the critic of rhetoric may render an accounting of the rhetoric of symbolic form.

Form and Rhetoric

If we adopt Burke's orientation toward the rhetoric of form, wha. led to see about the nature of rhetoric itself? I believe there are three major observations which warrant attention and study.

First, we see that symbolizing is a more fundamental process than we usually imply when we talk about the symbolic process as a "mediational process." Symbolic capacity is the basis for all human knowing, and all knowing is constrained by the principles of that capacity. The capacity is an a priori, which allows the infinitude of manifestations of symbolic forms we see all around us. All meaning, from the level of primal perception to the level of sophisticated technical manipulation, is formed.

Although Burke acknowledges the compulsive nature of human symbolizing, that is to say, man necessarily symbolizes because he has the capacity to, Burke also postulates that symbolizing is volitional, an act of will guided by purposing. Man wishes to comprehend, and he wishes to comprehend in such a way that he can conceptualize and label his environment in order to influence it, act upon it, and act in ways that make a difference. The symbolic formings which comprise all human interaction are shaped and used with an eye toward outcomes, effects and affects, results of some kind. To appreciate this is to appreciate the fundamental importance of what we have called "invention" in rhetoric. And this appreciation opens the way for us to study the epistemic nature of rhetoric, and the function of rhetoric in human knowing.

The inventional process is involved with much more than just the selection of ideas to be used in a rhetorical act from among those available. Invention is the forming and shaping of meaning which "fixes" human phenomenal reality. The fixing is imbued from its beginning with intention and purpose, guided by the forming and already formed constraints of valuing, and freighted with perceptual expectancies and implications for actional outcomes. Thus, on the primal level of cognition, the form-content, and invention-judgment dichotomies are rendered specious.

A second observation follows from the first. When we talk about symbols as mediational devices, we are actually referring to symbol systems or codes which have been developed by man over time. Myth, language, and mathematics are examples of such systems. In their development and use, they follow logical principles partly, but not completely, unique to themselves. And in their use, they mediate, that is, further shape and modify the primal forms of symbolizing. Given this perspective, there is reason for rhetorical critics to give attention to the particular rhetorical qualities of such phenomena as the sciences, art, literature, physical behaviors, and film, to determine the principles which constrain such forms and the peculiar rhetorical valences of each.

Finally, the rhetorical critic is compelled to move far beyond the arrangement of materials approach, and to begin to study, in richer perspective, the rhetorical functions of form and the forming potential of rhetorical messages. The critic is prompted to see that rhetorical messages are comprised of levels of formings, which, through subconscious and conscious maneuvering, constitute a "way of envisaging what it's all about." It is just these "ways of envisaging," these summative manifestations of the processes of symbolic forming, that profoundly underlie all rhetorical invitation and entreaty.

Epistemology and Ontology as Dialectical Modes in the Writings of Kenneth Burke

James W. Chesebro

In his seminal essay in 1967, Robert L. Scott concluded that, "In human affairs, then, rhetoric . . . is a way of knowing; it is epistemic" (p. 17). Scott's conclusion has permeated the discourse of rhetoricians for over twenty years now. As Orr (1978, p. 263) has aptly noted, the "view-point . . . increasingly pervades the thinking of communication and rhetorical theorists." Indeed, this conception has reinvigorated the centrality, significance, and pervasiveness of the "rhetorical perspective."

Yet, the epistemic function assigned to rhetoric has not uniformly impressed all. Kenneth Burke, for example, has argued that, "The practice of rhetoric can lead to new knowledge because the doing or experiencing of anything can lead to new knowledge" (1985, p. 92). In greater detail, he has noted:

> As for rhetoric as a form of knowledge, any bug can contribute to the science of entomology if it helps fill out a theory such as Darwin developed about evolution. Along Freudian lines, the stupidest dreams of the dullest person can be a contribution to knowledge. And the same goes for what we might learn by systematically analyzing any rhetorical text and subjecting it to modes of analysis we consider information. (1985, p.91)

The purpose of this essay is *not* to deny the epistemic function ascribed to rhetoric. Rather this essay explores a viewpoint which holds that a solely epistemic view of rhetoric is restrictive, for it de-emphasizes other useful conceptions and functions which rhetoric serves. More directly, this essay examines the claim that the ontological understandings generated by rhetoric have been neglected. Indeed, in his landmark and definitive 1967 essay, beyond arguing for rhetoric as epistemic, Scott also concluded that an ontological emphasis "offers no legitimate role to rhetoric" (p. 17). Others have apparently followed his lead. Embracing a solely epistemic conception

Reprinted from *Communication Quarterly* 36 (1988), with permission of Eastern Communication Association.

of rhetoric, McGuire has argued that, "rhetorical theory does not apply to empirical reality" (1980, p. 138). Similarly, Cherwitz and Hikins hope to "avoid attaching any of the traditional philosophical baggage represented by such terms as 'objective,' 'absolutism,' 'positivistic,' or the like to our definition of knowledge. What we offer is a concept of knowledge which makes no ontological statement regarding the nature of the objects of reality" (1982, p. 140). Likewise, Brummett (1979) has argued that epistemic modes of inquiry create all sensations, ultimately denying the existence of any independent, physical, and phenomenal reality.

This essay focuses upon the writings of Kenneth Burke, and it identifies a radical transformation in Burke's conception of rhetoric. Particularly, it is noted that in his earlier writings, Burke attributed an epistemic function to rhetoric. However, since 1968, he has posited a decidedly dialectic view in which both epistemic and ontological functions govern rhetoric. In this reconception, rhetoric is both an active and reactive medium. Rhetorical concepts and constructions enact environments, creating "situations" and shaping human attitudes and espouses to these events; simultaneously, rhetorical concepts and constructions must adequately, usefully, and wisely account for and accurately name the functions and relationships within environments. Ultimately, for Burke, a dialectical relationship—an epistemic and ontic interaction—defines and determines the functions of rhetoric, fostering creative human responses to environments but also responding reactively to the nature of environments.

In offering this view, a three-fold analysis is offered. First, definitional in nature, a common set of reference points are provided. Definitions are offered for terms such as *epistemology* and *ontology*, and a framework is established for conceiving an epistemic-ontological dialectic. Second, critical moments and stages in the writings of Kenneth Burke are traced which highlight the emergence of Burke's epistemic-ontological dialectic. Third, rhetorical implications of Burke's dialectical epistemic-ontological perspective are identified.

Specifying Types of Philosophic Systems

Seldom functioning in a value-free context, terms such as *epistemology* and *ontology* require definition. Most frequently cast as antithetical terms, *epistemology* has become the study of knowledge generated and constructed by human beings, while *ontology* is conceived as the study of phenomena independent of human experience (Chesebro, 1985b).

√Epistemology

Marking a distinction between what human beings know and what exists, the *Oxford English Dictionary* (1971, p. 246) defines *epistemology* as "the theory or science of the method or grounds of knowledge," particularly noting that a given work can meaningfully address questions of

"epistemology, ontology, anthropology, and ethics." *Webster's Third New
International Dictionary* (1986, Vol. 1, p. 765) more pointedly defir
epistemic as the "type of" knowledge derived from "experience," and
specifically equates epistemic to the "purely intellectual or cognitive" a
"subjective," which requires that particular "reference" be given "to its lim
and validity," in contrast with a "phenomenological sense" of knowing. Th
Angeles (1981, p. 78) has defined *epistemology* as the "study of (a) 1
origins, (b) the presuppositions, (c) the nature, (d) the extent, and (e) 1
veracity (truth, reliability, validity) of knowledge."

✓Ontology

Noting its metaphysical origins and emphasis, the *Oxford English
Dictionary* (1971, p. 131) defines *ontology* as "the science or the study of
being" and as a "department of metaphysics which relates to the being or
essence of things, or to being in the abstract." *Webster's Third New
International Dictionary* (1986, Vol. II, p.1577) reports that *ontology* deals
with questions of "being and existence," and it particularly notes that
ontological questions frequently deal with "the kinds of abstract entities that
are to be admitted to a language system." Thus, Angeles (1981, p.198) has
defined *ontology* as the "study of the essential characteristics of Being in
itself apart from the study of particular existing things."

The Shift from the Ontological
to the Epistemic in Communication

During the last fifty years, the methods governing rhetorical criticism
have increasingly shifted from an ontological to an epistemic view of
communication. The initial reliance upon neo-Aristotelian methods has given
way to a host of new methods (see, e.g., Brock & Scott, 1980). Historical
methods, for example, have been displaced by a stronger reliance upon
Bitzer's (1968) notion of a rhetorical situation and by the recognition that
history itself is rhetorical (Andrews, 1968). Reality itself is increasingly
viewed as socially constructed (Berger & Luckmann, 1966/1967), with
science itself cast as rhetoric (see, e.g., Simons, 1978). Indeed, for an
increasing number, reality itself is never directly experienced, for metaphors
and fantasies—symbolic forms—enact and mediate all understandings
(Hastings, 1970; Bormann, 1972; Fisher, 1984). Thus, rhetoric has increasingly been viewed as epistemic or as a creative, experiential, and
frequently unique mode for understanding what is (Scott, 1967; Scott, 1976;
Brummett, 1976).

Yet, rhetorical criticism is not unique in its shifting emphasis from the
ontological to the epistemic.

The transformation from the ontological to the epistemic has
characterized the evolution of virtually all theories of communication.
Krippendorff (1984, p. 22) has reported a fundamental "shift" in the basic

"paradigm" in the discipline of communication "from ontology to epistemology." In terms of existing models of communication, Krippendorff has specifically argued that:

> Ontology is the branch of philosophy that is concerned with the nature of reality or what exists independent of its observation. In a philosophy of science, ontological assumptions imply a one-way process of communication from an unvarying and disinterested object to an intelligent and interested observer; patterns in nature are taken to be involuntary, given and waiting to be discovered. By insisting on objectivity, established scientific methods are designed to prevent the properties of observers from entering their domain of observation. By insisting on replicability, such methods are limited to detecting stable phenomena only. The ontological commitments that observers may make in their work detach them from and make them intellectually superior to the object they describe. (1984, pp. 22-23)

Emphasizing the social and interactive nature of the epistemic perspective, Krippendorff has argued that an ontological conception is appropriately contrasted to epistemic orientations in communication:

> In contrast to ontology, epistemology is the branch of philosophy that is concerned with knowledge, not with what exists. From my acquaintance with epistemology generally, epistemology has become more specific, emphasizing "processes by which we come to know,"— perhaps at the expense of its products or what it is that becomes - known thereby. Probably the most important consequence of regarding communication between the observers and the observed to flow both ways is that the properties of observers enter their domain of observation and render the established standards of objectivity and replicability unachievable. (1984, p.23)

Because an epistemic view of rhetoric ultimately holds that an essential relationship exists between the observer of the communication process and the participants within that process, Wander (1983, p. 18) has explicitly concluded that any assessment of communication will necessarily reflect the "ideological" orientation of the observer, an orientation which he believes should not and cannot be "averted" or "ignored."

The Ontological-Epistemic Dialectic

While the shift from the ontological to the epistemic would appear decisive, an ontological-epistemic antithesis is the foundation for the "shift" from the ontological to the epistemic as an "evolution." However, an antithetical conception is but one of many ways of casting the relationship which can exist between questions of existence and knowing. A rhetorician can also legitimately ask how ontological and epistemic views of language systems mutually affect and define each, ultimately focusing upon the interaction of the ontological and epistemic as a basis for a grammar, rhetoric, and ethic of communication. When cast as enduring and interacting conceptions, an ontological-epistemic dialectic is at least theoretically conceivable.

Such a dialectic would necessarily posit two essential principles for understanding human communication, accounting at least for the methods or modes of inquiry used to study human communication and the nature of the human being to be understood.

First, a comprehensive view of human communication must necessarily invoke both ontological and epistemic modes of inquiry. While the dual modes may not be explicit, all methods of rhetorical criticism presume that distinct substantive entities exist, an ontological assumption, while simultaneously holding that human beings create, construct, or impose—to some degree—their own understandings regarding these entities, an epistemic assumption. The duality emerges whenever a rhetorical fantasy is cast as a product distinct from the small group participants who initiated the fantasy (a distinction which presumes a particular theory of ontology), while simultaneously holding that the fantasy possesses the potential of altering the attitudes, beliefs, and actions of the participants who create the fantasy (an epistemic presumption).[1] Similarly, the ontological-epistemic dialectic figures in a rhetorical concept on which posits that the story teller, story, and those who listen to the story are discrete (an ontological assumption), while likewise holding that the story may redefine the understandings of both the story teller and those who listen to the story (an epistemic assumption). Indeed, the ontological-epistemic might even be said to permeate a theory of communication which apparently posits a solely process orientation. Thus, when Berlo (1960, p. 23) proposed a theory of communication in which "any phenomenon" was to be treated as in "continuous change in time" (an epistemic assumption), he also held that it was essential to "isolate certain elements that all communication situations have in common" (an ontological assumption).

Second, beyond providing a more comprehensive view of human methods of inquiry, an ontological-epistemic dialectic posits a more viable conception of human nature. A solely ontological system is forced to ignore human creativity and human control, for its attention is necessarily fixed upon the phenomenal, and not the intangible motives which constitute the foundation

---

[1] The example used at this juncture is literal rather than hypothetical reflecting a clash which occurred in 1982 between an ontological and an epistemic scholar. Reflecting a concern for ontological issues, G. P. Mohrmann (1982a; 1982b) suggested that proponents of fantasy theme analyses had failed to specify adequately their philosophical and phenomenal base. Reflecting a concern for epistemic issues, Ernest G. Bormann's (1982) response emphasized the way in which the fantasy theme system of analysis emerged. Because the two orientations were so discrete in this exchange, many had a sense that a "non-debate" had occurred. Yet, the exchange does clearly reflect the potential importance of the epistemic-ontological distinction.

for ideals such as "creativity" and "control." In much the same vein, a solely epistemic system is forced to ignore the power of external circumstances and situations. A question of validity, an ontological-epistemic dialectic ultimately posits that human nature is both determined and telic.

Such an analysis of the methods and view of human nature employed by rhetoricians reveals, in part, some of the definitional features of an ontological-epistemic view of communication. Yet, the full dimensions of an ontological-epistemic dialectic view of communication are most evident in the writings of Kenneth Burke as they have evolved during the last seventy years.

The Emergence of Kenneth Burke's Epistemic and Ontological Theory

Prior to 1968, Kenneth Burke's conception of dramatism was flagrantly grounded in an epistemic orientation which was most readily revealed in his decidedly pragmatic focus. In 1945, for example, Burke directly isolated what he identified as the "Five Key Terms of Dramatism" (1945 & 1950/1962, p. xvii). He noted that the five key terms of dramatism provided a functional foundation for determining "what people are doing and why they are doing it" (p. xvii). In this view, Burke's rhetoric and symbolic of motives were "required if one would examine *in detail* the ways in which the Grammatical resources are employed for the purposes of persuasion and self-expression" (p. 442). Thus, as originally cast, dramatism was to function as a practical art, explaining persuasion and self-expression.

It should also be noted that prior to 1968, Burke's conception of symbol-using possessed a metaphorical, if not comedic, emphasis. For example, in his *Rhetoric of Motives* in 1950, Burke proposed that courtship might be viewed as a kind of "embarrassment in social intercourse" and "as a sign of a corresponding mystery in communication" (p. 732). While such a view of courtship may strike our fantasy, more particularly Burke's descriptors are predominantly metaphorical, if not ironic. Accordingly, Burke's pre-1968 writings often entertained as much as they informed.

Predominantly epistemic in their emphasis, few of Burke's earlier writings reflect a concern for the ontological; in his early writings, Burke seldom overtly examined the relationship between phenomenal existence and rhetoric. Indeed, one is hard pressed to isolate specific passages in Burke's pre-1968 writings which reflect an explicit concern for a theory of ontology. Yet, some examples apparently exist:

> "Action" by all means. But in a complex world, there are many kinds of action. Action requires programs—programs require vocabulary. To act wisely, in concert, we must use many words. If we use the wrong words, words that divide up the field inadequately, we obey false cues. We must name the friendly or unfriendly functions and relationships in such a way that we are able to do something about them. (Burke, 1937/1959, p.4)

Yet, such passages can mislead and overstate Burke's concern for the ontological during this early period. For example, while the passage immediately above possesses an explicit ontological emphasis, it must also be noted that Burke introduces this passage with a frame of reference which is predominantly epistemic as its governing mode: "One constructs his notion of the universe or history" by defining "the 'human situation' as amply as his imagination permits" (p. 3). Thus, while some exceptions might be noted, we are left with the conclusion that Burke's earlier writings, prior to 1968, are grounded predominantly, if not exclusively, in an epistemic function of rhetoric.

The Introduction of Ontological Inquiry

In 1968, Kenneth Burke posited a fundamental change in his conception of symbol-using.[2] His comedic posture was replaced by a far more serious mood and tone. Burke's theory of symbol-using was no longer to be perceived as solely a system for explicating the ways in which particular individuals employed symbols to create and to control specific social settings. Burke proposed to offer "a philosophy of language" and "a general conception of man and of human relations" (1968a, p. 416). Burke's conception of symbol-using was to be expanded to provide, not only a method for explication of symbol-using in practice, but also a foundation for identifying basic literal or phenomenal distinctions which determined how and why human beings communicate. Thus, in 1968, Burke asked if dramatism functioned only as a way of characterizing ongoing symbolic interactions: "Is dramatism merely metaphorical?" (1968b, p. 448). His answer was decidedly no. He held that dramatism also provided a "literal" definition of the human being "as an animal characterized" by a "special ability for 'symbolic action,' which is itself a literal term" (1968b, p. 448). He concluded that dramatism might deal with a particular nomenclature, but he also argued that "in a wider sense any study of human relations in terms of 'action' could to that extent be called dramatism" (1968b, p. 448).

By 1983, Burke had more clearly attributed two primary functions to his theory of symbol-using. In applied arenas, symbol-using might be examined as pragmatic instrumentations, creating and altering self and social expressions. He identified this mode of inquiry as *logology* and held its concern to be the exploration of epistemic issues. Yet, a second function was

---

[2] I employ the year 1968 as the landmark point when Burke introduced his epistemic-ontological dialectic view of symbol-using. The year 1968 appears particularly appropriate for it is the year Burke associates with the formulation of the epistemic-ontological dialectic view of symbol-using (see Burke in Brock, Burke, Burgess, & Simons 1985 p. 22) and because it is the year in which Burke's essay entitled "Dramatism," was widely circulated in the *International Encyclopedia of the Social Sciences*. However, it should be noted that Burke's first major and detailed published statement regarding the dramatisim-ontological equation is to be found in 1967 (see Burke, 1967).

also to be associated with his theory of symbol-using. Burke sought to describe the literal nature of symbol-using itself. He identified this mode of inquiry as *dramatism* and held its concern to be the exploration of ontological issues. Thus, two terms had been formally coined to describe Burke's theory of symbol-using. As Burke explained the distinction:

> This might be the place to explain why *two* terms for the *one* theory. Though my aim is to be secular and empirical, "dramatism" and "logology" are analogous respectively to the traditional distinction (in theology and metaphysics) between ontology and epistemology. My "Dramatism" article (in *The International Encyclopedia of the Social Sciences*) features what we humans *are* (the symbol-using animal). Logology is rooted in the range and quality of *knowledge* that we acquire when our bodies (physiological organisms in the realm of non-symbolic motion) come to profit by their peculiar aptitude for learning the arbitrary, conventional mediums of communication called "natural" languages (atop which all sorts of specialized nomenclatures are developed, each with its particular kind of insights). (Burke, 1983, p. 859)

By 1985, Burke began to reshape his conceptions of his earlier books to conform to his distinction between dramatism and logology. He noted, for example, "In my early book in 1935, *Permanence and Change,* I used rhetoric and ontological as synonymous terms. Later, I had to modify this equation; I made the shift in my 1968 article, "Dramatism," in the *International Encyclopedia of the Social Sciences* (in Brock, Burke, Burgess, & Simons, 1985, p. 22).

This analysis suggests that Burke would ultimately leave us with two theories of symbol-using, not one.

One theory is labelled and identified by Burke as *logology.* The logological theory examines rhetoric in practice. Burke's logological theory of symbol-using seeks to explain how different kinds of rhetorical systems are created and sustained by specific groups of agents. A logological analysis might examine, for example, how law functions as a rhetorical system which creates, maintains, and alters certain human norms during a particular era or specific time and place. The province of a logological symbolic analysis is thus upon particular constructions of socially shared symbolic realities. Thus, the logological theory focuses upon the study of how and why people use certain symbols in particular circumstances to create and to control specific social settings. It deals with particular social management applications of rhetorical principles designed to achieve specific objectives within a certain context. In terms of a philosophical placement, then, Burke's logological philosophy of symbol-using is decidedly epistemic in nature.

Burke's logological or epistemic inquiries are amply illustrated in his *Grammar, Rhetoric* (1945 & 1950/1962), and *Rhetoric of Religion* (1961/ 1970). Moreover, these epistemic principles have received extensive treatment within the discipline since 1952 (Hochmuth, 1952). In this context, Brock has argued that paradox and metaphor constitute the controlling features of this epistemic system (in Brock, Burke, Burgess, & Simon, 1985, pp. 18-22; also, see Brock, 1985), an epistemic system revealed through key concepts such as *strategy, symbol, hierarchy, acceptance* and *rejection,* the dramatistic process, *identification,* the *pentad, substance,* and *form* (Brock & Scott, 1980, pp. 348-360; Blankenship, Murphy, & Rosenwasser, 1974).

Burke's second theory is labelled and identified by Burke as *dramatism.* The dramatistic theory of symbol-using deals with universals of the human condition and universals of communication. Burke's dramatistic theory of symbol-using would seek to provide a general conception of all human beings as symbol-users. In this context, of Burke's many dramatistic claims, his most popular statement functions as an excellent example of his dramatistic theory of symbol-using. Burke has maintained that a human being is "an animal characterized" by a "special ability for 'symbolic action.' " Or, as Burke has otherwise put it, "bodies that learn language." The claim is intended, in Burke's view, to be a "literal," not metaphorical, definition of the human being. In terms of a philosophical placement, then, Burke's dramatistic theory of symbol-using is decidedly ontological in nature.

Burke's dramatistic or ontological views of symbol-using are scattered throughout Burke's writings during the last twenty year period in several less popular essays. In addition, while these ontological principles have been a subject of extended and intense disagreement by several rhetoricians (Brock, 1985; Brock, Burke, Burgess, & Simons, 1985; Tonn, 1988; Roundtree, 1988; Williams, 1988), the particular principles of Burke's theory of ontology have yet to be systematically articulated. Moreover, in Burke's writings, these ontological principles have yet to appear as one coherent compendium. Accordingly, Burke's ontological mode of inquiry is appropriately explicated.

Dramatism as Ontology

Five ontological principles emerge in the writings of Kenneth Burke which define dramatism ontologically.[3]

First, there is a world of external phenomena, and it is distinct from the realm of human symbol-using. For Burke, the realm of symbol-using is unique to the human being. Symbol-using is a solely conventional, arbitrary, and social process. It allows human beings to become self-conscious, create motives independently of physical phenomena, and ultimately to create social constructions of reality. In contrast, the world of external phenomena is a world of "motion," governed by instinct and intuition, without self-reflection. In this view, nature is not a conscious force; and, nature can do no right or

---

[3] In assessing whether or not the formulation of these five principles constituted a complete and sufficient description of his view of dramatism as epistemic and ontological, Burke has noted of the conception offered here, "Your outline of the dramatism-logology (ontology-epistemology) structure is as trim and accurate as I could e'er imagine" (K. Burke, personal communication, May 12, 1985).

wrong. As Burke (1985, p. 90) has put it, "Nature can do no wrong (whatever it does is 'Nature')." In greater detail, Burke's action-motion dichotomy is critical to this first ontological principle. *Action* specifies the province or realm of the symbolic which provides human beings with their most unique definition, while *motion* specifies the extrasymbolic or nonsymbolic operations of nature. As Burke has put it, " 'Action' is a term for the kind of behavior possible to a typically symbol-using animal" (1968b, p. 447). Action involves the ability to distinguish between "symbol and *symbolized* (in the sense that the *word* tree is categorically distinguishable from the *thing* tree)" (Burke, 1968b, p. 447). The ability to distinguish the thing and its name stems from the nature of a symbol system as a self-conscious, "conventional" and "arbitrary" system of communication (Burke, 1978, p. 809). In contrast, the "intuitive signaling system in such social creatures as bees and ants" would reside in the realm of motion and "not be classed as examples of symbolic action. They are not conventional arbitrary symbol systems such as human speech, which is not inborn but has to be learned" (Burke, 1978, p. 810). Moreover, a symbol system involves a "reflexive" aspect in which agents "can talk about themselves" (Burke, 1978, p. 810). Finally, symbol-using involves the use of a medium which "provides motives intrinsic to itself," shaping the self "in the modes of role, of sociality" (Burke, 1978, p. 813). In contrast, the realm of motion is defined by "the existence of speechless nature [which] does not depend upon man's ability to speak" (Burke, 1968b, p. 447).

Second, the world of external phenomena and the realm of symbol-using are unbridgeable. For example, while a vocal mechanism is required to talk (the world of external phenomena), what a vocal mechanism does—how it works—will not explain the meaning of symbols as human beings understand them. Yet, while the "motion-action 'polarity' is unbridgeable" (Burke, 1978, p. 815), action is dependent upon, but not understood in terms of, the existence of the realm of motion. In this view, behaviors are required to symbolize, but the behaviors themselves do not account for the meanings or symbols conveyed. These particular corollaries reveal Burke's position:

   (1) There can be no action without motion—that is, even the "symbolic action" of pure thought requires corresponding motions of the brain.

   (2) There can be motion without action. (For instance, the motions of the tides, of sunlight, of growth and decay.)

   (3) Action is not reducible to terms of motion. For instance, the "essence" or "meaning" of a sentence is not reducible to its sheer physical existence as sounds in the air or marks on the page, although material motions of some sort are necessary for the production, transmission, and reception of the sentence. (Burke, 1968, p. 447).

In this regard, Burke employs the origin of the Story to illustrate his principles:

Surrounding us wordy animals there is the infinite wordless universe out of which we have been gradually carving out universes of discourse since the time when our primordial ancestors added to their sensations *words* for sensations. When you could duplicate the taste of an orange by *saying* "the taste of an orange," that's when STORY was born, since words *tell about* sensations. Whereas Nature can do no wrong (whatever it does is Nature) when STORY comes into the world there enters the true, false, honest, mistaken, the downright lie, the imaginative, the visionary, the sublime, the ridiculous, the eschatological (as with Hell, Purgatory, Heaven; the Transmigration of Souls; Foretellings of an Inevitable wind-up in a classless society), the satirical, every single detail of every single science or speculation, even every bit of gossip—for although all animals in their way communicate, only our kind of animal can gossip. There was no story before we came, and when we're gone the universe will go on sans story. (Burke, 1983, p. 859).

As a related corollary, Burke holds that symbolic activity always constitutes a response to a situation in which it occurs; the response prescribes the range of actions which are believed reasonable in the situation (Burke, 1968b, p. 450).

Third, human beings are uniquely symbol-using animals. Burke defines the human being "literally as an animal characterized by" the "special aptitude for symbolic action" (Burke, 1968b, p. 448). As Burke notes, "So far as is known at present, the only typically symbol-using animal existing on the earth is the human organism" (1978, p. 810). As a symbol-using creature, the human being is uniquely able to impose associations or to create meanings about phenomena beyond the physical characteristics and physical functions of the phenomena. The most vivid illustrations of this symbol-using capacity are found in the creation of concepts which exist independent of any phenomenal reality such as *the negative, morality, hierarchy,* and *perfection:*

Man is
the symbol-using (symbol-making, symbol-misusing) animal
inventor of the negative (or moralized by the negative)
separated from his natural condition by instruments of his own making
goaded by the spirit of hierarchy (or moved by the sense of order)
and rotten with perfection. (Burke, 1966, p. 16)

Fourth, symbols are actions which create potentialities. For Burke, symbol-using is a creative activity which generates motive and potentiality (Burke, 1968b, p. 448). The symbolic frameworks human beings employ create social linkages which do not exist within the realm of motion. As Burke observes, "in contrast with the *immediacies* of the body, we confront our overall 'reality' in an indeterminately interwoven complexity of symbols, reports about local, national, and international affairs, about history, psychology, geology, astronomy, expectations true or false, promissory or forbidden, and so forth." Through this symbolically constructed "'reality'" or "'world,'" concludes Burke, "is embraced a potential 'universe of discourse' far beyond the realm of physiological sensation" (1978, p. 814). While not an essential feature to Burke's ontological analysis, he has held that these constructions frequently embody a dramatic construction in which pollution, guilt, purification, and redemption govern symbolic constructions:

> Here are the steps
> In the Iron Law of History
> That welds Order and Sacrifice:
> Order leads to Guilt
> (for who can keep commandments!)
> Guilt needs Redemption
> (for who would not be cleansed!)
> Redemption needs Redeemer
> (which is to say, a Victim!).
> Order
> To Victimage
> (hence: Cult of the Kill!). . . . (Burke, 1961/1970, pp. 4-5)

Fifth, chaos—not the regulating laws of nature—is the ultimate foundation of symbol-using. In this view, symbolic action is a function of the human will (Burke, 1968b, p. 450). The human will is capable of positing potential options which go beyond "what is." Or, as Burke has put it, "imagination falls on the side of disorder insofar as it encourages interests inimical to the given order" (Burke, 1968b, p. 450). In scientific terminologies, "chaos" functions as an appropriate explanatory metaphor and base for viewing the origins of symbol-using as an "irregular" variable in natural and social ordering schemes (Gleick, 1987). Moreover, the concept of will may also potentially transcend the action-motion dichotomy insofar as the overt recognition and "sensation" of a human will functions as a motivational or persuasive appeal for specific actions. Thus, Burke has rather specifically noted: "Ontologically, action is treated as a function of the will. But logologically the situation is reversed: the idea of the will is viewed as derivable from the idea of act" (1968, p. 450).

An overview of Burke's conception of symbol-using is appropriate. As I see it, Burke now employs a dialectic view to explain symbol-using. Rather than deny the epistemic view of rhetoric, Burke would argue that rhetoric is both epistemic and ontological. Specifically, rhetoric is viewed as both an active and reactive medium. As an active medium or epistemic system, rhetorical concepts and constructions enact environments, creating "situations," and shaping human attitudes and reactions. Simultaneously, as a reactive medium or ontological system, rhetorical concepts and constructions must adequately, usefully, and wisely account for and accurately name the functions and relationships within environments. In more concrete terms, the dialectic functions of rhetoric as both epistemic and ontological are revealed

in and can range from a carefully crafted verbal description perceived as
aesthetically persuasive to nonverbal cases of psychosomatic illness.
Ultimately, for Burke, a dialectical relationship—an epistemic and ontic
interaction—defines and determines the functions of rhetoric, fostering
creative human responses to environments but also responding reactively to
the nature of environments.

Thus, while functioning as different perspectives, the ontological and
epistemic conceptions are not inconsistent for Burke. Ontological and
epistemic perspectives mutually define symbol-using. The ontological
addresses the question of what the nature of the human being as symbol-user
is. The epistemic addresses the question of how human beings use and are
used by symbols. For Burke, both questions must be addressed if a
comprehensive view of symbol-using is to be provided. The ontological
recognizes the literal nature of symbol-using and posits the ways in which
human beings can be understood as symbol-using creatures; the epistemic
accounts for the specific kinds of knowledge-inducing activity generated by
symbol-using. While they may not be explicitly recognized and identified,
Burke holds that every theory of symbol-using posits basic axioms regarding
the ontological and epistemic status of symbol-using. But, Burke's axioms are
explicit. He deals overtly with both the ontological and the epistemic
dimensions of his theory of symbol-using.

Implications

First, Burke's reconception reinvigorates the epistemology-ontology
debate. As previously noted, in 1967, Scott set a tone for the next twenty
years when he concluded that rhetoric was epistemic and that the ontological
offered "no legitimate role to rhetoric" (p.17). Others have attributed a solely
epistemic function to rhetoric (McGuire, 1980; Cherwitz and Hikins, 1982;
Brummett, 1979; also, see Orr, 1978). This epistemic focus has meant that, in
many ways, rhetoricians have committed themselves to the study of fictions,
fictions in the form of fantasies and narratives. Indeed, for the last two
decades, the epistemic view has made the fictive the principle object of study
of rhetorical theory and criticism. Burke's reformulation attributes both an
epistemic and ontological role to rhetoric, suggesting that every theory of
rhetoric posits a theory of ontology in which basic features of reality are
specified as well as explaining how humans seek to construct understandings
of these basic features of reality. Burke's epistemic-ontic reformulation of the
functions of rhetoric reflects and explains recent debates which have emerged
within the discipline.[1]

Second, the ontological-epistemic features of Burke's theory require that
greater care be given to the ways in which Burke's system is understood. A
growing corpus of essays about Burke deal with his writings as if they were
solely epistemic (e.g., Crowell, 1977; Durham, 1980; Feehan, 1979; Heath
1979 & 1984). Some appear to intentionally dismiss Burke's dual mode of
inquiry (e.g., Brock, 1985). Few seem to recognize that the epistemic is but

one feature of Burke's system of thought (e.g., Lake, 1984). An example, for illustrative purposes, may serve our ends here. In discussing "Kenneth Burke's Realism," Fisher and Brockriede (1984) sought to identify "the philosophical ground of Kenneth Burke's dramatism and logology," which they have argued "is a variant of *realism*" (p. 35). They propose that Burke's "philosophical orientation" is not unlike the kinds of philosophies proposed by "Plato, Aristotle, George Campbell, and Chaim Perelman" (p. 35). In so doing, they treat Burke's action-motion dichotomy and the pentadic notion of "act" as equivalent support for their conception of Burke's emphasis on realism (p. 36). The placement, while flattering in many respects, reduces Burke's theoretical conception to a solely epistemic mode of inquiry. At the very least, the analysis confuses Burke's efforts to distinguish the ontological and epistemic dimensions of his theory. Burke himself has already described "realism" as but one of seven "philosophic languages" or "idioms" (1945 & 1950/1962, p. 127) rather than as an ontological system. It is unclear if a placement of Burke as a realist deals with both his ontological and epistemic concerns. Moreover, Burke employs the action-motion dichotomy to deal with the ontological mode of his theory (1978) while the pentadic term of "act has been reserved as a grammatical feature useful in an explication of a particular nomenclature" (1945 & 1950/1962, p. xvii). To employ both the action-motion dichotomy and the pentadic term of *act* as supporting evidence for a placement of Burke as a "realist" blurs Burke's effort to distinguish ontological and epistemic nodes of inquiry related to his theoretical analysis.

Third, the distinction between the ontological and epistemic modes contained within Burke's theory may be essential to the continued effectiveness of his entire system. If Burke's set of critical terminologies are perceived as solely epistemic, his system is aptly viewed as a kind of "tool box" from which any scheme of concepts can be extracted for any purpose. The integrity of the Burkeian system is ignored, if particular sets of Burkeian concepts are employed without regard to the ontological and epistemic contexts from which they are extracted. Under such conditions, a "stripped down" listing of Burkeian concepts might well be devised and employed as a pre-fabricated "cookie cutter" for any and all criticism. Such a use of the system is more likely to destroy rather than purify it. By analogy, the "outline" of the neo-Aristotelian method proposed by Thonssen and Baird in 1948 (pp. 292-293) and then extended and expanded by Thonssen, Baird, and Braden in 1970 (pp. 308-311) did not promote the insightfulness of neo-Aristotelian analyses; in fact, for some (Black, 1965), the outline began to constitute a "mechanization" of the method, ultimately emphasizing the categorical nature of the system rather than its insightfulness.

Fourth, the ontological-epistemic dialectic proposed by Burke allows us to more carefully explore the literal functions of symbol-using as an ontological dimension of criticism. Burke has provided a base for such exploration (1968b, 1978, 1983, 1985). Once the distinction between the ontological and epistemic functions of Burke's theory are recognized, other works begin to take on a refreshingly important function. Hugh Dalziel

Duncan (1968) has explored some twelve axiomatic propositions guiding Burke's system. These propositions might well be re-examined for their utility identifying the ontological base of Burke's theory.

Fifth, the ontological-epistemic distinction provided by Burke may yield important insights into the essential nature and function of symbol-using and symbol-users. We need to more carefully explore and to recognize the limits of symbol-using. We are in a media age which has blurred the distinction between what is real and what is understood (Hardt, 1972). Television frequently departs radically from what has occurred, often creating "pseudo-events" (Boorstin, 1961), promoting a "defect-ridden quality of reality" (Berg, 1972, pp. 256 & 258), and generating "unwarranted empirical beliefs" (Smith, 1982; also, see: Gerbner & Gross, 1976). Without overstatement, it is now possible to argue that the electronic media constitute a distinct reality which has displaced experientially understood reality (Chesebro, 1984). The most challenging task for the rhetorical critic is to reassert and to employ the distinction between the epistemic and ontological, to specify what is real and what has been constructed through human symbol-using, to identify the symbolic-constructions which mislead, and to isolate the range of life-affirming options which can be employed to enhance the quality of human life.

Sixth, an ontological-epistemic dialectic conception of symbol-using raises significant issues about the nature of symbol-using itself. Symbols have traditionally been defined as conventional and arbitrary verbal and nonverbal constructs. In the strictest sense of these words, insofar as they apply to symbols, *conventional* and *arbitrary* constructions would have no necessary relationship to environmental conditions, for solely conventional and arbitrary constructs would apply only to actions executed within the human realm. Accordingly, by definition, a symbol is an epistemic, rather than ontological, construct. While definitions are strategic and context-bound (Chesebro, 1985a), they are also designed to account for "what is," an ontological issue. In all, then, the relationships among a symbol, the epistemic, and the ontological require re-examination, with a concerted effort directed at reconceiving the definition of a symbol within the parameters established by the epistemic-ontological dialectic proposed by Burke.

Seventh, Burke's renewed interest in the ontological may constitute an alternative to a solely ideological conception of rhetorical criticism. As conceived by Wander (1983), rhetorical critics have paid increasing attention to the ideological component of persuasive messages, and, with increasing self-consciousness, to the ideological dimension of criticism itself. In this context, feminism has exerted its influence. Feminism has functioned, not only as an object of study, but also as a perspective reflecting an alternative ideological orientation. In such conceptions, ideology becomes an explicit component of the critical process. And, the ideological dimension of criticism is not without its power. The ideological dimension underscores and highlights the role of commitment and individual responsibility in criticism. It likewise de-emphasizes the social engineering metaphor which can control criticism. Finally, the ideological is a way, albeit indirect, of discussing the empowering and depowering capabilities of symbol-using. At the same time, the ideology is an awkward component to assess, if one wishes to determine the worth of rhetorical criticism itself. Many would wish to judge rhetorical criticism as a kind of discourse other than persuasion. Certainly, the value of rhetorical criticism becomes extremely difficult to assess if all rhetorical criticism becomes solely personal reactions. In this regard, an explicit theory of ontology may provide a common base for judging rhetorical criticism as a humanistic process which promotes the quality of life. Criticism is a personal commitment and responsibility of the individual critic. At the same time, criticism is more than a personal statement of taste. Criticism is also deliberative and forensic in means. Future and past facts, the foundations of deliberative and forensic communication, presume a theory of ontology.

Eighth, Burke's reconception of symbol-using offers an alternative to a solely postmodern view of rhetoric. Postmodern critics, such as Michel Foucault and Jacques Derrida, have argued that every symbol inherently conveys multiple and contradictory meanings (see, e.g., Sturrock, 1979). In this view, as Grossberg (1987, p. 90) has aptly argued, the meaning of a single concept depends upon the context in which the concept is used and the perspective of the person reacting to the concept. By extension when a concept becomes a symbol which dominates others, challenging the quality of life of others, a deconstructive method is invoked which exposes the self-defeating assumptions of the symbolic system. This postmodern perspective cannot be easily dismissed. It promises a profoundly participatory approach to symbol-using. It promises to challenge oppressive power systems. It promises to reinvigorate individual self-determination. At the same time the postmodern perspective does not emphasize the commonalities and the socially shared which also characterize communication. It places less attention than we might want on what is commonly understood during communication. Burke's effort to specify a theory of ontology directly seeks to identify what is common to all human beings as symbol-users and to determine the universals which define the communication process. Thus, if we seek a comprehensive theory of communication, Burke's notion of a theory of ontology may provide an extremely valuable adjunct to the postmodern perspective.

Conclusion

In his later writings, Kenneth Burke has proposed that a comprehensive examination of symbol-using requires that both the epistemic and ontological functions of symbol-using be recognized as mutually defining dimensions of the communication process. In this view, communication functions within two domains, in the human arena in which symbols create and construct socially understood and shared knowledge, and, in the nonsymbolic arena in which symbols must be thoughtfully selected which respond appropriately to the circumstances which govern human beings as animals. Rather than viewing the epistemic and ontological functions of rhetoric as antithetical, Burke posits that the epistemic and ontological constitute and operate within a dialectic relationship. Ultimately, while the commitment to a dual exploration of both the epistemic and ontological enlarges the critical task, the duality also promises to make the critical act a more responsible and moral endeavor.

References

Angeles, P. A. (1981). *Dictionary of philosophy.* New York: Barnes & Noble Books/Harper & Row, Publishers.

Andrews, J. R. (1968, November). The rhetoric of history: The constitutional convention. *Today's Speech, 16,* 23-26.

Berg, D. M. (1972). Rhetoric, reality, and mass media. *Quarterly Journal of Speech, 58,* 255-263.

Berger, P. L., & Luckmann, T. (1967). *The social construction of reality: A treatise in the sociology of knowledge.* Garden City, NY: Anchor Books/Doubleday & Company, Inc. (Original work published 1966)

Berlo, D. K. (1960). *The process of communication.* New York: Holt, Rinehart and Winston.

Bitzer, L. F. (1968, Winter). The rhetorical situation. *Philosophy & Rhetoric, 1,* 1-14.

Black, E. (1965). *Rhetorical criticism: A study in method.* New York: The Macmillan Company.

Blankenship, J., Murphy, E., & Rosenwasser, M. (1974, Winter). Pivotal terms in the early works of Kenneth Burke. *Philosophy & Rhetoric, 7,* 1-24.

Boorstin, D. J. (1961). *The image: A guide to pseudo-events in America.* New York: Harper & Row.

Bormann, E. G. (1972). Fantasy and rhetorical vision: The rhetorical criticism of social reality. *Quarterly Journal of Speech, 58,* 396-407.

Bormann, E. G. (1982). Fantasy and rhetorical vision: Ten years later. *Quarterly Journal of Speech, 68,* 288-305.

Brock, B. L. (1985). Epistemology and ontology in Kenneth Burke's dramatism. *Communication Quarterly, 33,* 92-101.

Brock, B. L., Burke, K., Burgess, P. G., & Simons, H. W. (1985). Dramatism as ontology or epistemology: A symposium. *Communication Quarterly, 33,* 17-33.

Brock, B. L., & Scott, R. L. (Eds.). (1980). *Methods of rhetorical criticism: A twentieth-century perspective* (2nd ed., rev.). Detroit, MI: Wayne State University Press.

Brummett, B. (1976). Some implications of "process" or "intersubjectivity": Postmodern rhetoric. *Philosophy & Rhetoric, 9,* 21-51.

Brummett, B. (1979). *Three meanings of epistemic rhetoric.* Paper read at the annual meeting of the Speech Communication Association, San Antonio, TX.

Burke, K. (1959). *Attitudes toward history.* Boston, MA: Beacon Press. Originally published in 1937.

Burke, K. (1962). *A grammar of motives and a rhetoric of motives.* Cleveland, OH: Meridian Books/The World Publishing Company. (Originally published 1945 and 1950)

Burke, K. (1966). *Language as symbolic action: Essays on life, literature, and method.* Berkeley, CA: University of California Press.

Burke, K. (1967). Dramatism. In L. Thayer (Ed.), *Communication: Concepts and Perspectives* (pp. 327-360). Washington, D.C.: Spartan Books.

Burke, K. (1968a). *Counter-statement.* Berkeley, CA: University of California Press. (Original work published 1931).

Burke, K. (1968b). Dramatism. In D. L. Sills (Ed.), *The international encyclopedia of the social sciences* (pp. 445-452). New York: Macmillan/The Free Press.

Burke, K. (1970). *The rhetoric of religion: Studies in logology.* Berkeley, CA: University of California Press. (Original work published 1961)

Burke, K. (1978). (Nonsymbolic) motion/(symbolic) action. *Critical Inquiry, 4,* 809-838.

Burke, K. (1983, August 12). Dramatism and logology. *TLS: The* [London] *Times Literary Supplement,* p. 859.

Burke, K. (1984). *Permanence and change: An anatomy of purpose.* Berkeley, CA: University of California Press. (Original work published 1935)

Burke, K. (1985). Dramatism and logology. *Communication Quarterly, 33,* 89-92.

Chesebro, J. W. (1984). The media reality: Epistemological functions of media in cultural systems. *Critical Studies in Mass Communication, 1,* 111-130.

Chesebro, J. W. (1985a). Definition as rhetorical strategy. *The Pennsylvania Speech Communication Annual, 41,* 5-16.

Chesebro, J. W. (1985b). Editor's introduction [for "Dramatism as Ontology or Epistemology Symposium"]. *Communication Quarterly, 33,* 17-18.

Chesebro, J. W. (1988, April). *Kenneth Burke's conception of reality.* Paper read at the annual meeting of the Central States Speech Association, Schaumburg, IL.

Cherwitz, R. A., & Hikins, J. W. (1982). Toward a rhetorical epistemology. *The Southern Speech Communication Journal, 47,* 135-162.

Crowell, L. (1977). Three Cheers for Kenneth Burke. *Quarterly Journal of Speech, 63,* 152-167.

Duncan, H. D. (1968). *Symbols in society.* New York: Oxford University Press.

Durham, W. B.(1980). Kenneth Burke's concept of substance. *Quarterly Journal of Speech, 66,* 351-364.

Feehan, M. (1979). Kenneth Burke's discovery of dramatism. *Quarterly Journal of Speech, 65,* 405-411.

Fisher, W. R. (1984). Narration as a human communication paradigm: The case of public moral argument. *Communication Monographs, 51,* 1-22.

Fisher, W. R., & Brockriede, W. (1984). Kenneth Burke's realism. *Central States Speech Journal, 35,* 35-42.

Gerbner, G., & Gross, L. (1976). Living with television: The violence profile. *Journal of Communication, 26,* 172-199.

Gleick, J. (1987). *Chaos: Making a new science.* New York: Viking.

Grossberg, L. (1987). Critical theory and the politics of empirical research. In M. Gurevitch & M. R. Levy, Eds., *Mass communication review yearbook* (Vol. 6, pp. 86-106). Newbury, CA: Sage Publications.

Hardt, H. (1972). The dilemma of mass communication: An existential point of view. *Philosophy & Rhetoric, 5,* 175-187.

Hastings, A. (1970). Metaphor in rhetoric. *Western Journal of Speech Communication, 34,* 181-194.

Heath, R. L. (1979). Kenneth Burke on form. *Quarterly Journal of Speech, 65,* 392-404.

Heath, R. L. (1984). Kenneth Burke's break with formalism. *Quarterly Journal of Speech, 70,* 132-143.

Hochmuth, M. (1952). Kenneth Burke and the "new rhetoric." *Quarterly Journal of Speech, 38,* 133-144.

Krippendorff, K. (1984, Summer). An epistemological foundation for communication. *Journal of Communication, 34,* 21-36.

Lake, R. A. (1984). Order and disorder in anti-abortion rhetoric logological view. *Quarterly Journal of Speech, 70,* 425-443.

McGuire, M. (1980). The ethics of rhetoric: The morality of knowledge. *The Southern Speech Communication Journal, 45,* 133-148.

Mohrmann, G. P. (1982a). An essay on fantasy theme criticism. *Quarterly Journal of Speech, 68,* 109-132.

Mohrmann, G. P. (1982b). Fantasy theme criticism: A peroration. *Quarterly Journal of Speech, 68,* 306-313.

Orr, C. J. (1978). How shall we say: "Reality is socially constructed through communication?" *Central States Speech Journal, 29,* 263-274.

Oxford English dictionary. (1971). Oxford, England: Oxford University Press.

Roundtree, J. C., III. (1988, April). *The most significant passage in Kenneth Burke's writing: The universal grounds of dramatism.* Paper read at the annual meeting of the Southern Speech Communication Association, Memphis, TN.

Scott, R. L. (1967). On viewing rhetoric as epistemic. *Central States Speech Journal, 18,* 9-16.

Scott, R. L. (1976). On viewing rhetoric as epistemic: Ten years later. *Central States Speech Journal, 27,* 258-266.

Simons, H. W. (1978). The rhetoric of science and the science of rhetoric. *Western Journal of Speech Communication, 42,* 37-43.

Smith, M. J. (1982). Cognitive schema theory and the perseverance and attenuation of unwarranted empirical beliefs. *Communication Monographs, 49,* 115-126.

Skodnick, R. (1983, Spring). Counter-gridlock: An interview with Kenneth Burke. *All Area No 2,* 4-33.

Sturrock, J. (1979). *Structural and since: From Levi-Strauss to Derrida.* New York: Oxford University Press.

Thonssen, L., & Baird, A. C. (1948). *Speech criticism: The development of standards for rhetorical appraisal.* New York: The Ronald Press Company.

Thonssen, L., Baird, A. C., & Braden, W. W. (1970). *Speech criticism* (2nd. ed.). New York: The Ronald Press Company.

Tonn, M. B. (1988, April). *Ontology or Epistemology: The Dramatistic Debate.* Paper presented at the meeting of the Central States Speech Association, Schaumburg, IL.

Wander, P. (1983, Spring). The ideological turn in modern criticism. *The Central States Speech Journal, 34,* 1-18.

Webster's third new international dictionary of the English language unabridged. (1986). Chicago, IL: Encyclopaedia Britannica, Inc.

Williams, D. C. (1988, April). *Re: Reading the history of rhetoric with Kenneth Burke.* Paper presented at the meeting of the Eastern Communication Association, Baltimore, MD.

Part Three:
Politics and Intervention

Towards a Better Life
Through Symbolic Action

by William H. Rueckert

In the twenties Burke worked for the *Dial* as contributor, reviewer, translator, and editor. His stories, poems, translations, critical pieces, and reviews of literary and critical works appeared in other journals as well. After 1929, Burke worked for the *Nation* and *New Republic,* primarily as a reviewer, but also as a music critic, and continued to contribute extensively to other journals. During the Great Depression, he moved into new fields, reviewing the works of anthropologists, economists, political theorists, psychologists, semanticists, and sociologists. To be sure, he continued to review critical and creative works and to publish essays of his own, but he finally abandoned his poetic career—a change symbolically re-enacted in the novel *Towards a Better Life*—and moved into the field of social criticism and theory. Though he gave up the writing of poetry as a vocation, he did not relinquish poetry; instead, he turned to it for permanent attitudes toward history which could be fruitfully applied to the problems of living in what he believed was a collapsing democratic society. The turmoil and intensity of this transformation from poet to spokesman for "poetic realism" are evidenced best by such things as Burke's extraordinary productivity between 1931 and 1941—five books and a large number of still uncollected essays and reviews; by such obvious signs of transition, new vision, and solidification as the nearly hysterical middle part of *Permanence and Change,* the apocalyptic last part of the same book, which is Burke's vision of the new way towards a better life, and the fragmented stylistics of *Attitudes toward History* (parentheses within parentheses, continuous digressions, and long, bewilderingly suggestive footnotes).

What caused Burke's change of direction was the historical situation in which he found himself. In the preface to *Permanence and Change,* Burke says that the book

> was written in the early days of the Great Depression, at a time when there was a general feeling that our traditional ways were headed for a tremendous change, maybe even a permanent collapse. It is such a

Reprinted from *Kenneth Burke and the Drama of Human Relations.* University of Minnesota Press, 1963, and University of California, 1982. Used by permission of William Rueckert.

> book as authors in those days sometimes put together, to keep
> themselves from falling apart. (PC,xiii.)

The book is a desperate attempt to locate analytically what is wrong with the
changing historical situation by setting it against the permanent universal
situation of man as it is revealed in the documents of the present and past.
Burke's general conclusion is that certain fundamental needs of man are
denied realization and satisfaction by the present scientific, rational,
technological, mechanistic, capitalistic orientation. These permanent, fundamental needs—what Burke calls "norms"—are denied realization and
satisfaction because the "technological psychosis" is negativistic, dissociative,
dehumanized, destructive, combative, deterministic, and selfish; anti-ethical,
anti-magical, anti-poetic, and anti-religious. This orientation advocates and
actually establishes a conception of self and purpose which leads, not toward
the better life of which man is capable, but away from it, toward the terrible
holocaust of total war. Burke felt with messianic urgency the need for a new
conception of purpose which would counterbalance the dangerously abnormal
emphasis of the "technological psychosis." To this end he devoted himself in
Permanence and Change and, I think, in all the rest of his works.

As Burke has pointed out, neither he nor any of his family ever missed a
meal or suffered any kind of physical hardship as a result of the depression;
yet so profound was its effect upon his thinking and career that it influenced
him in the most complete way during the rest of his life. After the depression
began, Burke saw and felt all around him the superstructure of economic,
ideological, and political certainties toppling. Always in need of these
certainties, always sensitive in the extreme to any weakening of or variation
in them, and profoundly aware that man defines and finds himself in terms of
these certainties, Burke felt that the very things which gave life meaning and
creative purpose were perhaps in the final stages of disintegration. He noted
that "when such a superstructure of certainties begins to topple, individual
minds are correspondingly affected, since the mind is a social product, and
our very concepts of character depend upon the verbalizations of our group"
(PC,173). At the time, Burke believed that the social system, or what he calls
the "system of coöperation" between individuals and groups, was so seriously
impaired that the very structure of rationality itself was threatened. "The
mind, so largely a linguistic product," he said, "is constructed of the
combined coöperative and communicative materials"; and, if "the system of
coöperation become[s] impaired . . . the communicative equipment is
correspondingly impaired" (PC, 163). The "system of cooperation," the
"social structure of meanings by which the individual forms himself"
(PLF,108), is what Burke calls an orientation. Any such orientation is
dominated by "reigning symbols of authority" which the individual naturally
and wholesomely wishes to accept in forming himself. But at certain periods
and for many reasons, a whole orientation, or certain key symbols of
authority, become "basically unreasonable" (ATH,II,52-53) and the individual
finds it necessary to reject the reigning symbols of authority because he loses

"faith in the [social] structure's 'reasonableness.'" (PLF,306.) The painful and bewildering consequence is alienation, or "spiritual dispossession" which causes "nostalgia and emptiness" (ATH,I,116,fn; II,67). Now, something like this is what happened to Burke and a great many other thinkers as a result of the Great Depression. The whole society in which they lived and most of the things for which it stood—in short the national-social orientation—had become unreasonable.

As early as the twenties Burke had characterized this orientation as scientific-technological, as rational-utilitarian, and said that "in contemporary America the distinguishing emergent factor is obviously mechanization, industrialism, as it affects our political institutions, as it alters our way of living, as it makes earlier emphases malapropos or even dangerous" (CS,107). And as early as the twenties, he had argued at length that artists, who are necessarily sensitive to dominant emergent factors in society as a whole because they have the more "barometric minds" (PC,173), must act as counter-agents by stressing the "humanistic" (CS,108), the anti-mechanistic, the anti-industrial (CS,111). Art and criticism should make counter-statements; together they should act as a counter-force to keep society from becoming too much itself. It did not take Burke long to discover that our own national-social orientation was but a part of the larger scientific orientation which began with the Protestant Reformation and, by the eighteenth century, had displaced the old hierarchic or religious orientation. This led Burke to study history and to discover that, preceding the religious orientation, there had been a third major orientation, the magical. He finally decided that each of these major orientations satisfies some of man's permanent fundamental needs, but no one of them satisfies all. In the course of history, which is marked by necessary and inevitable change, one major orientation is established, rigidified, and formulated only to collapse when it no longer satisfies the needs of a given period or is discredited by new knowledge. After a chaotic transitional period, a new orientation is gradually established, rigidified, and systematized. According to Burke, the tendency is for this process to be non-cumulative; often those things in a discredited orientation which actually satisfy fundamental human needs, as well as those things which do not, perish with the orientation. Though a radical shift of emphasis in the new orientation may obscure one or more of the permanent fundamental needs, the needs remain and must be satisfied by one means or another if man is fully and adequately to realize himself. In short, what is permanent, necessary, and valuable may be lost, or lost sight of, or dismissed in the course of the inevitable changes of history. Men often become so absorbed or lost in the historical situation that they fail to remember the universal one. Or, because of what Burke calls the "entelechial" ("to the end of the line") principle, a given orientation, which arose in answer to certain historical and universal needs, becomes too much itself by perfecting its outstanding characteristics at the expense of everything else. This, according to Burke, is exactly what happened with the scientific orientation; it gradually became a "technological psychosis," an aberration, a kind of mechanistic monomania which, absorbed in itself and intent upon its own distorted view of the world, man, and human purpose, could not satisfy some of man's basic, permanent needs, and could not lead toward that better life for which all men yearn.

Crucial to all of Burke's thinking in these matters is the idea of counter-statements, or counter-balances. He says, for example, that "a corrective rationalization must certainly move in the direction of the anthropomorphic or humanistic or poetic, since this is the aspect of culture which the scientific criteria, with their emphasis upon dominance rather than upon inducement, have tended to eliminate or minimize" (PC,65). And he argues that

> any point of reference by which a philosophic corrective of the scientific rationalization would be guided must almost necessarily show some superficial affinity with the religious rationalization. For man is essentially human, however earnestly he may attempt to reshape his psychological patterns in obedience to the patterns of his machines—and it was the religious rationalization which focused its purposes upon the controlling of human forces (the organic productive forces of the mind-and-body itself). (PC,63.)

Elsewhere, Burke says that "scientism" needs to be counter-balanced by a stress on "intuition," "imagination," "vision," and "revelation" (*Chimera*, I,24). Those things which have been omitted or de-emphasized in the scientific rationalization must be replaced and re-emphasized in the corrective counter-rationalization; and those things which have been overstressed in the scientific orientation must be unstressed in the same corrective orientation.

For example, Burke speaks repeatedly of scientism's over-emphasis on the profit motive, the competitive aspect of work, and the combative element in general which has "plagued the Western world with increasing violence" and "is a grave stimulus to war" and ultimately to universal holocaust (PC,268; PLF,317,319). Burke calls this "the romantic, 'Faustian' concept of effort that went with the rise of business enterprise," and says that

> in contrast with the classical notion that one developed himself by the harmonious apportionment of many different ingredients, you got the notion that development meant the intensification of some one peculiarity or aptitude. Hence . . . there was great opportunity for those warped by inordinate hungers. In the older [religious] frame, they might have tried to *restrain* these hungers—in the new [scientific] frame, they sought only to *embody* them in material attainments. (ATH,I,202-203,fn.)

This "Faustian" concept of effort—"ambition as a disease"—is but part of a larger set of identifications which are characteristic of the scientific orientation. Speaking of the Renaissance and Reformation, which he calls the "watershed" moment in western history, Burke says that

> at this point, a *negativistic* [combative] emphasis becomes organized,

both in the materials of pure thought and in economic imple-
mentation. Beginning with a plea for the separation of church and
state, we formally inaugurate the dissociative process that will end
with the theoretical separation of everything—a few centuries later,
religion will be in one bin, politics in another, art in another, science
in another, business in another—and there will be subdivisions, each
in its own separate bin. (ATH,I,171-172.)

This particular emphasis of scientism must be counter-balanced in the
corrective philosophy by a stress on the "coöperative" and "participant" or
non-combative aspects of action (PC,268-270). In the course of his analysis
of the scientific orientation Burke concludes that it over-stresses the "rational,
scientific categories of linkage" and under-stresses or even ignores the
emotional categories. Burke illustrates the point with this example and draws
the following conclusion from it:

> The lion, if the usual psychoanalytic theory of symbolization is
> correct, is the male or father symbol *par excellence*. Yet the lion is
> scientifically included in the cat family, whereas the cat emotionally
> is feminine. In both great poetry and popular usage, it is associated
> with female attributes. Here we have, in our rational categories, an
> association which runs counter to the associations of our emotional
> categories. A linkage emotionally appropriate becomes rationally
> inappropriate.
>
> In such cases, where the rational order of symbols would
> establish a congruity wholly alien to the emotional order of symbols,
> is it not possible that intense conflicts could arise, with the result that
> anguish or unrest could follow any really thorough attempt to
> embrace the rational category? (PC,72-73.)

It is not Burke's contention that the rational categories of linkage are wrong,
for he would be the first to admit that in bone structure and in other essential
ways, the lion does belong to the cat family; rather, the rational categories are
inadequate and may be disastrous, when it is argued that one can *only* define
and understand the lion in terms of the rational categories. According to the
rational categories of linkage a tree is a tree and is very useful as building
material and fuel. But according to emotional categories of linkage, a tree is
a parent and usually a father symbol. Hence, Burke argues, if a man takes an
axe and fells a great tree,

> we need not be surprised to find a strange misgiving permeate him as
> the noble symbol of shelter comes crashing to the earth. For however
> neutral his act, though the tree had been felled to satisfy the simple
> utilitarian needs of firewood, there may also be lurking here a kind
> of symbolic parricide. Not only firewood, but a parent-symbol, may
> be brought down in the crash. (PC,71.)

Burke then goes on to make the central point:

It is possible that much of the anguish affecting poets in the modern world is due to the many symbolic outrages which a purely utilitarian philosophy of action requires us to commit. In primitive eras, when the utilitarian processes were considerably fewer, and more common to the entire group, definite propitiatory rituals seem to have arisen as a way of cancelling off these symbolic offenses. In the magical orientation (so close to that of poetry) if the felling of a tree had connotations of symbolic parricide, the group would probably develop a corresponding ritual of symbolic expiation. The offender would thus have a technique for cleansing himself of the sin he had committed. (PC,71-72.)

Finally, Burke says that this radical dissociation between the rational and emotional categories and the tendency in the scientific orientation to deny the validity of the emotional and to ignore what he calls "hidden offenses," has resulted in "the loss of a definite, generally recognized technique for cancelling off these hidden offenses." Burke suggests that "much of the criminality in modern life might be explained psychologically as due to [this] loss" and argues that what we need is "a set of symbolic expiations . . . to counteract the symbolic offenses involved in [the many] purely utilitarian actions" forced upon us by the nature of existence in the modern world. (PC,74.)

The scientific orientation is inadequate as a description of the scene and the drama of human existence in that scene; it must be supplemented and corrected by a re-affirmation of those things in the religious and magical orientations—what Burke calls the "collective revelation" of mankind—which more adequately locate, describe, and satisfy the permanent, fundamental needs of man. There must be a re-affirmation of the universal situation, of the universals of experience, of what is common to all men in all places; a new attempt must be made to redefine the norms of human existence and, working from them, to find a new way, or rediscover the old ways towards a better life. We must, Burke says,

> . . . emphasize the underlying similarities, we [must] return through symbolism to a philosophy of *being,* [to] the Spinozistic concern with man *sub specie aeternitatis.* We [must] replace the metaphor of progress (and its bitter corollary, decadence) with the metaphor of a *norm,* the notion that at bottom the aims and genius of man have remained fundamentally the same, that temporal events may cause him to stray far from his sources but that he repeatedly struggles to restore, under new particularities, the same basic patterns of the "good life." (PC, 163.)

To be sure, there was a good deal about the "norms" in *Counter-Statement;* in fact the whole aesthetic theory developed there turns upon the idea that the norms of psycho-physical experience are the materials of art, that these norms link poet and audience and make possible the triple function of poetry as revelation, ritual, and rhetoric. However, in *Permanence and Change* and especially in *Attitudes toward History,* Burke attempts a much more comprehensive and specific treatment of the norms, aiming finally at some kind of description of the permanent fundamental needs of man and their relation to a current historical situation. Later, in the tetralogy of *Motives,* and as the culmination of a continuous effort, Burke arrives at Dramatism, which is offered as a complete system adequately locating what is permanent and fundamental in the drama of human relations. *Permanence and Change* and *Attitudes toward History* are perhaps best understood as stages in this continuous effort to find a way toward the better life through a study of the norms of psycho-physical experience.

In *Permanence and Change* and *Attitudes toward History,* as in *Counter-Statement,* Burke starts from the irreducible biological-neurological norm: "situations do overlap," he says,

> if only because men now have the same neural and muscular structure as men who have left their records from past ages. We and they are in much the same biological situation. Furthermore, even the concrete details of social texture have a great measure of overlap. And the nature of the human mind itself, with the function of abstraction rooted in the nature of language, also provides us with "levels of generalization" . . . by which situations greatly different in their particularities may be felt to belong in the same class (to have a common substance or essence). (PLF,2.)

The permanent and fundamental biological-neurological similarity between all men results in certain universal situations and certain universal strategies adopted by men as means of coping with the situations. Beyond these rather obvious norms, there are, Burke maintains, three factors at work in every human situation: the threat of disorder, division, and disintegration; "the yearning to conform with the 'sources of one's being'" (PC,69); and the yearning for unity, merger, and integration (PLF,205-206). Existence is a kind of dialectic of division and merger, disintegration and reintegration, death and rebirth, war and peace; the dialectic is the natural and inevitable result of the complex and ever-changing conflict relation between the human agent and his scene. This dialectic of existence—the drama of human relations—centers in what Burke speaks of as every man's attempt to build himself a character in order to establish and maintain an identity. Burke says in *Attitudes toward History* that all the "issues" with which he has been concerned "come to a head in the problem of identity" (ATH,II,138). And this is true not only of that book but of almost everything Burke has written. Man in search of himself and a way toward the better life is, for Burke, *the* universal situation; and the almost unbelievably complex drama of this quest is a major subject of all Burke's work. The mystery of the self in quest is Burke's point of departure; and the ideal self—one which follows uninterruptedly the "transcendental spirals of [its] moral grows" (ATH,I,108)—is his goal. It is the course of the self in quest which Burke charts, endlessly, ingeniously, and with extraordinary perceptiveness; in fact, it would be more accurate to say that Burke attempts to rechart the self, to direct it out of the waste land towards a better life through symbolic action.

As Burke and others have pointed out, the self is usually found and defined in terms of a number of motivational grounds or scenes. Among these are the natural, the biological, the psychic, the personal or reflexive, the familial, the social-political, and the religious or supernatural. The self, some mysterious and irreducible core of being, some changeless yet changing identity, is, in its growth, constantly subjected to radical pressures from within and without in the form of biological and neurological changes, the solidification and dissolution of family ties, sexual initiation and marriage (or vice versa), changes of setting, assumption of social responsibilities, setting of personal goals, religious crises, and the like. The self identifies with one thing or another, consciously or unconsciously; it accepts and rejects various alternatives, merges with and separates from certain things; its growth is the drama of ethical choice and its ideal is that unity of being which constitutes the determined and forward-moving self. Though the search for the self is a universal pattern of experience, though the pattern is almost always similar no matter who undergoes it, and though all selves are basically alike in so far as they have similar biological and neurological equipment, the individual self and the quest are capable of almost infinite variation. So, to say that the search for the self is central to Burke is to add very little unless one goes on to discuss in detail his concept of the self, to lay out Burke's main co-ordinates—what he later calls the great moments in the drama of human relations.

For Burke, as for Freud, the idea of the self begins with a biological-neurological potential: each individual begins, not with a blank self which is finally completely formed from without, but with a self which has as part of its essence this biological-neurological potential. The self embarks on its quest with something intrinsic to it: it has a certain kind of neurological equipment (the potential for speech and reason); certain permanent fundamental needs; and a certain biological potential (physical growth). In the course of its journey through experience the self builds an identity by making contact with various externals, such as nature and society. This constitutes the drama of the self in quest—the continuous interaction between agent and scene and between the conflicting impulses within the agent. Burke speaks of this gradual evolution of the essential self as "the sojourn of the personality in its different 'glandular [and other] environments'" (ATH,II,97), and points out that the central problem is "how much of one's past identity must be forgotten, how much remoulded, as he moves from one role to the next?" (ATH,II,98). "The maturing of the individual," for example, "exposes him to 'climacteric stages' of one sort or another." Even if there were no important historical changes taking place in society which called into doubt accepted values and conceptions of human purpose,

the mere changing of one's glandular system would involve him in "new situations." And each change of "situation" [scene], in this purely physical sense, would require a reorganization of the mind with relation to the public, forensic structure. Similarly, a man must be "reborn" in order to fit himself for genuine partnership with a woman—and if this partnership is ended, he must again be "reborn" in order to take new problems of identity into account. (ATH,II, 215-216.)

The drama of the self in quest, then, consists of the self confronting new internal and external factors in the form of radical alterations in its biological, natural, familial, social, intellectual, and religious environments. The new factors and the radical alterations necessitate changes in the self's perspective, in its "structure of interpretations, meanings, values, purposes, and inhibitions" (PLF,270). The self must either confront these issues and adjust to them by making such changes as are necessary or retreat into the abyss of itself and perish.

The drama of the self in quest is an extraordinarily complex life-long ritual of death and rebirth, rejection and acceptance, purification and change, disintegration and reintegration; essentially, it is the drama of moral choice. Confronted by such problems as evil, unchangeable brute realities, the trackless maze of unresolved and even undefined personal and social conflicts, and by an always fundamentally chaotic world, the self attempts to build its individual character and adopt its proper role by constructing a "frame of acceptance" (ATH,I,204-205)—a "more or less organized system of meanings by which a thinking man gauges" the world (ATH,I,3-4). In attempting to build an individual character—to find its real self and live purposefully in the external world, satisfying its permanent fundamental needs by conforming to the sources of its being—the self is almost continually in crisis-conflict situations. In some situations, the choice is simple and obvious and the conflict can be solved by direct physical action; but in others the self confronts "overlapping contradictions," where the choice is enormously complex and direct physical action seems impossible. Where conflicts are not resolvable by direct physical action, one "symbolically erects a 'higher synthesis' . . . that helps him to 'accept' them" (ATH,I,120). According to Burke, this "process of transcendence [is] basic to thought" (ATH,I,113), and is most commonly effected through the symbolic action of language whereby one can erect "a series of transcendental . . . poetic and critical" bridges which produce "a synthesis atop the antithesis by the organizing of a unifying *attitude*" (ATH,I,120). The unifying attitude becomes part of a coherent set of attitudes which make up a "frame of acceptance." With the help of such "transcendental bridges" as are necessary, a man "builds his character"; he attempts to put his self together, to discover and maintain his identity so that he can act purposefully and feel at home in the world. Such, Burke maintains, is man's "natural vocation." The potential for language is built into man's cells and it is natural that a self, which has language as part of its essence, would use the symbolic action which language makes possible to effect some of the transformations necessary to its continued moral growth toward final unity of being.

Burke's main coordinates are essentially moral-ethical, and his drama of human relations is an elaborate and deliberately worked out *secular* version of the Christian drama. Whether fact or myth, Burke says, both the Garden of Eden story and its sequel, the story of Christ, the sacrificial redeemer, are true in "essence," for they state, in narrative terms, certain essential truths about the human condition. By reducing both stories to the level of naturalistic discourse and explaining them in terms of the biological-neurological norms, Burke accepts the essential truths while rejecting both the doctrines and the organization (church) with which the stories are associated. The Garden of Eden, for example, has its biological analogue in the womb; there, "food simply descends benignly . . . and the organism has but to open itself and receive the bounty. There is no competition here. The organism . . . thrives by pure receptivity. It is truly at one with its environment . . . [for] the separation of the part from the whole . . . has not yet taken place" (PC,200-201,fn.). The Fall and expulsion from Eden have their biological and neurological analogues in the birth trauma and the agent's capacity for reason and social intercourse. The separation of the part from the whole, however, does not occur as a result of pride and original sin; it is natural and inevitable: man is not expelled because of original sin, but is expelled into it, for implicit in the nature of reason and the relationship between the individual and society is the potential for "sin" (ATH,I,211,fn.). Reason itself, man's neurological inheritance, is the very factor which causes the "categorical guilt" or "original sin" from which all men naturally suffer. Man "falls" every time he follows the impulse towards abstraction which reason and language make possible, and conceives of ideals ("god-terms") which are incapable of being perfectly realized. Man is naturally of "guilt-laden substance" (PLF,50); guilt as a permanent part of man's condition makes purification and redemption a continuous necessity, for, if unrelieved, guilt fragments and corrodes the self. The secular analogue for Christ, the sacrificial redeemer, is symbolic action; however, the purpose of this secular rhetoric of rebirth is *internal* rather than *eternal* rebirth and salvation, and it leads toward the better life rather than toward Heaven.

One of the most important things the scientific orientation denies to man is some means by which "the sense of the unclean [can be] periodically mitigated by purificatory rituals" (ATH,II,41). This is one reason why Burke believes that the scientific, rational account of the human condition is inadequate; it fails to take into account the fact that man is essentially a moral-ethical animal of guilt-laden substance, in continuous need of purification and redemption. This inadequacy must be remedied, Burke says, by a reassertion of the fundamental truths about the human condition contained primarily in the religious but also in the magical orientations. What the church recognized as well as exploited was the fact that man is essentially a moral-ethical animal. "With astounding exactitude, . . . [the church] built upon the foundations of human guilt, subtly contriving both to intensify people's sensitivity to the resources of guilt (making two opportunities for guilt grow where but one had grown before) and to allay this guilt by appropriate rituals and by acts of loyalty to the social status established by custom" (ATH,I,163). "The church founded the notion of brotherhood on the concept of original sin, the preoccupational basis of a guild of the guilty" (PLF,50). The church recognized that original sin and the guilt natural to it is a powerful goad to "collectivist" effort; it recognized that "the most normal mode of expiation is that of socialization" (what Burke calls the "socialization of losses") for by sharing, one's guilt is partly absolved. Finally, Burke argues, the church "well understood the disastrous accumulative power of silence. . . . [It] knew that speech [symbolic action] is curative," and invented all kinds of confessional and purificatory rituals whereby a man was able to strip himself bare, periodically and symbolically to slay the guilty part of himself (ATH,I,166,fn.). The church provided man with an elaborate network of "transcendental bridges" which enabled him to cope with one of his most fundamental and permanent conflicts—guilt. Though Burke believes that the church, which he describes as "a big deserted building, with broken windows and littered doorways" (PC,65), can no longer perform this necessary function for man, he does believe that some secular variant of religion must perform it if man is to be saved from the disastrous end implicit in the scientific rationalization.

According to Burke (in 1935) to act in a creative, assertive, synthetic way is man's ultimate motive (PC,259). For these three adjectives Burke uses, almost interchangeably, a whole cluster of others: religious, ethical, volitional, poetic, cooperative; action, communication, participation; unifying, integrating, transcending; and redemptive. The master term—what Burke calls the god-term—is "ethical-moral." "It is the moral impulse that motivates perception, giving it both intensity and direction, suggesting *what to look for* and *what to look out for*" (PLF,164). In typical fashion, Burke takes this "god-term" and links most of his other key terms to it:

> Action is fundamentally ethical, since it involves preferences. Poetry is ethical. Occupation and preoccupation are ethical. The ethical shapes our selection of means. It shapes our structures of orientation, while these in turn shape the perceptions of the individuals born within the orientation. Hence it radically affects our coöperative processes. The ethical is thus linked with the communicative (particularly when we consider communication in its broadest sense, not merely as the purveying of information, but also as the sharing of sympathies and purposes, the doing of acts in common, as with the leveling process of communicating vessels) . . . all universe-building [which includes the self] is ethical. (PC,250.)

Having isolated the moral-ethical as the primary "*underlying motive or set of motives that activates all men*" (PC,221), Burke then selects Poetry (symbolic action) as the paradigmatic example of this "ultimate motive" in human experience. The building of a self is compared to the writing of a poem (PC,78); the finding of the true self is compared "to the writing of a great poem," for "the poem is a sudden *fusion,* a *falling together of many things formerly apart*" (PC,158). "All action," Burke says, "is poetic," for "all acts are 'synthetic,' each being a new way of putting things together, quite as each line of a drama is" (PC,215,254). "Life itself," Burke maintains, "is a poem in the sense that, in the course of living, we gradually erect a structure of relationships about us in conformity with our interests" (PC,254). Burke believes, in other words, that poetic symbolic action expresses and embodies the essence of the drama of human relations and that through an intensive study of the nature and function of poetry the moral-ethical part of man denied or ignored by the scientific orientation can be rediscovered and re-affirmed. It is not the church to which we must turn for the way towards a better life, but to poetry, to symbolic action. In a passage which states these central ideas as clearly as anything he has written, Burke asks:

> might the great plethora of symbolizations lead, through the science of symbolism itself, back to a concern with "the Way," the old notion of Tao, the conviction that there is one fundamental course of human satisfaction, forever being glimpsed and lost again, and forever being restated in the changing terms of reference that correspond with the changes of historic texture? All that earlier thinkers said of the *universe* might at least be taken as applying to the nature of *man.* One may doubt that such places as heaven, hell, and purgatory await us after death—but one may well suspect that the psychological patterns which they symbolize lie at the roots of our conduct here and now. (PC,183-184.)

The belief that "the way" was to be found in and through poetry appeared in Burke's thought as early as the late twenties. In the middle works (1932-1941), however, Burke takes this essentially Romantic idea and follows it to the end of the line; in his theory of symbolic action he arrives at one of the most extreme defenses of poetry as knowledge and as a rhetoric of rebirth to be found in contemporary American literary criticism. Central to all his thinking about poetry during this period is the premise from the aesthetic of *Counter-Statement* that the poet is a superior man—a kind of ideal norm—with superior knowledge of the psychological universals and superior powers of articulation. These three "abilities" enable the poet to create symbolic structures which "illustrate . . . [the] major psychological devices whereby the mind equips itself to name and confront its [historical and personal] situation" (ATH,I,129). They also enable the poet to have a "clear awareness of the fact that a man's need of 'integration' or 'fusion' involves factors more complex, and closer to 'magic,' than rationalistic oversimplifications of political necessities can reveal" (SoR,I,171). Working from these premises, Burke makes a number of additional hyperbolic assertions about the poet and poetry, all of which illustrate the thoroughness with which he developed the Romantic belief in the superiority of the poet and poetry. Burke says that "the devices of poetry are close to the spontaneous genius of man" (PC,66); that "to learn what is really going on in the world" "one must watch the 'poetry exchange' " (ATH,II,240); that poems "are like 'meter readings' " for they are "the dial on which [the] fundamental psychological processes of *all* living are recorded" (ATH,II,35); that "the processes of social commerce operating in life as a whole" are all clearly revealed in poetry (ATH,II,35-36; PLF,308); and that "points of view"—attitudes toward history—"first make themselves apparent in the realm of 'fancy' " (PLF,234). Burke believes that *the* most fundamental psychological process of all living is the "ritualistic naming and changing of identity (whereby a man fits himself for a role in accordance with established coordinates or for a change of role in accordance with new co-ordinates which necessity has forced upon him)" (ATH,II,169-170). Poetry not only functions actively in this "ritualistic naming and changing of identity" in the sense that the poet uses it as a rhetoric of rebirth to effect changes in "role," but, Burke asserts, *the processes of* change of identity *are* [also] *most clearly revealed by analyzing formal works of art and applying the results of our analysis to the 'informal art of living' in general*" (PLF,308).

All of the above quotations are based upon a single assumption and all of them really affirm the same thing: that the poet is of all men the most extraordinary and that poetry is not only the mirror which reflects and the lamp which lights up the world, but the balm which heals it. Few people have ever taken this assumption and these ideas so seriously as Burke. Working out from them he constructed a poetic orientation which he conceived of as a solution to the historical situation in which he found himself and his society. He proposed the poetic orientation as a counter-statement for the scientific orientation: he asserted that its ideal was peace rather than war, action-without-combat instead of physical violence; he claimed that the poetic orientation gave a more complete account of man, that it was closer to the sources of man's being, that it recognized man as an essentially moral-ethical animal who must move toward the better life through symbolic action. In short, Burke proposed to extract a philosophy of living from poetry itself and with this "fresh unity of purpose" (PC,268) to rechart the self towards a better life. Between 1924 and 1941 Burke moved from writing poetry to theorizing about poetry to converting a theory of poetry into a philosophy of living.

According to Burke—and his own development surely bears it out—"a theory of poetry is likewise a theory of reality, a psychology, and an ethics; and its perspective may even be transferred to an account of historical or economic trends, if the times are such that we ask for the transference" (*Poetry,*XLVII,52). Evidently the times were such, for Burke made his theory of poetry into a theory of everything. In the long summarizing passage at the end of *Permanence and Change,* Burke presents his position as follows:

> . . . the ultimate metaphor for discussing the universe and man's relations to it must be the poetic or dramatic metaphor. Many metaphors are possible [e.g., man as warrior, man as machine, man as

animal] . . . and though any of these simplifications can serve as a postulate from which important and useful considerations . . . will follow, we suggest that the metaphor of the poetic or dramatic man can include them all and go beyond them all.

In adopting such [a] metaphor as key, we have a vocabulary of motives already at hand, evolved through the whole history of human thought. Indeed, beginning with such a word as *composition* to designate the architectonic nature of either a poem, a social construct, or a method of practical action, we can take over the whole vocabulary of tropes (as formulated by the rhetoricians) to describe the specific patterns of human behavior. Since social life, like art, is a *problem of appeal,* the poetic metaphor would give us invaluable hints for describing modes of practical action which are too often measured by simple tests of utility and too seldom with reference to the communicative, sympathetic, *propitiatory* factors that are clearly present in the procedures of formal art and must be as truly present in those informal arts of living we do not happen to call arts.

Would we not be actually living an onomatopoeia, for instance, if in a moment of anger we abruptly disarranged the furniture in our room or our relations with our friends? Are not such clinical words as fetishism and transference discussing much the same phenomenon as was discussed in the old books of rhetoric under the name of synecdoche, or part for the whole? Does not the "egoistic-altruistic merger" involve in practical life that same intimate relationship which we observe in the identity of poet and material, of internal attitude and external embodiment? Is not the civic process everywhere marked by acts of ingratiation and justification quite analogous to the motivations of art? Is not the relation between individual and group greatly illumined by reference to the corresponding relation between writer and audience? . . .

The [poetic] metaphor also has the advantage of emphasizing the *participant* aspect of action rather than its *competitive* aspect, hence offering a prompt basis of objection when the contingencies of our economic structure force us to overstress competitive attitudes. . . . Projecting the metaphor by analogical extension, we find that the entire universe again takes life, as a mighty drama still in progress. And even if we are led to fear that this drama is essentially tragic, the poetic metaphor reminds us that in a perfect tragedy there is "catharsis," hence we may be heartened to inquire what form this catharsis may take. (PC,263-266.)

The poetic or dramatic metaphor, Burke argues, is a purposive or teleological one. It stresses man's nature as a moral-ethical animal and takes into account the drama of choice which the self necessarily experiences in its quest (PC,260-261). The poetic metaphor is deliberately opposed to the mechanistic, scientific one which treats human acts and relations in terms of stimulus, response and conditioned reflex. From the poetic or dramatic metaphor Burke proposes to derive a "*calculus* [a grammar]—a vocabulary, or set of coordinates, that serves best for the integration of all phenomena studied by the *social* sciences" (PLF,105). In short, he proposes to derive a view of reality from poetry itself; and at the same time to derive from poetry an ideal program of action which the self may adopt.

Few people have investigated so thoroughly as Burke the uses to which poetry can be put for extra-literary purposes. In *Attitudes toward History,* for instance, he examines the various literary categories to show how "each of the great poetic forms stresses its own peculiar way of building the mental equipment (meanings, attitudes, character) by which one handles the significant factors of his time" (ATH,I,41-42). He begins with the epic, which he calls a "typical frame of symbolic adjustment under primitive conditions" (ATH,I,42). "The epic," Burke says,

> is designed . . . to make men "at home in" those [primitive] conditions. It "accepts" the rigors of war (the basis of the tribe's success) by magnifying the role of warlike hero. Such magnification serves two purposes: It lends dignity to the necessities of existence, "advertising" courage and individual sacrifice for group advantage— and it enables the humble man to share the worth of the hero by the process of "identification." The hero, real or legendary, thus risks himself and dies that others may be *vicariously* heroic (a variant of the symbolic cluster in Christianity whereby the victim of original sin could share vicariously in the perfection of Christ by his membership in the Church, the *corpus Christi*). The social value of such a pattern resides in its ability to make humility ["peace"] and self-glorification ["war"] *work together*: the sense of one's limitations (in comparison with the mighty figure of the legend) provides one with a realistic attitude for gauging his personal resources, while his vicarious kinship with the figure gives him the distinction necessary for the needs of self-justification. (ATH,I,44.)

The epic, then, promotes the attitudes of humility and resignation, for the flaw in the hero prompts one to seek the flaw in himself, to take "the inventory of one's *personal* limits" (ATH,I,46) and to realize that even the god-like men have their personal and human limitations. In one of his many statements on tragedy, Burke claims that, like the epic, it promotes the attitudes of humility and resignation. Tragedies admonish "one to 'resign' himself to a sense of his limitations." (ATH,I,49.)

> This state of resignation is produced through fusing, in aesthetic symbols, mental conflicts which cannot be fused in the practical sphere. The maintaining of a strict family pattern, for instance, gives rise to certain proscriptions or taboos which conflict with desires arising out of the same pattern. One could not practically destroy these taboos without breaking up the family pattern. Hence, by symbolic fusion in tragedy, an ability to "accept one's fate" is

established. This, in a general way, is the explanation of the "catharsis" of tragedy, which is the essence of "pure" art. It enables us to "resign" ourselves by resolving in aesthetic fusion trends or yearnings not resolvable in the practical sphere. (PLF,320.)

The "trends" or "yearnings" which are expressed and "resolved" in tragedy are the "criminal" and "expiatory" (PC,195). Tragedy, Burke says, is "a complex kind of trial by jury," and hence is "essentially concerned with the processes of guilt and justification" (PC,195). All kinds of "secret offenses" and unspeakable conflicts, such as incest, matricide, patricide, and regicide are expressed and purged in the subterfuges of symbolic action. The humility comes from the fact that tragedy universalizes the "trends" or "yearnings" by making them public and by asserting that all men are guilty and must expiate their crimes; the resignation or "acceptance" comes from the fact that the tragic catharsis temporarily or even partly solves (resolves) an intolerable conflict and thus enables one to "resign" himself to himself and life by enabling him once again to "accept" both. Tragedy, like the epic, performs a purgative-redemptive function which can and often does effect a change in attitude.

In *Attitudes toward History*, Burke attempts briefly to show how other poetic categories—notably the ode, the elegy, burlesque, and satire—may help to form our attitudes and become part of the equipment necessary for sane living. Satire, like tragedy, performs a purgative function which enables one symbolically to "sterilize" those trends or yearnings in oneself which might lead to physical violence and war. The satirist "attacks *in others* the weaknesses and temptations that are really *within himself*" (ATH,I,62). Hence, satire "*gratifies* and *punishes* the vice" which one has within himself. The satirist whips himself with his own lash in a kind of grotesque ritual of negative purification. The elegy, Burke shows, functions like homeopathic magic and a vaccination: it helps one to "develop tolerance to possibilities of great misfortune by accustoming him . . . to misfortune in small doses, administered stylistically." The "homeopathic style," which Burke feels is characteristic of all poetry, is "based . . . on the feeling that danger cannot be handled by head-on attack, but must be *accommodated*," controlled by "channelization" rather than by "elimination" (ATH,I,56,fn.). Burke calls this the "lightning rod" theory of art; and some of the ways in which he applies it have been briefly illustrated in the previous paragraphs. To switch the metaphor, Burke believes that "the symbolic manipulations of art [can] supply the vents for 'anti-social' [war-like] impulses, taking up the slack . . . between [a] . . . given society's norms and the individual's necessarily imperfect fit with these norms" (ATH,II,15-17). Now a vent "takes off" impurities and a lightning rod diverts what is dangerous and extremely destructive, rendering it harmless. In a similar way, impurities within the self may be taken off by means of "symbolic manipulations of art," and certain destructive trends may be diverted and rendered harmless through the expression or experiencing of them in the "symbolic manipulations of art." Or, an attitude towards either impurities or dangers expressed in a single work, or category of works, or by a particular author, may be adopted as part of one's equipment for living; and even though the impurity or danger may not be removed, the change in attitude towards it may make it easier to control and live with.

This particular phase of Burke's development of a philosophy or psychology of human relations derived from the nature and function of poetry is perhaps best illustrated in the use to which he puts comedy. "Like tragedy," Burke says,

> comedy warns against the dangers of pride, but its emphasis shifts from *crime* to *stupidity*. . . . The progress of humane enlightenment can go no further than in picturing people not as *vicious,* but as *mistaken* [i.e., in need of correction rather than destruction]. When you add that people are *necessarily* mistaken, that *all* people are exposed to situations in which they must act as fools, that *every* insight contains its own special kind of blindness, you complete the comic circle, returning again to the lesson of humility that underlies great tragedy. The audience, from its vantage point, sees the operation of errors that the characters of the play cannot see; thus seeing from two angles at once, it is chastened by dramatic irony. (ATH,I, 51-52.)

The comic attitude, Burke believes, "would enable people *to be observers of themselves, while acting. Its* ultimate would not be *passiveness,* but *maximum consciousness.* One would 'transcend' himself by noting his own foibles. He would provide a rationale for locating the irrational and non-rational." (ATH,I,220-221.) From this attitude Burke develops what he calls a "comic" or "dialectical" methodology which has its final realization in dramatism. Comic or dialectical criticism is a "methodology of exposure"; it attempts to demystify things, or, to use Burke's analogy, like the sun in Aesop's fable, it makes things "strip" and wash in the river. By systematically trying to show that nothing is what it seems to be on the surface, comic criticism tries to get at the full reality of things. Comic criticism, which approaches life in the way a "new critic" approaches a poem, attempts to "provide important cues for the composition of one's life, which demands accommodation to the structure of others' lives" (ATH,I,224).

As I pointed out earlier, Burke makes man as poet the ultimate metaphor for the study of man and human relations. As a result, the poet becomes the ideal man, and living, as well as each individual life, is treated as "a poem in the making." All the acts of a single man, like the parts of a good poem, are treated as if they were necessarily related and organically unified. Acts and things are treated as if they were symbols, and lives as if they were unified dramas of the self in quest. Western history is studied as a drama in five acts. Poetry becomes the expression of the essence of man and human relations and is thus studied as a true image of reality. Oddly enough, and seemingly without worrying about the possibilities of logical contradiction, Burke sees poetry as the expression of the ideal essence of man and human relations and thus studies it as a true image of both the real (or indicative) and the ideal (or optative). Not only does poetry express the real and ideal, but as symbolic action, it mediates between them by performing some of the most complex functions necessary to man if he is to progress toward the better life. Consequently, Burke studies poetry both for a knowledge of how it functions as a rhetoric of rebirth, and so that he may, priest-like, disseminate the good word.

All of these ideas led finally to Burke's theory of symbolic action. Mentioned first in *Permanence and Change* and partly developed throughout the germinal *Attitudes toward History*, the theory is fully developed in the title essay of *The Philosophy of Literary Form*. Ultimately, the theory of symbolic action is developed into a theory of language—dramatism—and is exhaustively worked out in Burke's tetralogy of *Motives*. Though Burke has been defining symbolic action for almost twenty years, he has never, as far as I know, given a concise and complete statement of the complex of ideas which constitutes the essence of the theory. When first introducing the idea of symbolic action in *Permanence and Change,* he makes a distinction between "*symbolic*" and "*necessitous*" labor; "drudgery," he says, "is purely necessitous labor, whereas symbolic labor is fitted into the deepest lying patterns of the individual" (PC,82). "'Symbolic' acts," however, "are grounded in 'necessitous' ones" (PC,168). Hobbies, for example, "are symbolic labor, undertaken as compensation when our patterns of necessitous labor happen for one reason or another to be at odds with our profoundest needs" (PC,237-238). Later, in *Attitudes toward History,* Burke makes the same kind of distinction between symbolic and other kinds of acts. "If a man climbs a mountain," he says,

> not through any interest in mountain climbing, but purely because he wants to get somewhere, and the easiest way to get there is by crossing the mountain, we need not look for symbolism. But if we begin to discuss why he wanted to get there, we do get into matters of symbolism. For his conceptions of purpose involve a texture of human relationships; his purposes are "social"; as such, they are not something-in-and-by-itself, but a function of many relationships; which is to say that they are symbolical. For eventually, you arrive at an act which a man does because he is interested in doing it exactly as he does do it—and that act is a "symbolic" act. It is related to his "identity." (ATH,II,165-166.)

In other words, according to Burke, "there are *practical* acts, and there are symbolic acts" (PLF,9). The distinction between them seems to lie in the fact that symbolic acts are representative, symptomatic acts of the self that performs them and, at the same time, perform some compensating function for that self. What the acts "represent," what they are "symptomatic" of, and their "compensating" function seem to constitute the symbolic or "hidden" meaning of the act. Symbolic action seems to be something which has hidden or private meaning and performs a hidden or private compensating function. Quite obviously almost any act, no matter how practical or necessary, could be a representative, and function as a compensating act. Yet Burke argues that "if one . . . carried out the motions necessary to attain some natural or mechanical end (as when picking up food in order to eat it, when the cells of the body really did need more nutriment), here would be a wholly 'practical' act" (HR,IX,214). The example seems patently absurd in view of the fact that such an act might well be representative and symptomatic of a particular person's essential self, and might be performing some profound compensating function for it. In a recent essay, Burke says that "insofar as an act is representative (or 'symbolic') of an agent, that act is the manifestation of some underlying 'moral principle' in the agent. Insofar as the act does not represent some underlying principle of the agent's character, some fixed trait of his personality, . . . it is not so much an act as an accident." (ChiR,VIII,97.) Certain obvious conclusions can be drawn from these attempts to define a symbolic act. Any act (whether physical or verbal) that is in fact representative of the self which performed it, and any act that has a compensating function for the self which performs it is a symbolic act. But, in vacuo, no act can be said to be purely practical, for, given the complexities of the human psyche and the findings of the psycho-analysts, analysis may show an act to be "symbolic" in either or both of the ways described above.

In view of these conclusions, one of Burke's most concise definitions of symbolic action seems absurd: "poetry, or any verbal act," he says, "is to be considered as 'symbolic action'" (PLF,8). This would seem to mean that all verbal acts are "representative," "symptomatic," and "compensating" acts of and for the person who performed them. The Sears, Roebuck catalogue, newspaper fillers, want-ads, and business letters—all of which strike one as eminently "practical" and "necessitous" verbal acts—become "the manifestations of some underlying 'moral principle' in the agent[s]" who wrote them, and compensate for the frustration of some of the agents' "profoundest needs." Now this is as ridiculous as the example given earlier of a purely practical act. The conclusion to be drawn from setting various definitions of symbolic action side by side is that Burke does not mean the same thing every time he uses the term. Hence, if one wishes to make sense out of the theory, and Burke's applications of it, one must establish the range of meanings it has for Burke and the way in which they are interrelated, and then determine from the context which of the meanings apply.

An examination of the many uses of the term reveals that it has three separate but interrelated meanings. When Burke says that "any verbal act" is "symbolic action" he means this in the most literal way, for words are symbols which stand for things and ideas, and verbalizations are symbols in action. Thus, when Burke speaks of "poetry, or any other verbal act" as symbolic action, or when he runs together "linguistic, or symbolic, or literary action" (PLF,vii), he is not making an absurd statement, but a literal one. All of the literary arts are indeed symbolic action, with symbolic, in this case, being little more than a synonym for verbal. So, when Burke says that "if a man crosses a street, it is a practical act [but] if he writes a book about crossings—crossing streets, bridges, oceans, etc.—that is a symbolic act"

(PLF,267,fn.3), the statement, though the term "practical" is misleading, makes perfectly good sense as a superficial distinction between non-verbal and verbal acts. But the statement carries another meaning which helps clarify the "representative" meaning of symbolic action, as well as Burke's consistently misleading use of the word "practical." The opposition between "practical" and "symbolic" suggests that verbal action is not practical, yet even a superficial reading of Burke reveals that he thinks symbolic action the most practical thing in the world. The distinction he is trying to suggest turns on the difference between an act and an accident. If, for example, a man deliberately wrote a book about crossings, or if he were obsessively interested in crossings and collected all kinds of works on the subject, both the verbal act of writing the book and the non-verbal acts of crossing and collecting would be symbolic in so far as they were significant representative acts of the agent or self which performed them. Representative-symbolic acts are images of the self which performs them, and analysis of such symbolic acts will reveal "some underlying principle of the agent's character, some fixed trait of his personality." Just as words are both what they are and what they stand for, so representative-symbolic acts, whether non-verbal or verbal, are both acts and images of the self. They are symbolic autobiography: acts symbolizing the essential self. Though any act may be a static, symbolic representation of some fixed trait of an agent's self, the act may also be performing some profound function for the agent over and above self-expression. For example, Burke says that "going nude" is "a symbolic divesting (unclothing) of guilt, a symbolic purification" (PLF,27,fn.3). He says also that poems function "as a symbolic redemptive process."

In order to be redeemed, one must be purified; according to Burke, "going nude" is a purgative-redemptive symbolic act because previously there must have been "the hiding of the shameful, [and] hence the clothing of the pudenda [becomes] . . . the 'essence' of guilt"; through an associative process, the "covering" takes on the quality of the "covered"; hence, "by removing the clothes, one may at the same time ritualistically remove the shame of which the clothes are 'representative'" (PLF,27,fn.3). These examples give us the clues for another important meaning of symbolic action and explain why it is the "manifestation of some underlying 'moral principle.'" Burke believes that man is fundamentally a moral-ethical animal, that he has built into his system a moral sense and the impulse toward alleviating the guilt naturally produced by moral consciousness. Man must continuously purge and redeem himself from the guilt that is as natural to him as breathing; such highly practical, purgative-redemptive moral action is the third kind of symbolic action. Any act, whether non-verbal or verbal, which performs this function, is a symbolic act.

There are, then, three general meanings for symbolic action; linguistic, representative, and purgative-redemptive. The first includes all verbal action; the second covers all acts which are representative images of the essential self; and the third includes all acts with a purgative-redemptive function. Clearly, symbolic action includes much more than poetry; and clearly almost anything from the full range of human action could be a symbolic act in one or more of the senses given above. As is usual with Burke, he makes his theory broad enough so that it will cover almost everything and permit repeated excursions away from and back to a fixed point. Burke's almost dogmatic assertion that all poetic acts are always symbolic acts in all three meanings is one of the unique features of his system. His argument is that though any act may be "symbolic" in one or more ways, all poems are *always* representative, purgative-redemptive symbolic acts. This means that every poem is the true image of the self which created it, and that every poem performs a purgative-redemptive function for the self. A poem, Burke tells us, is "the *dancing of an attitude*"; it is the internal self externalized, enacted in symbolic form (PLF,9,10-11). Poems "symbolically enact" the poet's characteristic "mental conflict[s]" (PLF,10), for "the poet will naturally tend to write about that which most deeply engrosses him—and nothing more deeply engrosses a man than his *burdens*" (PLF,17). And poems, Burke adds, are private rituals of rebirth (ATH,II,37-38), "salvation" devices (ATH,I,173), "purificatory ritual[s]" (PLF,130,131); they are "rituals of redemption . . . a kind of 'private mass' . . . communion services" (PLF,87-88).

Always profoundly personal, always about what deeply engrosses the ideal poetic self, poems (those "charismatic vessels" of grace) function for the poet as a private and, Burke believes, highly necessary and effective purgative-redemptive rhetoric of rebirth. They not only enable the poet to move toward the better life through symbolic action, but they chart the quest of the ideal self with extraordinary exactitude and richness. To use Burke's own word, they not only chart the way, they "dredge" it: they search out the hidden dangers in it and clear the way for others. The theory of symbolic action extends Burke's notion—first developed in *Counter-Statement*—that poetry is a necessary part of one's equipment for sane living. Because poems are the poet's solutions to problems faced in the search for the self and the better life, they may be considered as "charts" or "maps" (PLF,6,294) which one may consult when lost in the wilderness of the world; or they may be used to study the various "routes" which the ideal self takes in its quest, and from such a study one may locate himself and derive some solace from the knowledge that others have traveled the same hard route. Again, since poems are superior solutions to the problems of living, they may be studied as "formulae," as "statements," as "definitions." In this respect, Burke speaks of poems as entries in an informal dictionary, to which we may turn for definitions of, and solutions to, the problems of living (PLF,1,283). Poems, he says, are like proverbs: they name the "typical, recurrent situations" (PLF,293), they help one to "organize and command the army of one's thoughts and images" (PLF,298). And since poems are representative-symbolic acts of the ideal poetic self in quest, they provide us with depth knowledge of the self and the way it behaves in various motivational scenes. As representative-symbolic acts, poems should be subjected to the kind of analysis which psychoanalysts use on dreams, and for the same reason, since poems are secular confessions in which one names one's number (PLF,280-

281) in the "labyrinthine subterfuges of symbolism" (*Chimera*,I,21).

But this is not all, for poems as purgative-redemptive symbolic acts are "catharsis by secretion," incantations (PLF,281), "salvation device[s]" (ATH,I,173); a poetic symbolic act is like a "private-enterprise Mass" (PLF,286-287), "a strategy for taking up the slack between what is wanted and what is got" (PLF,54). It is a kind of "prayer" in which the poet makes himself over in the image of his imagery (ATH,II,113,fn.). In poetic symbolic action one can place one's burdens on the back of a symbolic scapegoat and whip it out into a verbal desert to die (PLF,45); or one can lift himself up by creating a symbolic hero. Burke thinks of poetry as "prophylactic" or "therapeutic," both for the poet and the reader. Poetry is "stylistic medicine" (PLF,61), and the poet is a "medicine man." As "medicine man" the poet "deals with 'poisons.' . . . [He] would immunize us by stylistically infecting us with the disease," or by providing us with an "antidote." (PLF,64-65.)

The central idea of the theory of symbolic action, and one of the main tenets of the "poetic realism" which Burke hoped would point the way towards a better life, is the belief that "poetry is produced for purposes of comfort, as part of the *consolatio philosophiae*. It is undertaken as *equipment for living,* as a ritualistic way of arming us to confront perplexities and risks. It would *protect* us" (PLF,61). Poetry, Burke says, is like the shield of Perseus, for "Perseus . . . could not face the serpent-headed monster without being turned to stone, but was immune to this danger if he observed it by reflection in [his shield] . . . The poet's style, his form (a social idiom) is this mirror, enabling him to confront the risk, but by the protection of an indirect reflection." (PLF,63.) The poet is like Perseus: his superiority is equivalent to the sword, shield, and winged shoes which Hermes and Athena gave to Perseus. His superiority enables him to do what Perseus was able to do with his gifts. Though Burke mentions only one of the gifts—the mirror-like shield which he compares to the poet's style and form—he must certainly have been aware of the others, for without the winged shoes Perseus never could have reached or left the island, and without the sword he could not have slain the serpent-headed monster. Poetry is not just an indirect reflection; it is symbolic *action.* The sword and winged shoes are as important as his shield if one is to take Perseus as Burke's figure of the poet. In moving from the poet-poem to the poem-audience relationship, Burke reverses the Perseus myth, for he contends that symbolic action is the poet's gift to humanity. The first gift—the verbal sword—enables man to do his symbolic slaying of the real or imagined monsters which menace him; the second gift—the verbal shield or mirror—enables man to observe and confront indirectly the monsters which might turn him to stone if they were observed and confronted directly; and the third gift—the verbal winged shoes—enables man to travel to and from the dangerous island and, ultimately, to return home. Together, the three gifts enable man to progress toward the better life.

As wise man, prophet, and medicine man, the poet will perform those charismatic symbolic acts which are the means of man's salvation; priest-like, the critic will mediate between the redeemers and those seeking redemption, interpreting the holy texts and preaching the gospel of the new secular religion. In this way, Burke hopes to effect a cure for the technological psychosis, directing the self away from the universal holocaust which he envisions as the ultimate end of the scientific orientation and toward the better life of purified war which he envisions as the ultimate goal of the poetic orientation.

Symbols in Society

by Hugh Duncan

Editor's Note: This selection begins with Section #3.

3. Structure and Function in Social Action: A Dramatistic Model

In great and established sciences such as physics, we do not need to ground every methodological statement on a theoretical base. But in a new science such as sociology, where we do not yet possess models of sociation which can match the classical models of motion in space and time, we must be careful to ground our methodology in some coherent body of theory.

Our concerns here are with the structure and function of the act considered as dramatic in form and social in content. The *form* of the act consists of five elements, namely, the stage (situation or environment) on which the act takes place, the kind of act it is (its social function), the roles involved in the action, the ways in which communication occurs within the act, and the kind of social order which is invoked as the purpose of the act. The *content* of the act exists in social interests as these are expressed in the basic institutions of society. Eleven such contents of social experience are distinguished. These are (1) the family; (2) ruling, being ruled, and reaching common agreement, as in political modes of action; (3) economics, or the provision of goods and services; (4) defense, or the means ranging from force to the apologetics and propaganda we use to defend ourselves from enemies within and without the community; (5) education, or the creation and trans-mission of culture; (6) sociability, or the purely social forms we use to court each other as superiors, inferiors, and equals; (7) play, games, entertainments and festivals, in which we learn to act together under rules, and in joy so that our social bonds will be strengthened in the euphoria of "togetherness"; (8) health and welfare; (9) religion; (10) art; and (11) science.

If we say that roles are "enacted" in their basic institutions, we must define what we mean by "enacted." Is "enactment" a "process," a "trans-action," a "performance," a "pattern of expected behavior," or a "position"? And whatever definition we select we must construct a model whose structure and function are derived from the same field of experience. If a role is a "performance," it is not a "transaction." If actors "cathect" to "patterns of behavior" they do not perform roles within an institution. Theoretical models, like metaphors, cannot be mixed. The theoretical monsters produced in modern American sociology almost rival the chimeras of antiquity; firebreathing monsters, with a lion's head, a goat's body, and a serpent's tail, have been matched by grotesques with mechanical heads and symbolic bodies. Actors, we are told, are being moved by mechanical processes which are the expression of patterns in which norms are cathected. Even if we know what this means, how do we observe it? What, in short, are the *data* of "process," and "pattern," and *how* is a norm "cathected"?

We must take into account what was communicated, the situation in which the communication occurred, the kind of person who communicated (that is, his role), the means he used, and the social purpose of his communication. If we stress media, or any of these five elements, to the exclusion of others (as does the Toronto school led by Marshall McLuhan), we make our special view so general that it risks loss of meaning, or, at least, loss of precision in meaning, as we have seen in Freud's use of "sex," or Durkheim's use of "society." We ascribe all kinds of affects to media, and then "derive" various effects from our ascription. The same may be said for all mechanistic theoretical constructs which reduce language to a series of signals. Signals do not set, create, or criticize themselves. The pattern within which they function was created by someone to serve a certain purpose.

Kenneth Burke, I. A. Richards, Bronislaw Malinowski, and George Herbert Mead differ in their models of symbolic action. But, in one sense, this is a difference in degree, not kind. In *The Philosophy of the Act* (1938), which is a compilation of unpublished papers Mead left at his death in 1931, and which is a mature statement of views foreshadowed in his early essays, notably "The definition of the Psychical" of 1903, Mead distinguishes four stages of the act, namely, impulse, perception, manipulation, and consummation. In *Mind, Self, and Society* (1934), he discusses the emergence of the self in role enactment. In *The Philosophy of the Present* (1932) he describes the temporal qualities of symbolic action. In *The Meaning of Meaning: A Study of the Influence of Language Upon Thought and of the Science of Symbolism* (in which the authors state, in 1923, the date of the first edition, that some of the pages were written as long ago as 1910), I. A. Richards and C. K. Ogden describe three factors in symbolic action, namely, "mental processes, the symbol, a referent—something which is thought 'of.'" The theoretical problem of symbolic analysis, as they see it, is how to describe the relationship between these three elements.

In his famous Supplement I to *The Meaning of Meaning,* "The Problem of Meaning in Primitive Languages," Bronislaw Malinowski distinguishes between languages as a "mode of action rather than as a countersign of thought" by the elaboration of his concept of "context of situation." In his view there are three fundamental uses of language; active, narrative, and ritual, which are analyzed through a model composed of three elements—symbol, act, and referent. In Kenneth Burke's works, notably *The Grammar of Motives* (1945) and *The Rhetoric of Motives* (1950), we find a synthesis of many views on the structure and function of symbolic action. Burke holds that while symbols are part of a communicative context which is not wholly symbolic, they do have a nature of their own. His task in the creati model of the symbolic act, as he sees it, is to conceive of symbols upon a scene" so that we give due importance to the structure of th well as to the relationship between the symbolic act and environmer act (which, Burke feels, has been stressed far too much in environr schools). In his model there are five terms: scene (the situation), a was done), actor (the kind of person who performed the act), age means of instruments used in performing the act), and purpose (why the act was performed).

Burke's pentad can be adapted to a sociological model of action easily enough if we think of the scene as a social stage, the act as the basic social contexts of action we find in social institutions, such as the family, govern-ment, economics, defense, education, entertainment, sociability, health, religion, art, and science; the actor as the various social roles enacted in these basic social institutions; agency as the medium in which communication takes place; and purpose as the struggle to achieve the consensus necessary to integration in social action. This is only a structural statement, of course, and if this theoretical approach is to be reduced to a sociological methodology, we must describe how this structure functions in social relationships, and, con-versely, how those elements of social action which are based in communi-cation are affected by their symbolic structure.

Freud, Malinowski, and Burke offer us many clues here. The basic socio-logical question on symbolic function is: How do symbols create and sustain order in social relationships? Mead taught sociologists that the self emerges in role enactment. We assume the roles of others to become aware of our self. When playing at being someone else, the self realizes its own nature at the same time it realizes the nature of the person whose role is being played. The self is born in gestures, and especially in vocal gestures since we hear our own vocal gestures as others hear them. In Mead's model the self arises out of a parliament of selves in which the self takes into account the attitudes of other selves toward the self. This is necessary because in situations which are problematic the self cannot act without the help of other selves. To act with others we need to put ourselves in their place, as they need to put themselves in our place. We can do this because we possess a common stock of public images made available to us in the various symbols we use in communi-cation. For without such public images, what Mead calls "universals" there could be no communication, and, hence, no community.

Granted then that the self arises in communication, what is the specific sociological component of this process? If the structure of the act is dramatistic, as Mead, Cooley, and notably, Burke, teach, what is the specific social nature of this drama? In short, how does the dramatistic structure function to achieve social integration? Of all questions asked in symbolic theory this is the most important to the sociologist. For, if we cannot explain *how* symbols function to achieve order in social relations, we cannot invoke "symbolic action" as a constituent element of the "social." Instead we must reduce symbols to "referents" in non-symbolic elements such as sex, work, or religion. If we say (as I have said in my works) that social structure (hierarchy, in my terminology) is created and sustained in symbolic action, we must say something about how all this happens.

All this seems obvious enough. For, how can we conceive of structure unless we reduce our abstractions to concrete social functions? Sociologists often neglect this question, and when they do, symbolic function within the act is explained not through structure as it functions in action in society, but as in thought within the mind, or as an "element" in some kind of "patterned" process. There is thought in the act, to be sure, but analogies of symbolic action derived from models of thought must be used with great care. Used carelessly they reduce all symbolic action to cognition (how we "perceive" or "apprehend" the world). How then are we to think about emotion, will, desire, affect, or attitudes, unless we consider them to be an inferior kind of thought, or as the "beginnings" of acts which end in cognition? Another source of confusion in thinking about symbolic function occurs when function is reduced to structure. The anthropologist Lévi-Strauss does this in his discussion of Indo-European languages when he says: "The languages have simple structures utilizing numerous elements. The opposition between *the simplicity of the structure* and *multiplicity of elements* is expressed in the fact that several elements compete to occupy the same position in the structure."[22] Marshall McLuhan's dictum that "the medium is the message" is another example of this.

Sociologists are aware of the dangers of echoing what has been said by synchronic linguists (who study languages as autonomous systems without reference to anything except other linguistic systems), and of talking about "structure," "pattern," or "form," as a way of avoiding the problems of talking about the function of language. They know, if others do not, that grammar cannot be separated from rhetoric. Inferences about symbolic function drawn from grammar must be made carefully. As Malinowski said in 1923, in his Supplement to *Meaning of Meaning:* "The lack of a clear and precise view of Linguistic function and of the nature of Meaning, has been, I believe, the cause of relative sterility of much otherwise excellent linguistic theorizing."[23] Even in 1923 the problem of relating linguistic form to function was not new. As J. R. Firth points out in his essay, "Ethnographic Analysis and Language with Reference to Malinowski's Views,"[24] Philipp Wegener had already developed a "situation theory" by 1885. In his first lecture in *A*

---

[22] In *Language in Culture: Conference on the Interrelations of Language and Other Aspects of Culture,* edited by Harry Hoijer (Chicago: The University of Chicago Press, 1954), there is an informative article, "Concerning Inferences From Linguistic to Nonlinguistic Data" by Joseph H. Greenberg (See pp. 3-19) with a discussion, "Inferences from Linguistic to Nonlinguistic Data," (pp. 127-47). The discussions of the Whorf Hypothesis (pp. 216-79) are very enlightening.

[23] C. K. Ogden and I. A. Richards, *The Meaning of Meaning: A Study of the Influence of Language upon Thought and of the Science of Symbolism* (New York: Harcourt, Brace and Co., 1945), p. 310.

[24] See *Man and Culture: An Evaluation of the Work of Bronislaw Malinowski,* edited by Raymond Firth (New York: Harper and Row, Harper-Torchbooks, 1964), pp. 93-118.

Treatise on Language: or the Relation Which Words Bear to Things, published in 1836, Alexander Bryan Johnson, the founding father of American semantics, declared that words must be understood as the "expositors of nature."[25]

4. The Problem of Function in Symbolic Analysis

How do symbols create and sustain social integration? Granted a dramatistic model of symbolic action, how does their structure function? If we abandon mechanical models based either on classical mechanics (in which symbols "gear" and "mesh") or on the new biophysical world (in which symbols "cathect"), what replacement do we propose, and why?

Symbolic integration is achieved through naming. We march to death in the name of God ("In this sign we conquer"), country, ideology, destiny, or way of life. We organize our creative lives in the name of wisdom, holiness, or beauty. We discipline our daily lives in the name of family, work, or what we owe (our social responsibilities) to others. In the name of status honor, we uphold styles of life as expressed in the drama of hierarchy. As Weber says: "The way in which social honor is distributed in a community between typical groups participating in this distribution we may call the 'social order.' "[26] Social order (in Weber) depends on "status honor." "In content, status honor is normally expressed by the fact that above all else a specific *style of life* can be expected from all those who wish to belong to the circle."[27] A style of life, like any style, is an expression through symbols of appropriate and inappropriate ways of acting. These "ways" are carried out under names which are not simply significations of "patterns," "triggers" to "latent forces," "indicators of attitudes," or "evocations" of archaic memories, but *goads* to action.

Honorable names give power because they endow actions with dignity, radiance, and glory. Dignity, as Weber argues, "is the precipitation in individuals of social honor and of conventional demands which a positively privileged status group raises for the deportment of its members."[28] This sense of dignity "is naturally related to their 'being' which does not transcend itself, that is to their 'beauty and excellence'. . . . Their kingdom is 'of this world.' The sense of dignity of negatively privileged strata naturally refers to a future lying beyond the present, whether it is of this life or of another. In other words, it must be nurtured by the belief in a providential 'mission' and by a belief in a specific honor before God."[29] Symbols, then, create and sustain

[25] See *Alexander Bryan Johnson: A Treatise of Language*, edited by David Rynin (Berkeley and Los Angeles, Calif.: University of California Press, 1959). This edition contains the full text of the *Treatise*.

[26] *From Max Weber: Essays in Sociology*, translated, edited, and with an introduction by H. H. Gerth and C. Wright Mills (New York: Oxford University Press, 1946), p. 181.

[27] Ibid. p. 187.

[28] Ibid. pp. 189-90.

[29] Ibid. p. 190.

beliefs in ways of acting because they function as names which signify proper, dubious, or improper ways of expressing relationships. As we are taught in religion, we act *in the name of* the Father, the Son, and the Holy Ghost.

Men believe that as they uphold the purity of sacred names they uphold social order. Whoever or whatever threatens this purity must be destroyed. There are, of course, many kinds of purity. We are moved deeply by invocations of holiness, beauty, or wisdom, but every social institution seeks to relate its particular symbols of order to universal symbols of social order. The sociological function of the dramatic structure of action is, therefore, an act of organization. If symbols are to become, and to remain, powerful in organizing social relationships they must inspire belief in their capacity to consecrate certain styles of life as the "true" source of order in society. For it is because of this "purity" that they can be used to consecrate actions believed necessary to social solidarity. When a king is consecrated, a debutante "comes out," a student is given his doctorate, a woman is married, they acquire a social role which they did not have before. In doing so the individual must leave a less worthy (or even a sinful state) and raise himself to a state of grace. Consecration is the apogee of an "upward way." We are familiar enough with religious consecration, but we forget that this is not the only form of consecration. Status consecration is another. Our social position may depend on religious consecration (as in cult membership) but our religion also may depend on status consecration for its worldly power.

In so far as symbolic action is social it is an act of identification with good, dubious, or bad principles of social order. The *structure* of such actions is dramatic, but from a sociological view the *function* of this drama is the creation and sustainment of social order. Style, how we express ourselves, is an identification with a social order. Such identifications are both positive and negative. As we respond to the manners of others we are aware that they have *not* acted improperly as well as that they *have* acted properly. Often, indeed, we honor people for what they have *not* done. Purity may be born in innocence (the "pure in heart") but it is preserved in struggles against the temptations of impurity. Principles of social order are kept alive in the glory of roles we use to sustain positions of superiority, inferiority, and equality in social position. So long as we believe that individuals err but that certain kinds of hierarchal roles are necessary to social order, there will be order. As John Dryden said in 1699 (in the introduction to his *Fables, Ancient and Modern*): "The scandal that is given by particular priests reflects not on the sacred function. A satirical poet is the check of the layman on bad priests. When a clergyman is whipped, his gown is first taken off, by which the dignity of his office is secured."

Symbols reach their highest state of power in struggles between good and bad principles of social order as personified in heroes and villains, Gods and devils, allies and enemies, and the like. As we say in vulgar American, the "good guys" and the "bad guys" must "shoot it out." The "bad guy" is called various things. In art he is the villain; in government, the enemy (within as well as without); in religion, the devil; in democratic debate, the "loyal opposition." But in the most profound and moving dramas of social life the "bad guy" is transformed into a victim whose suffering and death purges the social order. In art this is called "catharsis," in religion "purification." As we read in Webster, purification is "the act or operation of cleansing ceremonially, by removing any pollution or defilement; hence, a cleansing from guilt or the pollution of sin; extinction of sinful desires or deliverance from their dominating power; spiritual or moral purgation; as, *purification* through repentance."

Symbols are kept pure through victimage or sacrifice. The pure symbol is used as an intermediary between the sacrificer (the hero), the person or thing which is to be socialized in the sacrifice, and the sacred principle of order to whom the sacrifice is addressed. Thus, all social order depends on consecration through communication, or, as we have said in more specific sociological terminology, through *naming,* and as our generation knows only too well, much blood is spilt in our world over the control of names. Names must be kept holy, sacred, honorable, dignified, and proper; for if they are not, we cannot apply them to ways in which we relate and create order in society. Those whose acts are named "communistic" must be killed by those whose acts are named "democratic." What is a "communist" or a "democrat"? Often, indeed, whoever we name so. What do these names "really" mean? We know they are simply god and devil terms, and as we all know, devils must be "driven out" of the community, as of the self, if law and order are to prevail.

We punish, enslave, torture, and kill in the name of principles of sociopolitical order. As the smoke of battle clears, and the cries of the wounded die out in the silence of death, we ask: What was this battle about, for what did we fight? The answer is always the same: We fought to preserve a name whose radiance and glory make life worth living. This is not to say that *all* the misery of war is to purify a name. We fight for food, clothing, shelter, territory, and other materials of life. We may even fight for life itself, just as we may refuse to fight in the hope that we may preserve life ("I'd rather be Red than Dead"). But as we plunge into battle, we cannot fight long and hard unless we fight in the name of some great principle of social order, for it is such names which give our relationship the glory and radiance we need to stave off the pressing horrors of decay and death.

Much has been said on the function of victimage in religion. In their brilliant monograph, *Sacrifice: Its Nature and Function*, Henri Hubert and Marcel Mauss, following in the tradition of W. Robertson Smith, E. B. Tylor, and James G. Frazer, define the nature and social function of sacrifice as a procedure which establishes "a means of communication between the sacred and the profane worlds through the mediation of a victim, that is, of a thing that in the course of the ceremony is destroyed.[30] As they point out, a victim does not come to sacrifice with sacred qualities already perfected and clearly

---

[30]Henri Hubert and Marcel Mauss, *Sacrifice: Its Nature and Function,* translated by W. D. Halls (Chicago: University of Chicago Press, 1964), p. 97.

defined; "it is the sacrifice itself that confers this upon it."[31] They conclude that religious sacrifice integrates worshipers because in appealing to power beyond the self we enhance the powers of the collectivity, and, at the same time, the drama of sacrifice makes possible continuous and intensive communication with powers which are sustained in group life.

Purgation through tragic victimage is not the only kind of purification. The comic victim in art stands beside the tragic victim in the purification of social order. As we laugh at him, we laugh at ourselves. In his degradation and suffering we *confront* the many incongruities that beset us as we try to live together in love and hate. Unlike the tragic victim, who puts us in communication with supernatural power capable of great evil as well as good, the comic victim keeps us within the world. We talk to *each other*, not to our gods, about the social ills that beset us. In doing so we bring into consciousness the hidden and dark mysteries of supernatural realms. Consciousness rises in discussion. When talk is free, informed, and public, there is hope of correcting our social ills because in such talk reason can bring to light much that is hidden in the dark majesty of tragedy.

Two great dramatic forms are struggling for audiences in our world. Communism is essentially a tragic drama of victimage in which enemies within the state are killed in solemn and awful rites called purge trials. The communist victim, like all tragic victims, must suffer and die because it is only through his suffering and death that the community is purged of weakness and evil. Democracy is more a comic drama of argument, bickering, disputation, insult, beseechment, and prayer. We elect our leaders, after long and heated discussion; but no sooner are they in office than we attack them furiously for all the incongruities which we recognized but could not cure as we voted them into office. Democratic leaders fall from power because they fail to measure up in discussion, debate, and all the forms of argument which make up the great public drama of politics in a free society. Whether the tragic or the comic will prevail cannot be decided here. But if the argument in the following pages points up any lesson, it is this: Failure to understand the power of dramatic form in communication means failure in seizing and controlling power over men. An opponent becomes a victim when his disagreement shifts in our minds from ignorance to heresy. When this heresy becomes sin and this sin in turn becomes "original" or "categorical" the first terrible step has been taken to war and to the kind of mass victimage Hitler's Germans created in their camps of torture and death known as concentration camps.

5. *Time in American Social Thought: The Destruction of the Past by the Future*

As I have indicated in my previous writings, I make no pretense whatever of writing without bias. I, and here of course I am typically American, would

---

[31] Ibid.

rather have acts determined by a future than a past—especially when it is assumed that knowledge of the past is blessed as "real" while our knowledge of the future is damned as "subjective" and "imaginary." The past may be pregnant with the present, and even with the future, as Tönnies, Spencer, Maine, Sumner, and the social theorists of the "organic" schools would have us believe. But if this is so, there have been far too many monsters born of these "irrevocable pasts" (as in Italy, Russia, and Germany) to take much comfort in this depressing doctrine. Like Ward, Dewey, Mead, and Cooley in American sociology, I hold to the future because the future can be treated purely as an image or an "idea" and is, therefore, open to criticism. Plans for the future are not always considered "sacred" or "inexorable," or if they are, it is because they are invented by people so steeped in historicism that they cannot conceive of a future different from the past. As Hitler taught his orators of evil, always begin addressing German audiences with a historical review which "proves" that present evils are "caused" by "deviations" from the past which the proposed future will "correct." In Hitler's prophecy the future is always a "return" to a hallowed German and Aryan past.

I do not think anyone needs to admonish Americans about the dangers of finding sanctions for every action, no matter how vile, in some kind of future, where, in proper Hegelian fashion, all the horrors of the present will be "transcended" in a future good. Our treatment of Indians, *American* Indians, is evidence enough of what happens when weak and defenseless people get in the way of "manifest destiny." Social action based on beliefs in Edenic myths of the future, as well as action based on "returns" to a sacred past, are marked by horrible and revolting crimes. Nothing is more painful to endure in American life than our blind belief in the "tradition of the new." Beautiful buildings are torn down to be replaced with parking lots. Meadows, streams, great sand dunes where earth and sky meet, are poisoned and ripped up, to make way for "progress." Whole populations are "dislocated" by urban "planners" to replace "substandard" housing with huge steel and concrete boxes (in "penal-modern" style) whose only virtue seems to be their newness. And our cities, the bright and shining hopes for a new world, are now choked and congested with traffic until movement within them has become almost impossible, and life and health are endangered as we breathe the poisoned air of "progress."

The European suffering from shock over the horrors of historicism now has a brother in America. We have each in our way learned to our sorrow that all forms of "inexorable destinies"—whether of the past or the future—are evil destinies unless they are submitted to critical inquiry. Men must be urged to belief, for we must believe to act, but they must also be urged to criticize, for reason lives in criticism. Admittedly, this places great burdens on reason, and, perhaps, merely supplants one "inexorable" law of society with another. And like all guardians of order who are placed above the order they themselves create and control, there are temptations to the misuse of power lurking in the leadership of those who have blind faith in reason. The melancholy spectacle of modern technicians, who confuse manipulations through instruments with manipulations of reason in critical inquiry, should warn us of this. But with all its dangers, critical reason, as free, open, informed, and widely communicated inquiry, still seems the best hope of men. Perhaps this kind of communication is our last hope, a hope which may exist only in the memory of future beings of another planet who will remember how we used to destroy each other. But if so, this is still a better memory than the memory of those who ended as slaves cowering before masters they despised. Americans may not survive, but the vision of a community where every man could walk in dignity will never die.

This vision of a community guided by critical inquiry, a community where sociology is used as a *method* of social diagnosis, is, admittedly, a vision of a commonwealth which lies far in the future. But it is a vision, not a dream, and as a vision formed by the minds of man it is subject to his will. Social scientists believe that this will, can, indeed, *must,* be guided by reason because it is only when we reason that our love for each other can be trusted. This is not a comforting doctrine, and certainly social science offers no fixed dogmas for those who fear change. But neither does social science offer shelter to those who find in their visions of a future justifications for the injustice and evil of the present. The social studies are essentially studies in how to face the incongruity between ends and means in social action. As sociologists we hope to create better ways of facing the many incongruities which beset men in their attempts to act together for the common good. We seek, in short, to create a *method* of criticism which can be applied to action in society.

We hear on all sides that Americans have no understanding of the tragic sense of life. We lack roots, we have no organic feeling for human relationships, we are materialistic, our lives are dominated by money, etc. All this may be true, but at the same time, it must be pointed out that many of us in America live in a world where no bombs have fallen, and no great armies have swept the land leaving hunger and death in their wake. We have seen no one walk in rags, or stiffen and die of cold and hunger. True, we have seen race riots, and we have heard members of minority groups vilified and cursed. We have seen the poor sicken and die. We have seen lives wasted for want of help. We still treat the symptoms, but not the causes, of poverty. When our unemployed are broken and sick, we treat their illness, but we do not yet train them to stand on their own as citizens of a free commonwealth. No one is more poignantly aware of America's broken promises to her people than those who must face daily the consequences of our failure. Poverty in the midst of plenty is not new to human experience. But to an American it *is* new, and it is horrible, for in America, thanks to modern communication, it is no longer possible to hide our failure in ignorance or false illusions.

What social theorist in Germany, Italy, Russia, France, *really* believed that authority could exist in a society of equals governed by rules? What have Marx, Darwin, Freud, Pareto, Durkheim, Michels, Sorel, Tönnies, or even Weber, contributed to our understanding of peer relationships? What do theories of social order based in custom, tradition, charisma, law, or primitive religion, have to tell us about a society where beliefs and laws are treated as *rules* of conduct? Much of European social theory is simply irrelevant to American life. This does not mean we should disregard it. On the contrary, we should study it carefully, if for no other reason than to understand how the great civilization of Europe could end in Hitler's death camps. If we reach such understanding we may never know a Dachau. We would be fools to assume that what happened in Birmingham, Alabama, is any different than what happened in Hitler's Germany. Fire hoses and dogs turned on American children dispel any illusions that "it can't happen here." It is happening, here and now, and we cannot be too sure that the battle of civil rights will be won in discussion and debate instead of riot and blood.

Sociological man in Europe is determined by his past, not as in America, by his future. This does not mean that we have no history in America. On the contrary, we have a great historical tradition in America, but it is the history of the future, not the past, which concerns us. There are few historical societies in American small towns (especially the newer ones), but few are without a chamber of commerce which busies itself with plans for a "greater" village. Babbitt, the prophet of a "greater" Zenith, still dwells among us. That he now promotes "culture" as well as real estate and commerce indicates a change of costume, not of heart or mind. Like the Chicagoans of 1890 who were planning the World's Fair, we are determined to "make culture hum." Beauty has left the groves of Academe and workshops of our artist to dwell among politicians. Few cities are without plans for a "Culture Center." These new urban visions of the "City Beautiful" now match the older visions of the village Athens so familiar to us in the work of Frank Lloyd Wright, Vachel Lindsay, and other visionaries of the Middle West who saw an American "Athens" arising out of the bogs and swamps of the Great Valley.

These visions of the future should not be confused with formless dreams or fervent wishes, any more than the European love of history should be confused with obscurantism or blind traditionalism. As Mead points out in his *Philosophy of the Present*, imagery drawn from *both* the past and the future must be used to organize activity in the present. The future and the past exist because they are always the past and the future of a specific present. Action in the present is always problematical, and we use futures, as we do pasts, to create images of perfected acts, not so we can dream, but so we can act. These may be drawn from the past, as when we invoke tradition, or from the future, as when we invoke images of perfected acts (ideal commonwealths, an ideal marriage, etc.), but in so far as they both serve as guides to action they serve a similar function. This American view of the act, on both philosophical and sociological levels, is blessed (or cursed) by adherents of the various schools who find their locus of social reality in the act. The problem of how we know the truth of the future or the past which we are using as a guide to action need not (fortunately!) be answered by the sociologist. But this does not mean that he need not concern himself with how people *think* they are arriving at the truth when they use such "truths" to create order in their relationships.

"Think" may be translated into "act" (as in the American pragmatic tradition), and the sociological data of "acting" reduced to symbols of relationship, as in role theory based on dramatistic view of social relationships (as in the work of Mead and of Burke), but the problem of *how* people think it proper to reach order in their relationships must still be faced. We may talk about "legitimation," "integration," or "consensus," but unless we say something about *how* integration is reached we have not said anything to justify our role as sociologists. American sociologists have been aware of this, and the attempts to face this problem have produced some of our finest work. Two seminal ideas of the "act" have emerged in American sociology. The first stems from the work of Mead, whose model of social integration was taken from the game; the second originated in the work of Kenneth Burke, who taught us that social relations are dramatistic. "Game" and "drama" as models of interaction are peculiarly American.

It is by the rules of the game, as well as by dramatic rules of action, that we achieve and sustain consensus in American society. Tradition, law, charisma, and usage, as Weber taught us, function in our society as they do in every society, but Americans integrate through rules to a far greater degree than any known society of the past or the present. As Tocqueville pointed out some hundred and thirty years ago, Americans are unique in their ability to form voluntary associations that are governed by rules. So while we accept Weber's forms of legitimation, we add another, the power of rules. Rules, it should be noted, are subject to agreement, and in the creation of such agreements those making them become equal. Rules are used to regulate games and contests in which opponents of varying skills struggle against each other to win, but to achieve honor they must win according to the rules. For if tact is the touchstone of sociability in purely social moments in group life, rules are the determinants of honor in games, play, and all forms of contest which are not determined by brute force, appeals to supernaturals, and other forms of relatedness among superiors and inferiors determined by charisma, tradition, convention, or "sacred" law.

6. Tradition and Debate in
Sociological Analysis of Symbols

The following propositions are a summary of my views about communication in society. In my previous works I have grounded my way of thinking about symbols in classical traditions of social thought. In *Language and Literature in Society*, as in *Communication and Social Order*, I have given many references to what has been said in the human studies on the social effects of symbols. These references could be expanded greatly, and, indeed, when the history of sociolinguistics is written, it will be clear that my discussion of precursors in symbolic analysis has not done justice to the traditions of communication theory as it exists in even so limited a field as sociological theory.

The problem facing symbolic interactionists who use dramatic images as models for sociological theory has shifted from struggle over the right to be heard to the necessity of saying something coherent now that we are being heard. The question is no longer one of how to think about social relations as drama, but, assuming the model of drama as our paradigm for a model of social relations, how do we distinguish between drama as art and drama as social? It is possible, of course, to assume no difference, just as our dedicated behaviorists assume that models of spatial relations in physics are adequate models for social relations in sociology. Those of us who follow in the great tradition of symbolic analysis and who desire to do more than repeat what has been said before, must ask: What is involved (for sociological theory) when we use theatrical analogies (such as the familiar social concept of role) for thinking about social relations? What, specifically, is a dramatic model of social relations? What form of drama do we select or create, to explain the social use of symbols? And, finally, what is *social,* as well as dramatistic, about it?

The following propositions are stated in answer to the questions which govern this study. These questions are simple enough. How can we think of communication as a *constituent* element in the creation of order and disorder in human relationships? What is the specific social function of communication institutions as compared with those of the family, religion, politics, or economics? If it is true that communication determines social order, how can this be demonstrated? Few theorists deny the importance of communication, yet, as I have argued, sociological theory fails as symbolic theory because it fails to deal with the effects of communication on social integration. Almost every major social theorist uses some theory of symbolic interpretation to substantiate his system, but his rationale is often very weak, and, indeed, sometimes non-existent.

The theorists reviewed in *Communication and Social Order* make heavy use of symbols. Yet a curious paradox haunts their work. Even though there is constant use of symbolic data, the social functions of symbols are often explained by non-symbolic contexts of experience. The social meaning of a symbol is not found in man's attempts to communicate, but in sex, religion, politics, or economics. Thus, while we "observe" religion (or any social institution) through its "symbolic manifestations," these have little to do with the latent and "real" nature of religion. Communication, it seems, must be explained by everything but communication. It must have, as we read so often, a "referent," and while this referent is social, the social, it turns out, has no "referent" in language. The communicator, like the ventriloquist's dummy, is simply the voice of interests, drives, or needs, none of which he originates or controls.

I do not accept this view. I argue in the following pages, as I have in all my work, that *how* we communicate determines *what* we communicate, just as others argue (and rightly so) that *what* we communicate determines *how* we communicate. Communication occurs in forms, and these forms are public as well as private, for if there are no common symbols there can be no common meanings, and hence no community. And since sociation in role enactment depends on public communication (just as the ego depends on "interior" communication among "inner" selves) a knowledge of communication is basic to an understanding of the structure of relationships within as without the self. All symbols are universals. No matter how "interiorized" symbols may be, or how particular our symbolic expression may become, it is impossible to say anything that is absolutely particular. Even in our wildest dreams, or our most haunting memories, the forms of phantasies and images, obscure and absurd though they may be, are yet drawn from symbols common to a given time and place. In his lecture on symbolism in dreams Freud asks how it is possible to understand dream symbols about which the dreamer himself can give us so little information. His answer indicates the need, in *any* theory of symbolic interpretation, of assuming a public content to private imagery.

His reply, that we learn from fairy tales, myths, buffoonery, jokes, popular manners, folklore, customs, sayings, and songs, as well as poetic and colloquial use of language, indicates the importance of the public content of symbols to Freud's thinking.[32] In Chapter VI of *The Interpretation of Dreams*, in his discussion on representation by symbols in dreams, Freud admits his failure to get at the meaning of dreams through free association. As he says: "The technique of interpreting according to the dreamer's free associations leaves us in the lurch when we come to the symbolic elements in the dream-content."[33] He decides that things "that are symbolically connected today were probably united in prehistoric times by conceptual and linguistic identity."[34] But, he warns, however great the interpreter's knowledge of symbols, the dreamer's associations must be analyzed carefully. Only "combined technique," in which the analyst relates universal meanings to the associations (symbolic cluster) of the individual patient, can be used.

---

[32] See "Symbolism in Dreams," lecture X of "Introductory Lectures on Psycho-Analysis" in *The Standard Edition of the Complete Psychological Works of Sigmund Freud,* translated from the German under the general editorship of James Strachey (London: The Hogarth Press, 1953-), Vol. XV, pp. 158-59. As the editors point out in discussion of this lecture (in footnote 1), it was not until the fourth edition of the *The Interpretation of Dreams* (1914) that a special section was devoted to dream-symbolism. This, Chapter VI, Section E, and the lecture cited here, are considered by the editors to be Freud's main discussion of symbolism. "The topic [of dream-symbolism] appears, of course, in many other places both in *The Interpretation of Dreams* and in other works throughout Freud's life.... It may be added, however, that the present lecture has claims to being regarded as the most important of all Freud's writings on symbolism." In *The Interpretation of Dreams* Freud argues that things that are symbolically connected today were probably united in prehistoric times by conceptual and linguistic identity. *(Standard Edition,* Vol. V., p. 352) He cautions against arbitrary use of "prehistoric" connections. "We are thus obliged, in dealing with those elements of the dream-content which must be recognized as symbolic, to adopt a combined technique, which on the one hand rests on the dreamer's associations and on the other fills the gaps from the interpreter's knowledge of symbols.... (Dream-symbols) frequently have more than one or several meanings, and, as with Christian script, the correct interpretation can only be arrived at on each occasion from the context." *(Standard Edition,* Vol. V, p. 353) Freud's genetic theories of symbolic interpretation should be compared with Mead's telic theory, in which images of the future, as well as the past, are used to organize action in a problem-solving present.

[33] Freud, *The Interpretation of Dreams,* in *The Standard Edition of the Complete Psychological Works of Sigmund Freud,* Vol. V, p. 353.

[34] Ibid. p. 352.

7. Sociodrama as a Source of
Power in Modern Society

The great social revolution of the twentieth century has been in communication, the means whereby those in power create and control the images, or names, that will legitimize their power. Sociopolitical ideologies are *created*; their terrible power to goad men into wounding, torturing, and killing others, and even into destroying themselves in confessions of guilt, are not simply mechanical reaction to interests. They are symbolic forms, they are *names,* and whoever creates or controls these names controls our lives. As any revolutionary handbook tells us, the first step in the seizure of power is the control of all symbols of power and means of communication. We may seize power through force, but it is the images used in daily communication that control us, and whoever controls the creation and communication of these controls society. Much has been said about how new kinds of media, such as television, are "determining" the public images that goad us to action. But media alone cannot determine images. The great communication revolution is rooted in new forms of relationships, not simply new media of communication. To understand them we must ask five basic questions: Under what conditions is communication taking place? What is being communicated? In what kinds of roles? By what means? For what kind of social integration?

The new relationships of our time are **sociodramas** which are mounted daily and hourly for mass audiences. As we increase the size and diversity of our audiences we must increase the range, diversity, and, above all, the intensity of our appeals. And we must do this in competition with others who seek to control the same audiences. As their appeals change so must ours. Today, permanence occurs in change. Leaders who think of permanence and/ or change, and who confuse change with disorder, soon lose power. The "thousand-year Reich" of Hitler lasted but a few years. Force must be *legitimized,* the people must be persuaded that it is "right," even a "sacred duty" (as Hitler convinced his Germans), to wound, torture, and kill. We do not seek annihilation, but conversion, of the enemy. Broken and dead enemies do not make good customers, staunch allies, or willing workers.

Sociodramas move us through the intensity, as well as the diversity and range of their appeal. The great publics of our time must not be thought of as inert masses waiting to be "triggered" into action. As members of an audience we identify, as elements in a mass we cathect or polarize. Identification is a dramatic process. All legitimation of power rests, in the last analysis, on the acceptance of a style of life. We may usurp power through force, but we secure victory only when the vanquished admire, honor, and, finally, imitate our way of life. Movies, radio, television, the popular press, all forms of modern mass communication, reach their greatest power in their creation of sociodramas which, like art drama, are staged as struggles between good and bad principles of social order. The people do not want information about, but identification with, community life. In drama they *participate.*

The high moment in traditional sociodrama is the moment of victimage, the *personification* of evil powers which threaten community order. The torture and burning of heretics, the execution of traitors, like the hanging of criminals, were once public dramas of salvation. The suffering of the accused in torture and imprisonment were "necessary" to break his proud and evil will. In the confession and guilt of the victim the scapegoat was born. It was not his individual will which led him to heresy and crime, but "possession" by evil powers. If the community is to survive these evil powers must be driven out. Thus the punishment of victims becomes a sacramental act of purification in which the community is purged. Hitler's Germans killed Jews to prevent contamination of Aryan blood, the "racially innate element" which alone could preserve human culture and civilization. Stalin killed opponents after "purge trials" in which victims confessed their treason, and sacrificed themselves (even willingly!) in great public dramas of purification.

The effect on mass audiences of these German and Russian sociodramas of violence and killing is grim proof of the social power of victimage. The popularity of war news staged as brief sociodramas of the kill, our television Westerns with their "shoot-outs," man hunts, as well as the sadistic depiction of murder and vengeance in crime films, are witness enough to our terrible need for real and symbolic victimage. Modern mass audiences identify with their leaders, and with each other, through violence. In factories, offices, stores, and schools the individual is losing his sense of identity. In the filth of our ghettos and the mud holes of rural slums the poor have no sense of community with each other, or with their leaders in American society. But when the Negro turns against his oppressors and applies the lessons in victimage he has been taught so well by his white oppressors in the Ku Klux Klan, he finds in riot and pillage what he cannot find in peace and work. Thus far his victimage has been symbolic. Cursing, looting, stone-throwing, random shooting, and burning stop short of the kill. But for how long?

8. Sociological Jargon

There is nothing more ludicrous than obscurity in communicating about communication. "Sociologese" is one of the horrors of modern discourse, and I have no desire to add to it. It stems from the belief that when you talk in mechanical metaphors you are talking "science." Confusion of technique with science, as when we present our techniques of research as the sole justification of the problem whose solution is supposed to establish our research, is rampant in American sociology. This confusion of science with technique is really a kind of magical thought which hides behind the mask of science just as magic once hid behind the altars of religion. The least we should do as sociologists is to define what we are talking about (as well as to "refine" our instruments of research), for until we do we cannot avoid the dark suspicions of thoughtful men that ignorance, not profundity or originality, is at the root of sociological obscurity.

Making sounds like a hard scientist, twisting sociological terminology into a jargon modeled after physical science discourse, or confusing abstract nouns with theoretical concepts, is much the fashion in current sociological discourse. The deficiencies of sociologese have been duly noted in Fowler's *Dictionary of Modern Usage*. Students of society (Americans, alas!) who call an informal talk "a relatively unstructured conversational interaction" are not talking science; they are using jargon. They are also being pompous, and attempting to mystify us through the use of an abstract terminology which is difficult to understand, not because it is profound, but because it defies definition. When we say that we do not know why we are doing something but that we are doing it "properly," we have abandoned all pretense to rational inquiry. Method has a magic of its own. We are warned against the incantations of tribal magicians, but we are not so well armed against the magic of technology where *how* we do something is considered sufficient grounds for the legitimation of what we are doing.

Deification of means, as well as ends, leads to mystification. When *how* we do something determines what we do, we are in the realm of magic and mystery. Veneration of means is no different from any kind of veneration. The decline and fall of our great urban centers as fit habitations for human beings should be warning enough of what happens when technological means displace humane ends. The engineer's mystique of "efficiency" turns out to be a spatial mystique. The shortest distance between two points may be a straight road, but if this road destroys neighborhoods where social bonds have grown over the years, and these roads glut cities with traffic, the shortest distance in space becomes the longest in time. Means must be tested by ends, just as ends must be tested by means. When what we study in society is deemed scientific because we use the language and instruments of physical sciences we are defining through analogy, not observation. False analogies lead to jargon, the mystification of technique.

9. Democratic Bias of this Book: Equality as a Form of Social Order

The social bias in this book is indicated by the inclusion of equality as a form of hierarchy similar to superiority and inferiority as a determinant of social order. In my view equality must be considered a form of *authority*, just as doubt must be considered *necessary* to social integration. I argue that equality as a sociopolitical factor in human relationships depends on rules which are possible only when the will of equals can manifest itself. Doubt, comedy, ambiguity, and all the phases of conduct we label "uncertain," I do not regard as aberrations or weakness, but as a source of strength in social relationships. Without them there would be few of the benign forms of social change which offer some hope for escaping the terrible kinds of victimage we have seen in our time. In relationships which depend on rules that can be changed at will, but that must be obeyed once agreed to by the majority of those who are to apply the rules, the test of a rule is a *rational* test. Rules are always open to discussion when those who created them, and subject themselves to them, find them to be unsatisfactory or unworkable. A rule, unlike tradition, law, or the dark mysteries of religion, never derives its power from appeals to a sacred or supernatural source.

Rules, like fashion, are ephemeral, but it would be a great mistake to confuse change under rules with disorder. Indeed it may be that the opposite holds true. Quick and frequent changes in human relationships may be signs of strength as well as weakness. Only when the *forms* (as well as the contents) of human relations can be changed swiftly and easily can there be a strong society. And if there is danger in too much change, there is equal danger in too much rigidity. It may be true, as Disraeli taught, that experiments mean revolutions, but it is no less true that dogma and sacred beliefs also lead to change by violence and discord. Rules are the realm of change and experiment in social relations. We change rules often, and in such change feel less threat than in change of law, tradition, or belief. The power of rules is derived from their form, the *ways* in which they determine action. Fair play is play according to rules which are the same for all. The superior is the guardian of an inferior's honor ("It is the nature of the many to be amenable to fear but not to the sense of honor." Aristotle: *The Nicomachean Ethics,* iv.), just as the inferior is a jealous witness to the honor of his superior (as when we say of a courtier that he is more royalist than the king). But equals are jealous guardians of rules, for it is only through rules that equals can reach agreements which bind them together in common action.

Nothing better illustrates the power of form in social relationships than rules. In play, games, manners, and all moments of pure sociability we are bound to each other by the form of the game. Such forms function as bounds and determinants of conduct. As Mead taught us, in games we play our positions in terms of assumptions about how other players will play theirs. But these assumptions, however internalized, are objictified in forms of play which must be followed if the game is to be played fairly. Once rules are made and codified so that all concerned may know them, we appoint an umpire to serve as guardian of the rules we ourselves have made or accepted. His power is derived from his knowledge of the rules and his ability to apply them quickly and surely in all moments of play. He "speaks from the book (of rules)" and can "throw the book at us," as we say in America. Like the judge in common law, the umpire must remember that he applies, but does not interpret or create, rules.

Reason in democratic society is born in discussion that depends on disputants who remain loyal to the rules of discussion. In a society based on discussion there are no "revealed truths," any more than there are "laws" (physical, biological, or historical) of social process which "determine" human conduct. Nor, for that matter, are there fixed logical canons of inquiry. What we do try to fix, and make binding on all, are *rules* for discussion. Opponents not only tolerate but honor and respect each other because in doing so they enhance their own chances of thinking better and reaching sound decisions. Opposition is necessary because it sharpens thought in action. We assume that argument, discussion, and talk, among free and informed people who subordinate themselves to rules of discussion, are the best ways to decisions of any kind, because it is only through such discussion that we reach agreement which binds us to a common cause. We assume also in democracy that the highest kind of human relationship is friendship, because friendship among people of very different ranks and capacities enlarges our understanding and thus strengthens the "will" of our social bonds. If we are to be equal, and if we believe discussions among equals is a way to truth, relationships among equals must find expression in many formal and informal institutions. Equals agree, inferiors obey, superiors command. Democracy lives in agreement and it remains strong so long as there are many ways of reaching agreement.

To assume that whatever opens up difference is good assumes that differences can be overcome in some benign way. Unless we assume that communication is a random affair, or simply a "message track" for some reality beyond symbols, such as religion or politics, we must assume that it has formal qualities, and that these forms, like forms of any kind, are subject to inquiry. The paradox of contemporary social thought is that we have discovered, and continue to discover, regularities in physical and biological nature, and in economic, political, and tribal "structures" (just as theologians discovered regularities in supernatural realms), yet the medium through which all these vast systems are discovered, and in which our discoveries are reported and talked about, namely language, is not studied (at least, not in sociology) as a determinant of human relationships. How we have been able to study human relationships at all without using the observable data of relatedness—how we communicate—will be a question of great interest to future students of sociology.

As we shall discuss at some length, rules in our society stand beside law, religion, and tradition, as guarantors of social order. In the first section of his *Manual of Parliamentary Practise,* entitled "Adhering to Rules," Thomas Jefferson tells us that "the only weapons by which the minority can defend themselves [against] those in power are the forms and rules of proceeding which have been adopted . . . and become the law of the House." Although Jefferson spoke in a political context, he could do so only because there already existed in the American society of his time a belief in rules as a means to social order. For, as Jefferson said in his *Manual*: "It is much more material that there should be a rule to go by than what that rule is; that there may be a uniformity of proceeding in business not subject to the caprice of the Speaker or captiousness of the members." For Americans rules are a form of authority, and their study must not be limited to their application in play (important as this is) but to their general use in social action.

10. Hopes and Fears

I wish that as a lover of democracy I could end this introduction with a ringing note of confidence in the future of democratic man. But I cannot do so. Democracy was, and is still, the fairest hope of mankind. Will it survive? I do not think it will unless there are vast and profound changes in men and society, and certainly in the way we study society. Men enjoy war too much, and are honored too often for torturing and killing each other. Great and powerful actors now strut before the people of the earth as heroes and villains, rattling weapons that can destroy the world. And even these sounds, terrible as they are, do not drown out the cries of the victims of Hitler and Stalin. In the face of this, the faith of Mead and Dewey that "sharing" necessarily implies sharing only the good becomes incredible. Even those of us brought up in the benign society of the Middle West of America have learned that men share evil as well as good. Perhaps the best we can do is to give form to the evil of our time so that those who come after us—if any do—can use our records to confront, better than we have done, the horrible human need to torture and kill. At least those who come after us can learn from our example that we cannot become humane until we understand our need to visit suffering and death on others—and ourselves. We *need* to socialize in hate and death, as well as in joy and love. We do not know how to have friends without, at the same time creating victims whom we must wound, torture, and kill. Our love rests on hate.

The sociology of our time must begin in anguished awareness that victimage is the means by which people purge themselves of fear and guilt in their relations with each other. These victims take many forms. They range from the hapless scapegoat, such as the Jew in Hitler's torture and death camps, to symbolic scapegoats like the tattered sweating clown who is reviled, beaten and killed (symbolically) so that we can confront evils we are not permitted "officially" to confront at all. Popular art abounds in such victims; the villains of television dramas are beaten, shot, and killed daily in the only kind of community catharsis our art gives us. There are victims within us too, inner victims locked within the dark regions of the self. But they do not always stay locked up, and even at best, as we know from our fantasies, dreams, and bursts of hatred and rage, the victimized self waits impatiently for his moment to turn on the self who acts as his keeper. As we face the victims of our time, their anguished faces and terrible cries remind us that the philosophical foundations of American sociology supplied by Dewey and Mead were far too shallow. They offered us no vantage point from which to confront evil, or even to consider the social pathology of daily life. Fortunately for the vitality of American social thought, the work of Kenneth Burke corrects this error, and we now join DeSade, Pascal, La Rochefoucauld, Swift, and Freud in facing the terrible fact that men come together to enjoy inflicting pain, suffering, and death on their fellow creatures as they enjoy inflicting pain on themselves.

A Dramatistic Theory of the Rhetoric of Movements

by Leland M. Griffin

The relationship between utopia and the existing order turns out to be a dialectical one.

-Karl Mannheim

The obligations of order hang over us, even if we would revolt against order. Out of such predicaments, ingenious fellows rise up and sing; thus promptly have all our liabilities been by symbol-using converted into assets.

-Kenneth Burke

The following study in dramatism, the critical perspective of Kenneth Burke, both supplements and complements previous essays by the writer.[1] The attempt here is to develop, for the student of movements, a dramatistic model, or abstraction, of the structure of a movement's rhetoric.[2] The essay involves a synthesis of materials—words, phrases, and concepts—which have been drawn, almost wholly, from the terminology of Burke.[3] The central effort is to identify the dramatistic form of rhetorical movement with the dialetical movement of tragedy, poetic expression in general, and theological or political transformation and transcendence. Taken as a whole, the essay might be regarded as the exegesis of a line from *Towards a Better Life* (which ends, like *The Rhetoric of Religion,* with the key term silence): "speech being a mode of conduct, he converted his faulty living into eloquence."[4]

Reprinted from William H. Rueckert (ed.), *Critical Responses to Kenneth Burke, 1924-1966.* University of Minnesota Press, 1969. Used by permission.

[1] It is intended as supplementary to my "The Rhetoric of Historical Movements," *The Quarterly Journal of Speech,* XXXVIII (April 1952), 184-188; and as complementary to my "The Rhetorical Structure of the 'New Left' Movement, Part One," *The Quarterly Journal of Speech,* L (April 1964), 113-135.

[2] "... the 'dramatistic' is a critical or essayistic analysis of language, and thence of human relations generally by the use of terms derived from the contemplation of drama." Kenneth Burke, "Linguistic Approach to Problems of Education" *Modern Philosophies and Education,* Fifty-Fourth Yearbook of the National Society for the Study of Education Part I, ed. Nelson B. Henry (Chicago 1955), p. 264.

[3] Terms have occasionally been shifted from one context to another, for heuristic purposes, in accordance with Burke's method of "perspective by incongruity." The citations that follow unless otherwise noted are from the writings of Burke.

[4] *Towards a Better Life* (New York, 1932), p. 211.

The essay assumes that all movements are essentially political, concerned with governance or dominion, "the wielding and obeying of authority";[5] that "politics above all is drama";[6] and that "drama requires a conflict."[7] It also assumes that all movements are essentially moral—strivings for salvation, perfection, the "good."[8]

The essay employs an imagery of killing—as, according to Burke, "a typical text for today should."[9] And it is frankly speculative. But, as Burke has noted, "this is a time for speculative adventure."[10]

1

Let us begin with a definition of man, and with a paradigm of his history—his "drama," or action. As to the definition,

Man is
the symbol-using (symbol-making, symbol-misusing) animal
inventor of the negative (or moralized by the negative)
separated from his natural condition by instruments of his own
    making
goaded by the spirit of hierarchy (or moved by the sense of order)
and rotten with perfection.[11]

Man is a being by nature divided, designed for striving, "endowed for struggle" ("if they do not struggle, they rot, which is to say that they struggle in spite of themselves").[12] Man is an *acter*, a maker, a mover; a being who lives by striving, and who "can be expected to err as long as he keeps striving" *(es irrt der Mensch solang' er strebt).*[13] Man is a being who lives by language; who moves and is moved by words; who rises and is redeemed, or fails and falls, through words. Man is a being who lives by purpose or meaning, value and desire; a being who yearns, in this "imperfect world,"[14] for a world of perfection ("the conformity of a reality to its concept").[15] And

---

[5] The definition of politics in "Linguistic Approach to Problems of Education," *op. cit.,* p. 280.

[6] *The Philosophy of Literary Form* (Vintage ed., New York, 1957), p. 267.

[7] "Catharsis—Second View," *Centennial Review,* V (1961), 130.

[8] For Burke on the opening sentence of the *Nicomachean Ethics* see "Towards a Total Conformity: A Metaphysical Fantasy," *The Literary Review,* II (1957-58), 203-207.

[9] *A Rhetoric of Motives* (New York, 1953), ix.

[10] "Art—and the First Rough Draft of Living" *Modern Age,* VIII (Spring 1964), 162.

[11] "Definition of Man," *The Hudson Review,* XVI (Winter 1963-64), 507.

[12] *Attitudes toward History* (Beacon ed., Boston, 1961), p. 124.

[13] Burke's translation of words spoken by The Lord in the "Prologue in Heaven" of Goethe's *Faust, Part One.* See "The Language of Poetry 'Dramatistically' Considered," *The Chicago Review,* IX (Spring 1955), 42, 46.

[14] One of Burke's key terms: e.g., *Attitudes toward History,* pp. 227, 295, 320.

[15] The definition is from Martin Foss, *The Idea of Perfection in the Western World* (Princeton, N.J., 1946), p. 8. I take this definition as concise, and harmonious with Burke's concept of perfection as presented in "Definition of Man" *op. cit.,* and in *Permanence and Change* (Hermes ed., Los Altos, Calif., 1954), pp. 292-294.

hence man is a maker of movements; a maker *(poietes)* whose motto might be "By and through language, beyond language. *Per linguam, praeter linguam.*"[16]

As to the paradigm of his history,

Here are the steps
In the Iron Law of History
That welds Order and Sacrifice:
Order leads to Guilt
(for who can keep commandments:)
Guilt needs Redemption
(for who would not be cleansed!)
Order
Through Guilt
To Victimage
(hence: Cult of the Kill) . . .[17]

So man moves through the moments of his drama, which are also the moments of his movements: moves, all told, from Order, Guilt, and the Negative, through Victimage and Mortification, to Catharsis and Redemption.[18] He moves, and is moved, through speech—through the rhetorical power of the word, the persuasive power of language (for rhetoric is the essentially human mode of striving). He is moved by words of meaning, value, and desire; words that draw him *a fronte*, futuristically.[19] And engaged in struggle, in the act of strife, he is cleansed by the dialectical power of the word, the purifying power of language (for dialectic is the essentially human mode of transforming).

And thus the study of a movement implies a study of its rhetoric. And thus the significance of "Order, the Secret, and the Kill": for "to study the nature of rhetoric, the relation between rhetoric and dialectic, and the application of both to human relations in general, is to circulate about these three motives."[20]

---

[16]"Linguistic Approach to Problems of Education," *op. cit.*, p. 263.
[17]*The Rhetoric of Religion* (Boston, 1961) pp. 4-5.
[18]See "On Human Behavior Considered 'Dramatistically.'" *Permanence and Change*, pp. 274-294; and the discussion of "the cycle of terms implicit in the idea of 'order'" in *The Rhetoric of Religion*, pp. 183ff. See also William H. Rueckert, *Kenneth Burke and the Drama of Human Relations* (Minneapolis, 1963), pp. 128-162.
[19]Cf. A. J. Ayer, *Man as a Subject for Science*, Auguste Comte Memorial Lecture 6 (University of London, 1964), pp. 12-17.
[20]*A Rhetoric of Motives*, p. 265.

2

Because they desire Order (the reign of reason and justice),[21] men build cooperative systems, or orders. All such orders are of necessity hierarchical, involving division, "a ladder of authority that extends from 'lower' to 'higher,' while its *official functions* tend toward a corresponding set of *social ratings,*" a set of "different classes" (or "principles," or *"kinds* of beings").[22] Yet though men, in any system, are inevitably divided, "identification is compensatory to division."[23] And through identification with a common condition or "substance," men achieve an understanding (a sense of unity, identity, or "consubstantiality").

Any system that endures implies an "adequate" understanding, a dynamic understanding ("the *understanding* which is active in that it performs the act of unification").[24] It is the understanding essential to the ultimate achievement of integration (ideal unity; "a complete and perfect whole").[25] For it provides the basis for communication; and men must communicate, being by nature symbol-makers. And hence it is the ground, in any system, of "mystery" (the Secret): for "mystery arises at that point where different *kinds* of beings are in communication."[26]

In any "good" system, men accept the "mystery," strive to keep the Secret, preserve the hierarchy. For reason and justice reign. There is a common understanding, an "adequate" understanding. Men agree on meaning, value, and desire; and hence they gladly submit to a code of control, obey the "commandments."[27]

And thus the relations between classes are harmonious, cooperative, symmetrical; and the communication between classes is beneficent and benign, "like the ways of courtship"—a communication that might be likened to the "rhetoric of courtship."[28] It is a rhetoric in the order of love; for it strives for perfect communion, and "the word for perfect communion between

---

[21]"The 'social' aspect of language is 'reason.' Reason is a complex technique for 'checking' one's assertions by public reference.... Hence, implicit in both language and reason *(logos,* word) there is a *social* basis of reference affecting the individual. Linked with this is the need to feel the 'reasonableness' of one's society, the reasonableness of its aims and methods. This reasonableness comes to a focus in symbols of authority...." *Attitudes toward History,* pp. 341-342.

"For 'justice' is the logical completion of language, leading one to round the circle by imposing upon oneself the negatives one would impose upon others...." See "Postscripts on the Negative," *The Quarterly Journal of Speech,* XXXIX (April 1953), 211-212.

[22]*Attitudes toward History,* p. 374; *A Rhetoric of Motives,* p. 115.

[23]*A Rhetoric of Motives,* p. 22.

[24]*A Grammar of Motives* (New York, 1945), p. 188.

[25]See the definitions for "integrate," "integration," *Webster's New Collegiate Dictionary* (Springfield, Mass., 1953).

[26]*A Rhetoric of Motives,* p. 115.

[27]"Order by its very nature involves modes of control and self-control that add up morally to 'mortification.'" "On Catharsis, or Resolution," *The Kenyon Review,* XXI (Summer 1959), 367.

[28]Cf. *A Rhetoric of Motives,* p. 115.

persons is 'Love!'"[29] It is a rhetoric in the order of peace; for it strives for pure identification, and "in pure identification there would be no strife."[30] And it is a rhetoric energized, and sustained, by the motive of piety ("the yearning to conform with the sources of one's being"; loyalty, or obedience, to one's "natural condition").[31]

And thus a "good" order is one marked by communion and identification, by the practice and persistence of piety. It is an order charged with attitudes of benevolence, and sustained by communication, the relevance of its rhetoric. For because men are pious they avoid error in the use of symbols, strive to use their language with propriety (for piety is also *"the sense of what properly goes with what"*; and "it is pious to exemplify a sense of the appropriate").[32]

And because in a "good" order men are pious, they are "free."[33] And their freedom equals a state of continual movement toward perfection: toward "a complete and perfect whole"; a cooperative system of pure symmetry, perfect harmony, and *"integration,* guided by a scrupulous sense of the appropriate"[34]—an Order marked by perfect communion, pure identification, and absolute communication. For piety is also "a system-builder, a desire to round things out, to fit experiences together into a unified whole":[35] and "if men were wholly and truly of one substance"—*truly integrated, united, in a relation of perfect love*—"absolute communication would be of man's very essence."[36]

But tragically, in this "imperfect world," love is bound to be a taut, potentially frangible relation. For "piety can be painful," a motive difficult to endure;[37] and hence the pious may yield to the temptations of impiety. For men are by nature divided: capable of rising, hence of falling; of accepting, consenting, obeying—hence of rejecting, dissenting, disobeying; capable of loyalty and love, hence of alienation and Victimage, "the *perversions* of love (forms of ill-will towards one's neighbor)"[38]—the malevolent attitudes of pride, envy, wrath, sloth, avarice, gluttony, lust; attitudes, ultimately, in the order of murder. And men are by nature symbol-makers, both users and

---

[29]*The Rhetoric of Religion*, p. 30. ". . . love involves the element of *desire*, a sense of union with something with which one is identified but from which one is divided." *Attitudes toward History*, p. 372. " 'Communion' involves the interdependence of people through their common stake in both co-operative and symbolic networks." *Attitudes toward History*, p. 234. ". . . note that communion is a *unification*. Such a feeling of unity implies the transcending of a disunity." *A Grammar of Motives*, p. 297.

[30]*A Rhetoric of Motives*, p. 25.

[31]*Permanence and Change*, p. 69.

[32]*Ibid.*, pp. 74-75.

[33]The relation between freedom and piety is discussed in note 108 below.

[34]*Permanence and Change*, p. 77.

[35]*Ibid.*, p. 74.

[36]*A Rhetoric of Motives*, p. 115.

[37]*Permanence and Change*, p. 74.

[38]"Catharsis—Second View," *op. cit.*, p. 112n.

misusers of symbols: capable of understanding, hence of misunderstanding; of reason, hence of absurdity; of justice, hence of injustice; of courtship, hence of impiety, the *perversion* of courtship—of a rhetoric of abasement, maleficent and malign, like the ways of "rape, seduction, jilting, prostitution, promiscuity . . . sadistic torture or masochistic invitation to mistreatment."[39]

And thus a "good" order may turn faulty; and the symptom of its turning is the growth of verbal corruption—vile error in the use of language, the inappropriate use of symbols. It is an order marked by misunderstanding, the growth of absurdity and injustice, the increasing loss of communion and identification. It is an order strained by impiety, the irrelevance of its rhetoric; an order tending toward Death, the ultimate failure of communication—toward disunity, disintegration, Disorder.

In sum: wherever there is Order there is hierarchy; wherever there is hierarchy there must be communication, and hence "mystery"; and wherever there is "mystery" there must be an understanding—the understanding that makes piety possible. But the maintenance of piety involves the need for obedience—which is to say, the painful need for self-control (self-restraint, self-moderation). And out of this obligation comes the possibility of disobedience:[40] for men are by nature ambitious, Faustian, "rotten with perfection"; and ambition is a disease that ends in pride, "the desire to excel by the abasement of others";[41] and pride is a fall, the initial perversion of love, the impious yearning that ends in the misuse of symbols—in negation, rejection, "the rebel snapping of the continuity."[42]

As the communication between classes grows ever more malign, men turn from acceptance to rejection of the "mystery," cease to identify with the hierarchy, the prevailing system of authority. And as disloyalty spreads and the bonds of love corrode, the sense of Guilt grows increasingly greater: for in man, the symbol-maker, Guilt is a function of impiety—error, or the yearning to err, in the use of symbols.[43]

Now alienated, divided from the existing order (separated from their "natural condition"), men stand alone, without purpose or desire, hope or direction. They stand in silence, in the hellish state of indecision: stand, until moved to speak. *And speak they will* ("as the gun *will* shoot because it *is*

---

[39] *A Rhetoric of Motives*, p. 115.

[40] "Looking into the *act* of Disobedience, we come upon the need for some such term as 'pride,' to name the corresponding *attitude* that precedes the act." *The Rhetoric of Religion*, p. 187. Burke would label his ideal education "Faustological," "since it would center in the study of ambition as a disease." See "Linguistic Approach to Problems of Education," *op. cit.*, p. 272.

[41] "Catharsis—Second View" *op. cit.*, p. 112. And see *The Rhetoric of Religion*, p. 184.

[42] *A Rhetoric of Motives*, p. 233.

[43] Cf. "In failing to abide by the tribal or institutional thou-shalt-not's, or in fearing that one might fail, one piles up a measure of guilt after the analogy of a debt that needs repayment by corresponding sums." "A Dramatistic View of the Origins of Language," *The Quarterly Journal of Speech*, XXXVIII (October 1952), 264.

loaded").[44] For men are by nature charged with symbols; and by nature they cannot bear Guilt ("for who would not be cleansed"). And hence, inevitably, they will dream of salvation, the transformation of their condition, a state of Redemption: will envision, consciously or unconsciously (being "rotten with perfection"), an ideal Order—"heaven," paradise, the "good society," Utopia.

And thus, perversely goaded by the spirit of hierarchy, moved by the impious dream of a mythic new Order—inspired with a new purpose, drawn anew by desire—they are moved to act: moved, ingenious men ("inventors of the negative") to rise up and cry *No* to the existing order—and prophesy the coming of the new.

And thus movements begin.

3

To study a movement is to study a striving for salvation, a struggle for perfection, a progress toward the "good." It is a progress that is grounded in Guilt; but "Guilt needs Redemption," and Redemption needs Redeemer—which is to say, a Victim, a scapegoat, a Kill. And thus to study a movement is to study the progress of a killing; which is to say, to study rhetoric. For rhetoric is "in the order of killing, of personal enmity, of factional strife, of invective, polemic, eristic, logomachy"; is *"par excellence* the region of the Scramble, of insult and injury, bickering, squabbling, malice and the lie, cloaked malice and the subsidized lie."[45]

Yet it must not be forgotten that rhetoric, though in the order of killing, is also in the order of love. For it includes communication; and " 'communication' is the most generalized statement of the principle of 'love' "—"the area where love has become so generalized, desexualized, 'technologized,' that only close critical or philosophic scrutiny can discern the vestiges of the original motive."[46]

And it must not be forgotten that rhetoric, at its farthest reach, mounts to the level of "pure persuasion"—"the saying of something, not for an extra-verbal advantage to be got by the saying, but because of a satisfaction intrinsic to the saying."[47] It is rhetoric for the "sheer love of the art," the sheer love of persuasion itself.[48] And it includes, as intrinsic, "a principle of self-interference"[49] (self-restraint, *mortification,* "a scrupulous and deliberate

---

[44]*A Grammar of Motives,* p. 336. I take the phrase as a metaphorical expression of Burke's "principle of perfection"—the notion that "there is a kind of 'terministic compulsion' to carry out the implications of one's terminology." See "Definition of Man," *op. cit.,* pp. 510-511.

[45]*A Rhetoric* of *Motives,* p. 19.

[46]*Attitudes toward History,* p. 347; *A Rhetoric of Motives,* p. 19.

[47]*A Rhetoric of Motives,* p. 269.

[48]*The Rhetoric of Religion,* p. 34n.

[49]*A Rhetoric* of *Motives,* pp. 269, 274.

damping of limitations upon the self").[50]

It must not be forgotten, in sum, that rhetoric, though in the order of Victimage, is also in the order of Mortification; nor that Mortification, at its highest mounting, is in the order of perfect love (*"Greater love hath no man than this, that a man give up his life for his friends"*).

4

To study a movement is to study a progress, a rhetorical striving, a becoming. It is a progress from stasis to stasis; for both the origins and "the objectives of a movement are motionless."[51] They begin in the stasis of indecision, and they end in the stasis of "decision persevered in." They begin with Guilt and the dream of salvation. They end with the achievement, and maintenance, of a state of Redemption—of a new identity, a new unity, a new condition or "substance": which is to say, a new *motive* (for " 'substance' and 'motivation' are convertible terms").[52]

Every movement thus has form. It is a progress from *pathema* through *poiema to mathema*: from "a suffering, misfortune, passive condition, state of mind," through "a deed, doing, action, act," to "an adequate idea; the thing learned."[53] It is a progress from *auscultation* through *creation* to *revision:* from "the heart-conscious kind of listening, or vigilance, that precedes expression," through "the expression in its unguarded simplicity," to a "modification of the expression in the light of more complicated after-thoughts."[54] It is a progress from *Inferno* through *Purgatorio* to *Paradiso*: from the hell that is indecision, through the purification that is decision, to the heaven that is "the arrival that follows decision persevered in."[55]

To study a movement is to study a drama, an Act of transformation, an Act that ends in transcendence, the achievement of salvation. It is to study the Scenes that bracket the Act, for any movement is a sequence of "moments between the limits of before and after."[56] It is to study the Agents that make the Act; for men are the *acters,* the makers, of movements. It is to study the essentially human Agency that men use in the making of movements; which

---

[50]"Thanatopsis for Critics: A Brief Thesaurus of Deaths and Dyings," *Essays in Criticism,* II (October 1952), 372. See also *Permanence and Change,* p. 289; and "Restatement, on Death and Mortification," *The Rhetoric of Religion,* pp. 208-212.

[51]*A Rhetoric of Motives,* p. 322.

[52]*A Grammar of Motives,* p. 376.

[53]For Burke's use of these terms, which he takes to be "at the very center of dialectical motivation," see "Dialectic of Tragedy" and "Actus and Status" in *A Grammar of Motives,* pp. 38-43.

[54]Burke's terms for the three stages of artistic production. See *Counter-Statement* (Phoenix ed., Chicago, 1957), pp. 213-214.

[55]". . . we might say Hell is indecision, Purgatory is decision, and Heaven is the arrival that follows decision persevered in." "Catharsis—Second View," *op. cit.,* p. 128.

[56]"But 'becoming' itself, in being analyzable as moments between the limits of before and after. . . ." "The Language of Poetry 'Dramatistically' Considered," *op. cit.,* p. 48.

is to say, to study rhetoric. And the purpose of all such study is to discover the motive, or motives—the ultimate meaning, or Purpose—of the movement.[57]

And hence to study a movement is to study its form: for if movements are acts, acts have form—and form is content,[58] content is meaning, and meaning is motive or Purpose. It is to study the forms, in their particularity and plenitude, within the dramatistic form of rhetorical movement itself: which is dialectical. anagogic, triple-tiered; an organic, progressive, contrapuntal unfoldment, through periods of inception, crisis, and consummation, "through the realms of the damned, the penitent, and the blessed."[59]

5

The inception period of a movement is a time of indecision; of alienation, auscultation, and the innovation of public tensions. It is a time for the identification of destination and devils, the "Mecca" of the movement, and the "evil principles" it opposes.[60] It is a time for the accumulation of individual conversions; for the organization of an opposition; and for the achievement of solidarity, *merger*, in the ranks of the converted.

Movements begin when some pivotal individual or group—suffering attitudes of alienation in a given social system, and drawn (consciously or unconsciously) by the impious dream of a mythic Order—enacts, gives voice to, a *No.*[61] This enactment of the Negative by a Saving Remnant ("prophets," aggressor rhetors, who "see through" the existing order and foretell the coming of the new) will itself be precipitated by some event or attitude, or cluster of events and attitudes, that symbolizes the unacceptable—the manifestation of intolerable pride, the unendurable perversion of reason and justice. The movement's Negative is in essence the announcement of a stand, a "standing together," an *understanding*. It may be called a constitution,

---

[57]See "The Five Master Terms," *Twentieth Century English,* ed. William S. Knickerbocker (New York, 1946), pp. 272-288; and *A Grammar of Motives,* x-xvi.

[58]A rhetorical movement is a social act; and "in social acts, form *is* content." Hugh Duncan, *Communication and Social Order* (New York, 1962), p. 320. If a rhetorical movement is an act "contained" by the "psychology of the audience," one might define it as "the creation of an appetite in the mind of the auditor, and the adequate satisfying of that appetite." To do so would be to borrow Burke's definition of "form." *Counter-Statement,* p. 31. The dramatistic approach "through the emphasis upon the act promptly integrates considerations of 'form' and 'content.'" *The Philosophy of Literary Form,* p. 76.

[59]The phrase is from "Catharsis—Second View," *op. cit.,* p. 121. For Burke's discussion of two kinds of poetic "unfolding" (the poet's and the reader's), see "Toward a Post-Kantian Verbal Music," *The Kenyon Review,* XX (1958), 543-546.

[60]Cf. The Philosophy of Literary Form, p. 165; and see Hugh Duncan, *Language and Literature in Society* (Chicago, 1953), p. 121.

[61]On the pivotal group, see *Counter-Statement,* p. 71; and Karl Mannheim, *Man and Society in an Age of Reconstruction,* tr. by Edward Shils (London, 1940). On alienation ("that state of affairs wherein a man no longer 'owns' his world because, for one reason or another, it seems basically unreasonable"), see *Attitudes toward History,* pp. 216, 342.

manifesto, covenant, program, proclamation, declaration, tract for the times, statement, or counterstatement. It may be expressed in the form of an essay, document, speech, poem, sermon, novel, play, pamphlet or song. Whatever its label or mode of expression, it constitutes the initial act of the movement— the axe raised to its full height, and permitted to fall; or less militantly, the vernal bud from which the movement will unfold into flower.

As the starting point of the movement, the enactment of the Negative may be taken by the student as a "representative anecdote," a moment that embodies, implicitly or explicitly, the key terms and equations of the movement.[62] With these terms and equations the study of a movement begins.[63] They identify *what equals what, what opposes what, what follows what*. They identify the "heaven" of the movement, as well as its "hell"; its gods, or god, as well as its devils ("faulty principles," scapegoats, "vile beasts"). And thus they suggest, however darkly, an answer to the question *why*, the ultimate question of motive. For the key terms prefigure (consciously or unconsciously) the lineaments of the "perfecting myth" that draws the movement futuristically, *a fronte* ("The vision says in effect: 'Only if the socio-political order is on such-and-such relations with the principles of all order, can the order be reasonable.' And thus, the 'perfecting myth' becomes like the originator of the order it perfects").[64]

Arising as it does out of the enactment of a Negative, the rhetoric of the inception period, in its initial phase, is the rhetoric of an *anti* movement, predominantly a rhetoric of negation. Thus the period begins with a rhetoric of dissent and corrosion. It is a rhetoric of dual strategy, designed to produce doubt, and to promote indecision and the sense of division. Its first strategy is to intensify misunderstanding: to permeate the prevailing scene with a sense of the absurdity and injustice of the existing order, the irrelevance of its rhetoric, the failure of its communication. It is a strategy designed to infuse increasing numbers of hearers (the corruptible—the potentially alienable, the uncommitted, the powerless, the "disadvantaged," the "simply curious"),[65] with attitudes of rejection toward the hierarchy—which is to say, with impiety, and with the Guilt that goes with impiety (for *"to flourish in the state of Glory, we must first be sown in Corruption"*).[66]

Its second strategy is to provoke conflict. It is a strategy designed to

---

[62]Cf. *A Grammar of Motives*, pp. 324ff and "The Poetic Motive," *The Hudson Review*, XI (Spring 1958), 60.

[63]See "Linguistic Approach to Problems of Education," *op. cit.*, pp. 270, 274-278; *Attitudes toward History*, pp. 232-235; *The Philosophy of Literary Form*, pp. 56-86; and "Fact, Inference and Proof in the Analysis of Literary Symbolism," *Symbols and Values: An Initial Study, Thirteenth Symposium of the Conference on Science, Philosophy and Religion*, ed. Lyman Bryson (New York, 1954), pp. 283-306. For an illuminating treatment of Burke's method, see Rueckert, *op. cit.*, pp. 83-111.

[64]*The Rhetoric of Religion*, p. 241.

[65]*Counter-Statement*, p. 179.

[66]Sir Thomas Browne, *The Garden of Cyrus, Works*, ed. Geoffrey Keynes, IV (London, 1928), p. 67. Cf. *The Philosophy of Literary Form*, p. 83.

infuse the "priests" of the existing order (the incorruptible—the unalienable, the committed "establishment," the "power structure," the guardian symbols of the prevailing system of authority) with attitudes of rejection and Guilt toward the movement; attitudes that will impel them to the act of opposition—to the organization of a counter-movement, a reactive corps of defendant rhetors that will give salience to the errant symbols ("faulty principles," "vile beasts") of the existing order.

The development of a counter-movement is vital: for "*it is the bad side that produces the movement which makes history, by providing a struggle.*"[67] The counter-movement provides the movement with the potential for crisis, and hence for consummation; for it provides a salient Victim, a scapegoat, a Kill—a rhetorical Vile Beast to be slain. Or put otherwise: it provides a Negation to be negated; and hence the potential for dialectical movement, the purifying struggle of contradictions, the purgative striving that ends in transformation and transcendence.[68]

As the rhetoric of dissent does its work of corrosion, and rhetor and counter-rhetor begin to flower into public notice, the movement enters the second phase of the period of inception—turns to a rhetoric of conversion and catharsis. Its first strategy is to promote decision, to *convert* the estranged; to "turn toward" the movement increasing numbers of the alienated, the undecided; to turn them from their hellish state of indecision and division (passive suffering, *pathema*) toward the movement as a negation of the errant symbols they oppose. It is a strategy designed to convert the impious, to convince them that by attitude they are of the movement, and by reason and justice ought to be *in* it; that the movement as the opponent of the counter-movement, which speaks for the state of Corruption, constitutes a Saving Rebellion—a striving for salvation, perfection, the "good."[69]

Its second strategy—since attitudes are but beginnings, mere "*incipient acts*"[70]—is to provoke action. It is a strategy designed to move the converted—through "pity, fear, and the like emotions"[71]—to rise up and cry

---

[67] Karl Marx, *The Poverty of Philosophy* (International Publishers ed., New York, 1963), p. 121. See James W. Vander Zanden, "Resistance and Social Movements," *Social Forces*, XXXVII (May 1959), 313; and Harvey Seifert, *Conquest by Suffering: The Process and Prospects of Nonviolent Resistance* (Philadelphia, 1965), p. 51.

[68] "When approached from a certain point of view, A and B are 'opposites.' We mean by 'transcendence' the adoption of another point of view from which they cease to be opposites." *Attitudes toward History*, p. 336. See also *A Rhetoric of Motives*, p. 53; and Marx, *op. cit.*, pp. 107-108.

[69] Conversion is here conceived as involving both attitude and act. Note Burke on the conversion of Augustine, *The Rhetoric of Religion*, pp. 49-117. The form of Augustine's conversion is singularly appropriate for the study of movements; for his turn was from "bad" words to "good," from the teaching of pagan rhetoric to the preaching of the word of God (i.e. "speech being a mode of conduct, he converted his faulty living into eloquence").

[70] *A Rhetoric of Motives*, p. 42; *A Grammar of Motives*, pp. 20, 42, 50.

[71] "Pity is said to be like a movement towards; and fear (or 'terror') like a movement away-from . . . And we are healed by being enabled to put opposites together in a way that transcends their opposition." "On Catharsis, or Resolution," *op. cit.*, p. 341.

No to the counter-movement (thereby say *Yes* to the movement);[72] to move them to the purgative act *(poiema)* that will purify their "faulty living," enable them to transform their "natural condition," transcend their Guilt—to "shift their coordinates," "acquire a new 'perspective,'" "see around the corner," and hence "prophesy."[73] It is a strategy designed, in brief, to move them to the negation of the counter-Negation; which is to say, to the rhetorical killing of the Kill.

For the killing is rhetorical, whether it is in the order of Victimage or of Mortification. The killing is impious, in the order of murder, when the converted rise up, in the arena of their minds, and negate the contradictions of the counter-movement; when having "suffered," struggled with, the errant symbols of the existing order ("faulty principles," "vile beasts"), they "see through," reject, and thus slay them.[74] The symbolic rejection of the existing order is a purgative act of transformation and transcendence. It affirms the commitment of the converted to the movement—to the new understanding, which is an "adequate" understanding (for it is a striving for reason and justice). And hence it endows them with a new condition or "substance"— with a new identity, a new unity, a new motive.

And the killing is pious, in the order of Mortification, when the converted negate the negations that they encounter in themselves: when—inevitably tempted to disobey, to deny the "commandments" of the movement—they suffer, "see through," reject, and thus slay the "vile beasts" within.[75] The decision to persevere in their assent to the movement—to say *No* to the errant negatives that rise up in themselves ("in the light of more complicated after-thoughts")—is an act of symbolic self-sacrifice, scrupulous self-restraint (self-control, self-moderation). It is a purgative act of obedience that provides them with a renewed understanding, a "dynamic" understanding ("the *understanding* which is active in that it performs the act of unification").

Yet it must not be forgotten that the killing in a movement may be physical, nonverbal ("beyond language"); and that such killing is also rhetorical. For men may murder, for the sake of terror, in the name of the

---

[72]Cf. Albert Camus, *The Rebel: An Essay on Man in Revolt,* tr. Anthony Bower (Vintage ed., New York, 1956), p. 13. And see *Attitudes toward History,* p. 21.

[73]*Attitudes toward History,* pp. 269-270, 314.

[74]The "desire to kill" a certain person "is much more properly analyzable as a desire to *transform the principle* which that person represents." *A Rhetoric of Motives,* p. 13. "Stated broadly the dialectical (agnostic) approach to knowledge is through the *act* of assertion, whereby one 'suffers' the kind of knowledge that is the reciprocal of his act. This is the process embodied in tragedy where the agent's action involves a corresponding passion, and from the sufferance of the passion there arises an understanding of the act, an understanding that transcends the act. The act, in being an assertion, has called forth a counter-assertion in the elements that compose its context. And when the agent is enabled to see in terms of this counter-assertion, he has transcended the state that characterized him at the start." *A Grammar of Motives,* p. 38.

[75]Mortification is "a kind of governance, an extreme form of 'self control,' the deliberate, disciplinary 'slaying' of any motive that, for 'doctrinal' reasons, one thinks of as unruly . . . it is a systematic way of saying no to Disorder, or obediently saying yes to order." *The Rhetoric of Religion,* p. 190; and see "Thanatopsis for Critics," *op. cit.,* pp. 369-370.

movement—knowing that their Victims, though silenced, may speak: for Death, though the ultimate failure of communication, is nevertheless, being a mode of conduct, in the realm of speech ("*O eloquent, just, and mighty Death! whom none could advise, thou hast persuaded. . . .*")[76]

And it must not be forgotten, Death being in the realm of speech, that men may die, for the sake of pity, in the name of the movement; nor that of all the modes of dying, none is more eloquent than *martyrdom*—ultimate Mortification, self-Victimage, "a total voluntary self-sacrifice enacted in a grave cause before a perfect (absolute) witness."[77]

Three dangers confront the movement during its period of inception, any of which may cause its abortion. There is always the danger that the counter-movement will triumph; that the movement will be "killed," in the minds of the public, by its opponents. There is the danger that the rhetors of the unfolding movement—confronted by retrograde or recalcitrant factors in the gradually shifting Scene—will fail to revise their strategies, or otherwise err in their efforts to adapt to exigencies unforeseen. And there is the danger that the movement, as its ranks increase, will "splinter"—fail to achieve solidarity, *merger*; that the myth which prefigures the Purpose of the movement, imperfectly conveyed or received (whether consciously or unconsciously) will yield in the minds of a crucial number of converts ("heretics," "sectarians," "extremists") to an impious new vision of Order.

The formal need to circumvent these dangers structures the rhetoric of the final phase of the inception period. It is a rhetoric of profusion and intensity; a rhetoric raised to the level of eloquence. It is a rhetoric charged, to the utmost, with "a frequency of Symbolic and formal effects"; and energized, and sustained, by the pious desire to make utterance "perfect by adapting it in every minute detail to the [natural] appetites" of its hearers. It is a rhetoric marked by a "fullness of preoccupation" with the movement and its myth; by an "exaltation at the correctness," or propriety, of the movement's procedure.[78] It is a rhetoric that achieves and maintains solidarity; that intensifies recruitment and the commitment of the converted; that assures the emergence of triumphant hosts of "prophets"—rhetors united in their identification with the movement, in their conviction that the movement is the way to Redemption. It is a rhetoric that generates, in brief, a moving, mounting, and decisive tide of discourse.

And thus—as the movement succeeds in circumventing the dangers that confront it; as the rhetorical strategies of the inception period, correctly conceived and conveyed and revised to meet the needs of the gradually shifting Scene, begin to touch increasing numbers with the aura of alienation, and to accumulate conversions; as ineffective appeals are abandoned, new

---

[76] Sir Walter Raleigh, *The History of the World* (Edinburgh, 1820), VI, p. 370.
[77] *The Rhetoric of Religion*, p. 248.
[78] The phrases quoted are from Burke's discussion of "eloquence." See *Counter-Statement*, pp. 165, 41, 170, 37.

modes of argument adopted, available channels of communication subjected to increasingly intensified use, and ever broader publics addressed; as the power of the "priests" wavers and wanes, and the ranks of the aggressor rhetors grow ever greater, maintain solidarity, *merger*—the movement comes to its moment of crisis.

6

The crisis period of a movement is a time of mass decision; of collective catharsis, purgation, the resolution of public tensions.[79] It is the time of the expression ("in its unguarded simplicity") of a determinative public judgment; the time of the death of allegiance to a former system of authority—the time of negation, rejection, "the rebel snapping of the continuity."

Customarily, the crisis period will be a development *gradatim,* the climacteric of a process of cumulative negation; for most movements, as they develop, acquire a complex of issues. Yet even a multi-issue movement, through the calculated or fortuitous intervention of some cataclysmic event, may experience a relatively sudden moment of crisis.

However it comes, the moment of crisis marks the time when a class (or "principle," or *kind* of being) that has represented "the culmination of a society's purposes," gradually arrives "under changing scenic conditions . . . at the point where its act (and therefore its status) is no longer representative of the new conditions in their totality."[80] It is the time when the movement—having spread "by radiation from the few who [were] quickest to sense new factors in their incipient stages"[81]—effects the collective killing of the Kill.[82]

Now the old order dies, the old gods go. And thus the period of crisis is a time of transformation; for "the *killing* of something is the changing of it."[83] And it is a time of creation, *poiema;* for "consubstantiality *is* established by common involvement in a killing,"[84] and the death of the old order is but the birth of the new. And it is also a time of transcendence; for "a genuine 'new order' is a new *social ladder,*"[85] and the birth of the new order is but the birth of a new hierarchy, a new system of authority.

---

[79]The period of rhetorical crisis I have previously defined as the time "when one of the opposing groups of rhetoricians . . . succeeds in irrevocably disturbing that balance between the groups which had existed in the mind of the collective audience." See "The Rhetoric of Historical Movements," *op. cit.,* p. 186.

[80]*A Grammar of Motives,* p. 420. Cf. "Periods of social crisis occur when an authoritative class, whose purpose and ideals had been generally considered as *representative* of the total society's purposes and ideals, becomes considered as antagonistic." *The Philosophy of Literary Form,* p. 23n.

[81]*Counter-Statement,* p. 71.

[82]". . . a shift in allegiance to the symbols of authority equals the symbolic slaying of a parent." *Attitudes toward History,* p. 211. Cf. Ernest Jones, "Evolution and Revolution," *International Journal of Psycho-Analysis,* XXII (1941), 198ff.

[83]*A Rhetoric of Motives,* p. 20.

[84]*Ibid.,* p. 265.

[85]*Ibid.,* p. 264.

And thus "the obligations of order hang over us," even when we have revolted against order. So the old gods go, the new arrive. The counter-movement yields dominion to the movement. Men are endowed with a new condition or "substance"—with a new identity, a new unity, a new motive.

It is a motive marvelously adequate to the needs of the movement. For if it is the marvel of dialectical movement that "the moment of crisis in transcendence involves a new motive discovered en route"[86]—it is surely the marvel of the rhetoric of movements that, with the transcendence of the moment of crisis, men discover the one motive that will keep them en route. It is the motive that sustains the movement throughout its period of consummation.

7

The period of consummation is a time of decision persevered in. For it is a time of Redemption: men have been purged of absurdity and injustice; and having been purged, they desire to remain so ("for who would not be cleansed"). Reason and justice now reign. Men agree on meaning, value, and desire. And they are charged with attitudes of benevolence—with humility, faith, fortitude, forgiveness, temperance, prudence, and patience; attitudes, ultimately, in the order of self-sacrifice.

So there is a new understanding, an "adequate" understanding; for the order that now exists is essentially "good." And thus the relations between the new classes are harmonious, cooperative, symmetrical; and the new communication between classes is blessed and benign, "like the ways of courtship"—a communication that might be likened, once again, to the "rhetoric of courtship." For it is a rhetoric in the order of love; a rhetoric in the order of peace; and a rhetoric energized, and sustained, by the motive men have discovered—or rediscovered—with the transcendence of the movement's crisis.

For the achievement of transcendence is the achievement of dominion; and with the achievement of dominion men inevitably find, in their totality, that their former act is no longer representative of the new conditions: for now they yearn to conform with the new sources of their being; to be loyal, or obedient, to their new "natural" condition. Or put otherwise: with the transcendence of the movement's crisis, men inevitably find ("under changing scenic conditions") that, having been "prophets," they must now become "priests"; which is to say that they discover, or rediscover, the motive of piety (*mathema;* "the thing learned"). And so they strive to avoid error in the use of language; struggle, without ceasing, to use their language with propriety.

Thus arising as it does out of an attitude of affirmation, the rhetoric of consummation, in the initial phase of the period, is the rhetoric of a *pro* movement, predominantly a rhetoric of assent and allegiance. It is a rhetoric

---

[86]*A Grammar of Motives,* p. 421.

of praise, edification, prayer, petition, courtship; for men accept the new "mystery," the new communication between classes (or "principles," or *kinds of beings*"). And the rhetoric that they practice is a rhetoric, once again, of dual strategy.

Its first strategy is to arouse, and to gratify, the natural appetite for obedience.[87] Its second is to strive, to the utmost, to actualize the "perfecting myth" of the movement: to achieve the incarnation, or embodiment, in the actualities of the material world ("the realities of a social texture"), of the movement's guiding vision of Order—its dream (conscious or unconscious) of "heaven," paradise, the "good society," Utopia.

They are strategies wholly appropriate to a state of Redemption: strategies designed to infuse the pious with the desire to persevere—to continue, in their obedience, to "exemplify a sense of the appropriate"; and to move them, in their perseverance, to complete the building of the new order—"to round things out, to fit experiences together into a unified whole." They are strategies, put otherwise, wholly rotten with piety; designed to achieve "the conformity of a reality to its concept"—which is to say, a state of perfection: "a complete and perfect whole"; a cooperative system of pure symmetry, perfect harmony, and integration ("guided by a scrupulous sense of the appropriate")—an Order marked by perfect communion, pure identification, and absolute communication.

But tragically, in this "imperfect world," "communication is never an absolute (only angels communicate absolutely)."[88] And while it is true, as "prophets" know, that "insofar as [an opposition] can unite in a new collectivity, progressively affirming its own title to the orthodoxy, tendencies toward the negativistic, satanistic, disintegrative, and 'splintering' fall away"—it is also true, as "priests" learn, that "insofar as [an opposition's] own imaginative possibility requires embodiment in bureaucratic fixities ['the realities of a social texture'], its necessary divergences from Utopia become apparent."[89]

Wherefore Utopia—as an existentially "good" order, the portion of paradise gained, a state which is—is inevitably bound, in time, to become an *is not.* And it is a state bound, moreover, while it exists, to stand always "on the verge of being lost":[90] a state of pious men, "huddling together, nervously loquacious, at the edge of an abyss."[91]

For "human beings are not a perfect fit for *any* historic texture";[92] and even in the "heavens" of this earth, the pious remain human. They may gladly submit to a code of control; persevere, strive to obey, struggle to keep

---

[87]"Obedience to the reigning symbols of authority is in itself natural and wholesome." *Attitudes toward History,* p. 226.

[88]*Permanence and Change,* xv.

[89]*Attitudes toward History,* pp. 226.

[90]The phrase is from Burke's discussion of "pure persuasion," *A Rhetoric of Motives,* p. 285.

[91]Cf. *Permanence and Change,* p. 272.

[92]*Attitudes toward History,* pp. 225-226.

the new "commandments" ("if they do not struggle, they rot"). But because they are human, they "can be expected to err" in their striving; which is to say that they can be expected, in time, to disobey—negate, reject, the prevailing system of authority ("for who can keep commandments").

Or put otherwise: while it is true, as "prophets" know, that "man is the only creature who refuses to be what he is"[93]—it is also true, as "priests" learn, that man is inevitably bound to remain what he is: a being by nature divided, ambitious, prone to pride; the symbol-making (symbol-using and misusing) animal, inventor of the negative, goaded by the spirit of hierarchy, ultimately separated from his natural condition by impious dreams of an ideal Order—forever striving, tragically Faustian, wholly "rotten with perfection."

8

"Out of such predicaments, ingenious fellows rise up and sing"—keep the harmony, preserve the symmetry, conserve the cooperative structure: which is to say that they strive, in the time of the new order, to keep the new tension. For the time of the new order, which is the time of a movement in its consummation, is of necessity a time of tension: the tension inherent in a state of harmony, symmetry—a state of solidarity, *merger* ("the comprehension of scattered particulars in one idea").[94] It is the very tension, not to strain for a metaphor, intrinsic to metaphor itself ("the unification of the heterogeneous").[95]

It is a "good" tension, *eutonia*; for it sustains the state of Redemption—which is a state of reason and justice, understanding, love and peace. Yet it is a tension increasingly dependent, as "priests" learn to their pain, on the maintenance of another tension—a private, inner tension—which the pious, being human, may find difficult to endure: the tension of men who must obediently sing *Yes* to the existing order—though they yearn, with mounting anguish, to rise up and cry *No*. It is the tension of men charged with piety, but increasingly ripe with impiety: loyal men who must embody, or make incarnate—in the very texture of their being—the mystic "principle of the oxymoron" ("the co-existence of conflicting orders").[96] For if the state of Redemption is to endure, men must continue their courtship—though they remain by nature divided, "endowed for struggle," prone to pride.

And thus the period of consummation is inevitably a time of revision (self-control, self-restraint, self-moderation). For courtship, which is in the order of love, entails communication ("the most generalized statement of the

---

[93]Camus, *The Rebel*, p. 11.
[94]*A Grammar of Motives*, p. 403.
[95]Philip Wheelwright, *The Burning Fountain: A Study in the Language of Symbolism* (Bloomington, Ind., 1954), pp. 101ff.
[96]"Mysticism as a Solution to the Poet's Dilemma," *Spiritual Problems in Contemporary Literature*, ed. Stanley Romaine Hopper (New York, 1952), p. 111.

principle of love"); and communication, in its essence, involves "a principle of self interference":

> In its essence communication involves the use of verbal symbols for purposes of appeal. Thus, it splits formally into the three elements of speaker, speech, and spoken-to, with the speaker so shaping his speech as to "commune with" the spoken to. This purely technical pattern is the pre-condition of *all* appeal. And "standoffishness" is necessary to the form, because without it the appeal could not be maintained. For if union is complete, what incentive can there be for appeal? Rhetorically, there can be courtship only insofar as there is division. Hence, only through interference could one court continually, thereby perpetuating genuine "freedom of rhetoric."[97]

And thus the period of consummation, the time of a movement in its ending, is ultimately a time of self-sacrifice, self-Victimage, Mortification. For if men are to continue their courtship, and thus preserve the new hierarchy, they must scrupulously, and deliberately, clamp limitations upon themselves: promptly slay the "vile beasts" that arise in their minds; negate, and thus kill, the errant symbols within.

And thus, by symbol-using ("speech being a mode of conduct"), men convert their liabilities ("faulty living") into assets. Now means become ends. The "rhetoric of courtship" rises to the level of "pure persuasion." Men "take delight in the sheer *forms* of courtship for their own sakes"; "in the process of appeal for itself alone, without ulterior purpose."[98] It is a time of pure praise, edification, prayer, petition; of "pure courtship, homage in general, the ultimate idea of an audience, without thought of advantage, but sheerly through love of the exercise."[99] It is the time of "the rhetorical motive dialectically made ultimate": rhetoric for the sake of rhetoric, courtship for the sake of courtship, harmony for the sake of harmony, symmetry for the sake of symmetry.

And thus it is also a time of eloquence: for what is symmetry but "formal excellence"; and "formal excellence" is eloquence.[100] It is the eloquence of men fully preoccupied with the movement and its myth; men in a state of exaltation at the correctness, or propriety, of their procedure. And it is an eloquence which can be expected, at the farthest reach of the movement, to transcend itself (or "abolish itself") by passing, "beyond language," into the region of Silence.

For it must not be forgotten that Silence, being a mode of conduct, is also, like Death, in the realm of speech. There is the "silence of

---

[97] *A Rhetoric of Motives*, p. 271.
[98] *The Rhetoric of Religion*, p. 34; *A Rhetoric of Motives*, x.
[99] *A Rhetoric of Motives*, pp. 293-294.
[100] *Counter-Statement*, p. 37.

understanding"[101]—communion so perfect that it transcends the need of words; identification so pure that it promptly fuses contradictions, and thus sustains the continuity, "the co-existence of conflicting orders." And there is the mystic "rhetoric of silence"[102]—the wordless discourse of the "silent inner teacher": the hierarchical god of the movement, the mythic originator of the harmony or symmetry, the "perfect (absolute) witness," "the beloved cynosure and sinecure, the end of all desire" ("though some lovers of such symmetry may insist that their god be named Atheos").[103]

And it must not be forgotten, Silence being in the realm of speech, that man is a maker *(poietes)*; nor that "the 'poetic state' is in its essence silent."[104] It is the silence essential to "the heart-conscious kind of listening, or vigilance, that precedes expression"—"the artist's preparatory silence (the silence that must precede the saying, until ripeness is near to rot)."[105] It is "the silence of the quest," the Hunt.[106] And hence it is the silence, *par excellence,* of the impious—the realm of the new Saving Remnant, the proud rhetors of the movement to come.

9

And thus a movement may be said to end in stasis. It is the stasis, in a sense, of Redemption—love achieved, peace attained; the dynamic stasis of "that harmony which is movement so perfect that it is imperceptible, like the movement of a spinning top."[107]

And it is the stasis, in another sense, of pure tension. For because men are pious, they are "free";[108] and their freedom equals a state of continual

---

[101]Cf. Joost Meerloo, *Conversation and Communication* (New York, 1952), p. 115.

[102]Cf. Joseph A. Mazzeo, "St. Augustine's Rhetoric of Silence," *Renaissance and Seventeenth-Century Studies* (New York, 1964), pp. 16ff.

[103]A conjunction of phrases from *A Rhetoric of Motives,* pp. 333, 291.

[104]"Towards a Post-Kantian Verbal Music," *op. cit.,* p. 537.

[105]"Thanatopsis for Critics: A Brief Thesaurus of Deaths and Dyings," *op. cit.,* p. 374.

[106]"For in the quest one is naturally silent, be it as the animal that stalks its quarry or as the thinker meditating upon an idea." *A Grammar of Motives,* p. 303.

[107]The phrase is from Herbert Read's "The Flower of Peace" in *The Forms of Things Unknown* (London, 1960), p. 223.

[108]"Freedom" is "self-movement." *A Grammar of Motives,* p. 74. In the final, utopian stage of a movement, men are naturally pious, obedient; and their piety is the essential source of their freedom. Because they are pious they negate their desire to say *No* to the existing order, and hence "court continually, thereby perpetuating genuine 'freedom of rhetoric.'" Cf. note 97.

Because they are pious they are concerned with rhetoric for the sake of rhetoric, *pure form;* and "there is no purer act than pure form"—and "a pure act is by definition pure freedom." *The Rhetoric of Religion,* p. 281. And because they are pious, they praise; and praise "wells up"—"in praise there is the feel of freedom"; "in total admiration, one is wholly free." *Ibid.,* p. 55.

And because they are pious they are necessarily in movement toward a state of perfect symmetry, and hence "free." For they are possessed by the principle of perfection, "the desire to round things out," "the delight in carrying out terministic possibilities 'to their logical conclusion,'" in so far as such possibilities are perceived." And "this 'entelechial' motive is the poetic equivalent of what in the moral realm is called 'justice.' It is equitable with both necessity and freedom in the sense that the consistent rounding out of a terminology is the very opposite of frustration. Necessary movement

Mortification—self-restraint, self-control, self-moderation (and "modera-
tion . . . is nothing but pure tension").[109] It is the tension inherent in a state of
sheer courtship; the tension intrinsic to the very motive of "pure persuasion":
"It is the condition of Santayana's transcendental skepticism, where the
pendulum is at rest, not hanging, but poised exactly above the fulcrum . . .
Psychologically it is related to a conflict of opposite impulses. Philosophically, it suggests the plight of Buridan's extremely rational ass. . . .
Theologically or politically, it would be the state of intolerable indecision just
preceding conversion to a new doctrine."

It is a state "uncomfortably like suspended animation." It is "the change
of direction, from systole to diastole, made permanent"; "the moment of
motionlessness, when the axe has been raised to its full height, and is just
about to fall." Or less militantly, "it is the pause at the window, before
descending into the street."[110]

10

But no material world, as Burke has noted, could be run on the motive of
"pure persuasion."[111] For since men are by nature divided, "every human
statement is partial." And if it is true that "there is a point at which rhetoric
in its perfection transcends itself or 'abolishes itself' by becoming sheerly
dialectical"—it is also true that there is a point at which "even the most
'universal' of dialectical manipulations will disclose partisan motives, willy
nilly, whereat we are brought back into the realm of rhetorical partisan-
ship."[112]

So the wheel forever turns. Man's movements, in time, come to an end.
And they come to an end in tragedy—for tragedy involves defeat, "the failure
of our ends,"[113] the ultimate death of the "good."

Yet if his movements are tragic, the fate of man himself is comic—for
tragedy also involves triumph, "the beyond of resurrection,"[114] an ultimate
"prosperous end."[115] And if the wheel forever turns, it is man who does the

---

toward perfect symmetry is thus free." "The Language of Poetry 'Dramatistically' Considered," *op.
cit.*, p. 63.
Put otherwise: the problem of freedom in "utopia" (taken as a metaphor for the ending, or
"perfection," of a movement) resolves itself in terms of the Hegelian formula, "freedom is the
knowledge of necessity." Yet the freedom that is grounded in man's capacity for the Negative also
remains; and hence even in "utopia" men are free to be impious—to negate the negations of the
existing order, to say *No* to the prevailing "thou-shalt-nots." Cf. *The Rhetoric of Religion*, p. 222; and
the dialog between Satan and The Lord in the "Prologue in Heaven" *ibid.*, pp. 282-283.
[109] Camus, *The Rebel*, p. 301.
[110] *A Rhetoric of Motives*, p. 294.
[111] *Ibid.*
[112] "Mysticism as a Solution to the Poet's Dilemma," *op. cit.*, p. 109.
[113] Foss, *The Idea of Perfection in the Western World*, p. 63.
[114] *Ibid.*
[115] "*Comoedia vero inchoat asperitatem alicuius rei, sed eius materia prospere terminatur . . .*" *Dantis
Alagherii Epistolae: The Letters of Dante*, ed. Paget Toynbee (Oxford, 1920), pp. 176, 200.

turning—forever striving, in an "imperfect world," for a world of perfection. And hence man, the rhetorical animal, is saved: for salvation lies in the striving, the struggle itself.

It is the message of the ascending angels in Goethe's *Faust, Part Two:* "whoever strives with all his power, we are allowed to save" *(wer immer strebend sich bemüht, den können wir erlösen).*[116]

It is also the message of Camus: "The struggle itself toward the heights is enough to fill a man's heart. One must imagine Sisyphus happy."[117]

And it is essentially the message, to round things out, of Kenneth Burke—the ultimate meaning, or purpose, of dramatism itself: for ". . . the nearest man will ever get to a state of practical peace among the many persuasions is by theoretical study of the forms in all persuasion.[118]

---

[116]*Goethe's Faust,* tr. Walter Kaufmann (New York, 1961), p. 493. On the relation between this passage and its companion ("man can be expected to err as long as he keeps striving"), a relation that epitomizes the tragic attitude toward value, see Henry Alonzo Myers, *Tragedy: A View of Life* (Ithaca, N. Y., 1956), pp. 12-13.

[117]*The Myth of Sisyphus,* tr. Justin O'Brien (Vintage ed., New York, 1955), p. 91.

[118]"Linguistic Approach to Problems of Education," *op. cit.,* p. 300. Dramatism, Burke's "project directed 'towards the purification of war,'" is conceived as a means of striving, through study, for a world of peace. The ultimate end is unattainable (or unmaintainable); for in this "imperfect world," where men are by nature divided, one man's "good" may be another's "evil"—and men may always make the Satanic choice, "Evil, be thou my good." Nevertheless, in a world of "many persuasions," dramatistic study in itself offers a measure of salvation. For dramatism would encourage "tolerance by speculation," make "methodical the attitude of patience"; and tolerance and patience are in the order of peace. A world infused with such attitudes would surely be a "better world"; even a world, one must imagine, in which men might be happy.

Reading History with Kenneth Burke

by Frank Lentricchia

Maybe the most fascinating thing about our relationship to Kenneth Burke is the clever way in which we have managed consistently to avoid him while seeming always to pay homage to his work. By way of homage: in the spring of 1981 the University of California Press completed its honorable project of republishing all of Burke's books in a spacious paperback format. In the meanwhile, however, the ambitious studies of contemporary critical theory, with few exceptions, continue to ignore Burke almost totally. When he is mentioned, it is only fleetingly, out of a sense of scholarly duty, as if to demonstrate to knowing readers no ignorance of his large presence. My sense is that Burke's brief recognition in these books assuages a traditional scholarly conscience that wants to dismiss him. Although to prove it would require a more far-ranging treatment than can be permitted in the confines of this essay, I think it true that contemporary theorists, critics, literary historians, philosophers, and other students of humanistic disciplines have needed to exclude Kenneth Burke, and I mean that harsh term ("exclude") with the force with which it is applied in the writings of Michel Foucault.

Until recent years the canons of truth and sanity that govern the writing of critical theory in the United States have implicitly decreed that much of what Burke does is a deviation from good sense, which I translate: disturbing, different, perhaps dangerous. Burke cannot be accepted in small, bearable doses; he must be taken all at once or not at all, but to take him all at once would require a radical reconception of the basis of what is usually called humanistic study. For more than fifty years, Burke—this man without tenure, a Ph.D., or even a B.A., who writes books that cannot be touched by conventional academic definition—has been telling us that the conventional division of the humanities, with literature, philosophy, history, linguistics, and social theory each self-enclosed within the fortresslike walls of the disciplines, housing experts too often ignorant and contemptuous of everything outside their respective castles, is all, at best, a lie of administrative convenience, and, at worst, a re-enforcement in our institutions of higher education of bourgeois-capitalist hegemony. As a start, we (and I mean American academic intellectuals) would need to cease reducing the richly

Reprinted from White, Hayden and Margaret Brose, eds. *Representing Kenneth Burke: Selected Papers from the English Institute.* The Johns Hopkins University Press, Baltimore/London, 1982. Used by permission.

integrated and socially urgent European conception of critical theory to the comfortably alienated ivory-tower formalism of literary theory. To take Burke seriously, therefore, requires a searching re-examination of our traditional values; no wonder that we continually put off our appointment with him.

To demonstrate adequately the several claims that I have made on behalf of Burke in these beginning paragraphs is the task of a book-length project. There is a route into Burke, however, that will at least afford us a number of rapid views of subjects he has opened up with his usual provocation. I am referring to his repeated turning to ideas of history and to his practice as a reader of history. Burke keeps coming back both to philosophical speculation on the nature of history and to the writing and doing of the historical discipline. These are not separate intellectual activities, as Hayden White has argued, and Burke is good evidence for White's point of view, as if the confrontation with history, more than the formulation of what he has called Dramatism, were the act that conferred identity upon his career. Dramatism is Burke's official program, the name he has given to his system. *Attitudes Toward History,* the title of his fifth volume, gives us access to what I think is a more fundamental Burkean activity; a process of formulating, exploring, and making forays—in so many words, the various acts of reading and writing history. Although in my opinion Burke brings off this sort of act with maximum penetration and originality, and although I think it (not Dramatism) his true project, the historical act of thinking evidenced in his texts is not—and cannot be, by virtue of what he makes it—systematic. What may define him best as an historical thinker, in fact, is a series of decisive engagements, spread over his entire intellectual development, with the idea of system itself. As we'll see, the desire to be systematic is met at critical points by a resistance to system and in particular by a resistance to the essentializing consequences of systematic thought.

I

With the work of Martin Heidegger, his student Hans-Georg Gadamer, and, from another quarter, Hayden White, now behind us, it need no longer be argued that the starting point for any consideration of "history" (whether as discipline or as the temporal record itself) is necessarily with the act of interpretation and the location of that act within a sociocultural matrix. Burke's major early work belongs to the late twenties and the thirties. *Counter-Statement* (1931), *Permanence and Change* (1935), *Attitudes Toward History* (1937), and *The Philosophy of Literary Form* (1941), while they can be read as preparation for the huge works on motives (*A Grammar of Motives,* 1945, and *A Rhetoric of Motives,* 1950), are interesting in their own right, as documents marked by the social and intellectual conflicts of the thirties. Burke is a man of the thirties, and when the *Grammar* and the *Rhetoric* are understood as productions of a man of the thirties, much of what appears forbiddingly abstract and even arid in those books comes richly to life.

In *Permanence and Change,* Burke's thought on history is marked by an antiHegelian impulse to revere and preserve human differences in their nominalistic particularity, and therefore to check and resist the homogenizing sweep of teleological process: at the same time, his thought is marked by a desire to move directly to a transcendental perch above historical process in an effort to find the essence of a single meaning for it all. *Permanence and Change* opens with a declaration that to our self-congratulatory retrospection sounds uncannily up-to-date: "all living things are critics."[1] Burke means that all living things are interpreters. He goes on to distinguish human interpreters from animals by proposing that human beings alone have the capacity to interpret their own interpretations, to reflect upon the very process of reading and interpretation itself.[2] Further along in the argument he adds that it is never reality in itself, but only and always interpretation of reality that we deal with. He points out that even those things that we tend to think possess the most stubbornly natural being—he names stimuli and motives as chief examples—are distinctly linguistic products, and, as such, texts *of* and *for* interpretation.[3] Burke would refuse to grant to the interpretive process the reassurances that we feel when we anchor (think we anchor) our various readings to the truth of natural reality's fixed rock. As a prolegomena to any future hermeneutics, we must investigate the basis of the interpretive act with the knowledge that "reality" cannot be that basis. To this end, at an agonized moment in *Permanence and Change,* he describes the hermeneutic situation as a "Babel of orientations." He asks "what arises as a totality" from this Babel? And he answers: "the re-enforcement of the interpretive attitude itself."[4] With no way of making a unified interpretation out of Babel, with no totality ("totalization") possible, Burke would seem to have denied a shared basis for the interpretive process, would seem to have plunged interpretation so deeply into the temporal and cultural differences of human particularity as to have engendered a vision of history as a chaos of interpretive attitudes, all inaccessibly locked away within their prison-houses. This is no theory of history; it is rather the despair of history.

However, at the end of *Permanence and Change,* Burke manages a double escape. By postulating an organic genius for freedom that exists "*prior* to any particular historic texture"[5] he finds a point of view outside of history from which to mediate (tame) the conflicting interpretations within it. Now, insofar as the notion of "point of view," in its strict sense of *spatially situated vision,* implies that other "points" are possible, Burke's is no point of view. To indulge a necessary contradiction, it is the spatially ubiquitous point

---

[1] Kenneth Burke, *Permanence and Change: An Anatomy of Purpose* (Los Altos, Calif.: Hermes Publications, 1954), p. 5.
[2] Ibid., pp. 5-6.
[3] Ibid., p. 35.
[4] Ibid., pp. 117-118.
[5] Ibid., p. 226.

of view of truth, an unsituated understanding of the congeries of interpretations that discerns an otherwise hidden principle of coherence: what all conflicting interpretations would commonly signify—a shared signified that may be called (after Jacques Derrida) "transcendental." Moreover, this thesis of the innate genius for freedom that is "prior" to history, grounded in human nature, assumes "that no given *historical* texture need be accepted as the underlying basis of a universal causal series."[6] The principle of freedom not only resolves the hermeneutic Babel of history by providing a universal motive for interpretation, but also prohibits, at the same time, any locally engendered reading of the historical process from establishing priority as the key to all of history's meaning. So the principle of freedom sanctions Burke's transcendent innocence as an interpretive subject, situated over history's local forces of determination, because, as the ultimate motor principle of interpretation, that which moves all interpretation but is not itself caught up in the conflicts and partialities of interpretation, it is identical with the origin of a history that, in itself, is an arena of confusion and unfreedom.

Burke's response to historical complexity in *Permanence and Change* is traditional, conservative, and aesthetic—world-weary and nostalgic for the purity of an origin called freedom. This is a side of Burke that cannot be ignored by his apologists; in various guises it reappears in each of his major texts. I have called it an "aesthetic" response because it harkens back to Greek philosophy and to a distinction in Aristotle's *Poetics* that has structured (and biased) much of Western thought on the relations of artistic and historical disciplines: I refer to the idea that history (both as a kind of writing, a discipline, and as the untextualized temporal process) is bogged down in intransigent, irrational particularity (to echo Sidney's neo-Aristoteleanism), while art traffics in the realm of the universal. The history of theories of history tends to show that if you begin with this assumption that historical process is an unintelligible chaos you will make it meaningful, you will textualize history (because you won't be able to stand your assumption) in approximately the way that Aristotle said that the poet would make human reality intelligible: you will constitute historical process in and through a literary mode. The aestheticizing textualization of history (in *Metahistory* White claims that this process is inevitable) is its essentialization. From the vast and confusing panorama of human motives one motive is selected as the essence (ground, core, true meaning) of motivation and all others are done away with, as forces in their own right, by being relegated to the status of variants or departures from the essence, which is single, unitary, fundamentally real and, in a genealogical formulation of great moment, what Burke calls the ancestral cause of all other motives.[7] Against this essentializing strategy of interpretation, which he defines as the normal ideal

---

[6] Ibid., p. 228.
[7] Kenneth Burke, *The Philosophy of Literary Form: Studies in Symbolic Action* (Berkeley and Los Angeles: University of California Press, 1973), pp. 261-262.

of science to explain the complex in terms of the simple, Burke places what he calls a "proportional" strategy, which rests with complex interrelations of motives. Such complexities cannot be reduced; the interpreter must let them be. These two strategies of interpretation are at work in Burke's texts from the beginning; although in his two interpretations of interpretation he clearly elevates one over the other, neither such valorization nor the mere fact of high-level hermeneutic self-consciousness permits him to master the essentializing impulse in his writing. I deliberately echo in this paragraph the language of Jacques Derrida's essay "Structure, Sign, and Play in the Discourse of the Human Sciences," not to lay his ideas over Burke's but to indicate two things. First, the rather complete anticipation of a major Derridean point of view in Burke's essay on Freud of 1939. Second, to emphasize in Burke's work a point easily missed, and too often ignored in Derrida's well-known essay: that there is never a question of choosing between these strategies; no single interpretive subject is free to work its will in the hermeneutic process because the subject cannot control the forces at work *in* reading and *on* the reader.

The relocation of the interpreter, as traditional Cartesian subject, from its place of mastery and freedom to a function of a process of interpretation larger and more powerful than itself, has crucial consequences in Burke's later writings. At this point, however, and in somewhat artificial fashion, I want to segregate the essentializing impulse in him in order to examine its implications in greater detail. In *Attitudes Toward History* Burke offers two interpretive keys to history: the basic historical process he calls, in a phrase of considerable wit, "the bureaucratization of the imaginative," and the central interpretive attitude that he will take toward this process, his attitude of attitudes toward history, which is comic.[8] But let us not take his distinctions at face value, for what is signified by the phrase "bureau-cratization of the imaginative" is not (Burke's philosophical principles would never permit it to be) the reality in itself of history's process but an interpretation of it, and the comic attitude is a perfectly complementary way of responding to (living with) such a reading of history. The comic response is a consoling and accommodating interpretation of interpretation.

After opening his definition of the "bureaucratization of the imaginative" by calling it "a basic process of history," Burke quickly reveals the utopian, pastoral, origin-oriented bias of his position: "Perhaps it merely names the process of dying. 'Bureaucratization' is an unwieldly word, perhaps even an onomatopoeia, since it sounds as bungling as the situation it would characterize. 'Imaginative' suggests pliancy, liquidity, the vernal. And with it we couple the incongruously bulky and almost unpronounceable."[9] With an aesthete's vengeance, Burke has set up a critique of the everyday life of the

---

[8] Kenneth Burke, *Attitudes Toward History* (Boston: Beacon Press, 1961), p. vii.
[9] Ibid., p. 225.

historical process as the Calabanization of Ariel—or is it that what he bemoans is not so much the historical process at large as the coming to being of repressive social organizations and the various hegemonic instruments which keep them in place? He continues:

> Gide has said somewhere that he distrusts the carrying-out of one possibility because it necessarily restricts other possibilities. Call the possibilities "imaginative." And call the carrying-out of one possibility the *bureaucratization* of the imaginative. An imaginative possibility (usually at the start Utopian) is bureaucratized when it is embodied in the realities of a social texture in all the complexities of language and habits in the property relationships, the methods of government, production and distribution, and in the development of rituals that re-enforce the same emphasis. It follows that in this "imperfect world," no imaginative possibility can ever attain complete bureaucratization. . . . In bureaucratizing a possibility, we necessarily come upon the necessity of compromise since human beings are not a perfect fit for *any* historic texture.[10]

With this thinly veiled scorn for any and all sociohistoric textures that have been, are, and will be, with this concomitant projection of human being as a sort of platonic essence that can only be soiled, distorted, and encumbered by any and all actual and possible modes of government, production, and property-relations, and with this keen perception of what Antonio Gramsci called hegemony—the educative strategy of the ruling class to rule consciousness and thereby to extend and perpetuate its domination intellectually, with no need to coerce through physical force ("the development of rituals that re-enforce the same emphasis")—Burke has given us a portrait of historical life as an arena of despair with no exit. Tragically, all hope is situated at the freshness of origins, where (and when) imagination freely creates and plays with its possibilities of utopian vision: all subsequent historical movement away from the playful and contemplative consideration of multiple visions and into actions—into the *act*ualization of vision—is synonymous with a process of degradation, of the loss of freedom, even of dying. No *telos* is discernible as an end to history's futility because historical process is not purposive.

However, Burke's response, his key reading of the bureaucratization of the imaginative, is precisely not tragic. If tragedy implies necessarily dangerous limitations upon our capacity to know, and if an inescapable consequence of these limitations is that we act accordingly—self-destructively, in partial darkness, never able to free ourselves from a fatal mesh of circumstances—then Burke has appropriately named his attitude toward history "comic," for it postulates not fatal ignorance and death but

---

[10]Ibid., pp. 225-226.

foolishness and embarrassing exposure for the human agent, and full consciousness for the comedic overseer of the twists and turns of the human drama, a confident and complete knowledge of how the game begins and how it will end. And Burke is that comedic overseer who would teach us the lessons of humility. With the security of his knowledge that history inevitably bungles imaginative possibility, that with amusing (because mechanical) repetition the insight of imagination will always, because it is materially embodied, produce blindness in the bureaucratizing agents, and that historical action necessarily ends in gaping discrepancies between intention and actualization, Burke himself becomes the exemplary humble man, no champion of a single program because he knows in advance how all programs will turn out. History is thus essentialized in the mode of dramatic irony, with privileged place given to the man of comedic knowledge who, though he must be foolish actor, is somehow wise spectator as well. As comedic overseer Burke becomes what he exhorts others to be—an observer of himself while acting, an achiever, therefore, of *"maximum consciousness"* who can "'transcend' himself by noting his own foibles."[11] How more openly can we aestheticize history than by seeing it through the lens of a literary category? How more openly can we essentialize history than by squeezing it all under the umbrella of a single genre? To jam history into the narrow room of a single comedic plot, as Burke has done, is surely to press, in most aggressive fashion, Aristotle's claim for the poet's universalizing power, while, as a consequence, such single-minded narrative conversion of historical process wipes out the differences of historical textures and moves in another way against the threatening Babel of interpretation that Burke had repressed in *Permanence and Change.*

Although neither the older nor the newer generation of Yale New Critics has shown much overt speculative or practical concern for history, some such essentializing and aestheticizing attitude as Burke's would seem to commonly underwrite their respective formalist projects for literary study, with paradox, wit, and irony constantly at work in the essays of Cleanth Brooks to essentialize literary history (collapsing Wordsworth into Donne), and with *différance, aporia,* and undecidability similarly at work in Paul de Man's writing (to wipe out the differences between Rousseau, Nietzsche, and Yeats). The recent essays of de Man are epitomes of comic vision and his key terms provide an unintended verification. His criticism of difference ends up affirming what the comedic overseer has always known—that in the end all human differences make no difference because all historical ("bureaucratizing") forces of differentiation are simply "torn apart"[12] (de Man's words) by a power that returns literature to radical freedom from all context, just as Prospero, in the end, permits Ariel's return to unfettered airiness. De Man's

---

[11]Ibid., p. 171.
[12]Paul de Man, "Political Allegory in Rousaeau," *Critical Inquiry* 2 (Summer 1976): 650.

earlier criticism of allegory and irony demonstrates that true comic mastery lies in the acute self-consciousness of the fall even as we fall—falling being inevitable.

The linkage of Brooks's and de Man's persistent formalist projects—their work stretches from the thirties to the present—with Burke's comic meditation on history might remind us of what we are likely to forget in our zeal to banish formalism in the name of a "responsible" scholarship of historical life: that the comedic formalism of Burke was born in the thirties, in the midst of the worst socioeconomic crisis this country has known. Comedic formalism may be denigrated as romantic escapism, but it is nevertheless one kind of response to crisis and certainly it is one kind of alternative to the aesthetic of social realism that Burke, Brooks, and de Man saw, especially in the earlier phases of their careers, as a major threat to the understanding of literary discourse. The inaugural step of any modern formalism constitutes a double negation: on the one hand, of naive theories of social realism, and, on the other, of the philosophical support of such theories in a vulgar version of Marxism. (To be a man of the thirties, as I have called Burke, is not necessarily to be a man of the left, although, as we shall see, in a sophisticated way he is that, too.) The formalisms of Burke, Brooks, and de Man have a social context, and they promise, for the contemporary literary mind, in the wisdom of their comedic sense of history, what another comedy—*commedia*—promised for the medieval theological imagination: a paradise, this one secular and literary, in which the fruit of transcendence is not the end of history but a maximum knowledge of what history is, has been, and will be, from a privileged vantage point beyond its conflicts.

What the comedic historian knows, what he takes to be the single truth of a history in which there is no truth but only fools of truth, is that:

> The progress of humane enlightenment can go no further than in picturing people not as *vicious,* but as *mistaken.* When you add that people are *necessarily* mistaken, that all people are exposed to situations in which they must act as fools, that *every* insight contains its own special kind of blindness, you complete the comic circle, returning again to the lesson of humility that underlies great tragedy. The audience, from its vantage point, sees the operation of errors that the characters of the play cannot see; thus seeing two angles at once, it is chastened by dramatic irony; it is admonished to remember that when intelligence means *wisdom* . . . it requires fear, resignation, the sense of limits, as an important ingredient.[13]

We need to distinguish the Burkean theory of comedy from its classical forefathers. For, whereas Aristotle and numerous of his Renaissance progeny

---

[13]Burke, *Attitudes Toward History,* pp. 41-42.

relegated to comedy the representation of man as worse than he is—more frail, more prone to error, with the implication that such representation is a deviation from a norm of human behavior—Burke and other modernists push the comedic deviation to normative status by declaring, in effect, that comedy is the representation of man as he really is. The Burkean comedic vision would encapsulate truth in a metaphysics of foolishness and failure. This comedic knowledge—this ultimate of "humane enlightenment," which we have no difficulty identifying as the repeated message of modernist literary theory from Brooks to de Man—this ironic vision that declares the inability of literature to declare, to refer, or to have a message, would term all injunctions to act at best naiveté, at worst fanaticism. This so-called "humane enlightenment" (which makes a dread of powerlessness) would, in the fatalism of its "wise" counsel of "resignation" and "fear," uphold the status quo. The criticisms of comedy, paradox, irony, *aporia,* and *différance,* far from being socially innocent, or socially indifferent, sum up for many liberal humanist intellectuals, particularly for those with memories of the thirties, a certain attitude, a social posture—I will not call it a philosophy—that now passes, especially in literary critical academe, for sophisticated worldliness; it is, in the end, I think, a mandarin cynicism that betrays itself in the bewildering variety of ways that it has found in which to declare *noli me tangere,* for I belong to despair.

II

With this approach to a theory of "maximum consciousness" in *Attitudes Toward History,* Burke is prepared to stake out his most essentialist program in the introduction to *A Grammar of Motives*—what he calls Dramatism, but what we would now, with hindsight, call structuralism. The *Grammar* of 1945 is full-blown structuralism well in advance, of course, of the French structuralist movement. Much more interesting even than his anticipation of Lévi-Strauss and company is the way Burke, in several keenly self-conscious moments in his text, forecasts the critique of structuralism mounted in the work of Foucault and Derrida. In less systematic form, Burke's involvement with a structuralist method dates from the title essay of *The Philosophy of Literary Form;* it is in evidence there very concretely in his analysis of the binary coordinates of Clifford Odets' *Golden Boy.* The binary code in Odets' play is shown to be the productive mechanism, or model, behind the actual discourse of the play; at a certain level of analysis, this binary code is an expression of the "psychic economy"[14] of Odets' mind—an economy that, in turn, is expressive of a larger cultural economy. In theoretical terms Burke's structuralism surfaces in *The Philosophy of Literary Form* when, in an attempt to claim an ur-form for drama, he argues that he is making no genetic

---

[14]Burke, *Philosophy of Literary Form,* p. 34.

or historical or empirical claim: "We are proposing it as a *calculus*—a vocabulary, or set of coordinates that serves best for the integration of all phenomena studied by the social sciences."[15] A few sentences later he drops a footnote to the discussion in which he explains that he is at work on a text— it will be called *A Grammar of Motives*—in which the study of motivation will be identical with the "*structure*" of texts, and that, further, structure in all kinds of texts—philosophical, theological, fictional, juridical, scientific, and so on—can be accounted for by five key terms that, in their hierarchically disposed interrelations, and in their subtle play, can be thought of as exhausting the structural possibilities of textual expression.[16] A little further on in the same general discussion, and in another footnote, Burke subtly qualifies this voracious synchronic totalization of history by introducing diachrony, difference, and dialectic into the system in such a way that the systemic power of his five key terms (act, scene, agent, agency, purpose) is prohibited from accounting for change before change in fact occurs.[17] Again with hindsight, we can say that *A Grammar of Motives* is generated, at least in what I would think most contemporary critical theorists should find its most significant sections, by a conflict of hermeneutical impulses—call them synchrony and diachrony. Again, as both Burke and Derrida would remind us, there is never any question of choosing between them, never any question of segregating them as if the interpreting subject (Burke, Derrida, or anyone else) could master the process of reading.

Burke introduces his dramatistic version of structuralism ("dramatistic" because his five key terms are derived from an analysis of drama) via a Kantian essentialism of mind that he converts into a plan for something like a "critique of pure motives": "The book is concerned with the basic forms of thought which, in accordance with the nature of the world as all men necessarily experience it, are exemplified in the attributing of motives."[18] Then very quickly he textualizes Kant's epistemological idealism by removing the "forms of thought" from their traditional Kantian intersubjective location to their contemporary home within intertextual space: "These forms of thought . . . are equally present in systematically elaborated metaphysical structures, in legal judgments, in poetry and fiction, in political and scientific works, in news and in bits of gossip offered at random."[19] This textualization of Kant is not quite enough in itself, however, to save Burke from the idealistic reduction of history at work in some of the theoretical sections of his earlier books. For when he speaks of this textualization he speaks of the forms of thought being "embodied"[20] in discourse—a term that would place

---

[15]Ibid., p. 105.
[16]Ibid., p. 106.
[17]Ibid., pp. 109-111n.
[18]Kenneth Burke, *A Grammar of Motives* (Berkeley and Los Angeles: University of California Press, 1969), p. xv.
[19]Ibid.
[20]Ibid.

ultimate value not on discursive practice but on the subjective and prediscursive origins of some disembodied geometry of mind. In this same vein, he recalls his preoccupation with the "bureaucratization of the imaginative" when he refers to his grammatical resources as "principles" and the various philosophies that apply these principles as "*casuistries*" that seek to insert principles, by definition ahistorical, into "temporal situations."[21] We are not surprised when Burke indicates in this introduction that he began his treatise not with the notion of writing what in fact turned out, but with the intention of developing a theory of comedy as a way of investigating human relations.

The statement of intention in the *Grammar* is structuralist through and through and a summation of where he has been as a thinker since *Counter-Statement:*

> We want to inquire into the purely internal relationships which the five terms bear to one another, considering their possibilities of transformation, their range of permutations and combinations—and then to see how these various resources figure in actual statements about human motives. Strictly speaking we mean by a Grammar of motives a concern with the terms alone, without reference to the ways in which their potentialities have been or can be utilized in actual statements about motives.[22]

This intention to concern himself with the internal legality of terminological rules that governs globally the production of texts constitutes the classical austerity of the structuralist ideal. By the end of his introduction Burke has indulged the cold-blooded platonism of the most extreme kind of structuralism when, with uncharacteristic contempt for cultural and historical differences and particularities and changes, he violently synchronizes the historical process, as he had done earlier in *Permanence and Change,* with this claim: "Our work must be synoptic . . . in the sense that it offers a system of placement, and should enable us, by the systematic manipulation of the terms, to 'generate,' or 'anticipate' the various classes of motivational theory."[23]

Kenneth Burke never played the role of the pseudoscientific structuralist god very well; other passages in the introduction to the *Grammar* and numerous places in the body of the text show that his heart was somewhere else. To be sure, as a synchronist Burke must necessarily endow his five key terms with a solidity and hardness massive enough to withstand diachronic pressure. Yet even in the process of formulating his high-flying platonic structuralism Burke introduces theoretical qualifications that open up his method to a level of historical analysis generally untouched by structuralists.

---

[21]Ibid., p. xvi.
[22]Ibid.
[23]Ibid., pp. xxii-xxiii.

In *The Philosophy of Literary Form,* Burke distinguishes "between positive and dialectical terms—the former being terms that do not require an opposite to define, the latter being terms that do require an opposite."[24] The distinction between positive and dialectical is not quite the distinction of Saussure's linguistics between "substantialist" and "differential" terms: "dialectical" sometimes implies a difference of a very special sort, a difference that eventually does not evade the metaphysics of a "postivie" or "substantialist" vocabulary. Nevertheless, the general intention of his distinction is clear and valuable. With it we move from a realm of natural, fixed, or eternalized meaning—where artichokes are pretty much always what they are—to the human arena, where meaning is made and unmade, enforced and subverted, and assented to and resisted in collective acts of will, and nothing, or very little, is natural, fixed, and eternal. The further Burke can manage to move his key terms, and the temporally frozen model they imply, toward dialectical or differential status, the closer he engages the inherent synchrony of his grammatical project with a fluid diachrony of historical process.

However, that is not quite a fair way to put the issue, insofar as I have implied that synchrony has nothing to do with history and that diachrony and "true" history are to be identified. What the joining of synchrony and diachrony does for Burke is to vastly complicate his idea of history and thereby to open up for analysis a historical reality that preserves the long endurance of a synchronic totality, the immense staying-power of certain deeply rooted habits of sense-making—we can call this activity in history "tradition" and "tradition-making"—and, at the same time, preserves forces of change internal to the totality (that untotalize, unsynchronize it), forces that provide a certain complexity within a system that is (this is one meaning of "system") inherently simplifying. These forces thicken and make hetero-geneous historical textures that tradition and system would homogenize. Like interpretation, history is never synchrony or diachrony, never essential or proportional ("playful")—it is both, and there should never be a question of choosing. Some time in the late thirties and early forties Burke develops theories of interpretation that begin to do justice to his practice as a reader of history's texts.

As he puts it in that very complicated introduction to the *Grammar,* "what we want is *not terms that avoid ambiguity,* but *terms that clearly reveal the strategic spots at which ambiguities necessarily arise.*"[25] The important words here are "ambiguity," "strategic," and "necessarily." Apparently, the terms do not merely reveal ambiguity, being themselves free of it in their essentialist heaven: the terms themselves produce ambiguity. They are the *"resources"* of ambiguity, to use Burke's word, and because they are the resources of ambiguity they are ultimately—as terminological grandfathers—producers of

---

[24] Burke, *Philosophy of Literary Form,* p. 109n.
[25] Burke, *A Grammar of Motives,* p. xviii.

what ambiguity itself produces, "transformation": "it is in the areas of ambiguity that transformations take place; in fact, without such areas, transformation would be impossible."[26] I think it important to recognize that Burke is giving us here, both as theory of interpretation and as theory of history, not the comfortable view of the structuralist lineage of sense-making, with principles of sense-making themselves outside the structural fields of history, nor the equally comfortable view of recent Yale critics in which "undecidability" is made over into an instrument to cancel out the conflicts of force within history, in which the highest level of what is called textuality (the "literary") is placed outside the domain of history. When Burke defines his task as that of studying and clarifying the resources of ambiguity, and hence of transformation, he is proposing the kind of genealogical approach to history that would situate itself between the misleading fictions of a sheer synchrony and a sheer diachrony; an approach so situated, with key structural coordinates enmeshed in historical texture, could properly be charged neither with the reductions of structuralism (or of his earlier theories), nor with the vaporization of history in the name of Derrideanism. The antidote to the sterilities of too much contemporary critical theory has long been available in some of Burke's texts.

If it is helpful to have a term for what Burke does best as a reader of history, then I think that the term "critical structuralist" might be fair. Since one of my purposes all along (however self-congratulatory) has been to argue his uncanny contemporaneity, then "critical structuralist" is doubly useful to me, for it indicates not only his anticipation of structuralism but also its most recent critique. If my claims for Burke as a continuing historical force are at all right, then we have good reason to understand the basis of his exclusion and repression. By 1945 Burke had not only articulated the structuralist vision, but had gone beyond it. The radically historical thesis of Harold Bloom (neatly summarized by his phrase "the anxiety of influence") may go a long way toward explaining the curious discomfort that contemporary theoreticians (Bloom excluded) have long felt in Burke's presence.

The crucial strategy in the service of this critical structuralism is Burke's ruthless investigation of his own terminological resources. The deep bias of his dramatistic system is unavoidably humanistic because the very notion of Dramatism (this is a point that Burke repeats tirelessly) rests on the distinction between "action" (a uniquely human movement) and "motion" (a process that presumably characterizes all nonhuman movement). At face value the five key terms (act, scene, agent, agency, purpose) are unarguably humanistic. It can be no accident that when Burke lists his terms, it is always in that order, with "act" leading off. His formulation of the master ratios (act-scene, agent-scene) only re-enforces the humanism of the system. Yet it is probably the humanist privilege granted to the autonomous actor-subject (with

---

[26]Ibid., p. xix.

its corollary values of freedom, creativity, activity, and self-presence) that is the primary focus of Burke's critical consciousness. He performs about as thorough an act of what is now called "deconstruction" as is possible, but when he is finished he has not destroyed the humanistic impulse of his Dramatism; he has only (and this by design) relocated the "free" subject within a system that is now understood in a more complex fashion than his usual bare-bones formulation of Dramatism would permit. Let me put that point in another way: humanism is understood in the widest context—it is seen as having a constraining context, which is precisely what humanism can never admit about itself. However, such understanding does not, cannot, eliminate all humanist desire for the free subject—a point that many of our recent antihumanists have not yet apparently grasped.

Burke's critique of what would be called structuralism is really a critique of systematic thought itself, including his own. A major portion of *A Grammar of Motives* is devoted to an investigation of the systematic dimension of the various schools in the history of philosophy. More specifically, Burke wants to show how each of the philosophical schools derives its distinctive character from the peculiar genius of an "ancestral term."[27] Although all of the classical systems find a significant role for each of the five terms to play, the identity of any given system will be generated by an ancestral term, and this term, to stay with Burke's metaphor, in effect fathers all the rest because they are conceived, not independently, as having terminological lives and rights of their own, but only in relationship to the father: *their* identity is simply flooded by father-influence. Systems, then, are essentialized by their ancestral terms, and it is Burke's greatest insight to point out that essentialization is the product of a genealogical will to power. By probing the notion of "ancestral term" Burke has uncovered the secret power of systematic thinking.

At this point we are ready to appreciate the depth with which Burke has probed the essentializing thrust of his own system. By moving critically against the terms "act" and "agent" he has gone directly for the jugular of Dramatism. This criticism of act and agent—it will recall, before him, certain passages in Nietzsche's *The Will to Power* and, after him, Derrida and de Man—not only deliberately sets off an undermining effect throughout the *Grammar,* but also retrospectively revises his attitudes toward those quintessentially actional terms "freedom" (in *Permanence and Change*) and "imagination" (in *Attitudes Toward History*). In order for an act to be itself, and not a disguised term for scene, Burke says that it must possess a wholly arbitrary (magical) dimension; the act that is truly an act presumes creativity in the literal sense.[28] No act is truly an act, then, unless it can be shown to have a radically originating function. No matter how assiduously secular the philosophical systems that feature it, all ideas of act will easily be traced to

---

[27]Ibid., p. 128.
[28]Ibid., p. 66.

some sort of theological conception: "God would thus be perfect action," and of course perfect agent, "in that there would be no motivating principle beyond his own nature. . . ."[29] The self-irony that runs throughout Burke's discussion of act is that, for an act to be truly itself, it cannot be permitted to have a place within a system of other terms—it must (like God Himself) stand in a perfect purity of isolation.

Now, if Burke's analysis of act reveals that even the most secular and liberal-minded celebration of the human subject as autonomous source of action and value rests on theological support, what about his own featuring of act? Let us recall, again, that Burke inaugurates the system with a distinction between action and motion, and let us also recall that he situates act and agent within a network of five terms. Do act or agent essentialize Burkean Dramatism? Are his five key terms only thinly masked versions of an ancestral term? Is he, after all, a naive humanist? Or is it the peculiar virtue of Burke's system to subvert the essentializing power of even his own ancestral terms? Burke answers our questions (which are not really ours, since it is his text that provides us with such ammunition). The answer sustains the highest level of philosophical sophistication:

> We may discern a dramatistic pun, involving a merger of active and passive in the expression, "the motivation of an act." Strictly speaking, the act of an agent would be the movement not of one *moved* but of a mover (a mover of the self or of something else by the self). For an act is by definition active, whereas to be moved (or motivated) is by definition passive. Thus, if we quizzically scrutinize the expression, "the motivating of an act," we note that it implicitly contains the paradox of substance. Grammatically, if a construction is active, it is not passive; and if it is passive, it is not active. But to consider an *act* in terms of its *grounds* is to consider it in terms of what it is not, namely, in terms of motives that, in acting upon the active, would make it passive. We could state the paradox another way by saying that the concept of activation implies a kind of passive-behind-the-passive; for an agent who is "motivated by his passions" would be "moved by his being-movedness" or "acted upon by his state of being acted upon."[30]

Burke's unhinging of the traditional conception of the subject and its central category of a consciousness whose *active* power is coincidental with itself, entirely in control, lucid, and self-present, is rooted in what he discovers to be the radical duplicity of the very cornerstone terms of Western philosophical discourse. What he has done to "act" could be extended to agent, agency, purpose, and scene and, more importantly even than those words, to the word of words for any mode of thought, philosophical or

---

[29] Ibid., pp. 68-69.
[30] Ibid., p. 40.

otherwise, that would consider itself disciplined. I am referring to Burke's glancing reference to the "paradox of substance." *Substance:* a term indispensable not only to all manner of metaphysical thinking but also (and perhaps this is a way of gauging the impulse to metaphysics in us all) in every attempt to *define*—something, anything at all—in every attempt, in other words, to be intellectually rigorous, precise, and above all, serious.

In his stunning discussion of the "paradox of substance" Burke locates in the term "substance" a strange self-difference. Substance differs from itself because it moves between a sense that denotes what a thing intrinsically is— that part of the thing that is uniquely there and nowhere else, that which makes the thing what it is, what confers its special identity—to a sense (etymologically evident) that denotes a thing's support: *substance,* that upon which the thing stands, what is beneath it (from the Greek: a standing under). The paradox, then, is that "the word 'substance', used to designate what a thing *is,* derives from a word designating what a thing is *not.* That is, though used to designate something *within* the thing, *intrinsic* to it, the word etymologically refers to something *outside* the thing, *extrinsic* to it."[31] Or, to sharpen the paradox still further: used ordinarily to refer to the special interior presence of a thing, etymologically the word refers us to a context, "something that the thing is *not.*"[32] In such a strategic terminological moment, when the "intrinsic and the extrinsic can change places,"[33] we confront the bedrock of the antinomy of definition. It is a perilous kind of "bedrock," however, since no secure footing is provided; it is precisely security that is being done away with. The concept of substance, the one thing that must not differ from itself if definition is to be definition, is endowed with what Burke calls an "unresolvable ambiguity,"[34] but which we can call, after Derrida, undecidability, since no choice can be made between two very different senses. This perverse playfulness of undecidability, in evidence in Burke's cultivation of the paradoxes of substance and of act, is the very condition of transformation that curtails the essentializing desire of interpretation and thereby makes a certain kind of history possible. With the self-presence of key Western terms like substance and act so profoundly fissured, so radically unstabilized by Burke's analyses, we are prepared to confront, in the terminological dimension itself, a more detailed level of historical process than we have been accustomed to knowing.

III

Burke's interest in philosophical history is focused on the power of systematic thought to reproduce and extend itself while at the same time

---

[31] Ibid., p. 23.
[32] Ibid.
[33] Ibid., p. 24.
[34] Ibid.

engendering internal fissures and conflicts—and in general the very possibility of the transformation of modes of thought that tend to essentialize and eternalize themselves. This kind of interest in the history of philosophy is not for its own sake; the history of philosophy for Burke is part of a larger sociopolitico-historical totality, and the analysis of philosophical discourse is meant to be exemplary, a way into that totality. Up to this point in this essay I have been concerned with exposing the theoretical bases of the act of interpretation in Burke, rather than with his analysis of any concrete historical texture. I turn only now to his practice, not because theory is a higher thing, and must come first, but because I don't think that his readings can be appreciated in their wider implications unless their theoretical qualities are grasped: his theories of reading imply an historical process of a particular sort—and the opposite is true as well.

The closer we move in Burke toward the analysis of specific historical textures the more we need the conception provocatively put forth by Antonio Gramsci in his *Prison Notebooks:* I refer again to the conception of "hegemony," Gramsci's great contribution to Marxist dialogue on the relations of an economic base to superstructural expressions of culture.[35] Although he could not have known Gramsci's writings until most of his own texts had long been written, Burke's dialogue with Marx has been persistent—and remarkably close to Gramsci's revision of the vulgarities of economism. In simplest terms: hegemony in Gramsci, and its counterpart in Burke—he gave it no name—is fundamentally a process of education carried on through various institutions of civil society in order to make normative, inevitable, even "natural" the ruling ideas of the ruling class. The hegemonic process is a way of gaining "free" assent to a dominating and repressive political structure without needing recourse to violence (the domination of bodies through the means of the military and the police). Hegemonic rule is therefore the mark of the stable, "mature" society whose ideological apparatus is so deeply set in place, so well buried, so unexamined a basis of our judgment that it is taken for truth with a capital letter. Because the process of domination is an educative one, involving techniques of psychological manipulation on behalf of ruling economic interests, its theory represents a certain union of Marx and Freud, of materialist and psychoanalytic views of history. The ground of Freudo-Marxism is a common one for Burke and Gramsci. If Burke as the comedic historian, or even as the programmatic theorist of parts of the *Grammar,* is a dispassionate observer of historical inevitability, and therefore an implicit affirmer of the status quo, then the critical structuralist and student of hegemony is (at the least) an implicit interventionist who teaches not comedic lessons of humble

---

[35]See, for example, *Selections from the Prison Notebooks,* edited and translated by Quintin Hoare and Geoffrey Nowell Smith (New York: International Publishers, 1971), pp. 5-14. For commentary see Walter L. Adamson, *Hegemony and Revolution: A Study of Antonio Gramsci's Political and Cultural Theory* (Berkeley and Los Angeles: University of California Press, 1980).

passiveness but the muscular exercise of a collective will for the ends of social change.

Gramsci's theory of hegemony has its parallel in Burke's idea of a silent ethico-juridical process that, mainly at subterranean levels, coerces consciousness to assent to the structure of property relations authorized by "rules, courts, parliaments, laws, educators, constabulary, and the moral slogans linked with each."[36] These various constituents of the ruling class, especially what Gramsci would call their "organic intellectuals," and what Burke calls the various "priests"[37] of the pulpit, schools, press, radio, and popular arts (and we add television), educate the socially dispossessed person to feel "that he 'has a stake in' the authoritative structure that dispossesses him; for the influence exerted upon the policies of education by the authoritative structure encourages the dispossessed to feel that his only hope of repossession lies in his allegiance to the structure that had dispossessed him."[38] Perhaps Burke's most complete example of how this works is his examination of the "medieval synthesis," the way Thomist philosophy was a thorough re-enforcement and a technique of maintenance of established property relationships.[39]

Now, if we add, as Burke does, that a sociopolitical structure of authority and the hegemonic process proper to it, and which keeps it in force, have astonishing stamina to dominate history over the longest duration—he explores, for example, the morphological parallels of Thomism and capitalism[40]—then it would seem to follow that visionary social programs, in utopian and Marxist varieties, with their desire for radical rupture in the movement of history, a desire to make it new in the literal sense, can only be frustrated without hope. For such desire has for its object the formation of an identity that would imply, in order to be achieved, the destruction of all genealogy, an obliteration of one's entire past lineage, a symbolic suicide that involves a symbolic parricide.[41] Burke is speaking of the personal desire for rebirth, but his analysis holds equally well for collective social desire to be reborn in a revolution that would destroy the historical lineage of every society's collective past.

Burke's lesson, easily missed with his stress on the marathon character of historical repression, is that radical rupture, not change, is impossible. The structure of hegemonic authority that he traces in the curve of history from ancient Greece through "periods" of Christian evangelism, medieval synthesis, protestant transition, naive capitalism, and emergent collectivism, while massive and ominously persistent, is not monolithic. Like the terminological keystones of Western philosophical tradition, the dominant

---

[36] Burke, *Attitudes Toward History*, p. 329.
[37] Burke, *Philosophy of Literary Form*, p. 307.
[38] Burke, *Attitudes Toward History*, pp. 329-330.
[39] Ibid., pp. 124-134.
[40] Ibid., p. 93-94.
[41] Burke, *Philosophy of Literary Form*, pp. 41-42.

sociopolitical structure of the West, despite its totalizing desire to saturate every corner of history, is internally divided, different from itself in its very "substance." One of Burke's ways of pinpointing that structural instability in the tradition is to declare that every so-called historical period is transitional; no period is there, in full presence—historical texture is ineluctably heterogeneous.[42] Another way is to point out that, unlike real estate, the language of privilege and authority is not the private property of any person or class. The linguistic symbols of authority, like "rights" and "freedom," are appropriable—they can be seized by a collective and turned against those who appropriated them in order to dispossess yet earlier appropriators. This oscillation of rights depends, of course, on the oscillation of power between possessors and dispossessed; the locus of power/rights is never fixed because the locus is not natural. This process, described by Burke as the "stealing back and forth of symbols,"[43] is the beginning of any hegemonic education and rule. The point is clear: no hegemonic condition is fatal because no hegemonic condition rests on natural or God-given authority, although it is one of the key strategies of hegemonic education to inculcate those very claims. Like the term "substance," and its paradox of intrinsic and extrinsic, the term "rights" is paradoxical, although in this instance the "inside" and the "outside" are not ontological but social terms, better given as the "ins" and the "outs." It is precisely the radical instability (appropriability) of terms like "rights" that makes for transformation in philosophical and social history:

> The divine right of kings was first invoked by secular interests combating the authority of theocrats. It held that God appointed the king, rather than the church authorities, to represent the secular interests of "the people." Later, when the church made peace with established monarchs, identifying its interests with the interests of the secular authorities, the church adopted the doctrine as its own. And subsequently the bourgeoisie repudiated the doctrine, in repudiating both monarch and state. It did so in the name of "rights," as the doctrine had originally been promulgated in the name of "rights." Among these "rights" was "freedom." And Marx in turn stole this bourgeois symbol for the proletariat.[44]

In another meditation on the same phenomenon of the passage of "rights," this rite of appropriation, which reflects the increasing stress on language as the ultimate center of his theory, Burke notes that it is precisely the ontological emptiness of the term—it is always differentially, or dialectically, or contextually defined—that permits it to be undecidable, unresolvably ambiguous at a high level of analysis, and yet at a more concrete level, set in place, stabilized, and appropriated by a particular class,

---

[42]Burke, *Attitudes Toward History,* p. 135.
[43]Ibid., p. 328.
[44]Ibid.

even though such settings, stabilizations, and appropriations will in turn be upset by other classes, other times. As if looking ahead critically to the current partisans of undecidability, Burke wrote in *The Philosophy of Literary Form:* "the statement that a term is 'dialectical,' in that it derives its meaning from an opposite term, and that the opposite term may be different at different historical periods does not at all imply that such terms are 'meaningless.'" Far from it: such terms shape the course of political history, as Burke demonstrates in his genealogical analysis of our Bill of Rights, from the emergence of the Magna Carta, to the American Revolution, to the early twentieth century and the origin and growth of the supercorporations and, once again, a critical revaluation and renaming of majority and minority rights, the will of the people, and the centralization of authority.[45]

One final, complicated example compresses Burke's interests in philosophy, science, and sociopolitical history: I allude to his section on Darwin in the *Grammar* and to an earlier provocative comment on Darwin in *Attitudes Toward History*. Burke is struck by the preservation, in a period so profoundly committed to liberalism, of a feudalistic mode of thought in the nineteenth century's "extreme emphasis upon *genesis, origin*."[46] The emphasis on genesis and origin is produced, as he shows in his analysis of Thomism and medieval economics, by a familial metaphor: "From this metaphor there flowed the need of obedience to authority, as embodied in customs. In families one does not 'vote.' Authority does not rise by deputation, as in parliamentary procedure—it is just where it is, being grounded in the magic of custom."[47] By developing this familial perspective to universal limits, Thomism interwove the hegemonic, symbolic architecture of medieval feudalism, a structure uncannily built upon "the foundations of human guilt."[48] "The Church bureaucracy was pictured as a large-scale replica of family relationships, with 'fathers,' 'mothers,' 'brothers,' 'sisters,' 'Father,' and 'Mother' (a particularly serviceable pattern in that it readily shunts the erring son into the role of symbolic parricide)."[49] Darwin's formula of the "descent of man" is genealogical (feudalistic) to the core in that it analyzes man "by reference to his parentage: *what he was*."[50] At one level, at least, what is preserved in Darwin's texts, great books of objective knowledge for the liberal nineteenth century, is the political vision of feudalism: the thorough crushing of individual liberty.

If Burke's earlier analysis stresses how a discourse presumably beyond ideology, committed to scientific truth, is strongly marked in its theoretical underpinnings by a repressive Thomist ideology, then his later analysis of

---

[45]Burke, *Philosophy of Literary Form*, pp. 109-111n.
[46]Burke, *Attitudes Toward History*, p. 66n.
[47]Ibid., p. 129.
[48]Ibid., p. 128.
[49]Ibid., p. 129.
[50]Ibid., p. 66n.

Darwin demonstrates that those same texts are marked as well by forms of political idealism more contemporary to Darwin's life. The long duration of feudalist hegemony that in one way captured Darwin's writing is resisted and interrupted by a newer (bourgeois) hegemony of liberalism. Despite his nominal, programmatic commitment to scenic principles, Darwin's philosophy of deterministic materialism, in which existence can only be explained by its conditions, is invaded by idealistic notions of "purpose" and "agent" that stress a quality of "action" internally motivated that cannot be reduced to the "motions" of environment. Many of Darwin's key terms "lend themselves readily to appeal by ambiguities of the pathetic fallacy."[51] Hence, although his conscious intention (his "act") seems purely materialistic, examination of his discourse reveals that a larger discursive force of intention—a political unconscious?—which no single subject can control, is at work in Darwin's texts, binding them over to a liberal political discourse more encompassing than his own scientific writing, and more encompassing even than its purely scientific history of evolutionary thought, even as those texts had been bound over in another way to the political discourse of feudalism.

Burke's analysis of this liberal phase of the politics of Darwin's science comes to sharp focus on the occurrence of the term "variability" in *The Origin of the Species*. In an effort to deny an internal force of change in an organism, a force appropriate to an agent, not a thing, Darwin finds himself conceding a minimal "tendency to ordinary variability"[52] that cannot be reduced to observable scenic factors. This pressure of an agent term on his vocabulary, while it points once again to the heraldic or familial perspective of his theory, and the consequences that Burke has read out of that metaphor, also points, as Burke concludes, to the politics of "nineteenth-century English liberalism, in stressing the selective factor of *competition* . . . and in deriving new species from *individual* variations."[53] All of this conflict is condensed in an exquisite ambiguity in Darwin's term "variability," which allows simultaneously "for two quite different meanings . . . one referring to a cause *ab extra* and the other to some internal principle of action. lt stands pliantly where scene overlaps upon agent."[54] With his rare integration of the resources of technical, formalist criticism and social and political investigation, in this analysis of the political forces struggling to dominate Darwin's biological texts, Burke set standards for the ideological role of intellectuals that contemporary critical theory would do well to measure itself by.

---

[51]Burke, *A Grammar of Motives*, p. 153.
[52]Ibid., quoted p. 154.
[53]Ibid., p. 156.
[54]Ibid., p. 158.

Kenneth Burke's Comedy:
The Multiplication of Perspectives

by Wayne Booth

In choosing Kenneth Burke as my second pluralist I am obviously making as sharp a contrast with Crane as possible without leaving the subject of critical pluralisms entirely. But Burke, who does not himself make much use of the word pluralism, could happily point out that any such statement can be played both ways: I must really have chosen him for his similarity to Crane. Otherwise how could he belong in the same book? In any case, as he likes to say, echoing Hegel: "Things farthest apart are also closest together."[1]

Among the many similarities between Crane and Burke, the one that naturally interests me most is their unflagging effort to deal with intellectual conflict by taking thought about it. Some critics (fewer now, perhaps, than twenty years ago), viewing this preoccupation of theirs as an unfortunate deviation from the *real* job of practical criticism, might say that those who invent theory of criticism, metacriticism, do so to protect themselves from encounters with living literature. I must admit that both Crane and Burke sometimes push very close to my own limits of patience, Crane chewing on bones long after I think all marrow has been extracted, Burke juggling Indian clubs that I am not quite sure are even there. Clearly, neither of them has managed to hit the one right ratio of theory to practice that I have always maintained in my own work. The rule is, of course, as follows: *my* abstract theory is essential, concrete groundwork; *his* is frequently quixotic indulgence in a perhaps harmless but irrelevant hobbyhorse; and M. Jacques Lacan's is lamentable proof that when the Germans conquered France in World War II Hegel came swirling in with them and sent traditional French lucidity forever underground.

Burke in Crane's Quadrate

It is implicit in what I have said of Crane that he could easily describe Burke's differences from himself in pluralistic terms. Though he never

---

Reprinted from Chapter 3 of *Critical Understanding* (Chicago: University of Chicago Press, 1979). Used by permission.
[1] For example, in the Impresario's introduction of God and Satan for the splendid dialogue, "Epilogue: Prologue in Heaven," that concludes *The Rhetoric of Religion: Studies in Logology* (Boston: Beacon Press, 1961), pp. 273-74.

discusses Burke at length, he places him clearly among the many who define poetry as one kind or use of language rather than, say, an imitation of human life or a making of "objects." Indeed, Crane lists him among those authors— "Professor Coomaraswamy, Maud Bodkin, Kenneth Burke, Edmund Wilson, Lionel Trilling, Richard Chase, Francis Fergusson, and Northrop Frye (to mention only a few conspicuous names)"—who depend on

> positive analogies between poetry, viewed in terms of its content of meanings, and the various other modes—not all of them verbal strictly—of objectifying the conceptions and impulses of the mind, and hence of ordering experiences symbolically, which have been set over against science and discursive logic, in the speculations of the past half-century, as so many pre-logical or extra-logical types of "language."[2]

This group contrasts sharply with another list of critics who also see poetry as a special use of language but who depend on *negative* analogies with scientific language—people like I. A. Richards and Cleanth Brooks.

If we pursue Crane's kinds of distinctions among critics, we can easily elaborate this initial placement of Burke by using Crane's four variables derived from Aristotle's "causes." The result should be, if we work with as much care as Crane would demand, a Burke considerably more coherent and plausible and essentially more challenging than the one presented to us by most of the critics who have commented on his work. Indeed, reassembled "in his own terms," he will be irrefutable.

His *subject matter,* in this view, is clearly language and the way symbolic communication is effected through language. He sees both poems and criticism as manifestations of a universal human activity, *symbolic action,* and thus not primarily as the making of objects or the formulation of static thoughts or truths.

There are two major kinds of critics who make this choice, and Burke's *method* places him with those who are primarily interested in pursuing the similarities between poetry as language and other symbolic actions, not with those who want primarily to pursue differences and to consider poetry in its unique quality. Though Burke attempts to do justice to poetry in its distinctiveness, and indeed often begins or ends with a sustained bow in the direction of Chicago, he is really much more interested in what poetry *does* for poets and audiences than in what it *is* or how it is constructed. He seeks its special way of doing what other human actions also do. Poems compete, console, warn, celebrate, attack, defend, lament, purge, build (or destroy) community; the list is potentially as long as the indefinitely long list of human motives.

---

[2] Crane, *Languages,* p. 109.

Similarly, his *principles* are finally holistic or assimilative, remaining constant as he moves from field to field, even while the surface of his work reveals an iridescent variety. His definition of man, for example, as the *symbol-making and symbol-using animal* is itself not subject to change but only to elaboration. And he always *thinks with* a two-term dialectic of symbolicity/animality. What is more, his mode of working from his definition—what he calls dramatism—is found in every word he utters. Both the definition and the dramatistic pentad—act, agent, scene, agency, and purpose—are intended to cover the world, the world of man's actions (symbolicity) and the scientist's world of sheer bodily motion (animality).

With such choices of subject, method, and principles, Burke can show beautifully how poetry fulfills the "motives" of poets and readers—how it *does* in poetic language what other symbolic actions do in nonpoetic language or with other symbolic means: fight wars, threaten to drop bombs, sell and buy cars, issue manifestos, make constitutions, and so on.

It is inevitable that Burke, in choosing to show what literature has in common with other human deeds, surrenders the possibility of showing what poetry does in its uniqueness. Even more obviously (and disastrously, from the point of view of anyone wanting to study poems as *poems*), he gives up the possibility of accounting for what each particular poem does that no other poems do. Indeed, his methods are, as he himself often claims, as applicable to one kind of discourse as to another, as useful applied to *The Maltese Falcon* or even a comic strip as to *Coriolanus*. All of which is a way of saying, finally, that his *purpose* is practical or "actional" or "operational" rather than cognitive or aesthetic: his words are deeds, acting on the world of words seen as deeds. And if you happen to care more about that sort of thing than about poetic knowledge, he is a good man to turn to.

Thus Crane's pluralism might lead us to "do justice" to Burke. His dramatism is one of the possible modes: his subject, language as action; his method, an assimilative dialectic; his principles, comprehensive and operational; and his purpose, actional or "rhetorical." To use his own words, he attempts "to cure" himself and society by doing verbal "therapy." His initial choice of mode enables him to answer certain questions and prevents his answering other questions. When we judge his answers as "relative to" that initial choice, we can both judge his effectiveness within his chosen mode and avoid the kind of dogmatism that would rule out his mode as illegitimate in the first place.

Anyone who knows Burke at all knows that he will refuse to stay pinned and wriggling on anyone else's wall chart. Indeed, I think I can hear him now.*

---

*I *thought* I could hear him. But his actual response to words somewhat like these, and to the entirely sympathetic words that follow, was even less predictable than I had expected. See his reply, in *Critical Understanding*, pp. 128 ff.

If ever there was a misguided and hopeless effort at resolving conflict, what we have heard here from Booth about Crane and the Chicago School, and now about Burke, is it. Clearly Booth set the whole thing up to yield a neat and finally resolvable contrast between Crane and us. Obviously, he intends to come along in his final chapters with a reconciliation in some sort of supreme pluralism, which will be nothing more than his own disguised monism. Just as clearly, he thinks that in choosing us he has found a voice that will yield him a second pluralism, finally reducible to a monism, in order to make his own open-mindedness look good.

About the only thing in his whole presentation that is not either downright wrong or askew is his claim that we would do things differently from Crane, and even there he ignores the fact that we believe in doing Crane's kind of job *first,* before we turn to the more important matters encompassed in our dramatism.[3]

How absurd it is to classify us according to a four-cause analysis that our own work finds largely unhelpful. It's true that some of the terms of that analysis overlap terms we often use. We can digest Aristotle and the Chicago school between lunch and supper. The account may be right in one sense, in claiming that we see poems primarily as a *form of discourse,* only secondarily as *made objects.* Poems *do* things for us that other symbolic actions can also do. But what a grotesque reduction those terms impose. How that hypostasizing mind, the composite Booth-Crane, despite its professed commitment to induction, wields those same four fixed categories! Though Booth-Crane have not made the usual mistake of ignoring our general philosophical program, he/they might almost as well have done so, for all the good it does *us.*

Note secondly how Booth's own program implicitly prejudges critical acts as good or bad. There are killers and maimers (bad), and there are inquirers (good). But anyone can see that the distinction is misleading. What Booth calls warfare—or, in his other metaphor, the skewering of straw men—is itself a form of inquiry, perhaps the chief form we have. Most of the best critical work gets done precisely by the kind of warriors Booth deplores. The very destructiveness, even the "unfair" destructiveness, that he would diminish is what prevents various monisms from "perfecting" themselves and taking over the world.

What is more, Booth protects himself by refusing to deal with

---

[3] Burke seems to suggest that I need to become acquainted with his words on the Chicago critics. But he is surely being sly: of all his sweet and troubling words, surely he could expect those to be most deeply inscribed upon my heart. See, especially, "The Problem of the Intrinsic" (n. 15, chap. 2).

literal war, which is a much more present threat to the world than critical warfare. It is in the analogies between critical warfare and bloody war that we find some of the most useful insights into how to diminish the latter. Just as literal killing can be a form of inquiry, as when a general says, "Let's see what will happen if we send 10,000 troops against *that* salient," so can critical warfare bleed off some of the energies that otherwise might go into killing. What Booth should have conducted is not a classificatory exercise but a dialectical exploration of his two terms, showing how warfare can be modulated into inquiry and how inquiry can achieve the ends of war.

In sum: what *does* he think he is himself conducting if not an aggressive act of critical warfare? He comes with a "motivated" program, some of the motives conscious, many of them no doubt unsuspected. He assumes that his readers have misconceptions about us and about Crane and about how to relate the two of us, and he uses all the resources of his literal-minded art to diminish conflict— by winning! There are, after all, only three possibilities in *his* encounter with *his* readers: his view prevails (that is, he wins); their preconceptions about Crane and Burke hold (that is, he loses); or there is continued confusion and disagreement (that is, stalemate). Is that warfare or inquiry? Obviously, both; but a deeper exploration of my own uses for stalemates could have helped him a lot. The same will hold for each of his distinctions. And while we're on the subject, Booth's heavy-footed, judgment-ridden reading of that poem by Auden needs a bit of comic discounting. He left out most of what interests us about it. Let us move in on it again, this time. . . .

My imagined Burke is surely justified in his reply. To "understand" a man by showing, in alien terms, what he is about, even when one works with a relatively rich set of questions and terms and tries hard not to be reductive, is still to use him for purposes other than his own. In Burke's terms, one has used "administrative rhetoric" on him, getting him under control. Let me, then, make a second try, this time attempting total immersion in the words of that wonderfully variegated mind. As I make the attempt, I sense, hovering above us, hierarchical choruses of angels and devils, singing and dancing their Burkean yeses and noes, so thoroughly blended that one hardly knows which way to turn. Through it all, one does hear two fairly persistent, distinct voices, one of the Lord, the great Logos, chanting, as at the end of *The Rhetoric of Religion,* "It's more complicated than that," the other of Burke himself: "That wasn't what I meant at all."

Burke in Burke's Pentagon

Burke often speculates about beginnings, and he notes that what are beginnings temporally are often logically the end. What is more, in our temporal beginning is always our logical end, and vice versa. Besides, every beginning, if questioned, can lead to a further explanation.[4] What, then, prevents an infinite regress of both logical and temporal beginnings? I must face that question again later, because it is the same as asking, Why is Burke not a relativist or skeptic?

But first I must emphasize how strongly the surface of Burke's writing seems to violate two of Crane's criteria for good criticism, even though to do so may initially seem like the experience of crawling backward into a world of exuberant dancers. He often seems blithely indifferent to Crane's insistence on coherence and common-sensical correspondence with what is "really there." His paths are seldom straight and clear; his allusions are often obscure; his arguments often seem to depend on puns or questionable etymologies or on conjectures so wild that he does not even try to defend them. Whatever the accepted canons are for organizing a proof seem as often violated as honored. His notorious translation of Keats's last line into "Body is turd, turd body," is only one of thousands of what have seemed debasements—or, at best, irrelevant private translations—of what "everyone knows" about the works he discusses.

Obviously, what has annoyed many people besides Crane is not simply Burke's frequent pursuit of scatology or his free-wheeling delivery. Most of us accept far more dirt per page in Rabelais or Swift or Joyce, and no one complains when Pascal and Wittgenstein give us disjointed fragments. What is troublesome, surely, is precisely Burke's claim to make connections in what appears disparate—the claim, for example, to connect bodily functions to surroundings hitherto seen as "poetic." The trouble, in short, is not that turds are flung at us but that they come labeled as truth. Burke seems to be claiming to know better than Keats himself something of what the poem "means," and the meaning he finds is antithetical not just to the poet's intentions but to any intentions Keats might conceivably have entertained!

Scarcely surprising, then, that in much of what has been printed about Burke there is an air of condescension. "Responsible scholars" early tended to treat him like a buffoon with a high I.Q. The tone, often, was that of René Wellek, who begins with praise, referring to "men of great gifts, nimble powers of combination and association, and fertile imagination," but who then deplores Burke's irresponsibility, repudiates his critical judgment, condemns his general method (without bothering to look closely at it), and in general makes him into some sort of *idiot savant*—a man who can from time to time for some reason play beautiful music but who obviously knows nothing about how it is done.[5]

---

[4] See, for example, *The Philosophy of Literary Form: Studies in Symbolic Action,* 3rd ed. (Berkeley: University of California Press, 1973), pp. 344, 347-48. (First published, 1941.) Also *A Rhetoric of Motives* (New York: George Braziller, 1955), pp. 189 ff. (First published, 1950.) The point about logical as opposed to temporal beginnings occurs again and again.

[5] René Wellek, "Kenneth Burke and Literary Criticism," *Sewanee Review* 79 (Spring 1971): 171-88. (Quotation on p. 187.)

Without pretending to defend all of Burke's moves, many of which he himself later repudiates or contradicts, I do want to argue that his is one of the great pluralizing minds of our time. Can I do so without repudiating Crane?

Strong convictions about any mode of greatness are arrived at only in direct contact with that greatness. But argument about it need not be pointless if it leads to renewed efforts at contact. If you had never heard Mozart's Thirty-sixth Symphony and I wrote a detailed analysis of its first movement, defending it as great, the most I might hope for would be that you would then listen to the music and expect greatness—unless, of course, my illustrations had been so full, and your skill with scores so refined, that your reading was in effect a hearing. But even that kind of exception is not possible here, for I shall not be able to quote enough Burke to give anything like a full experience. I am not even sure how much that would have to be, since in my own case I had to read him and re-read him in large doses for many years before I got beyond my initial prejudices, imbibed in part from Crane.

Method: Beginnings and Endings

We can at least begin with Burke's own kind of defense when under attack. Having seen man's world as a drama of symbolic actions, convinced that man's "symbolicity" is disastrous whenever any symbolic direction is followed to some kind of logical "perfection," he has consistently sought ways of mitigating, or undermining, the rage for perfection that each monistic mode of thought exhibits. We can see what this means in his fairly recent defense of his excremental talk about Keats. We must think of him as seeking always to modulate the excesses both of eulogistic languages, which would treat man as a creature of pure mind or spirit, and of "dyslogistic" languages, which would reduce him to mere body, never acting but only reacting. In that light, what he calls his "joycing" of Keats can indeed be seen, in his words, as "but heuristic, suggestive, though it may put us in search of corroborative observations. And any such bathos, lurking behind the poem's pathos, is so alien to the formal pretenses of the work, if such indecorous transliterating of the poem's decorum had occurred to Keats, in all likelihood he would have phrased his formula differently, to avoid this turn."[6]

Such emphasis on stirring things up by probing beneath the "formal pretenses" of the work tells us what was most obviously wrong with the placement of Burke that I attributed to Ronald Crane. While it explicitly described Burke's purposes in pragmatic terms, it silently assumed that he shared, or should share, Crane's passion for knowledge about distinctions of constructional excellence. But even a superficial dip into Burke will show that the search for such knowledge is for him suspect when it is allowed to

---

[6] "As I Was Saying," *Michigan Quarterly Review* 11 (Winter 1972): 9-27; quotation on p. 22.

set the conditions of all critical endeavor. He does not flatly repudiate the search for demonstrable conclusions about literature in general or about particular works, for scientific pursuits have their place under his own kind of pluralistic umbrella; but he repudiates many of the canons of demonstration that most traditional scholars would take for granted. Now, when we find a critic not just deliberately flouting but making an overt attack on Occam's razor, when we find him not only "guilty of circular reasoning" but hailing circular reasoning as what every thinker inevitably commits, we can either rule him out of court or we can try to understand what critical purposes are thwarted when we insist that all discourse fit models imported from the sciences.

Consider Burke's discussion, in *Attitudes toward History*, of what he calls the "heads I win, tails you lose" argument. It is "a device," he says,

> whereby, if things turn out one way, your system accounts for them—and if they turn out the opposite way, your system also accounts for them. When we [Burke always refers to himself as "we," a stylistic choice that for many years offended me, until I finally figured out his reasons for it] first came upon this formula, we thought we had found a way of discrediting an argument. If a philosopher outlined a system, and we were able to locate its variant of the "heads I win, tails you lose" device, we thought we had exposed a fatal fallacy. But as we grew older, we began to ask ourselves whether there is any other possible way of thinking. And we now absolutely doubt that there is.

So what do "we" do now? We merely ask of any thinker that he "*co-operate with us* in the attempt to track down his variant" of the strategy.[7]

If Burke is right here—and I think he is, provided we understand that to "track down the variant" is in his view never easy—we have the basis for a special kind of free-wheeling inquiry into other critics' views. Instead of thinking that we can refute a given position by showing that it cannot be experimentally or logically falsified, we are invited by it to *one* perspective on the world, a perspective that is likely, by the very nature of perspectives, to be self-demonstrating. Every perspective expressed in a symbolic language becomes a "terministic screen" which both reveals some truths—obviously "demonstrated" to anyone employing the language—and conceals others.

Taken seriously, this position means that no refutation of Burke that I have seen has any relevance to what he is really doing, because they all employ some version of a scientistic calculus to show either that Burke cannot prove what he says, or that what he says can be refuted from some other perspective, or that all of his proofs are circular. But since all screens will be vulnerable to the same charges, the question becomes, not whether a given perspective can be shown to be distorted—because it always can be from any other perspective—but whether it is more or less adequate to the

---

[7] *Attitudes toward History* (1937; 2d rev. ed., Los Altos, Calif.: Hermes Publications, 1959), p. 260.

kinds of problems it reveals. The result of such a position is not relativism, although it is not surprising that inattentive readers have confused it with relativism; having cut his moorings from conventional norms of proof, Burke is naturally accused of having no norms at all.

He in fact rejects more than conventional norms. His dialectic of similarities and differences is so deliberately flexible and so aggressively opposed to neatly fixed meanings that in a sense all literal proof is made suspect. In the opening pages of *A Grammar of Motives* we find a series of claims that any action or statement can be considered as evidence for or against almost any concept. In defining any substance, for example, we necessarily place it in its context, its *scene*, which is to define it in terms of what it is *not*, leading to the "paradox of substance": "every positive is negative."[8] Before we know it, Burke has moved through statements like "any tendency *to* do something is . . . a tendency *not* to do it" (p. 32) to a series of paradoxes and oxymorons and "ambiguities of substance" that stagger the literal-minded:

> Hence, Pure Personality would be the same as No Personality: and the derivation of the personal principle from God as pure person would amount to its derivation from an impersonal principle. Similarly, a point that Hegel made much of, Pure Being would be the same as Not-Being; and in Aristotle, God can be defined either as "Pure Act" or as complete repose. . . . And Leibniz was able to propose something pretty much like unconscious ideas in his doctrine of the "virtual innateness of ideas." (We might point up the oxymoron here by translating "unconscious ideas" as "unaware awarenesses.") [P. 35]

Here we find Burke not simply claiming that everything is *like* everything else but asserting universal identity, identity not only of positives but of positive and negative. In this world, perfection "equals" nonperfection, purity "equals" corruption, action "equals" passion; everything equals everything else and, as he playfully puts it, vice versa.

Obviously such talk is nonsense to anyone who insists on a literal meaning for phrases like "the same as" and "amounts to." Burke seldom uses such words in a sense that would satisfy someone like Crane as strictly literal; even the word "literal" is not quite literal; thinking about the concept as Burke might, we would no doubt extend my questioning of Crane's usage in chapter 2. Indeed, a major part of his persistent program is to remind literalists that behind their claims to precision lurk confusions that can be acknowledged and lived with only by qualifying every copulative verb with some sense of ambiguity. It is not just that the words need semantic scouring. What something *is* is always too rich and complex for any one statement. Thus Burke can, without violating his own canons, say at one point that

---

[8] *A Grammar of Motives*, p. 25.

literary form as the gratification of needs *is* the appeal in poetry[9] and, in other contexts, say that literary form is a *disguise* for the true appeal; and he can really mean both statements.

But we must not be un-Burkean in what we mean by a phrase like "really mean." We are not—it should be clear by now—in pursuit of a meaning that is knowledge in a scientific sense of fixed concepts proved by tests of certainty or levels of probability. We are pursuing a truth-of-action, a meaning that is more probed than proved—a *way* of knowing, a knowing that is itself a kind of action.

Consider more closely the beginning of *A Grammar of Motives*. Like Burke's other books, it depends on a conceptual beginning in "dramatism": *if* man-as-symbol-user, *then* action (in the sense of symbolically motivated choices between various yeses and noes—the opposite, in short, of mere motion); *if* action, *then* conflict; *if* conflict, *then* drama. And *if* drama, *then* surely you must want to find a critical language that deals dramatically with the great symbolic drama of the whole of man's life.[10] But note how he says the project began, as distinct from how the finished book begins:

> We began with a theory of comedy, *applied* to a treatise on *human relations*. Feeling that competitive ambition is a drastically overdeveloped motive in the modern world, we thought *this motive might be transcended* if men devoted themselves not so much to "excoriating" it as to "appreciating" it. . . . We sought to formulate the basic stratagems which people employ, in endless variations, and consciously or unconsciously, for the outwitting or cajoling of one another. [P. xii; my italics]

He soon found himself trying to construct a rhetoric, symbolic, and grammar of human motives, a three-in-one inquiry that would potentially accommodate all particular doctrines and provide for their meeting without mutual destruction. In short, he set out, like certain others, to build a

---

[9] *Counter-Statement*, 2d ed. (Los Altos, Calif.: Hermes Publications, 1953; reprinted Berkeley: University of California Press, 1968), p. 138. (First published, 1931.) I refer here to article 11, "The Individuation of Forms," of "Lexicon Rhetoricae." Here, as elsewhere when Burke "identifies" something with something else, one can find in his immediate context clues about how the equation should be qualified: "Form, having to do with the creation and gratification of needs, is 'correct' in so far as it gratifies the needs which it creates. The appeal of the form *in this sense* [my italics] is obvious: form *is* [Burke's italics] the appeal."

[10] The sequence can be found in many places, e.g., in the first of the "Five Summarizing Essays" in *Language As Symbolic Action: Essays on Life, Literature, and Method* (Berkeley and Los Angeles: University of California Press, 1966), "Definition of Man," p. 18. (I shall from now on use the abbreviation *LSA*). Seeing inquiry as probing processes rather than proving results, Burke has naturally heard threatening prophetic voices on his left flank, considerably more willing than he to give up traditional standards of evidence. In the late sixties he tried to show that Marshall McLuhan's "probes" were both less responsible and less adequate to the world than Burke's own ("Medium as 'Message'" *LSA*, pp. 410-18). A fair number of new "rivals" have come on the critical scene a bit too late for full confrontation: the continental deontologizers and deconstructionists and their American cousins. I would not want to claim that Burke foreknew *everything* that Barthes, Derrida, de Man *et cie* have shocked the academic world with, but I am sure that, if they ever get around to reading him, they will be tempted to moderate their claims to originality. (See note 12 to chapter 2 of *Critical Understanding*.)

pluralism that would save himself and the world by reducing meaningless and destructive symbolic encounter.

The further one goes in Burke, the clearer it becomes that every consideration is subordinated to this master program. Though he has a passion for learning matched by few, though he is deeply responsible to his kind of truth, that truth cannot be summarized in ordinary cognitive terms. The world is threatened with kinds of conflict, symbolic and literal, that may destroy us. Can we, by taking thought about conflict, diminish the chances either of physical destruction or of that other kind that critics inflict on each other: the annihilation of one view by the "perfection" of another?

Consequences

One good way to see what this means is to imagine a modern-day Plato setting out to save mankind through thought but purged by Kant and others of any hope of discovering solid substances or ideal forms or essences. His hope cannot be for goodness or justice or wisdom but rather for *good ways* of talking and acting, *just ways* of talking and acting, *wise ways* of talking and acting. What will be some consequences of such a program?

1. Most of Crane's distinctions among kinds of discourse and kinds of action will no longer matter very much. Every action can have symbolic value, every statement can be a good or bad symbolic action, depending on its context. A pure poem, so called, may be more useful in curing us of our various isolationisms than an obviously didactic plea to be tolerant. By the same token, efforts at speculative discourse like Burke's will at times become more like "poetry" than like argument. Every generic distinction ever made can be thrown into what Burke calls his alembic and distilled into new visions of unity. Or, for curative purposes, any distinction can be left as it was or be tempered slightly, warmed or cooled, as it were. Consistency will be of method, not of definitions, distinctions, or conclusions, and our statements will often look inconsistent or ungrounded to critics seeking literal coherence.

Burke offers a revealing metaphor for how genuine meetings of conflicting views might take place in this new world in which process is more important than formulation. "Distinctions," he says,

> arise out of a great central moltenness, where all is merged. They have been thrown from a liquid center to the surface, where they have congealed. Let one of these crusted distinctions return to its source, and in this alchemic center it may be remade, again becoming molten liquid, and may enter into new combinations, whereat it may be again thrown forth as a new crust, a different distinction. So that A may become non-A. But not merely by a leap from one state to the other. Rather, we must take A back into the ground of its existence, the logical substance that is its causal ancestor, and on to a point where it is consubstantial with non-A; then we may return, this time emerging with non-A instead. [*Grammar,* p. xiii]

This vision, revealing what he sometimes calls his critical "machine" as a great smelter of his own distinctions, applies to the differences among all philosophical systems. What causes warfare among systems is that all terms are inherently ambiguous, and we therefore consider it "our task to study and clarify the *resources* of ambiguity" (p. xiii). Philosophical systems "can pull one way and another" just because the terms *are* inherently ambiguous. But the energetic student of ambiguities can pursue the "margins of overlap" in order to "go without a leap from any one of the terms to any of its fellows" (p. xv).

Everything in this world of process is, then, related to everything else. And similarities are somehow realer, in that molten center, than differences.

2. Suppose we accept this pervasive view of ambiguity and then try to find a way of talking that will potentially encompass all views, not by reducing them to convenient plus or minus signs, but by identifying with them and then incorporating them, in their richness, into a great dialogue. Our ultimate purpose is to save the world from the kind of warfare that would make good talk, including conflicting talk, impossible; in sum, we set out with the goal of *keeping the options open,* and that means that we are trying to act with *our* symbols on both the world of symbolic action and on the world of motion or body where there are no symbols to act on us in return. Various forms of warfare threaten on every hand: sheer critical confusion, motives for self-destruction and destruction of others, authoritarian censorship programs in new totalitarian form, and new weaponry capable of silencing the dialogue once and for all. Anyone who cares for *anything* human will thus surely have an interest in following us. The goal, stated as slogan, is to learn to "get along with people better,"[11] by inquiring into and explaining to them and to ourselves how we talk together.

The test of any action or piece of discourse will thus no longer be primarily "Is it true?" or "Is it beautifully made?" but rather "Is it curative?" Did the probe turn up something helpful, or help us discard something harmful?

3. When we do literary criticism, the elements of any poem, and thus of poetic analysis, will not be elements of a known form, formally considered, but elements of an action, actionally considered. We shall of course want very much to be able to do justice to every aspect of discourse, including its "poetic" form as analyzed by a Ronald Crane or a Cleanth Brooks, and we may thus borrow their terms at particular moments, trying only to do *their* job better.

> I shall grant to our current neo-Aristotelian school (by far the
> most admirable and exacting group a critic can possibly select as his
> opponent) that the focus of critical analysis must be upon the

---

[11]Burke puts his own motives in many different ways, but his statement at the beginning of *A Grammar of Motives* is representative; see esp. pp. xvii ff.

structure of the given work itself. Unless this requirement is fulfilled, and amply, the critic has slighted his primary obligation. It is my contention, however, that the proposed method of analysis is equally relevant, whether you would introduce correlations from outside the given poetic integer or confine yourself to the charting of correlations within the integer. And I contend that the kind of observation about structure is more relevant when you approach the work as the *functioning* of a structure (quite as you would make more relevant statements about the distribution of men and postures on a football field if you inspected this distribution from the standpoint of tactics for the attainment of the game's purposes than if you did not know of the game's purposes). And I contend that some such description of the "symbolic act" as I am here proposing is best adapted for the disclosure of a poem's function.[12]

If we think about what the key words in this passage mean for Burke as distinct from what they would mean for Crane—"relevant," "outside," "inside," "functioning of a structure," "purposes," "function"—we see that he is inevitably importing into his standard a notion of *poems as deeds,* and it is no idle boast at all for him to claim that his method is flatly superior for analyzing purpose and structure in *his* definition. But his definitions are not of autonomous forms, or of principles, purposes, materials, and methods for making such forms, but rather of actions and scenes, the principles of action, actors and their qualities, the means of action, and, most important, the purposes of actions. He seeks out whatever causes and conditions seem pertinent to or determinative of actions, and "motives" become even more important than the forms they lead poets to make.

What he means by action is that kind of behavior peculiar to a choosing agent, what nonagents like stones and plants and animals cannot perform. We must note, following this program, that many modern thinkers deny that such action is possible; for them men only *think* that they act, whereas they are really, just like plants and stones, in motion determined by previous motions. We shall know better than to try to refute such scientistic monists, because we know that their position will be self-proving, according to the heads-I-win-tails-you-lose form of argument. But we shall also cheerfully note that they try to persuade us to choose their views; that is, they act *as if* they could really act on us in our symbolicity, not in our animality—*as if,* in short, we could *act* in response.[13]

Thus the kind of action that we see as the center of our own endeavor as we try to change our readers will also be the center of every human drama

---

[12]*The Philosophy of Literary Form,* p. 74.

[13]Burke's attack on behaviorist reductions has been unrelenting (see, for example; part 1 of *LSA* and chap. 7 of part 3), but it is always made in terms that attempt to incorporate the validities in the partial view. His most recent restatement is in "(Nonsymbolic) Motion/(Symbolic) Action," *Critical Inquiry* 4 (Summer 1978): 809-38, esp. 833 ff.

(though as pluralists we must remember that we are at best pursuing only one of many possible ways of talking about the center). And, since it is genuine action that interests us, we note that even if people only think they act, even if they are really only body in motion, the actions they *think* they perform entail conflict, conflict entails drama, and drama entails the need for dramatistic terms for our analyses. Though behaviorists cannot be directly refuted, they can be shown to provide no language for talking about the drama their proponents engage in when they try to persuade us to accept their language.

We shall therefore always look, in every human situation, for the elements of drama, the five most obvious being the *action* itself, the *agent* doing the action, the *agency* or means by which he performs it, the *scene* in which it is performed, and the *purpose* it is intended to achieve. Sometimes we may want to add others, like *time* as a distinguishable part of the scene and *attitude* as a subdivision of agency, but usually the dramatistic pentad will do our job. We shall use these elements, however, not as some use Aristotle's four causes—unvarying, frozen, literal categories—but as fluid reagents, applicable in different "ratios" for different problems. What is one agent's action is another agent's scene. A given agent can be of someone else's agency—a tool to other ends—or he can be, again, a part of someone's scene. And we shall find that philosophies and critical theories can be classified and accommodated according to their proportionate emphases on one or another of these and the ratios among them. Scene, for example, may be elevated by materialists to become the supreme and only agent. Agent may be elevated by some religionists into supreme agent or turned, by pantheists, into supreme scene that is supreme agent (*Grammar,* part 2).

4. Every chosen language, even the least philosophical, is a "terministic screen." Without choice of terms, human beings would be incapable of their unique and defining gift, symbolic action. But each choice becomes a screen that is both a reflection of reality and a deflection of reality.[14] In fact each screen tends to superimpose a greater and greater distortion as it strives for its own perfecting; each symbolic actor is thus tempted to transcend all limitations by climbing a hierarchy of values implicit in his language in the hope of finally discovering the full and final meaning of his initial choice. Each screen tends thus to distort the whole of things by exploiting a partial view that pretends to be the whole and that struggles to perfect itself by triumphing over all other views. The result is of course more conflict—conflict of a kind that shows an inherent drive toward total confrontation.

5. In the resulting struggle, one glowingly tempting possibility is that mankind might find a way to transcend the conflicts, leave behind the partialities, and achieve some kind of ultimate harmony—what Burke calls

---

[14]*LSA,* p. 45.

the marriage of all to all. This is the happy route of transcendence that dialectical thinkers are almost always tempted by. The fact is, however, that no one can really hope for such a happy outcome of the dialectic of warring positions.

> I'm not too sure that, in the present state of Big Technology's confusions, any educational policy, even if it were itself perfect and were adopted throughout the world, would be able to help much, when the world is so ardently beset by so much distress and malice. The dreary likelihood is that, if we do avoid the holocaust, we shall do so mainly by bits of political patchwork here and there, with alliances falling sufficiently on the bias across one another, and thus getting sufficiently in one another's road, so that there's not enough "symmetrical perfection" among the contestants to set up the "right" alignment and touch it off.[15]

There is thus a second, potentially "gloomy route," much more probable: if action, then drama; if drama, then conflict; if conflict, then "victimage" and tragedy. By their nature as actors men will produce tragedies, both symbolic and real, and, as creatures "rotten with perfection," they are likely to strive toward supreme, "perfect" tragedy (*LSA*, pp. 54-55). Any one voice will strive for its perfection and will thus attempt to dominate all the others. Since men are not likely to relinquish their freely enacted disagreements voluntarily, this route promises that uniquely human kind of perfection, the annihilation of the opponent. Indeed, in this century, we can envisage a supreme and supremely gloomy transcendence of conflict in universal annihilation, as we realize the "perfect" victimage implicit in all drama.

The best we can hope for, then, is Burke's own "comic" choice: to produce and exploit stalemate, a kind of undivine comedy. We develop a dialectic of muddling-through, a deliberate interference with perfection by enforcing on every terministic screen an ironic reminder of other truths according to which it should be discounted. (Note here the contrast with the way Crane's key terms are kept distinct. The further we pursue any of Burke's key terms for method, the more alike they look, until finally comedy equals dialectic equals irony equals drama.) Since we have no real hope of transcending verbal wars with an ultimate harmony that will not be ultimate annihilation of man's essence, his symbol-making and using, our best hope is for this third route, neither radiantly happy nor especially gloomy but comic: we shall try to cure mankind by keeping things off balance, by dissolving fixities, by turning the potential tragedy of fanatical annihilation into the comedy of muddled mutual accommodation.

---

[15]*LSA*, p. 20. I am indebted to Tom Tollefson for his unpublished tracing of Burke's "comic" alternative to the two unacceptable or impossible routes.

Literature and Criticism as "Equipment for Living"

The dramatistic pentad can be used to explore any human action, including action by statement. Burke's own lifelong critical act, for example, can be viewed according to ratios among any of the terms, and the result may be what looks like contradictory language as we move from ratio to ratio. Suppose we say that Burke (as *agent*) is to be viewed as responding to the twentieth century (as *scene*), performing the *act* of literary criticism, through the *agency* of critical talk about language (he might instead have used boycotting or political revolution) for the *purpose* of cure. We read the scene as one of threatening chaos and ultimate annihilation, a scene that has led others to straightforward sermons defending eternal verities. But *if* the scene *is* chaotic, who will hear the sermons? How will such rhetoric work? Will it not probably contribute to further chaos? If it wins followers, they will surely be embattled and largely ignorant followers, and we will have contributed to the very factionalism that threatens to destroy us. *Our* agency, then—the kind of discourse we shall use in *this* scene—must be largely a disorienting discourse in order to build communities of explorers who are forced, by our criticism, to listen to each other.

Literary criticism will thus be only one of many *agencies,* an aspect of the disorienting but finally irenic discourse we need. The world of such criticism has its own gloomy route to match the "perfection" of total annihilation by the bomb. That route would lead to the annihilation of free discourse about the poem by establishing a single, final reading that readers must accept. To fix readings would be to limit the kind of actions poems and readers can perform with each other.

What we will seek, then, is a way of doing justice to many critical voices without letting any one of them achieve its destructive perfection. Knowing that the poem comes from a poet who is an inhabitant of both the world of body and the world of symbolic action, we shall expect it to show evidences of a variety of cures, bodily and spiritual, that the poet performs for himself and for his readers. It is true that when we treat a poem as an act, a piece of symbolic rhetoric, we shall find some aspects of its "medicine" in one sense timeless; for the poet and his audience share a human nature, and in the poetic part of our analysis we can do justice to what does not change from audience to audience. But we shall think it ridiculous to nail ourselves to such fixtures, since we all know that the same poem does different things for different audiences at different times. To allow a pedantic concern for permanent and fixed proof to prevent communal probing of meanings in dimensions not clearly "objective" or provable is to insure critical warfare rather than diminish it.

A Way into and around "Surgical Ward"

We must not, however, support simple skepticism or relativism; these always in practice feed the fanaticisms that destroy. Confidence must be maintained in the difference between good criticism and bad, and we must develop criteria for distinguishing the discourse that curses from the kind that cures.

We can see what this means by looking again at what "Surgical Ward" really is. It really *isn't*. Rather, it *does*. That whole chart that Crane led us into in chapter 2 was haywire. It should have been headed "Some Views of What 'Surgical Ward' *Does*."

I confess that at this point I spent some time trying to draw a chart that I wouldn't be ashamed to let Burke see. I failed, because I knew that any such chart must be a record of flowings and processes, not entities. To illustrate my problem, I here duplicate a chart Burke once made of an entirely different matter. You can see the difficulties.[16]

Suppose, then, that "Surgical Ward" comes up between us. We are not so foolish as to spend hours and hours trying to decide what it is and how it relates to its siblings and second cousins. We want to know how it works, of course, and we will thus spend some time on a "poetic" interpretation—but not, finally, for the purpose of judging Auden's skill. How it works will be important mainly as leading us to what it does, as an action produced by and thus pertinent to many motives. But this action will be received in many ways, depending on the receiver's "motives." We thus know that it *must* be viewed in many lights, all shining, as it were, simultaneously. But we shall never be satisfied with Crane's pluralism, which attempts to be a kind of supreme adding machine: there is *this* aspect of structure, pursued by *this* kind of criticism, and then there is *that* aspect of structure, pursued by *that* kind. . . . And when they are all accumulated together (but without essential communication among them?), the health of criticism is insured. No, we shall try to force all pertinent views into confrontation. We shall thus risk appearing hopelessly confused, since we shall be trying (in a sense) to do everything at once.

But we are really not all that confused. We can learn a lot about this poem. We can explore first its *literary*, its *poetic*, motives. Sonnets make demands of their own, as do statements about pain and happiness. In exploring the poetics of the piece, what the act *qua* act can tell us about itself, we can discover that the poem *is* in some sense motivated by the need to perfect the "act."

Such a poetic analysis reveals most obviously that curious contrast between the octet and the sestet that Booth's Crane made so much of. The poet ostensibly contrasts a world of isolated suffering and a shared world of health and happiness. "We," the healthy, "stand" together and "cannot imagine" that other world, where each person, reduced to a part of his ailing body, knows no truth but self-centered pain. But when we look more closely, we discover that Auden has played a curious game with us. First, only the

---

[16]*The Rhetoric of Religion*, p. 184.

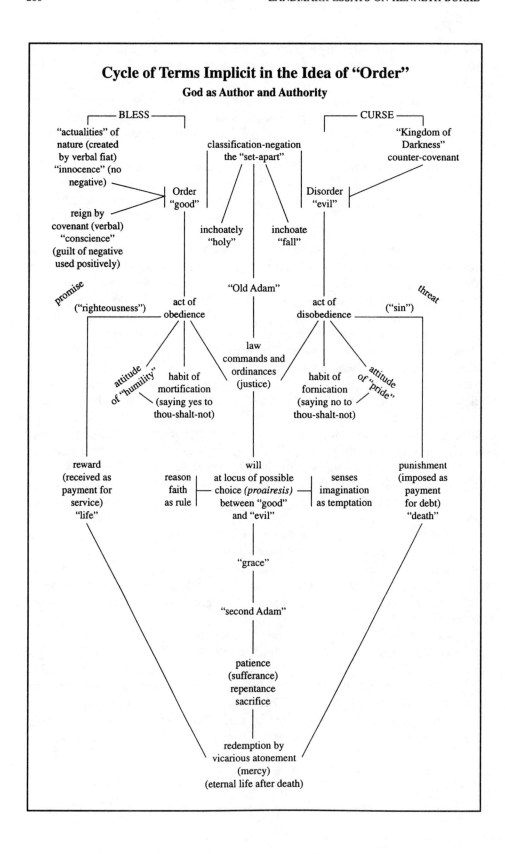

world of pain is fully imagined (despite the claim that we cannot imagine it when healthy), while the world of happiness is all abstraction, climaxed by a stress on the *idea* of love, presumably in contrast with love itself. Second, the rhyme, absolutely regular in the world of pain, becomes almost private, and therefore almost unshared, in the "shared" world. The meter not only turns free, but the free verse is hard to read aloud: *shared* regularities are thus violated, and the sonnet form almost disintegrates. Thus the speaker casts the greatest possible irony upon the claim that "we *stand* elsewhere"; we might rather almost say that we fall apart. The world of suffering is both imaginatively richer and prosodically stabler, and it is thus, as poetry, less private than the abstract world of happiness. For eight lines—or seven and a half—we *share* conventions, and author and reader in fact stand together securely in their knowledge of conventional form. Only in the sestet, with its skittish rhythms, rhymes, and half-retracted assertions, do we enter upon intellectual and prosodic ironies that leave us neither knowing nor seeing precisely where we *do* stand.

But no matter how far we took such a beginning in poetic analysis, it would still leave us with the main "dramatistic" questions unanswered. Surely we shall want to attempt answers to other, inherently more interesting, questions. Why *this* act by this poet at this time? Why *this* structure, when Auden has shown himself master of so many others? What does the poem do for Auden, and what does it do for us?

It seems inescapable, once we ask such questions, that the poem is an attempt at secular exorcism of pain and the fear of a pain-ridden world. It addresses the threat of suffering—a threat almost too awful to endure—and prays, in ironic secular style, for a way out: "about suffering they were never wrong, the old masters"; "those who suffer, suffer alone." Body is pain, pain body, that is all you know, in that surgical ward, and it is not enough. If that world is the ultimate reality, then "all the instruments agree" that the day of this hospital visit is indeed a dark, cold day. All of our observations in that ward would, like the impersonal instruments of science, teach us that we are hopelessly isolated in pain and death.

And what can we offer to ourselves to counter that life that is death? Not, in this poem, the God who in a later poem, "Thanksgiving for a Habitat," combats the

> Vision of Hell, when Nature's wholesome genial fabric
>   lies utterly discussed and from a sullen vague
> wafts a contagious stench, her adamant minerals
>   all corrupt, each life a worthless iteration
> of the general loathing (to know that, probably,
>   its cause is chemical can degrade the panic,
> not stint it).

The converted Auden will later find that the Holy Four, the Gospel-Makers, can, allied with prayer, combat the threat of isolated suffering. But here we have no Holy Four and no God, only a secular "defense": a shared happiness that turns ironically to a shared anger and then to a love that is not an assured love but only the idea of love. It is obviously not enough.* The struggle for transcendence of an isolated pain calls for something more than this; it cries out, once begun, for its logical or "logological" perfecting in a genuine salvation. We could surely prophesy from this poem alone, though admittedly "after the event,"[17] that Auden must some day convert to a God who offers a more convincing answer to the unredeemed world of that surgical ward or of the war-torn world for which it stands. And can we not surely prophesy that if Auden revises the poem after that conversion is secure, he will find intolerable the near-dissolution of the original? Will he not tighten things up into a fairly regular sonnet, one that somehow masters the world of pain in a way that the original, like so many of its companions in "In Time of War," visibly failed to do? With the world of happiness less problematical, he will attend more to "art" and less to the awful, intolerable pain of viewing man's fate in 1939.

For us readers the original poem will express a similar unsatisfied hunger. The resolution is, after all, deeply unsettling, undercut by the verbal irony, by the disintegration of the verse, and by the lack of vital images. The poem thus offers none of the kinds of sharp resolution characteristic of Auden's most admired pieces. It does not, like many early poems, teach the free man how to praise, but it also does not yield any of the wonderful wry satire that helped make the youthful Auden famous. Nor does it offer anything comparable to the brilliantly sharp ironic climaxes that we find in Auden's anthologized pieces: she "answered all of his long, marvelous letters but kept none"; "Dance, dance, dance till you drop"; "The question is absurd: / Had anything been wrong, we should certainly have heard."

Like many of those early poems, "Surgical Ward" offers us a kind of suffering scapegoat in those patients enduring the non-drama of unredeemed body, the in-action of those who are not agents and cannot act. Unlike them,

---

*My colleague, Richard Strier, plausibly objects to my seeing (that is, my "Burke's" seeing) the sonnet as strongly ironic. "What disturbs me is your argument that the 'breakdown' of the meter and rhyme scheme *itself* establishes an irony. This argument seems to me to be based on a number of ad hoc assumptions. Why is it *necessary* to see the relation between the formal and the thematic elements of the poem as ironic? First of all, I don't see why half-rhymes are 'private'; they are surely as verifiable and public a linguistic phenomenon as full rhymes. Second, it seems to me that one could view the prosodic phenomena to which you are pointing non-ironically, in the following way: the octet is consciously formal, distanced, tense; the metrical formality keeps us 'apart'; the sestet, on the other hand, relaxes into a more colloquial and easy-going mode. The 'irony' disappears if the prosody of the sestet is viewed as 'relaxed' rather than as 'private' and 'unstable,' as relying easily and assuredly upon the 'common world.'" Highly plausible, Burke might reply, and somewhat closer to what Crane would see in it. If Strier is right, then of course we have evidence that Auden's conversion is prefigured in the embodied motives of the poem, *before* Auden had consciously recognized, or at least declared, his turning to God. Should we not play it both ways?

[17]Burke often uses this suggestive verbal formula for his unpacking of the implications of any position. One might say that his life-work is to study such prophecy, using past symbolic actions, in order to speak prophetically about the consequences of present symbolic actions. If I can prophesy after the event about how (let us say) Hobbes's reduction of world to body led to Hobbes's conclusions, I should be able to show where Skinner's choice of motives will lead.

it attempts a kind of catharsis, but the catharsis is as yet either deliberately muted or fumbled. I here resist the temptation to do a Burkean exploration of how obscene bodily functions get into the poem; in fact we don't need them, because the octet is openly about the obscene reduction to "pure" body, the perfection of mere motion. But it is clear that Auden does not see any satisfactory escape from the reduction; he can share the unshared world of misery, but, instead of a "cure," he escapes into muted ironies.

We have of course only scratched the surface of what, viewed in Burke's terms, such a poem does or might be thought to do for its readers or for Auden.* Research into Auden's life, and guesswork about it, could lead to specific operations, specific angers, specific lonelinesses. And we can discover or imagine other audiences for whom it would either succeed or fail in different ways. We have no need to confine ourselves either to what Auden could plausibly have intended or to what seems clearly *in* the poem, viewed as a poetic structure. If we want to think of that foot, for example, as somehow related to the *"suffering"* Icarus's legs in "Musée des Beaux Arts," and then think of that scratch as somehow related to the horse scratching its innocent behind on a tree, that's our privilege. If we want to hear the breathing of an oxygen tank in the *th*-sounds of lines 1 and 6, why not? If we want to see a pun in *bear,* emphasizing the bare exposed body, or an ambiguity in the *it* of line 7, making it refer both to truth and to groans, let us do so—if we see any good reason to.

The Tests of a Good Terministic Screen

But what, then, are the criteria of good critical reasons in this view? What are the limits to such seeming improvisations? Why not turn the word "truth" to "turd" again here, the word "bear" to "burden," and then bring in an allusion from my childhood patois, in which "to cut your foot" meant to step unintentionally into cow dung? Why not, indeed? Is not this pretended pluralism then simply a relativism after all, one that allows anything to be said provided it can be said with enough brashness and verve, one that can only lead us to skepticism about the possibility of *knowing* anything about poetry?

Burke himself often raises the question of relativism,[18] and his way of answering is implicit in what I have said so far. There will be no single set of literal criteria for proper talk, no catalogue of logical fallacies applicable to all occasions, no easy reference to intentions or structure or historicity. No

---

*For Burke's own revision of my hunches, see *Critical Understanding*, pp. 134-36.

[18]Perhaps Burke's best summary of how languages work as screens, without leaving us helpless to deal with the screens, is in *LSA*, part 1, chapter 3. The contrast between his kind of pluralism and relativism is fundamental to his program, but it is not easily slated in short form. To me, his own summary, "Our Attempts to Avoid Mere Relativism" (in *LSA*, pp. 52-54), is cogent. But I find that everyone who reads it without knowing much of Burke finds it cryptic. See also *The Philosophy of Literary Form*, pp. 73-74.

one can list in advance all of the legitimate—that is, healing—uses a poem
can be put to. If someone has a private association with "Surgical Ward" like
cow dung, let him use it. But we shall insist that he discount that association
by recognizing many views of the poem to which it will be irrelevant, and we
shall insist that he enrich his view by learning to move logologically up to
spiritual and even theological readings and back down to other secular
simplifyings.

When we look for Burke's criteria, then, we find no short fixed list of
tests. There is nothing here to match Crane's persistent effort to build and
defend a coherent, testable, comprehensive method. Instead we have hundreds
of hints and guesses.

First, what can we say about the decision to start—and end—with
dramatism? There are clearly many philosophical and scientific languages,
each offering itself as the language of languages. All of them will prove
useful for some purposes, but few of them offer us much help in our general
program of dealing with the great drama of symbolic actors. If we set out, as
Burke says, "working for the purification of war," if we seek some alternative
to what he calls "dissipation" and "fanaticism" (his rough equivalents for the
extremes of what I have been calling skepticism and dogmatic monism), if
we seek to maintain the possibility in the world of a "neo-liberal, speculative
attitude," then surely our terms must be those that will describe and deal with
the symbolic actions we encounter—and perpetrate.

According to Burke, then, we do not simply have the right to choose a
dramatistic vocabulary, as one among many; rather, this vocabulary is forced
upon us by our choice of task. We could avoid it only by confining ourselves
to questions about those things and bodies in the world that do not commit
symbolic actions or by choosing, as the neo-Aristotelians do in their literary
criticism, to deal with a small aspect of any given act. As he says at the
beginning of *A Grammar of Motives,* "If you ask why, with a whole world of
terms to choose from, we select these [the dramatistic pentad] rather than
some others as basic, our book itself is offered as the answer. For, to explain
our position, we shall show *how it can be applied*" (p. x; my italics). Though
all other philosophies would have a right, in Burke's view, to begin with
exactly the same kind of unproved beginnings, they could not hope to deal
with *his* problem—the conflict of symbolic actions—unless they employed
the terms of dramatism.

What is more, we can distinguish, among other languages, some that are
inadequate even to the tasks that they claim to work on. Some philosophies
do with richness and power what they set out to do; many fail to do so. Plato
and Kant and Aristotle are in effect doing in other terms much of what we
try to do in our linguistic terms. Plato has a dialectic that leads from
substance to substance and ends only in transcendent reality. We will build a
dialectic that leads from term to term and ends in alternative visions of
possible transcendent terms—terms for order, for beauty, for right action, for
God. Similarly, Kant attempts a transcendentalism concerned with the
necessary forms of experience and reason; our pentadic ratios "name forms

necessarily exemplified in the imputing of human motives" for action. Thus even these giants are easily incorporated without essential distortion.

But most languages will be less important than these, deficient in one respect or another. The language of behaviorism (Burke often repeats the example, and so must I), though indispensable in studying mere motion, gets its users into trouble when they try to apply it to the human drama. There is no place here for a tolerant bow to the behaviorists, saying, "You explain the human drama in your terms, and we'll explain the human drama in our terms." Because for them there *is* no human drama, since there is no concept of *action.* Having reduced their language, for the sake of efficiency, to the language of motion, they deny in their terms what their own competitive treatises display: man's symbolic drama. Reducing action to motion, the behaviorists do not tell "a representative anecdote" when they tell us their stories about man-as-animal. Anecdotes about rats in mazes lack the "circumference" or scope needed if something like justice is to be done to the drama of man.[19]

As we have seen, it would be an equally misleading reduction, possibly even more dangerous, to move in the opposite direction and pretend that man is not in any sense undergoing mere motion. What we offer is a language that can incorporate the essential truth of both reductions—a language that can move dialectically to encompass the precritical facts of both our animality and our symbolicity. In short, our language requires us to be polyglots.

The first test of our terministic screen might, then, be summarized by Burke's demand that our "anecdotes" be *fully* "representative"—that the "circumference" of our terms be large enough to include at least the action that is performed as we tell our story about man and his actions. As in Crane, the validity of a neatly closed system is in itself not very impressive if it is not adequate to a richness in the subject that every inquirer knows to be there.

The second test could not be more different. As we have seen, Burke wants to prevent that kind of perfection of views that eliminates all other views. Burke would say that the superiority of any language would lie partly in its refusal to be perfected, its roughness about the edges, its celebration of ambiguities, its capacity to resist freezing. It is true that the language of dramatism is forced upon us by our task, but its terms are, as we have seen, inherently fluid and inexhaustible. Their use is kept molten by the systematic cultivation of incongruities. Methods that freeze the options mislead us because the reality that interests us is itself dramatic, in process, fluid.

The superiority of Burke's own terministic screen is thus in part its capacity to point out to other views the ironies that must discount them. But

---

[19]The goals of comprehensiveness, scope, and representativeness are implicit throughout, but see especially *Grammar,* chap. 3 of part 1: "Scope and Reduction."

it is clear that to do a proper job of discounting, a position or language must be potentially as powerful as what it corrects. Those who improvise carelessly will simply not do the job and will be cast aside. But it is only in the fires of dialectic, not in the application of abstract tests like that of falsifiability, that we can decide what to attend to.

It would require many pages simply to list the standards that Burke explicitly discusses at different times. I must content myself with a selection from the "Dictionary of Pivotal Terms," in his *Attitudes toward History.* Note how greatly most of them differ from the tests of rigorous coherence proclaimed by system-builders and from the tests of simplicity and falsifiability that reign supreme in many modern philosophies.

Any good—that is, useful—language will, for example, protect us from being "driven into a corner"; it will provide us with bridging devices (or what Burke elsewhere calls "devices of pontification"); it will provide a "machine" that will "mass-produce" incongruous perspectives; it will make us "at home in the complexities of relativism"; it will combat "dissociative trends" by integrative thought, while at the same time correcting integration with "latitudinarianism"; it will make new forms of communion possible; it will help make us sensitive to the oblique clues to meaning that authors consciously or unconsciously give us; it will provide systematic devices for avoiding efficiency, because efficiency always misleads; it will encourage exposure to the "total archives accumulated by civilization (since nothing less can give us the admonitory evidence of the ways in which people's exaltations malfunction as liabilities)"; it will help us watch for "unintended by-products" of our views, stressing always knowledge of limitations; it will remind us that we are not the independent, separate egos that some modernist views have claimed—rather, the so-called "I" is merely a unique combination of partially conflicting "corporate" "we's" (and it is here that we find Burke's reason for avoiding the first-person singular); it will encourage us to subject every insight to the tests provided by the collective body of criticisms (about the closest Burke comes, incidentally, to worrying about "objectivity"); it will provide ways of transcending what look like opposites by finding how they are not opposites; it will remind us that all arguments are not what they seem, and especially that linear argument is always "merely a set of interrelated terms . . .; the writer seeks to avoid subjectivity by reading the documents of other men"—documents that were organized by terms having similar functions; it will provide tests of "convertibility"—the ways by which one critic's terms can be shown to have cooperated in the formulation of another's. Finally, to cut short this summary of more than 200 pages, the useful language should apply to three different "spheres" of action: it should apply to intimate relations (the individual), to public relations, and to the "process of engrossment whereby works of art are organized." In *The Rhetoric of Religion* Burke adds a fourth sphere to these: the useful language should apply to the sphere of the supernatural or divine, because, whether or not divinity exists, men have always talked as if it did, and our language must do justice to how symbolicity works in religion. To demand that a

critical language do justice to these four spheres is to insist that our "anecdotes" be "representative" indeed! The demand is reasonable, but we should
not underplay the challenges that taking it seriously will give to a world
taught for centuries to hone Occam's razor.

The Dance as Cure

In discussing Burke, we never come to an end, as he himself never can
draw a project to a full stop. I hope to have shown, however, how his pluralism can embrace *all* meanings, potentially, and still repudiate relativism of
the kind that threatens critical understanding. "Charts of meaning are not
'right' or 'wrong'—they are relative *approximations* to the truth."[20] Dramatism is both an open system, encompassing all possible systems, and an
aggressive pursuit of one possible critical language, a language dictated to
anyone who chooses to treat symbols as actions in the human drama. As
Burke says,

> There is an infinite number of things that can be said about a
> poem's structure. You can, for instance, chart the periodicity of the
> recurrence of the definite article. You can contrast the versification
> with that of any other poem known to man. You can compare its hero
> with the hero of some work three centuries ago, etc. What I am
> contending is that the mode of analysis I would advocate will give
> you ample insight into the purely structural features of a work, but
> that the kind of observations you will make about structure will deal
> with the *fundamentals* of structure [namely, its true function for poet
> and reader], and will deal with them *in relation to one another,* as
> against the infinite number of possible disrelated objective notations
> that can be made. [*PLF,* pp. 73-74]

Immediately he is off on a brief effort to show why his analysis of structure
is superior to that of his most serious rivals, the "current neo-Aristotelian
school" (pp. 74-75). Why is it superior? Why of course because his method
"is better adapted for the disclosure of a poem's function"—that is, his
method is better for solving the problem that his method has chosen to solve.
"Function" in this sentence is not at all the same concept as it is in Crane.

In Crane, the pluralism and the chosen critical language were relatively
distinct; working on the problem of critical warfare was for him very
different from the problem of talking about a poem, and the two tasks
required different definitions and different methods. For Burke, the great
assimilator, the two problems are of course assimilated: critics perform acts
in a drama; metacritics, regardless of their differences, perform acts in a
similar drama.

---

[20]*Philosophy of Literary Form,* p. 108.

Thus if we were to ask these critics, "Which of you works more closely with poems?" we can be sure that each would answer, "I do," and that the answer would mean something different for each. For Crane, the act of moving close to the particular poem consists in discriminating it more and more precisely from its similars. Regardless of whether one in fact begins with a poem, as I did in chapter 1, or works around to it through discrimination after discrimination, as I did in chapter 2, one is always attempting to "begin" with what is the most real substance that we value: the "concrete" thing worth pursuing precisely because of its distinction from everything else. But Burke could argue that he never even leaves the poem, the poetry, the symbolic dance; while Crane is performing all of that preliminary analysis, Burke is at every moment performing his own poem, his symbolic act in the great drama. Every act in that drama is worth attending to, and when Burke turns to look explicitly at what we call poems, and commits the obscene act of connecting them even to our bodily life, the poetry has in his sense been with him everywhere, from the beginning. He thus lives with all poems more intimately, he could claim, than any analyst who sees himself as "working on" a poem, not "performing with" it.

Similarly, if you ask them, "Which of you is a more responsible critic?" each would have every right to answer, "I am." For Crane, Burke is irresponsible because he commits anachronisms and violates the author's intentions. But Burke can easily reply that nothing is more irresponsible than to isolate "poetry" from our deepest motives. He is supremely responsible, responding to everything anyone can say, embracing the task of curing us by joining us in the dance.

For proponents of certain kinds of rigor, to defend Burke in my way would no doubt seem a kind of dismissal, even a refutation: he has a self-proving, self-validating system, a method that invents problems that are essentially beyond solution and then claims to solve them by using principles that can be assumed only as part of his invention. His whole enterprise is impossibly, outrageously, shockingly ambitious, yet it finally frustrates intellectual ambition by undermining all solutions. But for anyone who will enter that enterprise, there is no reason why Burke's circularities, or even his imprecisions, should be condemned. Traced out in their richness, his circularities should trouble us no more than the circularities pursued by a Plato or a Cicero or a John Dewey—or by Crane or you or me. Unless the defender of rigor can refute Burke's claim that all thought is in one sense circular, that all conclusions are in a sense chosen "in the beginning," at the moment a thinker chooses his "terministic screen," he should attend closely to Burke's richer music: even the most linear and logical of critics is finally only spreading out in temporal sequence the individual notes from the musical chord that is sounded the moment he chooses his terms and begins.

Consider a true story that I used to tell as if it reflected against Burke. In the late forties I took part in a discussion with him and others of—well, *I* thought the subject was *Huckleberry Finn,* which for me at the time meant that we should talk only of *the* structure of that *made object*. Soon we were aware that Burke was talking about the balloon trip that Huck and Tom and Jim take over the Atlantic. Finally, in some embarrassment, one of us broke in and said, "But Kenneth, that episode is from another book!"

Burke turned on him.

"What the hell does that matter?" And he continued on his way, making points that I did not understand, deplored as irrelevant, and to my sorrow cannot now remember.

Today I see myself as mocked in the tale. I would give a good deal to know what original and shocking point about Mark Twain—or about nineteenth-century America or about the way literature works or about balloons—that monologuist was making. There were at least ten people in the room who could work with me, in our emulation of Crane, to perform the by no means contemptible task of discovering what we called the "unity" of *Huckleberry Finn*. There was only one Burke, and I could not hear him, monist that I was.

Post-Burke: Transcending the Sub-stance of Dramatism

by Celeste Michelle Condit

Kenneth Burke has offered us one of the most important corpora of works of the twentieth century. The historical contexts that generated most of Burke's work—the battle between communism and capitalism, Adolf Hitler, and World War II—have, however, been substantially altered. As Burke himself might suggest, in a new scene, the agency must change, and so it may be necessary to generate a post-Burkean discourse to fit this new scene. To move "post-Burke" is not, however, to turn away from Burke's insights, as might be suggested were we to employ as our analogy the term "post-modernism," which takes its "post" as an oppositional one. Rather, the turn post-Burke might be after the model of the "post-marxists" and "post-feminists," who use the prefix "post" to demarcate an effort to extend the essence of an older program into new contexts in light of new under-standings. Such an effort will, of course, require some alterations in earlier doctrine, but we hope to do it in a way that is in keeping with the spirit of Burke.

In Burke's case, of course, we ought to keep within his "sub-stance," rather than to any "spirit." In the Burkean corpus, substance is the key term, identifying the ultimate compromise (or dramatistic dialectic) upon which Burkeanism is built.[1] Substance is key to Burke because the term allows him to combine "spirit" and "matter" and hence to arrive at the ultimate trope whereby he defines human beings as "bodies that learn language." This definition allows Burke to play both sides of a series of important intellectual fences: universalism and particularism, psychoanalysis and sociology, tragedy and comedy, structure and function—all this built on the decision to endorse both body and mind. Although a thousand different perspectives on Burke can be sustained, and at least a hundred have been printed, as a rhetorical critic, it is this Burke—the one who embraces both sides of old dualisms—that I

Reprinted from *The Quarterly Journal of Speech* 78 (1992). Used with permission of the Speech Communication Association.

[1] Many commentators on Burke ignore the role of "substance" in Burke, or suggest with Bernard Brock, that it was an early "phase" that was later repudiated. However, I see such interpretations as simply an attempt to "cleanse" Burke of his materialism in order to make him fit into contemporary relativist epistemologies with which Burke is not, in fact, wholly isometric.

find constructing a Dramatism which is more enticing than any of the possible alternative discourses that cover similar ground—including structuralism, general semantics, psychoanalysis, and post-marxism.[2]

Therefore, to move post-Burke requires an identification of the substance of Burke upon which, as "Bodies that learn language," we stand and may transcend. Burke offers three subsidiary notions of substance: geometric, familial, and directional. He identifies all of these as special cases of dialectical substance. By examining the Burkean corpus for each of these types of substance, we might point out both the essences to be retained and the scenic baggage to be discarded on a post-Burkean trek.

I take Burke's *familial* substance to be constituted, in one half of his parentage, of the set of literary figures to whom he frequently returns—Coleridge, Shakespeare, Poe, Mann, etc. His other line of descent comes from literary critics, notably Caroline Spurgeon (although he seems to claim her more as "sister" than parent), and from a series of social critics—most notably Freud, Marx, and Korzybski. (Somewhere in the familial history, as in that of all academics, lurk Plato and Aristotle, and their generation of "rhetoricians" as well).

Burke's *geometrical* substance can be located against two landmarks. The socio-political canyon is that marked by the Great Depression and the greater depression of Adolf Hitler. The academic mountain is B.F. Skinner (or his "brother" Watson, who actually gets more ink from Burke). Burke's *directional* substance is far more complicated, and it would take me a great deal of space to defend my description of it against the myriad of other directions proposed for Burke, so I merely sum it up by this statement of Burke's: "if we get involved enough in the using of words, the words in turn begin using us" (*Attitudes Toward History,* p. 399, amplified in his statement of educational goals on p. 375).

To construct a post-Burkeanism, then, we might maintain Burke's directional substance, while adjusting as needs be the familial substance to our own geometrical context. As a rhetorician immersed in the tradition of public oral rhetoric, I would obviously set aside Burke's lineage of literati and replace them with figures such as Abraham Lincoln, Maria Stewart, Frederick Douglass, and Elizabeth Cady Stanton. The problem is more difficult with regard to Freud, Marx, and Korzybski, for I believe that Burke built his program both by working through the patrimony of this troika and by in part repudiating their heritage. I am not at all certain that the relationship of post-Burkeanism to post-Marxism and Lacanianism can be the same; and, I fear that general semantics has all but died out without surviving heir (other than Burke himself). These other fields of discourse are now

---

[2] I do not wish to over-relativize Burke. Although many positions can be sustained by isolated quotations from Burke, I believe that if we were to turn a cluster analysis to the task, it is this combination that would identify the "essence" of Burke. A Forum essay, however, seeks to stir up debate, rather than to close it off with indisputable evidence.

"kissing-cousins" rather than parents; they offer more as dialectical opposites than as progenitors. But let us set that issue aside.

The most pivotal concern is the shift in the "geometric substance" within which Dramatism must do its work. There are many important differences between the context offered by the Great Depression and World War II and the present year. While Burke has addressed some of the trends that were then incipient (race and gender conflict, globalism, Big Technology, and environmental devastation), the shift from incipient trends to dominant concerns produces a qualitative shift. And that shift shows itself most potently in the dialectic of universal and particular as it played itself out in Burke's work. For Burke, the fact that we are "Bodies that Learn Language" led him to place greater emphasis upon universals than upon the particulars that divide humans. Burke did not deny that there were differences of particularity and that these were both interesting and important. Nonetheless, his philosophical or medicinal project clustered around what he assumed to be universals grounded in the common characteristics of the human body. Our present contexts require that we pay greater attention to particulars. Three contexts in particular require modifying extensions of Burke's dramatism: gender, culture, and class.

Sex and Gender

In Burke's historical moment, most public discourse indicated that there were basically two sexes of people—two kinds of human bodies—which they labelled "male" and "female." In Burke's writing there is basically one gender—man (e.g. the definition of "man"; male-gendered nouns and pro-nouns dominate Burke's texts). Burke referred supportively to the women's movement and to the expansion of women's rights, but he portrayed this expansion as the inclusion of women under the sign of "man." In the historical moment, this was a progressive move, since women had been virtually excluded by being classed as "not-man." Inclusion under the sign of "Man" was a distinct improvement over exclusion from public life.

Today, however, the scene has changed. Today we are beginning to recognize that there are at least four genders (and increasingly simply a range of gendering), based more or less directly on six biological sexes (hetero-sexual xy, homosexual xx, heterosexual xx, homosexual xy, xxy and xyy). One cannot use a pseudo-generic term such as "Man" to refer to all these people, because of the dynamics of the intervening stage we have passed through (or are at least passing through). For the past two decades, we have rigorously recognized two genders (male and female), emphasized the differences between these two genders, and promoted the "female" gender to a status of equality or supremacy (as in the flourishing of essentialist or "radical" feminism). That phase has highlighted the inadequacy of male-gendered language for including non-male sexed persons. Today, in going beyond that dualistic stage, we must extend our language beyond duality to a broad "humanity" and to "human beings," discovering ways to speak that emphasize human plurality.

To talk in this way, is not, of course, a simple matter of inserting new words. It is a matter of coming to think in new ways or, as Burke might allow, letting the words use us. As an example, let us spin out what such a fragmentation of gender would allow us to do in revising Burke's definition of "Man." Burke defines Man as

> the symbol-using (symbol-making, symbol-misusing) animal
> inventor of the negative (or moralized by the negative)
> separated from his natural condition by instruments of his own
>   making
> goaded by the spirit of hierarchy (or moved by the sense of order)
> and rotten with perfection (*Language as Symbolic Action,* p. 16).[3]

This strikes me as a fairly perceptive summary of the average Euro-American heterosexual XY. But essentialist feminism has taught us that it is not a good summation of the majority of experiences of the other genders. For example, for most Euro-American heterosexual XX's of the past, it is the positivity of particular experiences (e.g. maternal love) that has formed the dominant influence on languaging. Consequently, for such women the *fact* that "the negative" is a *unique* creation of language does not mean that it forms the *essence* of language. Similarly, as radical feminist critics of science and technology, especially critics of the new birth technologies, have pointed out, it is *men* who have created the instruments that separate *women* from their natural conditions and it is largely for this reason that the separation has been so oppressive.[4] Furthermore, women have been largely shut out of the hierarchy game and have been involved in "orderliness" (i.e. housekeeping) rather than Order. Women are, therefore, rotted by men's vision of female perfection, specifically by the demands that women appear as the ultimately seductive ideal of *The Sports Illustrated Swimsuit Issue* and simultaneously as virtuous, unstained mother-saints. Thus, the essentialist or radical feminist would be forced to project this definition of Man's woman:

> Woman is
> the symbol-receiving (hearing, passive) animal
> inventor of nothing (moralized by priests and saints)
> submerged in her natural conditions by instruments of man's making
> goaded at the bottom of hierarchy (moved to a sense of orderliness)
> and rotted by perfection.[5]

---

[3] I choose here Burke's "middle" definition. The earlier one omitted the material in parentheses and was hence most univocal. The later one explicitly recognized plurality, but only in a codicilic second stanza.

[4] See eg. Patricia Spallone, *Beyond Conception: The New Politics of Reproduction* (MA: Bergin and Garvey Publications, Inc.).

[5] I have previously employed a modified form of this definition in a forthcoming essay, in "Oppositions in an Oppositional Practice: Feminist Rhetorics," *Feminist Critiques of Speech Communication,* ed. Nancy Wyatt and Sheryl Permlutter Brown (Ablex, in press).

But, as I suggested, I think we must move to post-feminism, beyond essentialist feminism to a philosophical gender deconstruction that allows people to construct their own genders from a wide range of genderings. In that vein, I offer a post-Burkean definition:

> People are
> players with symbols
> inventors of the negative and the possibility of morality
> grown from their natural condition by tools of their collective
> making
> trapped between hierarchy and equality (moved constantly to
> reorder)
> neither rotten nor perfect, but now and again lunging down both
> paths.

Culture

Enough sex. Let us turn to the issue of culture. Burke's emphasis on the body, as well as the discursive and sociological contexts of his time, led him to focus on race rather than culture. Because the differences between the bodies of persons of various races are clearly only of the most minor sort (difference within groups being greater than difference between groups), I believe that this led Burke to underestimate the impact of particularity and over-estimate the importance of universality. In a context where cultures, not biological race *per se,* are the issue, we must move post-Burke. All I can do here is to point out a direction.

Burke makes very many statements emphasizing universality. Most in point here is his statement that, "a Dramatistic definition of man requires an admonitory stress upon *victimage* as the major temptation in the symbol systems by which men build up their ideas, concepts, and images of identity and community" *(Language as Symbolic Action,* p. 2, also p. 373; also see *Permanence and Change,* pp. 35, and 49). Burke does not, however, work from multi-cultural materials in establishing this claim. He reads almost exclusively what he openly describes as the texts of "Western" civilization.[6] This proves repeatedly to be a fatal choice. For example, he argues, in the *Rhetoric of Religion,* that religion is language used with thoroughness and that we therefore can understand the essence of logology by understanding the essence of theology. But he assumes, without any questioning of that assumption, that Christianity is a representative anecdote for all religion. *Rhetoric of Religion* is about Christianity and logology is therefore about language in a Christianized social system. The same tendency pervades his other work. Thus, in place of the universal description of the symbol using

---

[6] At times he mentions anecdotal support from China or Buddhism, etc., but he takes as his "representative anecdote," western christianized tradition.

animal that Burke thought he was offering, we have gotten only a description of the way westerners use symbols. It may be that the cycle of guilt-victimage-purification-redemption is the single strongest motive in American discourse, but Burke leaves us with insufficient evidence to claim that it is the *dominant* motive of *all* cultures.

I am not denying that victimage is a universal *possibility* for all human cultures. I suspect that at some time, in more or less perfected form, persons in all cultures engage in victimage rituals. What I am suggesting is that victimage may not be the *dominant* motive structure of all cultures. What Burke's ethnocentric version of Dramatism threatens to blind us to is the multiplicity of different motive structures available in language. To move post-Burke is not, then, to deny that victimage is a universally tempting potential growing out of the nature of languaging. Instead, it is to suggest that we should look for other universally available potentials in language and add them to the Dramatistic dictionary. Additionally, it is to hint that while victimage might show up in many cultures, the nature of victimage might vary substantially. The Burkean definition of "victimage" may need casuistric stretching.

To move post-Burke requires, therefore, that we begin to work in other languages and cultures. Instead of taking the Christian mythic structure as our paradigm, we need to look at the quite different structure of other narrative forms. To seek for non-victimage oriented forms, we might turn to the mythologic structure of Buddhism. To seek out victimage forms which are structurally different from the Christian version, we might examine the trickster tales, so important in AmerIndian, African, and African-American discourse.[7] These stories can shallowly be described as "mortification" tales, but such a classification is Procrustean. To understand trickster tales simply as mortification of the powerful by the weak misses much that is crucial. A good post-Burkean analysis might clear this up for us. But in addition to dealing with cultural division, we need also to deal with class division.

Class

Unlike the topics of gender and culture, Burke spent a great deal of effort on characterizing class. In many ways, his milieu was one where class was the dispute par excellence. Much of Burke's analysis of class is brilliant. His concept of the "socializing of losses" is, I think, definitive for our present

---

[7] I use the term "AmerIndian" because I wish to be sensitive to the objections to the term "Indian," but I believe the more politically current phrase "native American" is unclear, given that "native" is often employed to mean a person born in a given place rather than to refer to the birthplaces of one's ancestors. We are left with this choice because the original voice of these peoples themselves is tribal, naming themselves as specific collective groups, rather than a universalized form naming themselves in terms of the continent they shared, which is the manner in which contemporary issues leads the naming process.

economy. Consequently, when I suggest the need for revisions in concepts of class, I am suggesting as much the need for revisions in the theories of "Burkeans" as the need for the revision of the Burke texts themselves.

The need for revision is made urgent by the fact that another great depression is reasonably likely in the near future. We are approaching the point in the business cycle where so much wealth is held by so few persons that consumption becomes inadequate to support industrial production. That we have reached such a point so soon after experiencing the Great Depression is frustrating, but a great deal of business money has been spent helping Americans to forget that unbridled capitalism tends toward monopolies of both production *and* wealth, and therefore, ultimately, towards temporary collapses. However, it is not merely that the public is gullible. Even academics never learned the lessons that those such as Burke taught the last time around.

Before spelling out that lesson in greater detail, we need to indict specifically the way in which critics within SCA, even Burkean critics, have failed to learn Burke's lessons. As A. Cheree Carlson has pointed out with such sharp aim, Burke argued for a comic perspective, not a tragic one.[8] Rhetorical critics, however, responding to the oppositional tragedies of the sixties, have written almost exclusively in the tragic frame. As Burke accurately suggests, discourse in the tragic frame always produces victims. Our critics, therefore, have merely participated in the oppositional processes that lead to a dialectic in which we indict the powers that are "in," urging that the "ins" become the "outs" and the "outs" become the "ins." In the end, we still have "ins" and "outs." We still have tragedy and victims. We still have the excesses of capitalism.

Burke would have us transcend this tragedy by adopting a comic frame. Burke accepted Marx's analysis of the class situation, but he rejected Marx's solution. At several points Burke suggests a preference for socialism, but he also indicates that a specific economic form is not the fundamental problem. In other words, he locates the problem of wealth and poverty outside of capitalism, at a deeper level, in language itself, where the urge to hierarchy tends to be generated (or, I would argue, at least exacerbated). Burke's analysis has been shown to be largely correct; we have learned that even in non-capitalist systems, dominated by discourses of equality, hierarchies reappear; and those "on top" systematically allocate to themselves more of the goods of social life than they allow to their "equals."

---

[8] "Limitations of the Comic Frame: Some Witty American Women of the Nineteenth Century," *Quarterly Journal of Speech,* 74 (August 1988), 310-322. I believe that while Burke argued in favor of the comic perspective, he actually himself held a tragicomic perspective, which may be the inevitable one for linguistically self-conscious human beings. Placed in an intellectual milieu dominated by tragic perspectives, however, the dialectic of logology led him to argue for the half that was missing, i.e. comedic elements. I owe my perspective here not only to Carlson, but also to a graduate student, Kim Powell, in her paper on the "AWSPL: A Movement in a Comic Frame."

The solution to "poverty," therefore, and the solution to the cyclical collapse of capitalism, lie in adopting attitudes more fundamental than a yes/no on capitalism vs. communism. When we set ourselves "against" the rich, we simply set in motion the tragic rhetoric of capitalism. The capitalists then simply and literally identify themselves with "middle America" and thereby set themselves and the majority "against" the critics (e.g. the "Reds"). Because of their greater access to the means of communication, the capitalists win and the critics become the tragic victims. The way out relies on the adoption of a tragicomic attitude.

The tragicomic attitude transcends Burke's expressed preference for the comedic, by adopting a realistic attitude, rather than a farcical or merely ironic one.[9] The tragicomic attitude might be summed up with the following quandary: **"human beings have the wondrous gift of life on a garden planet, and look what they keep doing with it!"** The tragicomic attitude would chart the progression of human motives from petty jealousy to greed to overpopulation to toxic waste dumps to war, as all of a piece. The tragicomic perspective sees implicit in the comedically petty jealousy of the SCA critic who fails to receive a coveted award the same response to hierarchy as that which leads to global war, with only a change of scene necessary. Actions that are comedic edge into high tragedy as the scene changes. From this perspective, learning to laugh at our petty jealousies is the prerequisite to calming our war-like fervors.

Such a post-Burkeanism would have us react to the next depression not by attacking "the rich" or the "capitalists"—"they" who got "us" here—but by an educational program that teaches us about ourselves as "bodies that learn language," so that we may learn to laugh at our petty jealousies, so that they may not pool their resources to become monopolistic tragedies. Such a program is logological disadvantaged—it is not as cathartic as angry attack. Oppositional discourses in feminism, African-Americanism, and Marxism flourish precisely because they feed the linguistic craving for victimage so well. But if we are truly to move post-Burke, we must first learn the lessons of Burke. We must learn to stop letting our language "use us" quite so facilely. We must step out of the tragedy and endorse the comedy. Let us laugh at Donald Trump and Lee Iaccoca and Frank Lorenzo and most hilariously with Stephen Job (as I write merrily away on my Macintosh Plus). These men are only the demons and villains of our drama if we make tragedy our plot. But let us not cast them even as murderous clowns; instead, let us dance them as poor buffoons naively trapped by the linguistic love of hierarchy. Understanding that, they and we together might dance our way out of the veneration of pernicious hierarchy. The expansion of Burkeanism through gender and cultural analysis is central to such a project because it

---

[9] Note the "comedic" is not "the humorous." Humor asks us to laugh against something, whereas comedy asks us to laugh knowingly and sympathetically with something.

provides a range of alternative hierarchies, exposure to which will allow us to make comparisons, and hence to construct the kind of broad wisdom needed to reject the identity frames into which we were born.

Ultimately, post-Burkeanism teaches us that linguistics is as important as economics, for they are both sign systems circulating within the presence of each other. Therefore, neither capitalism nor communism can make us rich as individuals or as gendered and cultured peoples. To do that, we must learn to know ourselves as *Diverse Bodies That Learn Many Languages.*

Bibliography

This bibliography, like the readings in this volume, concentrates on primarily theoretical rather than primarily critical studies of Burke. Books and essays published in the latter half of this century were generally preferred over earlier works. An attempt was also made to choose works so as to reflect the wide range of academic disciplines that Burke has influenced.

Abdulla, Adnan K. *Catharsis in Literature.* Bloomington: Indiana University Press, 1985.

Abbott, Don. "Marxist Influences on the Rhetorical Theory of Kenneth Burke." *Philosophy and Rhetoric,* 7 (Fall 1974), 217-33.

Aeschbacher, Jill. "Kenneth Burke, Samuel Beckett, and Form." *Today's Speech,* 21 (Summer 1973), 43-47.

Ambrester, Roy. "Identification Within: Kenneth Burke's View of the Unconcious." *Philosophy and Rhetoric,* 7 (Fall 1974), 205-16.

Aune, James A. "Burke's Late Blooming: Trope, Defense, and Rhetoric." *Quarterly Journal of Speech,* 69 (August 1983), 328-40.

Baer, Donald M. "A Comment on Skinner as Boy and on Burke as S—." *Behaviorism,* 4 (Fall 1976), 273-277.

Baxter, Gerald D., and Pat M. Taylor. "Burke's Theory of Consubstantiality and Whitehead's Concept of Concrescence." *Communication Monographs,* 45 (June 1978), 173-80.

Bennett, W. Lance. "Political Scenarios and the Nature of Politics." *Philosophy and Rhetoric,* 8 (Winter 1983), 23-42.

Benoit, William L. "Systems of Explanation: Aristotle and Burke on 'Cause.'" *Rhetoric Society Quarterly,* 13 (Winter 1983), 41-58.

Berthold, Carol A. "Kenneth Burke's Cluster-Agon Method: Its Development and an Application." *Central States Speech Journal,* 27 (Winter 1976), 302-09.

Blau, Herbert. "Kenneth Burke: Tradition and the Individual Critic." *American Quarterly,* 6 (1954), 323-336.

Bloom, Harold. *Agon: Towards a Theory of Revisionism.* New York: Oxford University Press, 1982.

Bostdorff, Denise M., and Phillip K. Tompkins. "Musical Form and Rhetorical Form: Kenneth Burke's *Dial* Reviews as Counterpart to *Counter-Statement.*" *Pre/Text,* 6 (Fall/Winter 1985), 235-52.

Brock, Bernard, and Robert L. Scott. *Methods of Rhetorical Criticism.* Detroit: Wayne State University Press, 1980.

Brown, Janet. "Kenneth Burke and the *Mod Donna:* The Dramatistic Method Applied to Feminist Criticism." *Central States Speech Journal,* 29 (Summer 1978), 138-46.

Brown, Merle E. *Kenneth Burke.* Minneapolis: University of Minnesota Press, 1969.

Burks, Don M. "Dramatic Irony, Collaboration, and Kenneth Burke's Theory of Form." *Pre/Text,* 6 (Fall/Winter 1985), 255-73.

Carpenter, Ronald H. "A Stylistic Basis of Burkeian Identification." *Today's Speech,* 20 (Winter 1972), 19-24.

Carrier, James G. "Knowledge, Meaning, and Social Inequality in Kenneth Burke." *American Journal of Sociology,* 88 (July 1982), 43-61.

Cheney, George. "The Rhetoric of Identification and the Study of Organizational Communication." *Quarterly Journal of Speech,* 69 (May 1983), 143-58.

Chesebro, James. W., ed. *Extensions of the Burkeian System.* Tuscaloosa: University of Alabama Press, 1993.

Combs, James E. *Dimensions of Political Drama.* Santa Monica: Goodyear, 1980.

Comprone, Joseph. "Kenneth Burke and the Teaching of Writing." *College Composition and Communication,* 29 (December 1978), 336-40.

Cowley, Malcolm. *Exile's Return: A Literary Odyssey of the 1920's.* rev. ed. New York: The Viking Press, 1951.

Crable, Richard E., and John J. Makay. "Kenneth Burke's Concept of Motives in Rhetorical Theory." *Today's Speech,* 20 (Winter 1972), 11-18.

Crowell, Laura. "Three Sheers for Kenneth Burke." *Quarterly Journal of Speech,* 63 (April 1977), 150-67.

Crusius, Timothy W. "A Case for Kenneth Burke's Dialectic and Rhetoric." *Philosophy and Rhetoric,* 19 (Winter 1986), 23-37.

Davis, Walter A. *The Act of Interpretation: A Critique of Literary Reason.* Chicago: University of Chicago Press, 1978.

Day, Dennis G. "Persuasion and the Concept of Identification." *Quarterly Journal of Speech,* 46 (October 1960), 270-73.

Donoghue, Denis. *Ferocious Alphabets.* New York: Columbia University Press, 1984.

Donoghue, Denis. "American Sage." *New York Review of Books,* September 26, 1985, pp. 39-42.

Duerden, Richard Y. "Kenneth Burke's Systemless System: Using Pepper to Pigeonhole an Elusive Thinker." *Journal of Mind and Behavior,* 3 (Autumn 1982), 323-36.

Duffey, Bernard. "Reality as Language: Kenneth Burke's Theory of Poetry." *Western Review,* 12 (Spring 1948), 132-45.

Duncan, Hugh Dalziel. *Communication and Social Order.* New York: Bedminster Press, 1962.

Duncan, Hugh Dalziel. *Symbols in Society.* New York: Oxford University Press, 1968.

Duncan, Hugh Dalziel. *Symbols and Social Theory.* NewYork: Oxford University Press, 1969.

Durham, Weldon. "Kenneth Burke's Concept of Substance." *Quarterly Journal of Speech,* 66 (December 1980), 351-64.

Edelman, Murray. *The Symbolic Uses of Politics.* Urbana: University of Illinois Press, 1964.

Feehan, Michael. "Oscillation as Assimilation: Burke's Latest Self-Revisions." *Pre/Text,* 6 (Fall/Winter 1985), 319-27.

Fiordo, Richard. "Kenneth Burke's Semiotic." *Semiotica: Journal of the International Association for Semiotic Studies,* 23 (1978), 53-75.

Fisher, Walter R., and Wayne Brockriede. "Kenneth Burke's Realism." *Central States Speech Journal,* 35 (Spring 1984), 35-42.

Fogarty, Daniel. *Roots for a New Rhetoric.* New York: Teachers College, Columbia University, 1959.

Foss, Sonja K.; Karen A. Foss; and Robert Trapp. *Contemporary Perspectives on Rhetoric.* Prospect Heights, IL: Waveland Press, 1985.

Frank, Armin Paul. *Kenneth Burke.* New York: Twayne Publishers, Inc.: 1969.

Gabin, Rosalind J. "Entitling Kenneth Burke." *Rhetoric Review,* 5 (January 1987), 196-210.

Griffin, Leland M. "When Dreams Collide: Rhetorical Trajectories in the Assassination of President Kennedy." *Quarterly Journal of Speech,* 70 (May 1984), 111-131.

Gronbeck, Bruce E. "Dramaturgical Theory and Criticism: The State of the Art (or Science?)." *Western Journal of Speech Communication,* 44 (Fall 1980), 315-30.

Gusfield, Joseph. "The Literary Rhetoric of Science: Comedy and Pathos in Drinking Driver Research." *American Sociological Review,* 4 (February 1976), 16-34.

Hagan, Michael R. "Kenneth Burke and Generative Criticism of Speeches." *Central States Speech Journal,* 22 (Winter 1971), 252-57.

Hartman, Geoffrey H. *Criticism in the Wilderness: The Study of Literature Today.* New Haven: Yale University Press, 1980.

Heath, Robert L. *Realism and Relativism: A Perspective on Kenneth Burke.* Macon, GA: Mercer University Press, 1986.

Hickson, Mark, III. "Kenneth Burke's Affirmation of 'No' and the Absence of the Present." *Etc.,* 33 (March 1976), 44-48.

Holland, L. Virginia. "Kenneth Burke's Dramatistic Approach in Speech Criticism." *Quarterly Journal of Speech,* 41 (1955), 352-358.

Holland, L. Virginia. *Counterpoint: Kenneth Burke and Aristotle's Theories of Rhetoric.* New York: Philosophical Library, 1959.

Howell, Wilbur Samuel. "The Two Party Line: A Reply to Kenneth Burke." *Quarterly Journal of Speech,* 62 (February 1976), 69-77.

Irmscher, William F. "Kenneth Burke." In *Traditions of Inquiry,* ed. John Brereton, pp. 105-36. New York: Oxford University Press, 1985.

Jameson, Frederic R. "The Symbolic Inference: or, Kenneth Burke and Ideological Analysis." *Critical Inquiry,* 4 (Spring 1978), 507-23.

Jay, Paul. "Kenneth Burke: A Man of Letters." *Pre/Text,* 6 (Fall/Winter 1985), 221-33.

Keith, Philip M. "Burkeian Invention: Two Contrasting Views: Burkeian Invention, from Pentad to Dialectic." *Rhetoric Society Quarterly,* 9 (Summer 1979), 137-41.

Kimberling, C. Ronald. *Kenneth Burke's Dramatism and Popular Arts.* Bowling Green, OH: Bowling Green University Press, 1982.

Kirk, John W. "Kenneth Burke's Dramatistic Criticism Applied to the Theater." *Southern Speech Journal,* 33 (Spring 1968), 161-77.

Knox, George. *Critical Moments: Kenneth Burke's Categories and Critiques.* Seattle: University of Washington Press, 1957.

Kneupper, Charles. "Burkeian Invention: Two Contrasting Views: Dramatistic Invention: The Pentad as a Heuristic Procedure." *Rhetoric Society Quarterly,* 9 (Summer 1979), 130-36.

Kostelanetz, Richard. "A Mind That Cannot Stop Exploding." *New York Times Book Review,* March 15, 1981, p. 11 ff.

Lentricchia, Frank. *Criticism and Social Change.* Chicago: University of Chicago Press, 1983.

Macksoud, S. John. "Kenneth Burke on Perspective and Rhetoric." *Western Speech,* 33 (Summer 1969), 167-74.

McCloskey, Donald N. *The Rhetoric of Economics.* Madison: University of Wisconsin Press, 1985.

Meadows, Paul. "The Semiotic of Kenneth Burke." *Philosophy and Phenomenological Research,* 18 (September 1957), 80-87.

Meisenholder, Thomas. "Law as Symbolic Action: Kenneth Burke's Sociology of Law." *Symbolic Interaction,* 4 (Spring 1981), 43-57.

Mullican, James S. "A Burkean Approach to *Catch-22.*" *College Literature,* 8 (Winter 1981), 42-52.

Nelson, Jeffrey. "Using the Burkeian Pentad in the Education of the Basic Speech Student." *Communication Education,* 32 (January 1983), 63-68.

Nemerov, Howard. "Gnomic Variations for Kenneth Burke." *Kenyon Review,* n.s., 5 (Summer, 1983), 23-25.

Nichols, Marie Hochmuth. "Burkeian Criticism." In *Essays on Rhetorical Criticism,* ed. Thomas R. Nilsen, pp. 75-85. New York: Random House, 1968.

Nimmo, Dan, and James E. Combs. *Mediated Political Realities.* New York: Longman, 1983.

O'Keefe, Daniel J. "Burke's Dramatism and Action Theory." *Rhetoric Society Quarterly,* 8 (Winter 1978), 8-15.

Osborn, Neal J. "Kenneth Burke's Desdemona: A Courtship of Clio?" *Hudson Review,* 19 (Summer 1966), 267-75.

Osborn, Neal J. "Toward the Quintessential Burke." *Hudson Review,* 21 (Summer 1968), 308-21.

Overington, Michael A. "Kenneth Burke as Social Theorist." *Sociological Inquiry,* 47, no. 2 (1977), 133-41.

Pattison, Sheron Dailey. "Rhetoric and Audience Effect: Kenneth Burke on Form and Identification." In *Studies in Interpretation,* vol. 2, ed. Ester M. Doyle and Virginia Hastings Floyd, pp. 183-98. Amsterdam: Rodopi, 1977.

Rod, David K. "Kenneth Burke and Susanne K. Langer on Drama and Its Audiences." *Quarterly Journal of Speech,* 72 (August 1986), 306-17.

Rosenfeld, Lawrence B. "Set Theory: Key to the Understanding of Kenneth Burke's Use of the Term 'Identification.'" *Western Speech,* 33 (Summer 1969), 175-83.

Rueckert, William H., ed. *Critical Responses to Kenneth Burke.* Minneapolis: University of Minnesota Press, 1969.

Rueckert, William H. *Kenneth Burke and the Drama of Human Relations.* 2d rev. ed. Berkeley: University of California Press, 1982.

Schwartz, Joseph. "Kenneth Burke, Aristotle, and the Future of Rhetoric." *College Composition and Communication,* 17 (December 1966), 210-16.

Shaw, Leroy Robert. *The Playwright and Historical Change: Dramatic Strategies in Brecht, Hauptmann, Kaiser, and Wedekind.* Madison: University of Wisconsin Press, 1970.

Simons, Herbert. W., and Trevor Melia, eds. *The Legacy of Kenneth Burke.* Madison: University of Wisconsin Press, 1989.

States, Bert O. *Irony and Drama: A Poetics.* Ithaca, NY: Cornell University Press, 1971.

Tompkins, Phillip K. "On Hegemony—'He Gave It No Name'—and Critical Structuralism in the Work of Kenneth Burke." *Quarterly Journal of Speech,* 71 (February 1985), 119-31.

Tompkins, Phillip K. *Communication as Action: An Introduction to Rhetoric and Communication.* Belmont, CA: Wadsworth, 1982.

Warnock, Tilly. "Reading Kenneth Burke: Ways In, Ways Out, Ways Roundabout." *College English,* 48 (January 1986), 262-75.

Washburn, Richard Kirk. "Burke on Motives and Rhetoric." *Approach,* 9 (1953), 2-6.

Watson, Edward A. "Incongruity Without Laughter: Kenneth Burke's Theory of the Grotesque." *University of Windsor Review,* 4, no. 2 (1969), 28-36.

Watson, Karen Ann. "A Rhetorical and Sociolinguistic Model for the Analysis of Narrative." *American Anthropologist,* 75, no. 1 (1973), 243-64.

Wellek, Rene. "The Main Trends of Twentieth-Century Criticism." *Yale Review,* 51 (Autumn 1961), 102-18.

Wellek, Rene. "Kenneth Burke and Literary Criticism." *Sewanee Review,* 79 (Spring 1971), 171-88.

Wells, Susan. "Richards, Burke, and the Relation Between Rhetoric and Poetics." *Pre/Text,* 7 (Spring/Summer 1986), 59-75.

White, Hayden. *Tropics of Discourse: Essays in Cultural Criticism.* Baltimore: The Johns Hopkins University Press, 1978.

White, Hayden, and Margaret Brose, eds. *Representing Kenneth Burke.* Baltimore: The Johns Hopkins University Press, 1982.

Winterowd, W. Ross. "Dramatism in Themes and Poems." *College Education,* 45 (October 1983), 581-88.

Winterowd, W. Ross. *Rhetoric and Writing.* Boston: Allyn and Bacon, 1965.

Yagoda, Ben. "Kenneth Burke: The Greatest Literary Critic Since Coleridge?" *Horizon,* 23 (June 1980), 66-69.

Burke's Major Works

Counter-Statement. New York: Harcourt, Brace, 1931; 2d ed., Berkeley: University of California Press, 1968.

Towards a Better Life: Being a Series of Epistles, or Declamations. New York: Harcourt, Brace, 1932; Berkeley: University of California Press, 1966.

Permanence and Change: An Anatomy of Purpose. New York: New Republic, 1935; 3d rev. ed., Berkeley: University of California Press, 1984.

Attitudes Toward History. 2 vols. New York: New Republic, 1937; 3d rev. ed., Berkeley: University of California Press, 1984.

The Philosophy of Literary Form: Studies in Symbolic Action. Baton Rouge: Louisiana State University Press, 1941; 3d rev. ed., Berkeley: University of California Press, 1973.

A Grammar of Motives. New York: Prentice-Hall, 1945; 2d ed., Berkeley: University of California Press, 1969.

A Rhetoric of Motives. New York: Prentice-Hall, 1950; 2d ed., Berkeley: University of California Press, 1969.

The Rhetoric of Religion: Studies in Logology. Boston: Beacon Press, 1961; Berkeley: University of California Press, 1970.

Language as Symbolic Action: Essays on Life, Literature, and Method. Berkeley: University of California Press, 1966.

Collected Poems, 1915-1967. Berkeley: University of California Press, 1968.

The Complete White Oxen: Collected Short Fiction of Kenneth Burke. Berkeley: University of California Press, 1968.

Dramatism and Development. Worcester, MA: Clark University Press, 1972.

Index